Navigating the Medical Maze with a Child with Autism Spectrum Disorder

of related interest

Kids in the Syndrome Mix of ADHD, LD, Autism Spectrum, Tourette's, Anxiety and More!
The one stop guide for parents, teachers and other professionals
2nd edition
Martin L. Kutscher MD
With contributions from Tony Attwood PhD and Robert R. Wolff MD
ISBN 978 1 84905 967 1
eISBN 978 0 85700 882 4

Autism Spectrum Disorders Through the Life Span
Digby Tantam
ISBN 978 1 84310 993 8 (hardback)
ISBN 978 1 849 05344 0 (paperback)
eISBN 978 0 857 00511 3

A Practical Guide to Mental Health Problems in Children with Autistic Spectrum Disorder
It's not just their autism!
Khalid Karim, Alvina Ali and Michelle O'Reilly
ISBN 978 1 84905 323 5
eISBN 978 0 85700 697 4

Autism and its Medical Management
A Guide for Parents and Professionals
2nd edition
Michael G. Chez MD
ISBN 978 1 84905 926 8
eISBN 978 0 85700 707 0

Navigating the Medical Maze with a Child with Autism Spectrum Disorder

A Practical Guide for Parents

EDITED BY SUE X. MING
AND BETH A. PLETCHER

Jessica Kingsley *Publishers*
London and Philadelphia

First published in 2014
by Jessica Kingsley Publishers
73 Collier Street
London N1 9BE, UK
and
400 Market Street, Suite 400
Philadelphia, PA 19106, USA

www.jkp.com

Library of Congress Cataloging in Publication Data
Navigating the medical maze with a child with autism spectrum disorder : a practical guide for parents /
edited by Sue X. Ming and Beth A. Pletcher.
    pages cm
 Includes bibliographical references and index.
 ISBN 978-1-84905-971-8 (alk. paper)
 1. Autism spectrum disorders in children--Handbooks, manuals, etc. 2. Autism in children--Diagnosis. 3.
Parents of autistic children--Handbooks, manuals, etc. I. Ming, Sue X. II. Pletcher, Beth A.
 RJ506.A9N34 2014
 618.92'85882--dc23
                        2014000905

British Library Cataloguing in Publication Data
A CIP catalogue record for this book is available from the British Library

ISBN 978 1 84905 971 8
eISBN 978 0 85700 860 2

Printed and bound in Great Britain

MIX
Paper from
responsible sources
FSC
www.fsc.org FSC® C013056

We dedicate this book to our patients and their families, whose inner strength, insight, passion, and humor amaze us and help us to help them along their journey into uncharted territory. We are grateful to them not only because they inspire us to be better doctors and to ask important clinical research questions, but also because they make it a pleasure to come to work each and every day.

Acknowledgments

We thank our colleagues and friends who worked individually and together in the creation of this book. Furthermore, we are eternally grateful to our husbands, Yong and Paul, as well as our children, Victor, Lilia, Brett, and Brittany, whose support, patience, and encouragement enabled us to forge ahead to complete the book. We are deeply indebted to Lilia, who spent many hours of her time assisting us in designing the chapter layout as well as searching for and verifying references.

Contents

Disclaimer

This book is intended for informational purposes only. It is in no way intended to be a substitute for professional medical advice, nor is it to be used for purposes of diagnosis or treatment. Neither the publisher, editors, nor contributing authors accept any responsibility for the results of any decisions made based on the information contained in this book.

Preface

Over the past decade, we have had the opportunity to meet many families of children with autism spectrum disorders (ASDs) and provide care for their children. When a child is diagnosed with an ASD, parents often feel overwhelmed and inevitably have a host of questions. Invariably, lengthy discussions ensue focusing on medical concerns, management and treatment, testing strategies, anticipatory guidance, as well as potential side effects of medications if these are recommended. After the initial visit, much time is devoted to patient and family education and counseling about individualized educational and behavioral approaches to the child with an ASD. We believe that parents or family members are the most valuable partners within the multidisciplinary team caring for a child with an ASD. Parental knowledge and education are essential to empower them to best advocate for their child.

This book represents the collective knowledge and opinions of many individuals who have provided care for children and young adults with ASDs. Our goal is to provide a practical guide for parents who are navigating the medical system and wish to get the most out of their medical encounters. For many parents, medical visits provide limited time to have all of their questions answered, and we hope that these chapters will augment what is discussed in a typical medical encounter and perhaps enable fully informed parents to formulate a list of specific questions that pertain to their child and may make the medical visit more efficient and productive. Several of the authors are not only medical professionals but understand this experience on a personal level, having a child of their own with an ASD. Because service delivery, resources, and legal ramifications for individuals with disabilities vary from state to state and country to country, some of what is discussed in the book relates specifically to service provision in the United States. For individuals living outside of the United States, you will need to access local and/or governmental resources and refer to pertinent legislation or regulations in your country.

We fully recognize that ASDs are a group of heterogeneous conditions. This means that the medical concerns, underlying causes, and responses to therapies of one child with an ASD may not be the same as those of another child with an ASD, no matter how similar the behaviors they display. As such, recommendations or suggestions gleaned from this book should *not* replace individual medical evaluation and recommendations by a team of physicians and ASD specialists. Two children with identical symptoms may have completely different underlying problems, and only in-person evaluation and assessment by experienced physicians and other medical professionals can be relied upon to determine an appropriate plan of action. Advice or recommendations generated from face to face interactions with the child and family are essential in developing an individualized care plan that addresses the full spectrum of care from the medical, to the behavioral, to the social, to the educational needs of the child.

We encourage our readers to not necessarily read each chapter in sequence but instead to read those that seem most relevant to their own particular child or circumstance. Each chapter can stand on its own and provide information about a specific aspect of ASD care.

Finally, we know that this book will not touch on all aspects of care for children and young adults with ASDs, and we cannot anticipate what future avenues of diagnosis and therapy await us as research discoveries emerge at a rapid pace. Therefore, much of what we know today may be replaced with new theories and scientific knowledge within a short period of time; however, for now we hope to review the most current and relevant information for parents and their primary care providers, including a discussion of both proven and some alternative therapies, how best to partner with members of the ASD medical team, as well as how to approach transitions of medical care for young adults with ASDs.

Chapter *1*

When Your Child Is Diagnosed with an Autism Spectrum Disorder

Sue X. Ming, MD, PhD

Introduction

When a child is diagnosed with an autism spectrum disorder (ASD), parents may be overwhelmed and may have many questions. This chapter discusses how ASDs are diagnosed, our current understanding of the causes of ASDs, as well as accompanying medical conditions and developmental manifestations that may be seen in individuals with ASDs. Once you have had a chance to review these topics, you may decide to explore individual chapters to learn more about specific medical issues in ASDs and what you can do to partner with your physicians and other health care providers to identify key resources to help your child achieve optimal physical and mental health.

What are autism spectrum disorders?

ASDs are a group of neurodevelopmental disorders. It is quite possible that autism was described thousands of years ago. In their book, *The Biology of the Autistic Syndromes*, Christopher Gillberg and Mary Coleman write, "Thousands of years ago in ancient Mesopotamia, between the Tigris and Euphrates rivers, medical information was written down on a set of durable clay tablets which have survived to the present day... If a woman gives birth and the infant rejects his mother... Could this be the first written description of an infant who is autistic?"[1] Many of us are more familiar with the modern description of autism by Leo Kanner in 1943, "extreme aloneness from the beginning of life and an anxiously obsessive desire for the preservation of sameness."[2] At that time, autism was regarded as "childhood schizophrenia" and parents were blamed for the child's behavior, "Children with early infantile autism were the offspring of highly organized, professional parents, cold and rational, who just happened to defrost long enough to produce a child."[3] Later on, more descriptions of social cognitive impairment emerged. Lack of social insight, emotional reciprocity, motivation for seeking social interaction and joint attention, and ability in mind reading (theory of mind) were described in children with autism.[4] Repetitive behaviors and restricted interests were also reported in children with autism along with communication impairment. Until 1980, infantile autism was classified in the *Diagnostic and Statistical Manual of Mental Disorders*, third edition (DSM-III) as a single disorder.[5] The separate diagnostic criteria for autistic disorder, Asperger disorder, and pervasive developmental disorder—not otherwise specified (PDD-NOS) were established with the publication of DSM-IV in 1994 and revised in DSM-IV-TR in 2000.[6,7] About a decade ago, autism was recognized to be a continuous spectrum of disorders and the term "autism spectrum disorders" was introduced. The DSM-5 combines all three pervasive developmental disorders (autistic disorder, Asperger disorder, PDD-NOS) back into a single ASD diagnosis while adding severity specifiers depending on the presentation of each individual child.[8]

It was absolutely wrong to attribute the cause of autism to the proverbial "refrigerator mother." It is now well accepted globally that ASDs are in fact a group of brain-based whole-body disorders with organic causes. Starting with the new millennium, the concept of an ASD as a biological disorder emerged. The Autism Center, now of Rutgers New Jersey Medical School, was established in 2001 with a mission to treat ASDs as biomedical disorders and conduct clinical research on a variety of aspects of these brain-based conditions.

It is likely that ASDs are biologically distinct groups of disorders that exhibit similar abnormal behavioral and developmental features. Many of us recognize the variability of ASDs in their behavioral presentations and especially in their medical/physical manifestations. While behavioral subtypes of ASDs (autistic disorder, PDD-NOS, Asperger disorder) are recognized, this classification by no means represents the diverse biological phenotypes (presentations) of ASDs. Many overlapping classifications of ASDs have been used in the literature, such as high- and low-functioning autism, regressive autism, autism with or without gastrointestinal (GI) disorders, and idiopathic or secondary autism. In my opinion, there has been no good methodological approach to subgrouping ASDs. Biomarkers are needed to more accurately classify the behaviorally grouped ASDs into biologically based ASDs.

So what are ASDs? They are a group of biological disorders resulting from abnormal brain development during early childhood, and the causes of ASDs are still largely unknown. It is difficult to have an inclusive term to describe all types of ASDs because ASDs represent behavioral symptoms of different disorders and diseases. Perhaps our readers will come up with their own description of ASDs after reading this book.

How doctors diagnose ASDs

Up until 2013, most clinicians have used the behavioral criteria described in the DSM-IV-TR[6] to diagnose and define ASDs. The diagnostic behaviors are grouped into three categories: qualitative impairment in social interaction; qualitative impairment in communication; and restricted repetitive and stereotyped patterns of behavior, interests, and activities. Qualitative impairment in social interaction is the hallmark of an ASD, while impairment in communication alone may be found in children with speech and language disorders who do not have an ASD, and restricted repetitive and stereotyped behaviors alone may be found in children with obsessive–compulsive disorder who do not have an ASD. To diagnose a child with an ASD, he or she should exhibit symptoms or behavioral criteria in all three domains. The emphasis is again on an abnormality in social quality of the behaviors. For example, a child with speech delay may use other means to communicate, such as gestures, pointing, and eye gaze, whereas a child with an ASD may not employ non-verbal communication. DSM-5 merges the social interaction impairment and social communication deficits into a single domain, while the repetitive and restricted interests, behaviors, and activity remain the same as in DSM-IV-TR. Although both DSM-IV-TR and DSM-5 emphasize impairment in social interaction, DSM-5 recommends only the use of the term "autism spectrum disorder" partnered with a severity indicator. Regardless of which DSM criteria are used to actually make a diagnosis of an ASD, we recognize that early diagnosis is critical to promote optimal developmental progress.

Types of ASDs

As stated earlier, the DSM-IV classifications of ASDs consisted of autistic disorder, PDD-NOS, and Asperger disorder. The core ASD, autistic disorder, required more stringent behavioral criteria for a diagnosis. Children diagnosed as having an autistic disorder were noted to have delays or abnormal functioning in all of the following areas, with onset prior to age 3 years: (1) social interaction, (2) language as used in social communication, and (3) symbolic or imaginative play. Children with autistic disorder were felt to have more typical social interaction impairment, higher rates of cognitive impairment, and delays in speech development. The criteria for Asperger's disorder in terms of social interaction, repetitive behaviors, and restricted interests were very similar to those of autistic disorder, but, according to DSM-IV-TR, "there is no clinically significant general delay in language (e.g., single words used by age 2 years, communicative phrases used by age 3 years)" and "there is no clinically significant delay in cognitive development or in the development of age-appropriate self-help skills, adaptive behavior (other than in social interaction), and curiosity about the environment in childhood";[6] however, individuals diagnosed with Asperger disorder were felt to have impairment in social use of language, or pragmatic communication using either verbal or non-verbal means. PDD-NOS is a less specific or less well-defined category of ASD. Children with PDD-NOS have qualitative impairment in social interaction but may not have at least two items listed in the criteria, and have either verbal or non-verbal communication deficits, or repetitive and restricted interests/activities. Other features that set PDD-NOS apart include later age at onset and/or atypical or mild symptomatology. With the DSM-5 guidelines, children diagnosed using the previous criteria may need to be reclassified.

Another way to classify ASDs is based on known causes. If a child fulfills the DSM-IV-TR diagnosis of an ASD and has another known disorder, such as tuberous sclerosis, Down syndrome, or Fragile X syndrome, the child's autism is classified as a "double syndrome." On the other hand, if a child has only an ASD and the cause of the ASD is unknown, this child is said to have an idiopathic (cause unknown) form of ASD.

What causes ASDs?

Despite all of the research and intensive studies that have been done, we still do not know the definitive causes for idiopathic ASDs. It is generally believed by the scientific community that a combination of genetic and environmental factors are responsible for manifestations of ASDs. Exposure to an environmental factor during a developmentally vulnerable time in a genetically susceptible child currently seems to be a commonly accepted theory. There continue to be debates about whether a child is born with an ASD or if ASDs develop during early childhood. There is evidence supporting both theories. The description from those ancient tablets suggests that a child with autism shows autistic behaviors at birth, and I have encountered many children in my practice whose mothers claim that their child was not cuddly, not interactive, and resistant to being touched right from birth. Some of the brain changes, such as cerebellar Purkinje cell abnormalities, described in children with ASDs appear to originate during brain development in fetal life. Based on this we could argue that for some children with ASDs, their autism stems from alterations in prenatal brain development. On the other hand, individuals with a regressive form of ASD are described to have apparently normal development early in life, and then between 18 and 36 months of age their parents begin to notice their child is losing skills and exhibiting autistic behaviors. I have seen many of these children as well. These variable presentations and many potential causes of ASDs reinforce our belief that ASDs do not represent a single entity but instead a group of biologically distinct disorders. Scientists have accepted the evidence that there are in fact many different pathways leading to ASDs and this is further supported by the recognition that ASDs can co-occur with a known genetic condition (a so-called double syndrome) which has distinct brain findings and, in many cases, an identifiable genetic cause.

Research on genetic causes of ASDs has produced a list of candidate genes that could be associated with idiopathic ASDs. Some genes have stronger associations than others, but the inheritance pattern of ASDs does not follow what we would consider traditional patterns of transmission. Even for identical twins who are not only genetically identical but also share the same prenatal environment, autism is not seen 100% of the time in both twins. In many cases, a responsible gene or combination of genes could be common variants of the normal gene, which confer a genetic predisposition, but do not inevitably cause an individual to develop an ASD. Carrying such a gene or genes may not be sufficient for an ASD to develop, but in certain susceptible individuals in conjunction with a specific trigger, such as an environmental factor or exposure, an ASD may occur. Scientists are working diligently on trying to tease out the genetic and environmental factors that may trigger autism in certain individuals. (See Chapter 7 for a detailed discussion on genetic causes of ASDs.)

While it is widely accepted that environmental factors play a crucial role in the development of an ASD for at least some individuals, research on environmental causes of ASDs is just beginning to clarify these relationships. Most of the studies published in this area are limited to detecting exposures and measuring levels of a group of toxins, usually by evaluating affected individuals retrospectively (looking backward over their history). Since it is clearly unethical and inhumane to willfully expose children to a known toxin, linking causative toxins to ASDs in humans is quite difficult. As such, researchers rely on animal models of autism to test the effect of a toxin on the occurrence of an ASD. I participated in research projects developing mouse models of autism by exposing mice to methyl mercury or valproate in

Dr. George Wagner's lab. Although we were successful in producing mice who exhibit some features of autism, it is clear that these mice are not identical to humans with autism; therefore, testing toxins in mice may clarify some general concepts about toxic compounds and how they may impact brain development, but such testing may not be directly relevant when examining autism in humans. (See Chapter 10 for more information on environmental risk factors.)

Medical conditions that may accompany an ASD

Many medical or physical problems have been increasingly recognized in individuals diagnosed with an ASD. These co-occurring medical disorders are called comorbidities. As stated earlier, ASDs are recognized as a group of brain-based whole-body disorders. The brain and the nervous system exert control in one way or another over all the organs and body systems, and conversely, many organs and body systems provide feedback to the nervous system or provide some type of regulatory signals (similar to two individuals having a back-and-forth conversation). It is therefore not surprising to see certain physical problems in individuals with ASDs. Since some form of brain dysfunction is expected in all individuals with an ASD, it is not surprising to see more serious disorders of the nervous system in some of them. These neurological disorders include epilepsy, sleep disorders, autonomic disorders, as well as motor and sensory disorders. Because both thoughts and behaviors are generated from the brain, brain dysfunction can lead to thought disorders and abnormal behaviors. As a result, individuals with ASDs are more likely to display symptoms of psychiatric disorders such as an anxiety disorder or mood disorder, and may be more likely to exhibit symptoms of irritability and/or agitation.

Gastrointestinal (GI) disorders are frequently reported in children with ASDs.[9,10] Experts believe that GI disorders are an important comorbidity of ASDs, to the extent that there was discussion as to whether GI disorders should be included in the DSM-5 diagnostic criteria for ASDs. There are many neurons (nerve cells) within the walls of the gut (intestinal tract) and multiple layers of interaction between the gut and the neurons within the gut, as well as between the neurons within the gut and neurons in the spinal cord and brain. The so-called gut–brain interaction has received increasing recognition and is associated with many brain disorders such as hepatic encephalopathy, central nervous system celiac disease, and enteric encephalopathy. In addition, the gut is home to some 10,000 species of bacteria that symbiotically cohabitate with humans. The role of this "microbiome" in contributing to disease and health is a new hot area of investigation that has attracted ample attention in the scientific world. Interestingly, I first heard a discussion about gut flora imbalance in ASDs during a presentation by Dr. Sidney Finegold at the Jonty Foundation Symposium on Autism in 2001. In 2012 we published our observation of increased gut bacterial products in children with ASDs who also exhibited GI dysfunction.[11] Our study showed that more than 50% of children participating in an autism research project had one or more defined GI disorders.[12]

Immunological disorders have also been frequently reported in individuals with ASDs.[13-17] Much like nerve cells within the nervous system, immunological cells are widespread throughout the body including the brain itself. Although the brain may be protected from some insults and substances due to what is known as the blood-brain barrier, the brain is not at all safe from immune system challenges. For this reason, scientists believe that brain dysfunction consistent with ASDs could be caused by immunological disorders in some individuals. Various symptoms related to immune dysfunction are reported in a subgroup of persons with ASDs, and I have evaluated and referred many of these individuals to our immunologists.

Recognition and treatment of comorbid medical conditions (when they occur) are very important for the well-being and developmental progression of any child with an ASD. For example, effective treatment of sleep disorders or epilepsy may improve daytime behavior, learning and well-being of the child. (For an in-depth discussion of the neurological, psychiatric, gastrointestinal, and immunological comorbidities, see Chapters 2, 3, 4, and 5, respectively.)

What we know about ASDs

Research on ASDs has exploded to an unprecedented level. During the writing of the first version of this chapter in June 2013, the keyword "autism" in the PubMed search engine produced 22,721 articles from 1947 to May 2013, while a search of Google Scholar, which includes scholastic articles in journals not indexed in PubMed, produced about 480,000 "autism" citations. A search of the same sources in November 2013 yielded 24,146 articles in PubMed (1425 new articles) and about 541,000 citations in Google Scholar (an increase of approximately 61,000) in just 5 months! In addition, there has been an emergence of more and more new journals dedicated exclusively to autism. In my opinion, the persistence, dedication, hard work, and focused efforts of parents through organizations such as Cure Autism Now, National Alliance For Autism Research, Autism Research Institute, Safe Mind, Simon Foundation, and Autism Speaks have had a tremendous impact on

(1) promoting autism research through lobbying congressional committees for increased funding, (2) recruiting many more scientists to work in the field of autism, and (3) establishing large human tissue repositories to support autism research.

There have been many large- and small-scale epidemiological studies done in various parts of the world, a few of which are referenced here.[18–24] Overall, the rate of ASDs is increasing. Currently, the most quoted rate is that 1 in 88 children is diagnosed with an ASD.[18] Among children with ASDs, there are four times more boys than girls; however, girls diagnosed with an ASD tend to have more severe symptoms. ASDs are not limited to a particular ethnic group or a particular region of the world.[19] ASDs can and do occur in families from any social or economic stratum. Older mothers have been found to have a higher chance of giving birth to a child with an ASD,[25,26] and older fathers were also found to have a higher chance of having an offspring with an ASD;[27–29] however, parents of all ages and walks of life face the possibility of having a child with an ASD.

Many studies report an increased propensity for developing a medical comorbidity in individuals with ASDs. Besides the previously described neurological, psychiatric, GI, and immunological disorders,[9,12,13] metabolic disturbances, such as mitochondrial dysfunction[30,31] and reduced ability to detoxify toxins,[32–35] have been reported in some individuals with ASDs. It is not clear at this point if these comorbidities (1) result directly from the ASD, (2) contribute to the development of the ASD, or (3) represent simply co-occurrence with the ASD, with both the ASD and medical problem resulting from the same common cause or pathogenesis. In other words, does A cause B, does B cause A, or is there a third factor C that causes both A and B?

There is increasing documentation of structural brain abnormalities in persons with ASDs. Studies in the 1990s by Kemper and Bauman describe regional brain abnormalities in the cerebellum and hippocampus;[36,37] however, the brains they studied were from individuals with ASDs who also had another serious medical disorder such as epilepsy. It is therefore unclear whether or not some of the abnormalities were in fact caused by the epilepsy. Similar problems exist in other brain studies done on individuals with ASDs after they have died.[38] Studies in living patients with ASDs have used volumetric magnetic resonance imaging (MRI) looking at differences in the size and shape of various brain regions comparing patients with individuals without an ASD. Various investigators have studied white matter tracks using specialized MRI scans and reported abnormalities in various regions of the brain in persons with ASDs.[39–44] At the International Meeting for Autism Research 2013 in San Sebastian, Spain, there were many presentations on MRI findings in individuals with ASDs, but it is still unclear how these variations in brain anatomy translate into functional abnormalities, or whether these findings can in any way help us to better understand the causes of ASDs. These particular MRI tools are available only for research purposes at present, but they may someday help us to diagnose, manage, and treat patients with ASDs. We analyzed the results of conventional brain MRIs performed on a clinical basis for our patients with ASDs and found a low yield for relevant brain abnormalities.[45]

While there is great interest from families and providers to pursue research to identify effective treatments and therapies for ASDs, the number of these types of studies is relatively small compared with research studies trying to identify the causes or pathogenesis of ASDs. Nevertheless, clinical trials directed at treating core symptoms and comorbidities of ASDs have been performed. Risperodone and aripiprazole were FDA approved to treat irritability in individuals with ASDs.[46] There have been a few small-scale trials looking at supplementary essential fatty acids, with some reporting reduced irritability and hyperactivity in children with ASDs.[47–49] N-acetylcystein, vitamin B6, vitamin B12, donepezil, probiotics, and oxytocin were/are under clinical trial evaluation for improving ASD symptoms.[50–54] There are studies on hyperbaric oxygen therapy, heavy metal chelation, acupuncture, and music therapy as well.[55–63] There has been even more research on interventional therapies, such as Applied Behavioral Analysis, Floor Time, TEACCH (Teaching Expanding Appreciating Collaborating and Cooperating Holistic).[60,64–68] While we are slowly making some appreciable progress in the field of autism research, for many children with ASDs and their families, it is not fast enough.

Despite the steadily increasing pace of autism research, our current understanding of ASDs is still quite fragmented, resembling pieces of a puzzle still needing to be assembled. The etiology, pathogenesis, relationship between the core symptoms and comorbidities, heterogeneity, and effectiveness of treatments or therapies are still under investigation. When I attend autism research meetings where various groups of investigators present their findings, as each of them reports their findings they are convinced that what they have uncovered is significant and critical to understanding one or more specific aspects of ASDs; however after these meetings, when I pause to try to pull all of these puzzle pieces together, I am unable to create a clear and coherent landscape. It reminds me a bit of the story of six blind-folded people who are placed in a room with an elephant and asked to describe what they feel. Although each individual is able to describe one specific part of the animal, none can produce a coherent picture without the input from the others. In the same way, I see groups of scientists touching different parts of the "elephant" and reporting their findings, but without coordination, communication, and shared knowledge, the giant elephant of ASD is so enormous that it has yet to be viewed in its entirety; however, with perseverance, sharing of research data, creative thinking, advances in technologies, and partnering with all stakeholders (providers, scientists, patients, and parents) there is hope that in the near future we will be able to not only diagnose and treat but to prevent the occurrence of ASDs.

Autism across the lifespan

Despite their struggles and need to confront their disabilities, children with ASDs eventually grow up to be *adults* with ASDs. Children with ASDs may take different paths to maturation; some improve slowly but surely and become functionally independent as adults, while others may embark on a less predictable, winding path but nevertheless reach functional independence. Still other people with an ASD endure frequent and persistent challenges of body and mind, requiring more intensive supervision across a lifetime. Some children and young adults with ASDs who have special talents are able to use their skills in adulthood to become extremely productive members of society. Because ASDs are quite heterogeneous, the developmental trajectories vary among these children.

The critical issues, manifestations, personal needs, and therapies change as the individual grows older, as does the focus of the interventions. During the first 3 years of life, parents of a child with an ASD are required to focus on addressing the symptoms of developmental disabilities and possibly regression. Some children may also develop sleep disorders, allergy/immunology disorders, or GI dysfunction during this period which may require subspecialist attention. Parents and caregivers during this time may begin to see some therapeutic benefits. During preschool to early school ages, insomnia may become more prominent along with behavioral disorders such as anxiety, mood disorders, hyperactivity, and irritability/agitation which also need to be addressed. Epilepsy may occur in a subset of these children. Other medical comorbidities may continue to pop up or gradually resolve. With therapy, many children develop functional use of language that may ameliorate some of the frustration and behavioral problems by the time they reach later grammar school ages. Sleep problems also tend to improve over time in most of these children; for some, their hidden intellect and cognitive abilities may start to be unveiled. Some children may also experience a leap in academic and/or extracurricular achievement. Adolescence poses interesting challenges for most teenagers (as well as their families and teachers), which may be magnified for teens with special needs. Hormonal surges, the adolescent's struggle for autonomy, defiant behaviors, and mood swings may pose even greater challenges for adolescents with ASDs compared with typically developing adolescents. The autonomic (adrenaline system) dysfunction in many adolescents with ASDs may contribute to their difficulty holding back angry outbursts; some may experience instantaneous rages or aggression toward others or themselves. Expression of their sexuality may be precocious and, if they also have reduced social awareness, it may lead to inappropriate behaviors. The adolescent growth spurt with increase in size and muscle mass can potentially pose a risk to others. In this case the individual may now have the ability to inflict injuries on their siblings, parents, classmates, or teachers when the adolescent uses his or her physical force in an emotional outburst. Sometimes, these adolescents benefit from a medication that inhibits a rapidly cycling mood disorder. In extreme cases, inpatient stabilization may be necessary to prevent injury to the child and others. Certainly not all the adolescents with ASDs go through a difficult phase. Some of them improve both academically and behaviorally, turning around during adolescence. For now we have no sensitive tool that helps us to predict which children with ASDs will have difficulty or make steady improvement during adolescence. Furthermore, the pubescent level of functioning and concomitant behaviors may not always predict the course of the condition in adulthood.

Level of functioning as well as physical and mental wellness during adulthood in persons with ASDs has been the least well studied. My limited experience is that adults with an ASD tend to stabilize and plateau shortly after the adolescent period. If we thoughtfully address any of the comorbid conditions and behaviors before and during adulthood, we give these individuals the best chance to maximize their developmental, social, and productivity potential. Data on life expectancy for individuals with ASDs are quite scarce and clearly cannot include the many newly diagnosed individuals with ASDs. Unless a person with an ASD has another serious comorbidity or underlying medical condition, such as a life-threatening birth defect, one would anticipate that the life expectancy would be similar to age-matched, typically developing children and adults.

TAKEAWAY POINTS

- ASDs are a group of biologically and clinically heterogeneous neurodevelopmental disorders.
- The causes of ASDs are currently unknown but are believed to depend on a combination of genetic and environmental factors.
- The diagnosis of ASDs is evolving but is still limited to behavioral criteria.
- Individuals with ASDs are at higher risk for developing medical and psychiatric comorbid disorders.
- Early diagnosis and treatment of ASDs and comorbid disorders are paramount to maximally improve developmental progress and maintain good health for children with ASDs.
- Much more research is needed on all aspects of ASDs and is especially critical for the identification of effective treatments.

Co-occurrence of Neurological Disorders in Individuals with Autism Spectrum Disorders

Sue X. Ming, MD, PhD

Introduction

Individuals with autism spectrum disorders (ASDs) may be more prone to developing certain medical conditions, among which are neurological disorders. Sometimes presenting symptoms of these medical conditions could be mistaken for a behavior related to the ASD. It is important for parents to be aware of these conditions and discuss their concerns with their child's physician. This chapter discusses neurological disorders experienced by some children and adults with ASDs, including but not limited to epilepsy, sleep disorders, autonomic dysfunction, movement disorders, and reduced pain perception. We introduce typical symptoms and signs suggestive of specific neurological problems and highlight certain behaviors that could be symptoms of an underlying medical disorder.

Why individuals with ASDs are more susceptible to neurological disorders

ASDs are a group of neurodevelopmental disorders. As described in Chapter 1, the diagnosis of an ASD is based on behavioral criteria that consist of a deviation from normal developmental milestones and the appearance of abnormal behaviors. It is quite reasonable to assume that changes in brain function or structure are responsible for the abnormal behaviors. Numerous studies have shown that both brain function and structure may be abnormal in individuals with an ASD. For example, the brains of individuals with an ASD show abnormalities in the Purkinje cells (a type of brain cell in the cerebellum) and hippocampus.[1] A special magnetic resonance study (volumetric MRI) shows that children with idiopathic ASDs (ASDs with no known cause) have significantly more white matter (the connection or "wires" within the brain) that might explain the larger head size seen in some young children with ASDs.[2,3] Post-mortem studies of patients with ASDs have found abnormalities in various parts of the brain including the amygdala, limbic system, prefrontal lobes, basal forebrain, brainstem, and cerebellum.[1,4,5] Additionally, studies of individuals with ASDs have found abnormal levels of neurotransmitters such as norepinephrine, serotonin, dopamine,[6] and neuropeptides such as oxytocin.[7–11] Although we cannot directly correlate specific behaviors in individuals with ASDs with precise structural changes in the brain reported so far, it is clear that the abnormal brain function is responsible for the behavioral symptoms seen in individuals with ASDs. Abnormal brain structures and/or function can no doubt lead to neurological disorders; therefore, neurological disorders can co-occur with ASDs.

Neurological disorders that may co-occur with ASDs

There are many neurological disorders identified and reported in persons with ASDs. These disorders include epilepsy (seizure disorders), sleep disorders, autonomic disorders, movement disorders, and sensory disorders/ disintegration. Increased rates of headache, visceral (abdominal) pain, and abnormal vestibular function (imbalance) are reported in individuals with ASDs; however, there have been very few systematic studies examining these disorders in children and adults with ASDs. We therefore focus our attention on neurological disorders that are better characterized and studied in this population.

Epilepsy

Epilepsy is a chronic seizure disorder. Seizures are generated when part of or the whole brain cells' electrical activity discharges spontaneously and unexpectedly. Depending on which area of the brain is the source of the seizure activity, the presentation of seizures can vary significantly from one seizure to another. For example, a seizure originating from the motor area of the brain manifests as jerky movements of a limb, twitching of one side of the face, the head turning to one side, or eyes deviating to one side. A seizure generated from the temporal lobe may manifest simply with staring and lip smacking. These seizures are called partial seizures. If the seizure focus spreads from the motor area to the entire brain, the person having the seizure could have stiffening of the entire body with or without jerky movements (so-called secondary generalized seizures). The patient is usually unconscious during generalized seizures. Altered consciousness is common during many seizure types. If a partial seizure does not result in a change of consciousness, the seizure is classified as a simple partial seizure. On the other hand, if a partial seizure causes loss of consciousness, the seizure is called a complex partial seizure. Complex partial seizures may be difficult to recognize if consciousness is not completely lost but merely altered. Alterations in consciousness may be mistaken for behavioral changes in a child with an ASD. Seizures tend to be stereotypic, which means that each seizure arising from the same seizure focus tends to manifest in a very similar if not identical way. Seizures are often provoked by fever, hypoglycemia, electrolyte imbalances, drugs, or medication overdoses. If seizures occur because of any of these problems and the seizures are not prolonged, they may not recur if the underlying problem is recognized and treated. Repeated, unprovoked seizures, on the other hand, are diagnostic of true epilepsy. Patients with epilepsy may have spontaneous seizures, or seizures may be triggered by illness, bright scintillating light, or sleep deprivation, for example.

In individuals with ASDs of unknown cause, epilepsy is reported to be several times more common than in the general population. The rate of epilepsy is even higher in persons with an ASD and other known disorders such as tuberous sclerosis. Epilepsy is estimated to be present in about 1% of the general population, while the rate of epilepsy in individuals with ASDs is reported to range from 7 to 40%.[12-14] Epilepsy is reported to be even more frequent in females with ASDs.[15-17] Although seizures can occur at any age, the peak onset of epilepsy in children with ASDs is between early school ages and adolescence. Many types of epilepsy have been reported in individuals with ASDs.[17-19] These epilepsies range from simple or complex partial epilepsy, to partial epilepsy with secondary generalization, to generalized epilepsy, to myoclonic epilepsy (a specific type of jerky seizure), to atonic epilepsy (a seizure causing a person to drop to the floor). There are no specific types of epilepsy that occur solely in persons with ASDs. Making the diagnosis of seizures in children with ASDs may be difficult, especially if the child is experiencing complex partial seizures. Many children with ASDs have stereotypic behaviors and may stare into space without responding to their surroundings. The language challenges faced by many children with ASDs make it more difficult to sort out these behaviors. Most children with ASDs exhibit their other behaviors in a random fashion, which could be distinguished from the paroxysmal, sudden onset and stoppage, and stereotypic nature of seizures. Most seizures involve changes of sensorium or altered consciousness which most parents can identify and differentiate from non-epileptic stereotypic behaviors.

There has been controversy about the possible existence of a special type of epilepsy in children with ASDs who demonstrate no clinically identifiable seizures. This condition, Landau–Kleffner syndrome (LKS), describes children with epilepsy who lose their acquired language and have an abnormal electroencephalogram (EEG) while not having seizures. Children with typical LKS usually do not have problems in their social interactions and, prior to their language regression, their language skills are most often normal for age. Children with LKS generally have continuous epileptiform activity (seizure activity on EEG, but there may not be any noticeable seizures in the patients) in the language area of the brain. The cause of LKS is believed to be an abnormal immune response or inflammation within the brain because some of these children respond to immunomodulation treatment.[20] Some children with an ASD may be felt to have atypical LKS, but authorities disagree about this issue. Although children with ASDs often have language regression and some develop epilepsy, not all children with ASDs (with or without epilepsy) have LKS. There is overlap between children with confirmed LKS and other children with an ASD, since both may be associated with regression and epilepsy. Immunological changes or other causes of inflammation of the brain are sometimes implicated in the development of an ASD.[21] Some children with ASDs lose the limited language they have and are found to have epileptiform activity in the language area of the brain but do not have LKS because they had earlier delays in language acquisition and function before the onset of speech regression. These children are also noted to have impairment in social interactions and more severe behavioral disorders than reported in children with LKS. Some children with ASDs are noted by their parents to have features of epilepsy, while parents of others do not report seizures. Regardless, children with regressive ASDs and signs of epilepsy deserve an evaluation for continuous epileptiform activity by prolonged video EEG monitoring. It is not clear whether all children with signs of regressive ASDs who have no signs of seizures should also have a prolonged video EEG. (The risks and benefits of such testing are discussed in Chapter 11.)

Immunomodulation therapy in children with ASDs and some LKS-like features is much less successful than for children with clear-cut LKS. The question of whether the continuous epileptiform activity in some children with regressive ASDs has any impact on language development remains unanswered. It is understandable that parents would like their physicians to consider treating epileptiform activity to determine whether or not their child's development and behaviors will improve; however, treatment with anti-seizure medications has failed thus far to produce consistent improvement in development or even suppression of the epileptiform activity. Perhaps an effective treatment is not far from reach with rapid progress being made through focused research on autism.

Sleep disorders

Up to 50% of children between birth and 6 years of age, and an average of 25% of all ages of typically developed children, have sleep complaints that improve over time.[22] Sleep disorders have been frequently reported in individuals with ASDs. The rate of sleep disorders of children of all ages who have ASDs ranges between 44 and 83%.[23,24] Children with ASDs are frequently reported to display problematic sleep patterns, which are often severe in nature.[25–27] These sleep problems include difficulty in settling to sleep, lengthy episodes of nighttime waking with or without confusion, crying or screaming during sleep (night terror), bruxism (teeth grinding), enuresis (bedwetting), rapid eye movement (REM) sleep behavior disorder (acting out of dreams), early-morning awakening, shortened nighttime sleep, daytime sleepiness, and irregularities of the sleep–wake rhythm.[27,28] In my clinical experience, the types of sleep disorders seen in children with ASDs are related mostly to sleep initiation and maintenance disorders (i.e., insomnia). The less frequent sleep disorders seen in my clinical practice include circadian disorder, sleep apnea, parasomnia, and movement disorders during sleep. Sleep disorders may develop during infancy and may present with so-called colic. Sleep complaints are most likely brought up by parents during early childhood, around 3–6 years of age. Sleep complaints tend to lessen gradually over time in the majority of children with ASDs but may reemerge as a significant problem again during adolescence in a smaller proportion of children with ASDs.

Insomnia is frequently associated with anxiety, depression, and mood disorders. For sleep to occur, one must be relaxed physically and mentally. The heart rate at sleep onset should be lower than one's average daily heart rate; breathing should also be regular. Many children with ASDs have difficulty relaxing, are anxious and hyperalert, or are hyperactive at bedtime. The need to perform rituals, or fear of sleep/darkness, could prevent them from falling sleep.[29,30] The same anxiety could wake them up and make it difficult for them to fall back to sleep. Night awakening could also be medically related. Children with ASDs have an increased rate of gastrointestinal (GI) problems, such as reflux, bloating, gassiness, bowel pain, constipation, or loose stools. Any of these problems, or a combination of bowel problems, could awaken a child and prevent the child from resuming sleep. Allergy symptoms and associated sinusitis may get worse during supine (back) sleep positioning and awaken a child. We know children with ASDs have a higher rate of allergies than the general child population.[31] Our own study showed that the children with ASDs and sleep disorders were significantly more likely also to have GI disorders and food intolerance.[32]

Other problems that disrupt sleep in individuals with ASDs include parasomnia such as confusional arousal, night terrors, nightmares and sleepwalking, obstructive sleep apnea, REM sleep behavioral disorders, and nocturnal epilepsy (nighttime seizures).[27,28] We documented in our sleep laboratory confusional arousals/sleep terrors in 14 of the 23 children with ASDs that we tested; 11 of the 14 children had multiple confusional arousals/sleep terrors in the same night, while only 3 of the 20 similar-aged typically developing children had one parasomnia recorded during the study.[28] The children with ASDs who appeared to be aroused but were not fully awake (partial arousal) during the sleep study in our lab were able to go back to sleep. Paavonen *et al.* reported that children with Asperger disorder have higher rates of nightmares than typically developing children.[29] Persons with nightmares usually wake up fully alert and have difficulty going back to sleep; such may be the case for children with ASDs as well. Sleep apnea was reported in children with ASDs, especially for children who were obese, had anatomical changes in the upper airway such as seen in some children with Down syndrome, or had periodic sinus nasal congestion. Nocturnal epilepsy can surely disrupt sleep, and therefore children with both ASDs and epilepsy may have sleep disruption due to nocturnal seizures.

The consequences of poor sleep are well recognized. In typically developing children, poor sleep quality can lead to poor school performance and daytime behavioral disorders such as hyperactivity, impulsivity, anxiety, aggressiveness, or excessive sleepiness.[27] Children with ASDs who have disordered sleep can certainly experience similar consequences, and treatment of sleep disorders in such cases can improve daytime behaviors as well as learning and performance in these children.[33,34] We should also be cognizant of the impact of poor sleep of children on their parents or caregivers. The impact is even more pronounced for parents of younger children who need to be supervised in the middle of the night, or even worse if these children have behavioral disorders as well that emerge during the night. Many families of these children with ASDs and disordered sleep are desperate to find relief from chronic sleep deprivation. Melatonin, a natural supplement, may be quite effective in improving the insomnia in some children. Over time, the dose of melatonin may need to be increased. Sometimes, another medication needs to be added to maintain nightly sleep. In a small-series case study, we reported good efficacy of clonidine in treating insomnia and improving daytime behaviors in children with ASDs.[34]

Autonomic dysfunction

The autonomic nervous system (ANS) is an involuntary nervous system responsible for many body functions. The ANS consists of the sympathetic, parasympathetic, and enteric nervous systems. The sympathetic nervous system (SNS) is mediated by adrenaline, which is responsible for the so-called fight-or-flight reaction. When the SNS is activated, heart rate, blood pressure, and respiratory rate increase. The pupils dilate and the skin becomes flushed or moist. The parasympathetic nervous system (PNS), on the other hand, is responsible for digestion, sleep initiation, and recovery from excitement or stress. When the PNS is activated, heart rate and blood pressure are lowered, breathing becomes regular and deep, pupils constrict to limit the entry of light, gut motility increases, and digestive enzymes are secreted. The enteric nervous system consists of neurons within the wall of the gut and regulates gut motility. The SNS and PNS counteract each other, balancing the ANS function level suitable for a given state of body function. Both SNS and PNS control the enteric nervous system. Multiple regions of the brain and spinal cord form a network of the ANS, producing layers of interaction and feedback.

Dysfunction of the ANS (dysautonomia) can cause mild symptoms such as exercise intolerance or more severe problems such as passing out (syncope). Dysautonomia can also lead to physical and behavioral problems, such as sensory hypersensitivity, hyperactivity, anxiety, mood swings, irritability, photophobia (light sensitivity), GI dysfunction (reflux, constipation, diarrhea, bloating), poor sleep, irregular breathing, blotchy or flushed complexion, or unexplained fever. We can identify quite a few symptoms from the list that are seen more frequently in individuals with ASDs.

Sensory disintegration is a frequently reported symptom, manifested by atypical responses to sensation.[35-37] The American Psychiatric Association's new DSM-5 diagnostic criteria for ASDs include hypo- or hyper-responsivity to sensory input or unusual sensory interests as one criterion fulfilling the restricted or repetitive patterns of behavior,[38] suggesting that sensory disintegration is prevalent in individuals with ASDs. Studies identified the ANS as being responsible for the atypical behavioral responses to sensation in children with sensory processing disorders *without* autism.[39-41] More recent studies indicate a similar link in children *with* autism.[42,43] Attention deficit hyperactivity disorder (ADHD), anxiety, obsessive–compulsive behaviors, mood disorders, aggression, and irritability all have been reported with increased frequency in children with ASDs.[32,44] Dysautonomia has been reported increasingly in children with ASDs.[45–47] Toichi and Kamio found that the mean resting parasympathetic activity of the heart was significantly lower in adolescents with ASDs compared with age-matched controls.[48] When we examined ANS activity during resting states we found that children with ASDs demonstrated significantly lower resting PNS activity and significantly higher SNS activity, measured by various parameters of blood pressure, than typically developing controls. Treatments and therapies for these comorbid disorders of dysautonomia are frequently targeted at modulation of the ANS. Clonidine, risperidone, and selective serotonin reuptake inhibitors, such as sertraline, produce their therapeutic effects via the ANS. Music therapy, yoga, relaxation therapy, and presumably cranial–sacral maneuvers all target improving parasympathetic function;[49–52] however, their effects in children with ASDs remain to be determined.

Abnormal motor and sensory functions

Motor and sensory dysfunction have been reported in individuals with ASDs. While gross motor deficits in children with idiopathic ASDs are rare, fine motor deficits or motor program problems (apraxia) are not uncommon. We reported hypotonia and motor apraxia in almost half of the children with ASDs evaluated.[53] The rate of children with ASDs who had fine motor deficits decreased with age, suggesting improvement over time. This improvement could be the result of a combination of therapy and the natural maturation of the brain and central nervous system.

Motor apraxia often manifests as body and limb incoordination. An example of such apraxia is difficulty with peddling a tricycle at 7 years of age. Hand motor apraxia is frequently reported by teachers, therapists, and parents. In such cases, hand grip may be described as "weak," yet the hands are not weak in muscle power; instead, they are clumsy or incoordinated. Hand posture while holding a pen or a utensil may be noted to be awkward. Older children may not be able to use scissors or staplers; however, the same child may be able to pinch his arm or pull his hair out without difficulty. Performance of a fine motor act may be variable, for example, a child may be able to use a pair of scissors at one time but not at another, especially when the child is stressed. Unlike regression, there is no permanent loss of the skill, only a temporary dysfunction. Motor apraxia may also affect the muscles responsible for speech production. When this occurs, the child is said to have oral motor apraxia. Such a child may not be able to pucker the lips, use the tongue correctly, or move the lips or laryngeal muscles at will. These muscles of speech production may be too incoordinated to work in harmony to produce intelligible words. Cook, Blakemore, and Press found that adults with ASDs had atypical body movement adjustments in responding to motor tasks as compared with typically developed adults. Adults with ASDs did not minimize jerky movements and moved with greater acceleration and speed.[54] Retrospective analysis of infant videos demonstrated that children with ASDs were found to have postural control difficulties.[55] Motor accuracy and sensory motor coordination were also found to be impaired in individuals with ASDs.[56]

Another motor problem noted in individuals with ASDs is dystonia. Some children with ASDs may show sustained muscle contraction, leading to a twisted posture of an arm, a leg, or a finger. Dystonia may be observed in children with ASDs during repetitive movements. Many children with ASDs habitually turn their head while looking at objects by way of a sideways glance, and as a result, some parents may report that the child's eyes are "stuck" in the corners. To my knowledge, however, this issue has not been carefully studied.

A third rare motor disorder in individuals with ASDs in my clinical practice is sudden motor freezing, much like the frozen gait of patients with Parkinson disease. At least one such child with a known ASD responded to L-dopa treatment (a medication for Parkinson disease). These are just anecdotal reports at this time; however, similarities between ASDs and Parkinson disease have been reviewed.[57]

In addition to the sensory disintegration discussed earlier, some children with ASDs may have reduced sensitivity to pain and temperature. Parents of these children report a reduced reaction to a cut, bruise, or other injury. It is not entirely clear if the reduced reaction is due to insensitivity to pain or reduced emotional response to pain. Sometimes these children may not even be aware of a painful cut or sore. Similarly, many children with ASDs are insensitive to cold. Walking in the snow with bare feet is not unusual for some children with ASDs.

When should you be concerned about these neurological disorders in your child?

Some of the neurological disorders described above need to be treated immediately with medication, while others may respond to therapy. It is clear that repeated or prolonged seizures need to be treated right away. Prolonged seizures can cause brain damage and generalized convulsive seizures can lead to falls and injury. Not infrequently, patients with epilepsy are brought to the emergency department for treatment of a seizure. If your child has had more than two unprovoked seizures, he or she should take a daily medication to prevent seizure recurrence. Your child needs to see a physician, preferably a neurologist, for seizure treatment. Chronic insomnia deserves an elective evaluation, especially if the impact of the insomnia on daytime behaviors and family life is significant. Frequent sleep terrors, confusional arousals, or sleepwalking should also be evaluated to ensure that these are not symptoms of a nocturnal seizure.

Identifying a neurological disorder in a child with an ASD may be somewhat more challenging. For example, autonomic dysfunction may not be identified if it presents in a child who consistently refuses to get up quickly from a sitting position. This behavior may be regarded as intentional willfulness rather than compensation for autonomic symptoms. In this case, the child has learned that if she gets up quickly, she feels dizzy and therefore compensates by taking her time to get up. She in fact has orthostatic (postural) hypotension[58] and a leisurely approach to changes in position (lying to sitting or sitting to standing) ameliorates symptoms. A symptom, sign, or behavior that is persistent and stereotypic (very similar if not identical in its presentation and triggering events each time it occurs) should be evaluated. Unexplained regression (loss of a learned skill) that lasts more than a few weeks should also be evaluated in a timely manner; however, children may temporarily lose a recently learned skill when they are physically sick or experiencing significant emotional stress such as the departure of a primary caregiver.

Many children with ASDs exhibit self-stimulatory behaviors, hyperactivity, or obsessive–compulsive behaviors. Although the theme or focus of the obsession may be the same for an individual child over time, the resultant compulsive behaviors are usually not stereotypic or identical each time the child engages in compulsion or self-stimulation. Most of these symptoms or behaviors are treated with behavioral therapy. Parents should bring these symptoms to the physician's attention during scheduled visits. Similarly, motor and sensory deficits are usually treated with specific focused therapies and should be addressed regularly when discussing comprehensive services for your child.

How to get your child evaluated for a suspected neurological disorder

If your child is having a seizure for the first time, you should take him or her to the nearest emergency department. He or she may need a test done immediately. If the seizure is prolonged, emergent treatment is required. Paramedics are equipped to give medication to stop a seizure before arriving at the emergency department. You should request an evaluation from a neurologist while in the emergency department or soon after discharge. Prolonged seizures (greater than 5 minutes) or multiple seizures during the same day generally require inpatient care.

If you suspect your child has a non-urgent neurological disorder that needs to be evaluated, you may find it helpful to prepare prior to an appointment. Videotape the symptoms or events if you can. Keep a log of the events, the antecedent events and aftermath of the behavior, circumstances surrounding the events, frequency and duration of each event, and so forth. In some cases the trigger may be something that happened the day before, such as a particularly poor night's sleep, an unusual meal the night prior, or a minor injury a few days before. Keep a detailed record of all the medications your child is taking and has taken. A pediatrician or primary care physician is usually the first physician you should contact with your concerns. The symptoms could be non-neurological and your pediatrician may be the best person to address these because they have more experience with non-neurological issues compared to a neurologist. If it is neurologically based, your pediatrician may help you to get an earlier appointment (if needed) with your own neurologist or a first-time visit with an appropriate subspecialist. In addition, in most cases you would prefer that your pediatrician or primary care physician serve as the "captain of the ship" in coordinating your child's care.

 ## TAKEAWAY POINTS

- Children with ASDs are at increased risk for neurological disorders.
- Epilepsy in children needs to be diagnosed and treated promptly.
- Sleep disorders are amenable to treatment and this can result in improvement in the child's behaviors and also the family's quality of life.
- Behavioral symptoms may be the clue to an underlying neurological disorder.
- Motor and sensory problems may respond to therapy and/or medication.

Co-occurrence of Psychiatric Disorders in Individuals with Autism Spectrum Disorders

Lisa Ford, MD

Introduction

Behavioral and psychiatric disorders are common among individuals with autism spectrum disorders (ASDs). Some estimates suggest that as many as 70% of children with ASDs present with at least one comorbid psychiatric disorder.[1] Behavioral problems sometimes are regarded nonspecifically as "autistic behaviors" rather than a specific psychiatric disorder. Early identification of a specific psychiatric disorder can help to devise a more focused behavioral therapy and treatment plan. This chapter gives an overview of various psychiatric disorders we have diagnosed and treated in children and adults with ASDs, among which are general anxiety disorders, mood disorders, and obsessive–compulsive disorder (OCD).

The co-occurrence of psychiatric disorders in ASDs has been recognized and may include mood disorders, depression, obsessive–compulsive behaviors, as well as aggressive and self-injurious behaviors. One study reported that subjects with pervasive developmental disorders—not otherwise specified (PDD-NOS) are more likely to have a medical disorder, whereas subjects with Asperger disorder are more likely to have psychiatric comorbidities.[2]

The diagnosis of psychiatric co-occurrences involving expression of affect, appreciation of self-value, or thought obsession in individuals with ASDs is challenging. This type of information can only be elicited in older, verbal, less severely affected individuals. Nevertheless, the psychiatric co-occurrence in this cohort appears to be higher than in the general population. For example, the frequency of mood disorders was found to be 26.3% in ASDs compared with 1–4% in youths ages 14–18 years in the general pediatric population.[2–4] Mood disorders appeared to be more common in older age groups and in autism in these studies. Affective disorder in autism first noted during childhood has been reported, and the rate of mood disorder rises with age. It has also been reported that individuals with intellectual disabilities have an increased risk for psychiatric disorders.[5] Because individuals with an ASD are more likely to have intellectual disabilities than those with PDD-NOS or Asperger disorder, this may partly account for their increased prevalence of mood disorders. It is not clear whether aggression or self-injurious behaviors, or both, are a symptom of another psychiatric disorder.

General anxiety disorders

In addition to autism-specific impairments, high rates of anxiety disorders are observed in individuals with ASDs. There is considerable evidence that children and adolescents with ASDs are at increased risk for anxiety and anxiety disorders;[6] however, it is less clear which of the specific DSM-IV anxiety disorders occur most in this population.

Prevalence of anxiety disorders in children with ASDs

Several studies looking at the prevalence of anxiety disorders in young people with ASDs have been conducted. One systematic review of the literature identified 11 studies involving 1353 young people (ages 6–18 years) with ASDs where rates of anxiety were reported based on observation, interview, or questionnaires.[7] Significant variation was found across studies with rates of clinically significant anxiety ranging between 11 and 84%. Another systematic review of the literature identified 31 studies involving 2121 young people (ages <18 years) with ASDs, and where the presence of anxiety disorder was assessed using standardized questionnaires or diagnostic interviews. Overall results revealed substantial comorbidity for anxiety in children and adolescents with an ASD; across studies, nearly 40% were estimated to have clinically elevated levels of anxiety or at least one anxiety disorder.[6] Studies show that a specific phobia was most common at nearly 30%, followed by OCD in 17%, social anxiety disorder and agoraphobia in nearly 17%, generalized anxiety disorder in 15%, separation anxiety disorder in nearly 9%, and panic disorder in nearly 2%.[1,7–9]

By way of comparison, anxiety disorders in typically developing children are estimated to occur in 2.2–27%.[10] In addition, with the exception of panic disorder, the rates of the specific anxiety disorders observed in children with an ASD are more than twofold higher than in typically developing children, and higher than those found in children seeking treatment for attention deficit hyperactivity disorder and learning difficulties.[10–12]

In children with ASDs, higher rates of anxiety in general were found in studies concentrating on a higher mean age. Contradictory results of studies reporting on anxiety in ASDs, however, have been found for the relationship between age, anxiety, and ASDs. Some studies found that older children with an ASD were more likely to report anxiety.[13,14] It is possible that the type of anxiety disorder under study is an important issue, which may be somewhat age dependent. For example, studies concentrating on a higher mean age also reported higher rates of generalized anxiety disorder and lower rates of separation anxiety disorder.[13,14] These findings are consistent with the results of studies examining anxiety disorders in typically developing children, which found (1) rates of anxiety disorders (generally) increase with age, (2) rates of generalized anxiety disorder (specifically) increase with age, and (3) rates of separation anxiety disorder are associated with younger age.[15,16]

There is some evidence that anxiety in general is more likely to be diagnosed in children with PDD-NOS compared with those with autistic disorder and Asperger syndrome. There is also evidence of certain anxiety disorders being more strongly associated with one or more ASD subtypes.[6] The severity of the communication, social interaction, and stereotyped behaviors associated with ASD subtypes varies, and this may lead the child more toward one form of anxiety than another. The presence of autistic disorder was associated with higher rates of OCD and a specific phobia but lower rates of generalized anxiety disorder, while the presence of Asperger syndrome was associated with lower rates of a specific phobia and OCD. Finally, the presence of PDD-NOS was associated with higher rates of a specific phobia, generalized anxiety disorder, and panic disorder, and lower rates of OCD. Across ASD subtypes, increased rates of anxiety disorders in general were associated with lower IQ scores.[17–19]

Obsessive–compulsive disorder

Once considered a rare phenomenon, epidemiological studies have found OCD to be the fourth most common psychiatric disorder, with prevalence rates between 1.5 and 3% in the general population. OCD encompasses a relatively frequent anxiety disorder characterized by repetitive thoughts, impulses, or images (obsessions), and repetitive behaviors or mental acts (compulsions) that cause marked distress. OCD is highly debilitating, and the World Health Organization has found it to be among the ten most disabling medical conditions. It has been suggested that OCD is part of the "obsessive–

compulsive spectrum disorders." Disorders belonging to this spectrum are thought to share similarities in clinical symptoms, associated features, etiology, and response to treatment. The obsessive–compulsive spectrum disorders include neuropsychiatric conditions such as Tourette syndrome, Sydenham chorea, and ASDs. Most of the research into the relationship between ASDs and OCD has been performed in pediatric patients with ASDs.

Interestingly and unlike studies that assess anxiety in typically developing children, studies that included younger children with ASDs reported higher prevalence rates of OCD than those that included older children with ASDs. OCD in typically developing children, however, tends to have a relatively late age of onset[10] and is found to increase with age;[15] however, OCD and the restricted, repetitive behaviors observed in individuals with ASDs share much overlap in symptoms, and therefore differentiation between the two disorders can be extremely difficult. There is some evidence that younger children with ASDs have more restricted, repetitive behaviors compared with older children with ASDs[20] and that children with ASDs "improve" in the ritualistic/repetitive behavior domain as they grow older.[21] These results seem to support the present finding that higher rates of OCD were seen at a lower mean age in children with an ASD.

Children with ASDs have shown increased rates of obsessive–compulsive symptoms. Conversely, pediatric patients with OCD show increased frequencies of autistic symptoms. Repetitive behaviors are among the core features of both ASDs and OCD, and comparison of ASDs with OCD has demonstrated more similarities than differences in obsessive–compulsive symptom characteristics between these groups. Some differences can be noted, with individuals with ASDs demonstrating more hoarding, touching, tapping, and self-damaging behaviors, and less checking, repeating, and counting behaviors, as well as less aggressive and somatic obsessions than others with OCD alone.[22,23]

Mood disorders

Psychiatric comorbidities in ASDs have not been well examined. Some of the older literature indicates that depression is the main psychiatric comorbidity reported in individuals with ASDs;[24] more recent data suggest that bipolar disorder is the major comorbid mood disorder in adolescents and young adults with ASDs, particularly those with a high-functioning ASD.[25]

According to a review of 17 older published cases of individuals with ASDs and depression,[26] half of the patients with mood disorders were female, even though ASDs are seen much more commonly in males. In these studies, the age of onset ranged from childhood to young adulthood, and almost all of the patients had intellectual disabilities. Although depression was the most common comorbidity in ASDs,[27] some cases of bipolar disorder (BPD) have been reported.[28-30] For example, in one study 14 of 66 consecutively referred children with ASDs demonstrated mania as a comorbid condition.[31]

Since individuals with ASDs, especially those with low intellectual abilities (IQ < 70), have limited verbal communication abilities and inappropriate facial expressions, it remains uncertain whether they are verbalizing their inner experiences, such as sadness or inflated self-esteem. Clinicians may try to detect depressive or hypomanic symptoms from facial expressions or behaviors, but this is quite challenging. Researchers have regarded a sad appearance, loss of interest in activities, frequent crying spells, insomnia, and loss of appetite as depressive symptoms, or a cheerful appearance, hyperactivity, pressure of speech, and increased appetite as hypomanic symptoms.

One study evaluated the comorbidity of mood disorder in adolescents and young adults with high-functioning ASD because patients with IQ ≥ 70 can often verbalize inner experiences more appropriately than low-functioning individuals. The results suggested that BPD was the major comorbidity for mood disorders in adolescents and young adults with high-functioning ASD. About one-third of patients in this series had a mood disorder, and the prevalence of BPD was three times that of major depressive disorder.[32] These rates of mood disorder were consistent with those of another study: Ghaziuddin, Weidmer-Mikhail, and Ghaziuddin found that 13 of 35 patients with Asperger disorder between 8 and 51 years old had a mood disorder based on DSM-IV.[24] Of these 13 patients, 8 patients had major depressive disorder, 4 patients had dysthymia, and only 1 patient had BPD.

Environment in the manifestation of psychiatric disorders

The environmental context differentially affects individuals with ASDs and it is an additional crucial factor that may influence the onset, expression, and severity of the psychiatric disorder or comorbidity. The variable expression of psychiatric difficulties in children with ASDs may be directly related to environmental factors and this points to the possibility of planning differential intervention. For instance, family and daily routines have to be considered as environmental factors that could potentially lead to differential burden of psychiatric comorbidities.

The importance of environmental context in psychiatric symptom expression has been investigated in a sample of youths with ASDs and their siblings, using an evaluation completed independently by parents and teachers. Reports by teachers show a much lower prevalence of psychiatric comorbidity, in particular for affective, anxiety, attention, conduct, oppositional, and somatic problems in these individuals, as compared with the reports of their parents.[33] Manifestations of psychopathology in people with Asperger disorder or high-functioning autism (HFA) may vary depending on the context; their identification depends on the type of observer, suggesting that informant discrepancies may constitute an additional variable element for the proper identification of comorbidities. In this regard, there is often a lack of consensus between reports by parents and teachers about the behaviors present in children with Asperger disorder or HFA, thus suggesting caution when interpreting results of surveys or drawing conclusions about the presence of comorbid psychiatric problems based on a single informant source or a single environmental context. Emphasis needs to be placed on the importance of gathering information from multiple sources and observations of the individual in various settings, which should also include direct observation by clinicians. Since the environment seems to considerably influence the expression of psychiatric comorbidities in individuals with ASDs, more attention should be focused on the interactions between these individuals and their various everyday life environments in order to provide better social support and help the individual, family members, therapists, and teachers to develop coping strategies that may, in the long run, contribute to a decrease in the incidence of psychiatric comorbidities.

Behavioral treatment

The management of behavioral problems in children and adolescents with ASDs is a challenge for clinicians and families. Even individuals with Asperger disorder or HFA may have difficulties describing their own feelings and emotions, so it is not easy to detect and recognize another psychiatric comorbidity that could be masked by the autistic symptoms themselves.

Comprehensive treatment programs for young children with ASDs vary in both the amount and types of support they provide and the presence of recommended components. The lack of a clear consensus on the superiority of one treatment model over others has led to many children with ASDs receiving any variety of interventions and techniques within home-based programs and/or school-based programs, which are often lumped together under the term "eclectic"; however, though specific program components and characteristics might vary, the importance of early intervention is now well established, and consensus that early intervention can improve adult outcomes is building.

The only psychoeducational treatment that meets the criteria as a well-established and efficacious intervention for ASDs is behavioral treatment, which is often referred to as applied behavior analysis (ABA). Within the National Autism Center guidelines, virtually all of the 11 interventions identified as established treatments are components of ABA; however, families may be unaware of the existence of ABA services, unsure how to find a qualified provider to access the services, or may mistakenly think that there is only one version of ABA services (i.e., early intensive behavioral intervention, or EIBI) when other forms of behavioral treatment have been proven effective for issues across the lifespan and at lower intensities.

There are at least three critical features for all behavioral treatments. First, the procedures should be derived directly from behavioral theory and research. Second, there needs to be an emphasis on frequent measurement of observable indicators of progress. Third, all aspects of the child's functioning (e.g., skills, deficits, problem behaviors) are considered products of the interaction between children and influential aspects of their environments. After careful examination of the interplay between the child and the environment (e.g., people, events) uncovers important interaction patterns, problematic interactions can be directly targeted using behavioral treatment procedures. Sometimes the interaction pattern is altered by teaching the child important new functional skills (i.e., the ability to request) and sometimes the interaction pattern is changed by modifying some aspect of the environment (e.g., availability of certain interactions and adult responses to problem behaviors). Substantial differences exist in behavioral treatments in relationship to the scope and goals of the therapy, the venue for delivering the services, and unique client characteristics, such as age and clinical presentation.

EIBI is a behavioral treatment based on the principles of ABA that is delivered early (before age 5 years) and intensively (25–40 hours per week), usually over a span of 2–3 years. For now, EIBI is the only current well-established treatment that produces positive outcomes for children with ASDs. The purpose of EIBI is to increase intellectual (i.e., communication, cognitive, academic) skills and adaptive functioning (i.e., social skills, self-care skills, safety) to prepare children with ASDs to learn from, and succeed in, typical home and school environments with the fewest possible supports.[34,35] These goals are achieved by creating a precise and sophisticated instructional environment for as many of the child's waking hours as possible, at the youngest age possible, to alter the developmental trajectory in all areas of functioning. Perhaps the most critical repertoires targeted are the learning-to-learn skills (e.g., imitation, following instructions, and initiating interactions) that allow children to learn from more typical environments in ways that are similar to those of their peers.[35,36] Large and sustained improvement in specific skills and in overall functioning increase the likelihood that a child will continue to be able to succeed throughout life with less intensive behavioral supports.[37]

The origins of EIBI are linked to the University of California at Los Angeles Young Autism Project model (also termed the Lovaas model). The core elements of EIBI involve (1) a specific teaching procedure referred to as discrete trial training, (2) the use of a 1:1 adult-to-child ratio in the early stages of the treatment, and (3) implementation in either home or school settings for a range of 20–40 hours per week across 1–4 years of the child's life. Typically, EIBI is implemented under the supervision of personnel trained in ABA procedures who systematically follow a treatment manual outlining the scope and sequence of tasks to be introduced and taught. Possible variables affecting child outcomes might be (1) who delivers the treatment (e.g., parent, clinician, or teacher), (2) treatment intensity and duration (dosage), (3) staff supervision schedules, and (4) intervention settings. Many families of young children receiving treatment, including EIBI, also seek out additional services to address residual symptoms of ASDs, such as speech therapy, occupational therapy, or group-based interventions. It is unclear which, if any, of these variables moderate treatment effects.

EIBI addresses the core deficits of ASDs; individual instructional programs are developed based on the child's current behavioral repertoires (e.g., communication and social skills), and a functional approach is used to address challenging behaviors that interfere with learning. Furthermore, EIBI generally includes a family component, so parents implement, manage, or assist in treatment planning and delivery. The specific intervention strategies implemented within EIBI programs include a variety of techniques such as antecedent packages, modeling, use of schedules, and self-management. Although EIBI is considered one of the most well-established treatment programs to date for young children with ASDs, questions remain about the methodology of EIBI research.

In addition to the components of EIBI listed earlier, effective programs always include a substantial segment of parent support and training designed to assist families in crafting a home environment that promotes optimal functioning for their child and minimizes the likelihood of the development of severe problem behavior.[35] Providers teach parents how to play with their children in ways that feel natural but are likely to promote better social interactions and more meaningful and appropriate play. They also learn how to prevent problem behaviors or how to change their interactions with the child if problem behaviors emerge, and how to teach daily living skills, communication, and social skills using behavioral instructional procedures.

Problem-focused behavioral treatment

Similar to EIBI, behavioral outpatient or consultation services typically focus on decreasing problematic behaviors or developing specific skill sets or behavioral repertoires; however, the purpose and model of implementation differ from those of EIBI. Outpatient and consultative behavioral treatment services are typically short-term, focused interventions requiring less intensive contact with the provider (i.e., 1–2 hours per week). Characteristics of behavioral consultation and therapy significantly overlap with those of EIBI, because the same theoretic approach is used for both forms of behavioral treatment.

The typical course of services involves targeted assessment of a few specific problems followed by development of a focused intervention plan. Subsequent implementation occurs either directly by the outpatient therapist or by the family or school personnel who have been trained by the therapist to provide the intervention.[38] This model is appropriate for children or adolescents with milder forms of ASDs, such as Asperger disorder, with no concomitant intellectual impairment, for children who have completed EIBI and are experiencing new behavioral issues across time, or if EIBI services or funding are unavailable.

Behavioral consultation and outpatient therapy services are usually provided in the community (e.g., private practice office or school) and often involve the development of a behavioral intervention plan for both home and school settings. Often the consultant or outpatient provider serves as a member of a multidisciplinary team that establishes and implements the child's individualized education plan. Some of the most common targeted skills for acquisition in this model include social skills, emotion-regulation skills, and self-management skills.[39] Common problematic behaviors referred for treatment include self-injury, noncompliance, tantrums, and disruptive behavior.[40] Before and during adolescence, individuals with an ASD may be increasingly affected by social difficulties, including teasing and bullying, and present with an unusually high rate of comorbid mental health concerns such as anxiety[41] and depression.[9]

In summary, behavioral treatment in the form of EIBI is currently the only better-established treatment for young children with ASDs.[42,43] In addition to EIBI for young children, many other behavioral interventions are available in outpatient treatment and consultation services that are effective for targeted concerns of children and adolescents with ASDs.[44]

Below are four specific recommendations for families considering behavioral treatments for their child:

1. Families are encouraged to pursue evidence-based practices such as those described above rather than treatments that have not been shown to produce powerful and replicable gains for children with ASDs.

2. Families should seek highly qualified providers of services using information outlined in this chapter, because the skills and qualifications of the provider make an important difference in treatment outcomes.

3. Families should maintain optimistic but realistic expectations for outcomes for their children (i.e., important skill improvements rather than recovery) and have appropriate expectations about their own role in achieving those outcomes (i.e., the importance of parent training, long-term planning, and consistent responses).

4. There should be active, ongoing collaboration and communication between the physicians and behavioral treatment providers.

Treatment of disruptive behavioral disorders

Children with ASDs may exhibit challenging behaviors; available literature using DSM-defined disorders indicates that approximately one in four children with an ASD has a comorbid disruptive behavioral disorder (DBD). Disruptive behaviors are important in ASDs because they contribute to poorer health and well-being of individuals with ASDs. For instance, one study reported that psychiatric hospitalization among people with ASDs was five times more likely for those who exhibited aggressive behavior compared with those who did not.[45] Disruptive behaviors also affect others; conduct problems, physical and verbal aggression, and other behavior problems have been associated with increased parental stress[14] and teacher burn-out.[46] These behavior problems often persist into adulthood, where they are associated with a more restrictive lifestyle, including increased residential or out-of-home placements.[47]

One review study reported the effects of behavioral treatment on DBDs in individuals with ASDs.[48] Eight studies focused on the psychosocial treatment of disruptive behaviors. One study was an observational study on the effectiveness of community-based services for this subset of individuals.[49] In this study, regardless of the background of the therapist, behavior problems were reduced after 8 months of treatment for children with ASDs. The authors also compared the effectiveness of community-based therapy for those with ASDs and those with a non-ASD diagnosis who were seeing the same therapists. They found that children with ASDs were receiving similar therapy for behavior problems as those without an ASD, and treatment outcome was similar as well.

Gabriels *et al.* investigated therapeutic horseback riding (THR), also known as hippotherapy. In this uncontrolled open-label study, irritability and other disruptive behaviors were reduced during the 10-week intervention.[50] THR has been reported previously to improve social functioning[51] or motor skills,[52] but this is one of the first studies to examine effectiveness on disruptive behaviors.

Cognitive behavioral therapy (CBT) for anger control has also been studied in the treatment of DBDs.[53] There was a significant reduction in instances of aggression for the treatment group that continued at the 6-month follow-up relative to the waitlist group. Children receiving CBT also demonstrated greater problem-solving skills in potentially difficult situations compared with children in the waitlist control group.

Other programs involved manualized parent training, where therapeutic teams used a structured treatment manual outlining the tasks for each session, including a therapist script, needed materials (e.g., instructive videotapes, activity sheets, homework tasks for families), and data collection forms. Parent training involves teaching parents skills, generally based on the principles of ABA, and then having them implement the skills at home. Several parent therapy programs have established efficacy in the treatment of DBDs among typically developing younger children.[54] Four different programs have been evaluated among children with ASDs: a program developed by the Research Unit on Pediatric Psychopharmacology (RUPP), the Incredible Years program (www.incredibleyears.com), Parent-Child Interaction Therapy (PCIT),[55] and Stepping Stones Triple P (SSTP).[56] Across these studies, parent therapy was very effective at reducing targeted DBD symptoms. Reduction in disruptive behaviors was found with a modified version used with preschoolers.[57]

The RUPP manualized treatment program has also been used in pharmacological studies.[58] McIntyre evaluated an adapted Incredible Years program.[59] These modifications maintained the primary intervention strategies from the toddler program, but they (1) added an initial discussion on the blessings and challenges of raising a child with a disability, (2) added a discussion about identifying applicable and inapplicable aspects within scripted vignettes, (3) excluded the content on time out, and (4) provided information on local disability services. The study focused on all children with developmental disabilities, but 50% of the treatment group had an ASD.[48] After treatment, the children's disruptive behaviors and the parents' less-than-helpful parenting behaviors were significantly reduced in the experimental group compared with the control group.

Solomon et al. modified PCIT to include use of redirection during the Child Directed Interaction phase, and incorporated higher frequency of praise for appropriate social interaction.[60] Ten children between the ages of 5 and 12 years received PCIT immediately and nine constituted a waitlist control group. PCIT resulted in a large reduction of DBD symptoms, though there was a smaller between-groups effect on the intensity of outbursts when they occurred.

The final manualized parent therapy program used for children with ASDs and disruptive behavior is SSTP, which was also first used among those with intellectual disabilities or other developmental delays.[61] In one study on youngsters with ASDs, parents were taught the original intervention and how to use comic-strip conversations and social stories to improve social understanding in their child.[62] Families receiving SSTP showed improved parenting skills and a decrease in the frequency and disruptiveness of problem behaviors compared with pre-treatment. Treatment gains were maintained for 6 months with problem behaviors no longer in the clinical range.

Behavioral treatment for anxiety disorders

Although anxiety disorders commonly co-occur with ASDs, no single treatment has been well established as effective across the board for anxiety in children with ASDs; however, emerging CBT modification trends have provided an important step in establishing a standardized treatment approach. Based on collective results from multiple studies, CBT can be an effective treatment for children who are diagnosed with an ASD and who also have anxiety disorders.[6] There is a small but growing body of evidence that CBT as designed to improve anxiety in typically developing children also has moderate but positive effects on anxiety disorders in children with ASDs.[63,64] Group studies have shown repeated success in utilizing CBT with children diagnosed with ASDs as well. The use of CBT for anxiety in children with Asperger disorder showed that the CBT group had fewer anxiety symptoms post-treatment and generated significantly more strategies for handling anxiety situations than those in the waitlist group.[63] Another group study of CBT for anxiety in children who had HFA found that the CBT group had significantly fewer anxiety symptoms than the waitlist group. At post-treatment 71.4% of the children in the CBT group no longer met criteria for an anxiety disorder, whereas 100% of children in the waitlist group still met criteria for an anxiety disorder.[64]

When to consider medication

There are no evidence-based pharmacotherapies to treat the core symptoms associated with ASDs, but advances in treatment continue to be made. In some cases pharmacological treatment could be effective in improving the psychiatric symptoms typically noticed in ASDs that frequently have a negative impact on quality of life, thus facilitating adjustment in a variety of settings such as the home, school, and community.

Aggression and related symptoms are the associated problems that often elicit the greatest concern in ASDs. Aggressive behaviors toward self and others displayed by some children with ASDs are a grave concern and may result in removal from less-restrictive classrooms or possibly more restrictive placements. Furthermore, these behaviors are significant predictors of inpatient treatment. Such behaviors can lead to injury to self or others and, consequently, many of the pharmacological investigations in this population are geared toward addressing this potentially dangerous set of behaviors.

Although behavioral and environmental approaches are recommended as the initial treatment, more severe or even dangerous behaviors usually result in requests for urgent pharmacological intervention. Patients can present with a variety of aggressive acts directed toward self, others, and property. Several classes of medications are used to treat aggressive behaviors. The atypical antipsychotics risperidone and aripiprazole are the most studied agents in ASDs, are approved by the FDA for treating irritability (not ASD per se), and have shown solid evidence of effectiveness.[65,66] Studies on the older typical antipsychotic haloperidol also provide favorable evidence for its off-label use; however, the level of evidence is also high for the risk of developing clinically limiting side effects for all antipsychotics, such as the extrapyramidal effects of conventional agents or the metabolic changes of atypical antipsychotics. Close monitoring of patients using these agents is essential. Divalproex and methylphenidate are off-label options with modest evidence of effectiveness. The decision to initiate pharmacological treatment should be based on severity of symptomatology, degree of impairment, risk to self or others, and prevention of hospitalization. While no widely endorsed clinical algorithms for treatment of aggression exist, physicians generally attempt initial treatment with lower-risk alternatives to antipsychotics.

The most commonly prescribed psychotropic medications are antidepressants, stimulants, and antipsychotics; however, non-psychotropic medications are also prescribed at high rates for individuals with ASDs, although few studies have been conducted to benchmark the prevalence of use of such medications to treat physical health symptoms in this population.

Antidepressants are the most common class of psychotropic prescribed for individuals with ASDs, and although their benefits have been described in many case reports and uncontrolled studies, such benefits have not been confirmed in large, rigorous studies. Rigorous studies have been conducted in youth with ASDs only for fluoxetine and citalopram.[67] (See Chapter 8 for details of medication use in ASDs.)

TAKEAWAY POINTS

- Psychiatric disorders or comorbidities occur frequently in children and adults with ASDs and may go unrecognized.

- Anxiety and anxiety disorders are more common in children with ASDs, and the types of anxiety symptoms often vary with the age of the child. Lower IQ scores are associated with an increased chance of having an anxiety disorder.

- Early evidence suggests that anxiety disorders may respond to cognitive behavioral therapy.

- Obsessive–compulsive disorder can be quite debilitating, is seen more often in individuals with ASDs, and is more likely to be seen in younger children.

- Mood disorders, such as depression and bipolar disorder, may also be seen more often in individuals with ASDs, but diagnosis may be especially difficult, especially in non-verbal or minimally verbal people.

- Behavioral management focuses not only on the behaviors themselves, but the context or environment in which they occur.

- Applied behavioral analysis (ABA) is the best-studied and most well-established behavioral therapy to treat children with ASDs. Early intensive ABA, as the name implies, is started in children before 5 years of age and is quite time and labor intensive. It has been shown to be effective in some children with ASDs.

- Problem-focused behavioral therapy may be used to treat specific unwanted behaviors and may require consultation with a consultant such as a behavioral therapist.

- Disruptive behavior disorders may be treated effectively in the community setting, and early evidence suggests that therapeutic horseback riding may be an effective intervention for these behaviors as well. Cognitive behavioral therapy has also been used to address disruptive behaviors as well as programs that incorporate parental training.

- Medications may be tried for behaviors that are severe, dangerous, or significantly impacting quality of life for both the child and the family.

Gastrointestinal Disorders That Can Lead to Both Physical and Behavioral Problems in Individuals with Autism Spectrum Disorders

Iona M. Monteiro, MD

Introduction

It has been increasingly recognized that gastrointestinal (GI) problems are more common in individuals with autism spectrum disorders (ASDs) than in the general population.[1] Constipation, loose bowel movements, food intolerance, excess gas or bloating, reflux, or stomach pain can affect the sleep and well-being of a child, and can cause irritability and aggression. This chapter discusses the conventional evaluation process for possible GI disorders and daily practices that may curtail the symptoms of GI problems.

Gastrointestinal-related symptoms in the non-verbal child

Many children with ASDs, even those who are verbal or minimally verbal, may not be able to indicate that they are in pain. A high level of vigilance is required on the part of the parent and the physician to determine if a non-verbal child is having GI symptoms. A recent study validates parental concerns for GI dysfunction in children with ASDs. Although parents were sensitive to the existence of GI problems in their children, they could not necessarily pinpoint the nature of the dysfunction.[2] Functional constipation is the most common GI dysfunction. It is seen more often in younger children and those with increased social impairment and lack of expressive language.[2]

The prevalence of GI symptoms reported in children varies from as low as 9% to 70% or higher.[3,4] The existence of specific GI disturbances related to ASDs has not been established. As in children without ASDs, the most common GI symptoms and signs reported for persons with ASDs are chronic constipation, abdominal pain with or without diarrhea, and encopresis (involuntary leakage of stool). Other GI abnormalities are gastroesophageal reflux disorder (GERD), abdominal bloating, and disaccharidase (enzyme for sugar digestion) deficiencies. Problematic behaviors may be signs of abdominal pain or discomfort. These behaviors include, but are not limited to, sleep disturbances, self-injurious behavior, tantrums, aggression, and/or oppositional behavior. A parent may suspect abdominal discomfort when the child is noted to be pressing his or her abdomen, holding the abdomen and crying, or exhibiting problem behaviors in relationship to meals.[3]

Unusual sleeping or eating habits and oppositional behavior were found to be significantly associated with GI problems in children with ASDs; however, they were frequently also noted in children without GI problems. This suggests that these behaviors alone may have limited utility in screening for GI problems in individuals with ASDs.[5] As compared with children with ASDs who had no GI problems, those with GI problems showed greater symptom severity on measures of irritability, anxiety, and social withdrawal.[6] Weight loss, fever, bloody stools, and/or intractable vomiting in a child with an ASD certainly merit an in-depth medical investigation.

Approach to common GI disorders in children with ASDs

The common GI disorders that we discuss are constipation, chronic diarrhea, chronic abdominal pain, GERD, and celiac disease. Warning signs that need to be looked for are blood in the stool, fever, poor growth, protracted vomiting, or diarrhea.

Constipation

Constipation is defined by the frequency, consistency, and difficulty with which stool is passed. Passage of hard stool associated with difficulty in passing the stool is considered constipation; however, passage of a soft stool without difficulty, even if after 2 or 3 days, is not considered constipation. The causes of constipation are varied. In the child with an ASD as with children without ASDs, it is commonly due to functional constipation, the perception of pain on defecation followed by stool-withholding behaviors that result in harder stool, and subsequent pain with passage leading to further stool-withholding behaviors. This can eventually lead to impaction stool blockage and secondary fecal soiling with loose or mushy stool that passes around an impaction and is then sometimes reported as diarrhea.

Evaluation of the child with constipation starts with a thorough history and physical exam. Warning signs that need to be looked for are poor growth, fever, vomiting, a history of constipation starting at birth and, on examination, a tight anal sphincter or increased sphincter tone. Some medications, such as antacids, opiates, phenobarbital, anticholinergics, and antidepressants, can also cause constipation. A dietary history is also a key as some children may not get sufficient fiber and/or fluids in the diet. Besides a general physical exam, an abdominal exam focused on the presence of palpable stool in the colon and inspection of the anus allows for recognition of perianal soiling or fissures. The rectal exam focuses on the presence of anal wink (neurological reflex), sphincter tone, and the presence and consistency of the stool in the rectal vault (stool-holding area).

Management of functional constipation includes disimpaction (removal) of feces if impacted, followed by maintenance therapy with stool softeners. The child can be disimpacted using magnesium citrate, glycerine suppositories, mineral oil or saline enemas, senna, bisacodyl, or polyethylene glycol. Enemas and suppositories may be difficult to use in the child with an ASD and may further perpetuate the pain, fear, and stool-withholding cycle. Maintenance medications that can be used to keep the stool soft are mineral oil, magnesium hydroxide, sorbitol, lactulose, and polyethylene glycol. Dietary changes that focus on increasing fiber and fluid in diet can sometimes present a problem in the child with an ASD who has very strong and/or limited food preferences. Behavior modification with regular toilet training is important, using the gastro-colic reflex to help evacuate stool after meals. Follow-up assessments with the physician are necessary to determine if therapy is working or changes are necessary.

Chronic diarrhea

Loose stools that persist beyond 2 weeks is considered chronic diarrhea. Common causes of chronic diarrhea are functional or non-specific toddler's diarrhea, malabsorption (which may be caused by things such as excessive juice intake, post-infectious lactose intolerance, celiac disease, or cystic fibrosis), inflammatory bowel disease, and chronic infections.

Evaluation of chronic diarrhea includes a thorough history and physical exam. History includes the age of onset of diarrhea and relationship (if any) to particular foods. A family history of allergies, celiac disease, cystic fibrosis, or inflammatory bowel disease directs the workup in a more specific direction. Warning signs or red flags, such as weight loss, fever, or blood in the stool, should be looked for and always reported to your child's physician. If lactose intolerance is suspected, a lactose breath hydrogen test (LBHT) can be done; however, if the LBHT is difficult to perform, either because the child is unable to fast overnight or unable to provide repeated breath samples, a 2-week completely lactose-free dietary trial can be attempted. Celiac disease can be assessed with a blood test for tissue transglutaminase antibody along with an IgA antibody level; if positive, the diagnosis is confirmed with an endoscopic small bowel biopsy. Stool can be tested for occult blood and inflammatory markers, such as leukocytes (white blood cells) and calprotectin, and if positive, a colonoscopy should be considered to rule out colitis. Stool is also tested for ova or parasites, *Giardia* antigen, and if positive for an infection, it should be treated appropriately. Stool for qualitative fat may uncover fat malabsorption and stool elastase may suggest a pancreatic cause for the fat malabsorption. Food allergy testing as a cause of the diarrhea is more difficult, as most food allergies are not IgE mediated and the help of an allergist may be required in the evaluation (see Chapter 5). If a child continues to have diarrhea while fasting, secretory diarrhea should be considered and stool studies should be sent for osmolality and electrolytes, and then evaluation for hormone-producing tumors will be needed.

Management of chronic diarrhea depends on the cause of the diarrhea. Functional or toddler's diarrhea is usually self-limiting, and eliminating excess juice intake may help. Lactose-free diets are used in the management of lactose intolerance. A lifelong gluten-free diet is recommended for individuals with celiac disease. Inflammatory bowel disease is treated with anti-inflammatory and immunosuppressive medications.

Chronic abdominal pain

Chronic abdominal pain is defined as the presence of at least three episodes of pain occurring over a period of 3 months or more that is severe enough to affect activities. The pain can be constant or intermittent. Chronic pain without the warning signs of fever, weight loss, hematemesis (vomiting of blood), bilious vomiting (vomiting of green bile), anemia, or blood in the stool is likely to be functional (i.e., not due to an underlying structural problem). The child with an ASD may be unable to indicate whether they are in pain and may have other behaviors like aggression, irritability, or sleep disturbances as signs of abdominal pain. Parental history is of utmost importance and a parent may be able to tell by behaviors like punching or pointing to the belly that the child is having pain.

Evaluation of the child with an ASD and abdominal pain includes a thorough history and physical examination. Pain related to ingestion of dairy products suggests lactose intolerance and a LBHT or trial of a lactose-free diet, as discussed above, should be considered. The physical exam may reveal stool masses and the child will need to be treated appropriately for constipation. Signs of chronic disease, such as pallor (paleness), clubbing (changes in the nailbeds), arthritis, hepatosplenomegaly (enlargement of the liver and spleen), abdominal masses, or perianal disease, should be sought. Tests that can be done on stool include testing for occult blood, leukocytes, ova or parasites, *Giardia* antigen, and *Helicobacter pylori* antigen. Blood tests that can be considered are a complete blood count looking for anemia, comprehensive metabolic panel, and a lead level (especially if there is history of pica, i.e., eating non-food items). Urinalysis and urine culture can be done to check for a bladder infection. An abdominal X-ray can be done to determine if there is colonic fecal retention. Invasive tests requiring sedation or anesthesia, such as esophagogastroduodenoscopy and colonoscopy, are used when certain warning signs are present.

Management of chronic abdominal pain includes treatment of specific disorders if found on workup. If the diagnostic workup is negative, the child should be monitored over time for any changes or progression of symptoms.

Gastroesophageal reflux disease

The effortless passage of stomach contents back up into the esophagus is termed gastroesophageal reflux. When this reflux causes complications it is termed gastroesophageal reflux disease (GERD). GERD includes complications like recurrent vomiting leading to weight loss and failure to thrive, heartburn, chest pain, irritability, apnea (periods of not breathing) in infants, feeding problems, wheezing, stridor (noisy upper airways sounds), and cough. GERD symptoms are often more common after meals or when the child lays down.

Evaluation begins with a thorough history and physical examination. A therapeutic trial with acid suppression medication may be of diagnostic value. A pH probe study can be done to determine if there is significant reflux; however, a child with an ASD may be unable to tolerate a probe that is placed through the nose into the esophagus and kept in place for 24 hours. A Bravo pH probe can be directly attached to the esophagus but requires sedation or anesthesia; however, if this is being done, a complete esophagogastroduodenoscopy (EGD) can be done at the same time and other causes of GI problems, such as esophagitis or gastritis, can be ruled out. An invasive procedure like the EGD should be reserved for children who have failed diagnostic acid suppression therapy or those who have symptoms like food refusal or hematemesis (vomiting of blood).

Celiac disease

Celiac disease is an immunological non-IgE-mediated enteropathy caused by a permanent sensitivity to gluten in a genetically susceptible individual.[7,8] Gluten is present in grains such as wheat, rye, and barley. Children with celiac disease may present with diarrhea, failure to thrive, abdominal pain, vomiting, constipation, and/or abdominal distension. Celiac disease may also present with non-GI symptoms or be totally asymptomatic. Given the varied presentation, celiac disease should be considered in the differential diagnosis of children with ASDs who appear to be having GI distress.[4] Hans Asperger initially described Asperger syndrome in 1961 and suggested a relationship between Asperger syndrome and celiac disease.[9] One group reported a case of a severely autistic child with celiac disease and micronutrient deficiencies whose behavior improved after instituting a gluten-free diet and treatment of micronutrient deficiencies.[10] Children with known or even undefined neurological disorders do not appear to have a higher prevalence of gluten sensitivity;[11] however, a subset of children with ASDs have been described to have increased antigliadin antibodies suggestive of celiac disease, in the absence of other markers for this condition, which could point to immunological changes and/or intestinal permeability abnormalities.[12] Buie did a literature search and concluded that there is insufficient evidence to support a gluten-free diet as a treatment for ASDs, though a subgroup might benefit from a gluten-free diet.[13] Still the symptom or testing profile for this group of patients remains unclear at this time. Tissue transglutaminase antibody testing is more sensitive and specific for the diagnosis of celiac disease. An EGD with small bowel biopsy should be performed to confirm the diagnosis of celiac disease, because treatment is not easy and is lifelong. For individuals confirmed to have celiac disease, a gluten-free diet has to be instituted for treatment, which includes elimination of all wheat, rye, and barley from the diet. Oats can sometimes be contaminated with gluten if they are processed in the same environment as the other grains, and therefore they may need to be eliminated too.

Food allergies/intolerances and GI disorders

The exact cause of ASDs is unknown, and various interventions have been tried including the exclusion of gluten, casein, or both in the diet. Available research data do not support the use of a casein-free diet, a gluten-free diet, or combined gluten-free, casein-free diet as a primary treatment for individuals with ASDs;[3] however, contemporary use of a gluten-free and/or casein-free diet is being instituted by parents in many settings despite the fact that there are no formal guidelines recommending this.[14] Multiple reviews have suggested caution in the use of gluten-free and/or casein-free diets and the need for further controlled research to determine if there is a significant effect.[15] Food allergy is defined as an adverse health effect arising from a specific immune response that occurs reproducibly on exposure to a given food.[16] Food allergies can be IgE (immunoglobulin E) mediated or non-IgE mediated. Diagnosis of IgE-mediated food allergies is based on the history, physical exam, and skin-prick testing or specific allergen IgE testing.[17] Non-IgE-mediated food allergies are more difficult to test for and are diagnosed on the basis of complete resolution of symptoms after an elimination diet, followed by recurrence of symptoms after an offending food is reintroduced. The two most common antigens (causative factors) in non-IgE-mediated food allergies are milk and soy proteins.[18] Non-immunological adverse reactions to food are termed food intolerances. An example of this is lactose intolerance where the lactase enzyme is not available to digest lactose (milk sugar) and the child has symptoms of carbohydrate maldigestion such as bloating, cramping, gassiness, and diarrhea. (See Chapter 5 for a detailed discussion of food allergies.) Williams *et al.* found deficiencies in disaccharidases and hexose transporters, and compositional dysbiosis of the intestinal flora, in children with autism and GI problems.[19] Jyonouchi *et al.* demonstrated more intrinsic defects of innate immune responses in children with ASDs and GI problems as compared with those with ASDs without GI problems.[20]

Stronger beliefs on the part of parents and practitioners about the causative role of food allergy in ASDs have been associated with higher use of detoxification treatments, special diets, and vitamins, and lower use of prescribed medications.[21] Some parents (27%) have endorsed the causal effect of food allergy. About 14% of parents of a child with an ASD reported that a doctor or other health professional told them that their child had a food or digestive allergy, compared with 3% of parents of children without ASDs.[22] Food allergies do occur in a subset of children with ASDs; however, all children with GI symptoms should not be automatically considered to have food allergies.[23]

Children with ASDs are often reported to have limited food preferences and behavioral difficulties associated with feeding. A study by Emond *et al.* showed that children with ASDs had late acceptance of solid food, were slow feeders as infants, and by 15 months of age they had a less varied diet; however, there was no impairment of caloric intake or growth.[24]

Gut flora in children with autism spectrum disorders

Disruption of the bidirectional interactions between the enteric microbiota (natural bacteria in the intestinal tract) and the nervous system may be involved in the pathophysiology of acute and chronic GI disease states, including functional and inflammatory bowel disorders.[25] Distinctive *Clostridial* bacteria populations have been shown to be present in more children with ASDs as compared with healthy controls.[26,27] Modulation of gut microflora by reducing the number of *Clostridia* in patients with ASDs and stimulating more beneficial gut bacteria may help alleviate related symptoms.[28] *Bacteroidetes* species were more common in children with severe autism, while *Firmicutes* was predominant in the control group.[29] Children with ASDs had lower levels of *Bifidobacter* and higher levels of *Lactobacilli*; however, yeast levels were similar to that in the control group.[30] Gondalia *et al.*, on the other hand, did not find a difference in the GI microbiota of children with ASDs with or without GI symptoms and those of their typically developing siblings, and concluded that their data do not support the hypothesis that the GI microflora plays a role in the symptomatology of ASDs.[31] Mulle *et al.* reviewed evidence that suggests that a deeper understanding of the gut microbiome could open up new avenues of research in ASDs and potential novel treatment strategies.[32] Probiotics can be used to restore the microbial balance in the intestine, to relieve GI problems, and to attenuate immunological abnormalities. Whether the use of probiotics by children with ASDs can lead to improvement in behaviors needs to be established in well-controlled trials with sufficient group sizes.[33]

Controversies regarding GI disorders in autism spectrum disorders

Wakefield *et al.* published a study that suggested that lymphonodular hyperplasia and a nonspecific colitis was linked to the measles, mumps, and rubella (MMR) vaccine in children with autism.[34] They purported that the MMR vaccine caused an insult to the gut of children who subsequently experienced regression and became autistic; however, this article was retracted in 2010. Taylor *et al.* reviewed medical records of 400 patients with ASDs and found that there was no increase in prevalence of GI problems or regression since the vaccine was introduced in 1979.[35] In an attempt to replicate the study by Wakefield *et al.*, D'Souza, Fombonne, and Ward looked for evidence of measles virus in tissue and bodily fluids and found none in children diagnosed with ASDs nor in healthy controls.[36] Hornig *et al.* found no relationship between the timing of administration of the MMR vaccine and the onset of either GI complaints or signs of autism.[37]

Is there a link between ASD and GI disorders? Ibrahim *et al.*, in a retrospective case study done at Mayo Clinic, concluded that the greater prevalence of constipation and food intolerance among children with ASDs could be behaviorally related.[38] Brown and Mehl-Madrona, in an editorial, point to the limitations of the Ibrahim *et al.* study and suggest that there may in fact be a subset of children with ASDs who have related GI disorders, and there is already sufficient evidence supporting the presence of a subgroup of children with ASDs who may suffer from concomitant immune-related GI symptoms.[39]

What parents can do to help children with GI symptoms

It is difficult to determine if a child with an ASD has a GI problem. A study done by Maenner *et al.* found that unusual sleep and eating habits as well as oppositional behaviors occurred more frequently in children with ASDs who had GI problems;[5] however, these behaviors were frequent in children with or without GI problems, limiting its utility as a screening tool. Keeping a food diary may help parents to determine if a particular food is related to the child's worsening behaviors. IgE-mediated food allergies present soon after the ingestion of the offending food; however, non-IgE-mediated allergies may present hours later, making this diagnosis more difficult.

Parents need to be keen observers of symptoms and document specific changes in behaviors or health that may be related to an underlying GI or other medical problem. Blood in the stool or vomitus, persistent vomiting, frequent episodes of abdominal pain (especially if these are interfering with normal daily activities), fever, weight loss, or listlessness should alert parents to a more significant problem that warrants a careful medical examination and possibly testing. Testing may include blood work, imaging studies such as X-ray or scans, and in some cases, direct visualization of the GI tract. (See Chapter 11 for more information on testing for children with ASDs.)

TAKEAWAY POINTS

- Gastrointestinal (GI) problems are quite common in individuals with ASDs.

- Making the diagnosis of a GI disorder in a child with an ASD may be hampered by verbal limitations and/or confounding behavioral disturbances.

- The history and physical exam may help physicians to determine if a child has an underlying GI problem such as constipation, chronic diarrhea, chronic abdominal pain, gastroesophageal reflux disease, celiac disease, food allergies, or food intolerances.

- Persistent abdominal pain with fever and/or weight loss, vomiting of blood or bile, anemia, or blood in the stool may represent a serious GI problem and warrants prompt medical attention.

Allergies and Immune-Mediated Conditions in Individuals with Autism Spectrum Disorders

Harumi Jyonouchi, MD

Introduction

While timely diagnosis and treatment of comorbid conditions are essential for children with autism spectrum disorders (ASDs), this sometimes presents a challenge because of limited expressive language and/or behavioral symptoms. As a result, busy primary care physicians may easily under-diagnose or under-treat even common pediatric conditions in these children. This may be especially true for allergy/immunology (A/I) associated conditions where careful history taking and physical examination are key elements in diagnosis and management. Medical professionals caring for children with ASDs may also tend to underestimate the effects of common medical conditions on neuropsychiatric symptoms (partly caused by pain and discomfort) secondary to their limited expressive language.[1] It has been our observation that, all too often, neuropsychiatric symptoms associated with underlying medical conditions are simply attributed to the autism diagnosis.

In the pediatric A/I clinic at our institution, we have evaluated many children with ASDs. In our experience, the difficulty associated with diagnosing and treating A/I disorders in children with ASDs may be best illustrated in the evaluation of food allergy (FA). The recent guidelines for FA diagnosis and treatment states that there are no definitive diagnostic measures for FA.[2] Currently, a FA diagnosis is largely based on clinical findings, including a comprehensive history coupled with a careful physical examination and the results of challenge testing if applicable.[2]

Given the importance of clinical findings in diagnosing FAs, the limited expressive language and often complex behavioral symptoms in children with ASDs make it very difficult to evaluate FAs. In addition, non-allergic conditions, such as chronic urticaria and intrinsic eczema, are often incorrectly attributed to FAs by primary care physicians and other medical specialists. Some medical professionals practicing complementary and alternative medicine may also utilize laboratory measures which are not validated for FA diagnosis and management. These issues may also arise with other allergic conditions as well as other common childhood diseases such as intrinsic asthma and chronic sinusitis.

In the previous paragraph, I suggested that the word "allergy" is used too casually. This is because, in many cases, medical professionals do not specify if an allergic reaction is caused by production of immunoglobulin E (IgE) or not, or if it is caused by a response by the immune system or not. Diagnosing IgE and non-IgE-mediated immune conditions is not as simple as it seems, even for typically developing children. Diagnosis becomes even harder for more complex immunological conditions; therefore, the focus of this chapter is on diagnosing and treating A/I disorders in a timely manner in children with an ASD and the challenges associated with this.

In the first part of the chapter, allergic disorders are discussed, focusing on FA diagnosis and treatment, since the role of FA in ASDs has been controversial. The latter part of this chapter focuses on non-allergic common medical conditions associated with immune mechanisms. This section also discusses less common, but more serious, immune conditions such as antibody (Ab) deficiency syndromes.

Common allergic conditions seen in children with ASDs: experience in the pediatric allergy/immunology clinic at Rutgers New Jersey Medical School

Food allergy

Food allergy is defined as an adverse health effect arising from a specific immune response that occurs reproducibly upon exposure to a given food.[2] Immune reactions are usually provoked by food proteins (FPs), but other ingredients in food, such as chemicals, can also trigger immune reactions. Reproducible but non-immune-mediated adverse reactions to food, such as lactose intolerance, caused by an enzyme deficiency, are called food intolerances. The prevalence of FA is thought to be higher in young children than in adults.[3] This may be associated with the immature gut mucosal immune system in young children.[4] To provoke FA reactions, regardless of types of immune responses, the immune system needs to be sensitized by the offending food prior to the FA reaction.

IgE-mediated food allergy (IFA) is provoked by the activation of effector cells (mainly mast cells and basophils) by IgE Ab. When food allergens bind to specific IgE, this can lead to a rapid release of inflammatory mediators, such as histamine, from the effector cells, causing reactions affecting not only the gastrointestinal (GI) tract, but also the skin and respiratory tract.

When a food component that can cause an allergic reaction, known as a food antigen (Ag), comes in contact with T lymphocytes (a subset of white blood cells), certain T cells may trigger B lymphocytes to become effector B cells and plasma cells. These effector B cells and plasma cells produce food Ag-specific IgE. IgE Ab has a short half-life in the bloodstream (2–3 days), but when IgE Ab binds to the effector cells, it remains stable for 4–6 weeks on their cell surface. When this happens, even a tiny amount of food Ag can cause the effector cells to activate almost immediately; thus, IFA is characterized by a rapid onset of symptoms (within 2 hours of exposure, and as quickly as 10–15 minutes) and involves multiple organs including the GI tract, skin, and respiratory systems. IFA can also cause systemic, potentially fatal reactions, such as anaphylaxis.

It is noteworthy that most FPs that provoke IFA are heat stable and acid resistant. Therefore, they are not affected by heating (cooking) or digestion; however, reports have shown that extensive heating of egg or milk proteins causes fewer immune reactions (better tolerance). Certain other proteins from fruits and vegetables which are cross-reactive to those in pollens or other aeroallergens are generally not resistant to heat or acid. Reactions to such heat- or acid-labile food allergens are generally limited to the lining of the mouth, causing so-called food protein–pollen syndrome, and is seldom associated with anaphylaxis.[5]

Diagnosis of IFA should be based on clinical features, including reproducible clinical symptoms by food allergens, although the presence of food-allergen-specific IgE Ab detected by prick-skin testing (PST) or enzyme-linked immunosorbent assay (ELISA) can be used as supportive evidence; however, positive PST or ELISA alone in the absence of clinical symptoms is not diagnostic for IFA.[2] Although a negative PST or ELISA is over 90% accurate, positive tests are not nearly as reliable, with a high false-positive rate.[6,7] In certain circumstances, when the causal relationship between clinical symptoms and a suspected food allergen is unclear, oral-challenge testing may be considered, provided such a challenge test is conducted at a medical facility that is equipped for handling anaphylaxis and other serious adverse reactions to food allergens.

Treatment of IFA involves avoiding offending food allergens. Because of the high risk of anaphylaxis with exposure to even a minute amount of food allergen, it is highly recommended that individuals with IFAs carry a ready-to-use epinephrine autoinjector (e.g., EpiPen, Mylan, Canonsburg, PA). Guidelines also recommend the implementation of a FA action plan at school as well as at home.[2] No subcutaneous allergen immunotherapy (IT) is available for food allergens; however, IT given by mouth or under the tongue may have therapeutic potential, although standard measures have not yet been established in the United States.[2]

Eosinophilic esophagitis and gastroenteritis

Certain FA conditions are elicited by mixed IgE- and non-IgE-mediated immune reactions, as typically seen in eosinophilic esophagitis (EoE) and eosinophilic gastroenteritis. Currently, EoE is defined as a "chronic, immune/Ag-mediated disease characterized clinically by symptoms related to esophageal dysfunction and distinguished histologically with eosinophilic mucosal inflammation in the esophagus."[8] Patients with EoE often have both IgE and non-IgE responses to FPs. The diagnosis requires that a biopsy of the esophageal mucosa (lining of the food pipe) show many eosinophils (another type of white blood cell). Neither PST nor food-allergen-specific IgE are diagnostic for EoE.[8] Other eosinophilic GI diseases are also diagnosed on the basis of clinical and biopsy findings.[2] Treatment of EoE is complex and should be managed by subspecialists.

Non-IgE-mediated food allergy

Non-IgE-mediated food allergy (NFA) is defined as reproducible immune reactions to FPs or other components of food in the absence of food-allergen-specific IgE,[2] and therefore PST and ELISA for food-allergen-specific IgE are negative. Onset of symptoms may be delayed up to 48–72 hours after ingestion of the offending food and are limited to the GI tract.[4,9] Milder forms of NFA may be called FP-induced proctocolitis syndrome, and more severe forms of NFA are often referred to as FP-induced enterocolitis syndrome (FPIES) and FP-induced enteropathy. NFA conditions were previously thought to occur predominantly in infants with bloody stool, but not all patients with NFAs have bloody stool, and NFA can be seen in older patients.[9,10]

Although the cause of NFA is not well understood, it is generally attributed to cell-mediated immune reaction to FPs.[4,11] Production of certain proinflammatory cytokines by FP-specific T cells are thought to cause NFA; however, diagnostic testing for these cytokines has not been established, having only been utilized for research purposes. Therefore, current diagnosis of NFA is solely dependent on clinical observations. These observations include (1) resolution of GI symptoms following avoidance of offending food, and (2) recurrence of GI symptoms with reintroduction of offending food.[2,4,11]

Among some medical professionals practicing complementary and alternative medicine, IgA and IgG antibodies against FPs have been used for diagnosing NFA; however, since NFA is likely caused by cell-mediated immune reactions, Ab levels against FPs have little diagnostic value in NFA.[2,12] Therefore, IgG/IgA Ab levels against FPs should *not* be used for diagnosing NFA.

Although NFA immune reactions are typically delayed and limited to the lining of the GI tract, in a small subset of patients with NFA, reactions can occur almost immediately, with systemic reactions that resemble anaphylaxis.[4,13] Such anaphylaxis-like reactions are usually seen in FPIES patients, with severe vomiting shortly (typically 1–3 hours) after intake of offending food, followed by lethargy and diarrhea.[10,14,15] Such severe, acute (sudden) manifestations of FPIES can be misdiagnosed as anaphylaxis, acute abdomen, or other diseases, leading to unnecessary invasive procedures.[16] As opposed to anaphylaxis caused by IFA, severe acute reactions caused by NFA do not have skin or respiratory manifestations.[13] Furthermore, this type of reaction, unlike anaphylaxis, is unresponsive to treatment with epinephrine.

Treatment of NFA involves avoiding offending food allergens. Many individuals with NFAs become tolerant to foods that once caused a reaction (mainly soy and milk) by 3–4 years of age; however, in some patients, especially those with severe reaction to multiple FPs, resolution of GI symptoms may only be achieved by an elimination diet and the use of free amino acid formulas for nutritional support.

The role of non-IgE-mediated FA (NFA) in causing ASD symptoms has been controversial. Given the difficulties associated with NFA diagnosis, this is not surprising. Previously, we conducted a study assessing how treatment of NFA can affect behavioral symptoms in children with ASDs.[17] In this pilot study, our results indicated improvement in certain behavioral symptoms (irritability, lethargy, and hyperactivity) after improvement in NFA symptoms following avoidance of offending food(s).

Aeroallergen allergy

Aeroallergen allergy (AA) occurs by IgE-mediated effector cell activation, as previously described for FA, following sensitization to aeroallergens by the lining of the respiratory tract; thus, clinical symptoms are limited to the areas of aeroallergen exposure, typically the eyes (allergic conjunctivitis), nose (allergic rhinitis, or AR), and lower airways (allergic or atopic asthma). AA exposure is usually chronic, resulting in chronic inflammation at the site of allergen exposure; however, symptoms can involve ears, sinuses (allergic sinusitis), and throat, including post-nasal drip.

The prevalence of atopic disorders caused by aeroallergen sensitization is increasing in developed countries, which is in part attributed to better sanitation and changes in environmental factors in early life. In other words, better sanitation and the resultant decrease in the variety of microorganisms in the respiratory and GI tracts have been implicated ("hygiene hypothesis"). It is noteworthy that the hygiene hypothesis is not simple, and increases in AAs are likely to be influenced by various genetic and environmental factors, as reviewed elsewhere.[18–21] Nevertheless, it is undeniable that the prevalence of AR, the most common manifestation of AA, is astonishingly high in developed countries, affecting up to 30% of the general population with an even higher prevalence in children.[22,23] Over 40% of patients with AR become symptomatic before age 6 years.[24] AA is as common in children with ASDs as it is in the general population.

Because seasonal AR requires repeated exposure to seasonal aeroallergens, children under 4 years of age are unlikely to become symptomatic. On the other hand, year-round AA caused by indoor allergens, such as dust mites, can cause nose, eye, and respiratory symptoms even before 4 years of age. The presence of atopic dermatitis in the first 2 years of life is a risk factor for aeroallergen sensitization.[25,26]

Diagnosis of AA is based on clinical features supported by PST reactivity and/or the presence of aeroallergen-specific IgE detected by ELISA. As opposed to FA, in AA a positive test is quite helpful in making a diagnosis, although positive results in the absence of clinical findings are not diagnostic for AA. As with FA, in some cases when the presence of AA is unclear, allergen challenge tests may be conducted in a clinical setting. Such challenge tests have been conducted by applying aeroallergen extracts to the nasal or ocular mucosa, or by inhalation of aeroallergens. Since AAs play only one part (as triggers) in asthma, diagnosis and treatment in asthmatics is discussed in the next section of this chapter.

Current first-line treatment measures for AA are (1) avoidance of relevant aeroallergens and triggers, and (2) medication. Commonly used pharmacological approaches to AR include intranasal corticosteroids, leukotriene receptor antagonists such as a montelukast, and oral or intranasal antihistamines. For allergic conjunctivitis, pharmacotherapy includes topical eye solutions with properties of antihistamines (such as ketotifen and olopatadine) and mast cell stabilization (cromolyn), in addition to oral antihistamines. For atopic (allergic) asthma, first-line therapy includes oral and inhaled corticosteroids, leukotriene receptor antagonists, inhaled ß2 agonists, and mast cell stabilizers, as detailed in the Expert Panel Report 3 (EPR 3) asthma guidelines.[27]

For individuals with AA who have suboptimal symptom control with the above-described first-line measures, allergen immunotherapy (IT) may be considered. Subcutaneous IT is currently the mainstay of IT, which is commonly referred to as "allergy shots"; however, recent studies show potential beneficial effects of sublingual IT, which is now more widely used in Europe and recently approved in the United States.[28] Another therapeutic approach is monoclonal anti-IgE antibody (omalizumab), which inhibits IgE-mediated effector cell activation.

Anaphylaxis

Anaphylaxis is clinically defined as an acute onset of severe systemic illness involving skin, mucosal tissues, or both, with exposure to an allergen, often accompanied by low blood pressure and compromised respiratory status.[29] The prevalence of anaphylaxis varies with estimates ranging from 0.05 to 2% in the general population. Under-diagnosis may be common in milder cases of anaphylaxis.

Common triggers of anaphylaxis include food allergens (e.g., peanuts, tree nuts, shellfish, fish, milk, egg, and sesame),[30,31] medications, bee venoms, latex, and many more biological agents that trigger activation of effector cells via IgE-mediated mechanisms, as described in the FA section. Anaphylaxis to medications is more commonly seen in middle-aged or older individuals, while food allergens are main causes of anaphylaxis in children.[31] Anaphylaxis occurring in the absence of an identifiable trigger is called idiopathic anaphylaxis. On rare occasions, anaphylaxis can also occur through non-IgE-mediated mechanisms. For example, over-sulfated, chondroitin-contaminated heparin can potentially cause anaphylaxis through activation of the complement system.[32] Physical stimuli, such as exercise, can also trigger anaphylaxis (so-called exercise-induced anaphylaxis) and this can be dependent on intake of certain food before or after exercise.[33]

Diagnosis of anaphylaxis primarily requires careful history; however, additional laboratory measures, such as skin testing, allergen-specific IgE, and presence of serum tryptase in the acute stage of anaphylaxis (within 4 hours), can be utilized as supportive evidence. Histamine concentration in urine collected over 24 hours is considered to be a more sensitive marker of mast cell and basophil activation, but this is not routinely used for diagnosis of anaphylaxis.[31] Regardless of the underlying pathology, the end result is systemic activation of effector cells, which can result in a life-threatening event. The most important treatment measures in anaphylaxis are administration of epinephrine and supplemental oxygen.[31] For individuals known to be at risk for anaphylaxis, preparation of a written action plan is highly recommended along with education of caregivers regarding proper use of epinephrine autoinjectors (e.g., EpiPen).[31] Anaphylaxis is likely to be under-diagnosed or delayed in individuals with minimal expressive language. For example, rapid onset of respiratory symptoms may cause severe anxiety and paniclike behaviors in those with limited expressive language.

Drug allergy and chemical sensitivity

Adverse drug reactions (ADR) are defined by the World Health Organization (WHO) as any noxious, unintended, and undesired effect of a drug that occurs at doses used for prevention, diagnosis, or treatment. The WHO categorizes ADRs into predictable (type A) and unpredictable (type B) reactions. Type A reactions are generally dose dependent, related to the known pharmacological actions of the drug, and account for about 80% of all ADRs.[34]

Type B reactions are generally dose independent, not associated with the pharmacological actions of the drug, and thought to occur only in individuals with genetic and environmental predisposition. Type B reactions are subdivided into drug intolerance, drug idiosyncrasy, drug allergy (DA) mediated by immune reactions, and pseudoallergic reactions which are largely attributed to direct activation of effector cells. DA can be caused by IgE-Ab-mediated immediate reactions, cytotoxic reactions mediated by IgG/ IgM Ab with activation of the complement system, immune complex (Ag–Ab complex), and cellular immune responses;[34] however, DAs can involve various immune mechanisms and often they cannot be categorized into one of the above-described hypersensitivity responses.

Hypersensitivity to chemicals can be caused by both non-immune and immune-mediated mechanisms. Because of a wide variety of causative mechanisms, it is difficult to narrow down the cause of DA to one specific hypersensitivity reaction. Absence of drug-allergen-specific IgE and negative skin-test reactivity are very helpful in ruling out DAs, and very likely rule out IgE-mediated immune reactions. For non-IgE-mediated DA, reliable laboratory diagnostics measures are not currently available.

As expected, due to the complex immune mechanisms associated with DA, clinical manifestations of DAs vary greatly and can involve multiple organs. This makes it particularly important to take a detailed history and carefully document DA. For example, in DA occurring as a delayed-type reaction without evidence of IgE-mediated effector cell activation, administration of epinephrine is not only ineffective but can potentially cause harm, especially in individuals with cardiovascular conditions.

Management of DA involves avoidance of causative drugs; however, for DA, if a particular medication is medically necessary, DA can be assessed by skin testing with incremental doses of the drugs and then challenges of small doses orally or intravenously. Alternatively, temporary tolerance status can be induced by a procedure called "desensitization." This procedure is used for both IgE-mediated and non-IgE-mediated conditions. It must be emphasized that successful desensitization is not permanent and is likely to be lost after discontinuation of the drug. Even during continuous intake of the drug, tolerance can be lost.

In summary, DA is caused by multiple immune mechanisms, and a detailed history is essential; therefore, diagnosing DA is more challenging in individuals with limited expressive language including children with ASDs.

Effects of allergic conditions on neuropsychiatric symptoms

Allergic diseases causing chronic inflammation in the gut, airway, and skin may induce or aggravate psychiatric conditions. This may be due to stress as well as pain, discomfort, and sleep deprivation. Studies addressing the effects of allergic diseases causing neuropsychiatric symptoms are scant. Nevertheless, the limited data currently available indicate the importance of recognizing underlying allergic conditions in association with neuropsychiatric symptoms.

Two studies examined effects of allergic rhinitis (AR) on neuropsychiatric symptoms in young children with pollen allergy.[35,36] The results showed impaired learning as well as impaired memory in patients with AR as compared with controls. Symptoms, such as fatigue, may be attributed to the use of antihistamines with sedative effects, but patients with AR treated with placebo also showed fatigue and impaired learning.[36] Another case-control study involving 1814 students (ages 15–17 years) evaluated school performance during grass-pollen season and supported previous findings showing a significant risk of lower national examination test scores in students who had symptomatic AR and who used AR medication or sedative antihistamines.[37] Other studies involving smaller numbers of subjects also yielded similar results.[38]

In addition to the negative effects of AR on cognitive skills, impaired sleep is a well-recognized complication of AR.[38] It is not unusual for individuals with AR to complain of a lack of "a good night's sleep." A study that examined the quality of sleep in adults with AR showed a positive correlation between disturbed sleep and the severity of AR.[39]

The effects of AR on behavioral symptoms have long been recognized by medical professionals; most studies focus on a potential association between attention deficit hyperactivity disorder (ADHD) and allergic disorders including AR, atopic dermatitis (AD), and asthma. A high prevalence of AR has been reported in patients with ADHD.[40] Tsai *et al.* reported an increased rate of ADHD among patients with AR in a nationwide population-based study involving 226,550 children (<18 years of age) conducted in Taiwan.[41] In another study, also conducted in Taiwan, individuals with ADHD as well as a tic disorder were reported to have a higher prevalence of allergic diseases, including AR, as compared with those with an ADHD diagnosis alone (43 vs 28%, p<0.001).[42] In our clinic, we have also observed worsening tic symptoms with a flare-up of AR in children.

Neuropsychiatric symptoms that have been reported to be associated with AR, such as hyperactivity and irritability, are commonly observed behavioral symptoms in children with ASDs. In addition, since AR is a common condition in the general population, AR symptoms are likely to impact behavior in children with ASDs too; thus, AR and its potential neuropsychiatric effects should be considered when evaluating children with ASDs who are symptomatic. It may be more time-consuming to examine children with ASDs, and they may be less tolerant of topical AR medications, such as nasal inhalers, than unaffected peers, but it may be very worthwhile to address chronic naso-ocular symptoms of AR in children with ASDs, since the efficacy and safety of topical allergy medications are well proven.

AD that is not well controlled causes persistent discomfort, pruritus (itchiness), and sleep disturbances. It is not unusual to see increased irritability, hyperactivity, and short attention spans in individuals with poorly controlled AD. Sleep disruption in children is known to cause daytime behavioral symptoms. The association between chronic eczema with sleep disorders and ADHD has been addressed in several studies. One study of 77 children (6–16 years of age) with eczema revealed a higher frequency of sleep problems which are positively associated with a higher ADHD index and oppositional behaviors.[43] Meta-analysis of four epidemiological studies showed a connection between AD and ADHD, with a 43% increased risk of ADHD in individuals with AD.[44]

Persistent skin conditions associated with AD can affect other neuropsychiatric conditions, possibly due to the discomfort associated with AD. Interestingly, when 112 adult subjects without known psychiatric diseases were assessed by the Hamilton Anxiety Scale and Hamilton Depression Rating Scale, the authors found a positive association between chronic allergic skin diseases and higher rate of anxiety and depression.[45]

In summary, AD can have significant effects on neuropsychiatric symptoms. Assessment and management of AD, which is easily executed in routine clinical settings, should be integrated into general health care for children with ASDs.

IgE-mediated FA (IFA) is observed in about one-third of individuals with AD; therefore, children with AD who do not respond to first-line AD treatments (i.e., emollients, topical corticosteroids, and topical antibiotics) should be evaluated for IFA. Again, it must be emphasized that clinical association with positive reactivity to PST and/or food-allergen-specific IgE is necessary to evaluate the role of FA in AD. In patients with both AD *and* FA, caretakers usually recognize worsening skin symptoms with intake of food to which a child reacts. IgG/IgA antibody levels against food allergens should *not* be used for diagnostic purposes.

Other immune-mediated disorders not related to allergies

Apart from the allergic disorders described above, other immune-mediated conditions are also frequently observed in children with ASDs. These disorders can also affect behavioral symptoms in addition to organ-specific symptoms. Such A/I conditions are discussed in this section.

Asthma

Asthma is a heterogeneous disease characterized by chronic airway inflammation, reversible small airway obstruction that causes wheezing, and airway hyper-responsiveness. Airflow obstruction in the small airway is generally reversible; however, this may not be the case in the advanced stage of asthma, secondary to progressive fibrosis (scarring) of airways and resultant loss of elasticity. Multiple genetic and environmental factors are associated with the onset and progress of asthma. Despite recent progress in research, asthma remains a major chronic respiratory condition in children. Moreover, the prevalence of asthma has been increasing in developed countries and the "hygiene hypothesis," as with AA, has again been implicated in the increased prevalence of asthma.[19,21,46]

Allergen exposure is not the only trigger of an acute asthma attack.[47] Other common asthma triggers include respiratory infection, non-specific irritants, such as tobacco smoke, exercise, weather changes, and gastroesophageal reflux, and use of certain medications such as aspirin.

For many patients with asthma, the onset is in infancy or early childhood, at a time when viral infection plays a major role as a trigger for wheezing. With viral infection, about 50% of infants wheeze and two-thirds of those that wheeze have persistent symptoms, which may become quiescent or persistent in adolescence.[48] Since asthma causes chronic airway inflammation and progressive airway remodeling if not treated, progressive loss of lung functions has been reported in individuals with asthma.[49] Surprisingly, several groups have reported that the greatest absolute loss of lung function in asthmatics occurs early in childhood.[50,51]

Decisions about asthma management are based on impairment of airway function and expected long-term outcomes as detailed in the Expert Panel Report 3 (EPR 3) asthma guidelines.[27] Like any chronic inflammatory disease, most patients with asthma require daily control medications for chronic airway inflammation. The EPR 3 guidelines emphasize daily use of asthma-control (anti-inflammatory) medications and step-up measures with worsening asthma symptoms.[52] The importance of avoidance measures for allergen exposure is also emphasized for atopic asthma. Other preventive measures for triggering events are encouraged as well, including minimizing exposure to environmental irritants such as tobacco smoke, prevention of respiratory tract infections with aggressive vaccination including a yearly influenza vaccine, and preventive use of ß2 agonist, which is a bronchodilator, before exercise (for exercise-induced asthma).

A mainstay for asthma treatment is inhaled corticosteroids (ICSs) via a nebulizer or meter-dose inhaler. Step-up measures include substituting ICSs with a combination treatment of ICS and long-acting ß2 agonists (LABAs). Additional anti-inflammatory medications, such as leukotriene receptor antagonists (LTRAs) and theophylline, have also been used. In children, LTRAs are preferentially used because of easy administration and fewer side effects. Worsening asthma symptoms may require frequent or persistent use of oral corticosteroids. Although over 80% of patients with asthma can achieve control with currently available control medications (ICSs, ICSs/LABAs, LTRAs, and theophylline), a subset of patients are resistant to such treatment measures and present with different clinical features.[53,54] As an additional therapeutic option, anti-IgE antibody (omalizumab) has been integrated into the asthma guidelines and appears to have an impact on control of severe atopic (allergic) asthma.[55]

Since asthma is a chronic inflammatory condition, early diagnosis and implementation of asthma-control measures (avoidance of triggers and daily use of asthma-control medications) are keys to successful asthma management and prevention of irreversible asthma complications, including loss of lung function. While part of asthma diagnosis depends on lung-function testing using a spirometer, most children with ASDs are unable to execute this testing effectively. In such cases, asthma diagnosis is solely dependent on good history taking and careful physical examination. It is noteworthy that wheezing is typically episodic in patients with asthma and becomes less evident with age. For children with limited expressive language, it is difficult to express common asthma symptoms such as shortness of breath or tightness of chest; therefore, common asthma symptoms can be easily missed in children with ASDs. The onset of asthma symptoms can affect behavioral symptoms by increasing anxiety in children with ASDs, and may be under-diagnosed and under-treated. In addition, many children with ASDs are unable to use a meter-dose inhaler effectively, requiring instead the use of a nebulizer; thus, the treatment of asthma can be especially challenging for children with ASDs.

Non-allergic rhinitis and rhinosinusitis

The cause of non-allergic rhinitis (NAR) is not well understood and is thought to be heterogeneous. NAR without eosinophilia (also called idiopathic rhinitis) presents with chronic nasal congestion in the absence of aeroallergen sensitization and microbial infection.[56] These patients appear to be sensitive to non-specific irritants such as tobacco smoke, odor, humidity, and temperature changes. This condition is also called vasomotor rhinitis. Young children often demonstrate nasal congestion with exposure to cold air, and although the exact mechanisms of this condition are not well understood, evidence points to neural hyper-responsiveness.[57]

Non-allergic rhinitis with eosinophilia syndrome (NARES) presents with year-round nasal congestion, profuse watery rhinorrhea (runny nose), sneezing spells, nasal itchiness, and occasionally loss of smell. NARES is also distinguished by the presence of eosinophils in nasal smears, despite negative skin-test reactivity and absence of allergen-specific IgE.[56,58] This condition is mainly seen in middle-aged adults and rarely seen in children.

Hormonal rhinitis can occur with hormonal changes, as illustrated with rhinitis seen in pregnancy, with the onset of puberty, and in those with hypothyroidism. Drug-induced rhinitis can occur with use of oral or topical medications. Oral medications known to cause chronic rhinitis include angiotensin-converting enzyme inhibitors, ß blockers, other anti-hypertensive medications, and non-steroidal anti-inflammatory drugs such as aspirin. Chronic use of topical α-adrenergic decongestants (>5–7 days) can also cause chronic rhinitis as well as withdrawal symptoms with decreased mucociliary clearance (often called rhinitis medicamentosa).[59]

Medications used to treat NAR are similar to those used for AR; however, if causative triggers are known, such as drug-induced rhinitis, avoidance measures should be implemented. Chronic nasal congestion may also be associated with enlargement of the adenoids and tonsils, which predisposes individuals to recurrent ear infections and sinusitis as well as obstructive sleep apnea. Careful physical examination and medical history taking will be helpful for diagnosing the above-described NAR conditions. Again, this can also be challenging in children with ASDs with limited expressive language and distracting behavioral symptoms.

Rhinosinusitis (RS) is inflammation of the nose and paranasal sinuses. Acute RS is defined as up to 4 weeks of purulent (pus-like) nasal drainage accompanied by nasal obstruction, facial pain/pressure/fullness, or both.[60,61] Subacute RS is defined as those symptoms lasting 4–8 weeks. Chronic RS (CRS) is defined as an inflammatory condition involving the nose and paranasal sinuses lasting more than 8 weeks despite attempts to manage this medically.[60,61] In addition to the above-described symptoms, patients often describe a decreased sense of smell. To diagnosis CRS, in addition to clinical features, evidence of sinus inflammation by imaging studies (typically computerized tomography scan of the sinuses) is required; however, it is noteworthy that there is a poor correlation between clinical symptoms and objective findings on computerized tomography scan.

Acute RS is usually caused by either viral or bacterial infection. On the other hand, CRS is not totally attributed to infection, although infection plays an important role.[60,61] CRS is currently classified into three subsets:

1. CRS without nasal polyposis which accounts for approximately 60% of CRS. This is most commonly seen in children.

2. CRS with nasal polyposis which accounts for 20–33% of CRS and has similar clinical symptoms to CRS with polyposis; however, reduced sense of smell is more commonly seen in these patients.[62] This condition is also more likely to be associated with aspirin-induced asthma.

3. Allergic fungal RS which is defined as CRS with presence of fungal allergen-specific IgE and allergic mucin in which fungal hyphae are identified. Fungi are colonized in the sinus but not invasive, and most trials of anti-fungal medications have failed to show any benefits.[60,61]

Chronic rhinitis, both atopic and non-atopic, is a leading predisposing factor for CRS;[63] however, other underlying conditions also predispose individuals to CRS, including immunodeficiency syndromes, cystic fibrosis, anatomical problems such as enlarged adenoids or tonsils and nasal polyps (mainly in adults), and the presence of systemic diseases such as vasculitis.[64] Mucosal susceptibility to exogenous (outside) stimuli is common in RS.[65] In addition, sinusitis is one of the major triggers for asthma.[65] This is also likely the case for children with ASDs as seen in our clinic, where we observe a high frequency of non-atopic asthma in children with ASDs diagnosed with CRS.[66]

Management of RS involves controlling nasal inflammation with topical steroid nasal inhalers and use of antibiotics (mainly for acute RS and CRS with purulent discharge). Patients with CRS and polyps may benefit from a burst of oral corticosteroids; CRS refractory to medical management may require endoscopic sinus surgery. Once again, diagnosis and management of sinusitis in children with ASDs is likely to be more challenging than in typically developing children.

Hypogammaglobulinemia and antibody deficiency syndrome

Impaired Ab production (hypogammaglobulinemia) typically manifests as increased susceptibility to bacterial infection, resulting in recurrent upper and lower respiratory infection (otitis media [ear infections], sinusitis, and pneumonia). These patients typically do not respond to the first-line antibiotics and often require intravenous antibiotics. In addition to respiratory bacterial infection, recurrent viral infection is common. Infections involving other organs (skin, joints, central nervous system, GI tract, urinary tract) can be seen more frequently in these patients. Primary Ab deficiency syndromes are known to be caused by multiple distinct gene mutations associated with B-cell development, maturation, and/or functions including those associated with T-cell and B-cell interactions. Depending on the mutations, clinical features vary in primary Ab deficiency syndromes. Describing each known gene mutation that causes primary Ab deficiency is beyond the scope of this chapter. Interested readers are encouraged to read recent review papers regarding this topic.[67–69]

A primary Ab deficiency syndrome should be considered as a part of the differential diagnosis in individuals with chronic sinopulmonary infections not responsive to the first-line antibiotics. Ab deficiency syndromes are not uncommon and thus may affect children with ASDs. In fact, in our clinic, we follow several children with ASDs who also fulfill the diagnostic criteria for Ab deficiency syndrome. In these patients, supplemental IV or subcutaneous immunoglobulin (IVIG or SCIG) treatment controls their recurrent infections. In addition, treatment with IVIG or SCIG resulted in a reduction in fluctuating behavioral symptoms in some of these children, possibly related to better control of pain and discomfort associated with recurrent infections.[70]

Secondary Ab deficiency syndrome (SADS) can also be seen with various medical conditions. This may be best illustrated in patients undergoing myeloablative treatment prior to stem cell transplantation, with increased susceptibility to infection secondary to temporary antibody suppression with reduction in white blood cells; however, SADS can also be seen in other conditions, such as malnutrition and chronic inflammation, that suppress Ab production, and also in conditions causing loss of Ab from the GI tract (i.e., protein-losing enteropathy), skin (such as burn injury), and kidney (i.e., nephrotic syndrome). In patients with severe FA, malnutrition as well as protein loss from the GI tract can occur, and thus management of SADS also may need to be integrated into FA treatment.

Other medications can also cause hypogammaglobulinemia. One of the most common causes of drug-induced SADS is anti-epileptic drugs (AEDs). In fact, multiple AEDs are reported to cause SADS, although the cause of AED-induced SADS is not well understood.[71-76] This may be an important consideration when children with ASDs who are on AEDs present with symptoms suggestive of an Ab deficiency syndrome. Also, seizure disorders are more common in children with ASDs, and AEDs may be prescribed to treat neuropsychiatric symptoms in children without seizures.

Pediatric autoimmune neuropsychiatric disorders associated with streptococci and pediatric acute-onset neuropsychiatric syndrome

Previous reports support a high frequency of autoimmune diseases in the immediate family members of children with ASDs, which may not be universally reproducible. Nevertheless, molecular genetics studies indicate a role for the immune system in at least a subset of such children. In addition, neuropsychiatric conditions associated with autoimmune or neuroimmune dysregulation in children with ASDs has become a research focus. The conditions most frequently examined are pediatric autoimmune neuropsychiatric disorders associated with streptococci (PANDAS) and pediatric acute-onset neuropsychiatric syndrome (PANS).

A PANDAS diagnosis requires fulfillment of all of the following five diagnostic criteria:[77,78]

1. presence of obsessive–compulsive disorder (OCD) or a tic disorder

2. pre-pubertal onset of symptoms

3. acute symptom onset and episodic (relapsing-remitting) course

4. temporal association between group A streptococcal (GAS) infection and symptom onset or exacerbation

5. association with neurological abnormalities (particularly motoric hyperactivity and choreiform movements).

PANDAS initially attracted attention in association with Sydenham Chorea (SC), since patients with SC are known to exhibit OCD symptoms at high frequency (60–75%);[79] however, it has been difficult to prove a temporal association between GAS infection and onset or exacerbation of neuropsychiatric symptoms in many cases, which is also our experience. Prospective studies of patients with PANDAS yielded negative as well as positive results in association with GAS.[80–83] This may result from differences in the criteria used to diagnose PANDAS. Unlike SC, use of preventative (prophylactic) antibiotics is not recommended, and its efficacy for PANDAS has not been established, although two small studies appear to support the efficacy of penicillin prophylaxis[84] and azithromycin or penicillin prophylaxis.[85]

Following the characterization of PANDAS, it subsequently became clear that many children present with similar clinical features, but without evidence of a temporal relationship with a GAS infection; instead, neuropsychiatric symptoms are associated with other bacterial and viral infections, and are not limited to one specific microbe; hence, broader diagnostic criteria encompassing both PANDAS and non-PANDAS were developed and published in 2012 under the umbrella term of PANS.[77] The diagnostic criteria for PANS were proposed as follows:[77]

•   abrupt, dramatic onset of OCD or severely restricted food intake

•   concurrent presence of neuropsychiatric symptoms with similarly severe and acute onset; presence of at least two of seven categories (anxiety, emotional liability or depression, irritability/aggression/severe oppositional behaviors, behavioral [developmental] regression, deterioration in school performance, sensory/motor abnormalities, and somatic signs/symptoms)

•   symptoms not attributed to a known neurological or medical disorder.

An abrupt, dramatic onset of OCD and severe symptoms causing significant distress and interference in the patient's daily activity are hallmarks of PANS. Acute-onset anorexia was an alternative first diagnostic criterion.[86] Other somatic signs and symptoms of PANS include sleep disturbance and enuresis or urinary frequency.[77] Sensory abnormalities can manifest as a sudden increase in sensitivity to light, sounds, smells, textures, and so forth. Motor abnormalities may include an abrupt deterioration of handwriting, tics, motor hyperactivity, and choreiform (writhing) movements.

It is noteworthy that authors described the PANS diagnostic criteria as "working criteria" with expected revisions and modifications in the near future. For patients with PANS, no therapeutic guidelines have been established. Current therapeutic measures typically offered are symptomatic relief with neuropsychiatric medications and behavioral interventions; however, it appears that patients with PANS are very sensitive to neuropsychiatric medications with a higher frequency of side effects.[87] Responses to these measures are rather limited, but like patients with PANDAS, some patients with PANS appear to respond well to antibiotics and anti-inflammatory treatments including IVIG.[77]

In a subset of children with ASDs followed in our A/I clinic, behavioral symptoms similar to PANS have been observed including: abrupt onset of behavioral or developmental regression, worsening school performance, onset of motor or sensory symptoms, and increased irritability or OCD behaviors, which followed some kind of microbial infection; however, the severity and acute onset of these symptoms are not as dramatic as observed in patients with PANS who do not have an ASD, and pre-existing behaviors associated with ASDs may make it difficult to distinguish the onset of PANS symptoms. Unlike other children with PANS, children with ASDs with fluctuating PANS symptoms do not appear to respond well to the first-line pharmacological or behavioral interventions. It remains to be seen whether PANS can be reliably diagnosed in children with ASDs. Some parents of children with ASDs seek treatment directed at PANDAS or PANS, such as prolonged antibiotics and IVIG, but such treatment should be reserved for children with a firm diagnosis, since these measures are not side-effect free.

Effects of immune-mechanism diseases on neuropsychiatric symptoms

It has been long suspected that asthma has an impact on mental illnesses and/or behavioral symptoms. An increased frequency of anxiety and panic symptoms/disorders has been reported in patients with asthma.[88] A large community study examined 4181 subjects, including 236 with asthma, between 18 and 65 years of age. Patients with physician-diagnosed asthma and asthma symptoms within 4 weeks of the interview were found to have an increased likelihood of anxiety disorders, specific phobias, panic disorders, and panic attacks.[89] A high prevalence of panic attacks in both adults and children with asthma was reproducible in subsequent studies that utilized both clinic and community samples.[88,90–93] In studies of groups of people without documented psychological disorders, asthma was positively associated with the later development of internalizing symptoms and panic disorders.[94–96]

Respiratory distress associated with asthma may aggravate anxiety, which then may trigger panic and anxiety disorders. Asthma symptoms cause discomfort and general ill feeling, which may in turn exacerbate irritability and hyperactivity. In a Swedish study involving 1480 twin pairs, authors reported that childhood asthma is associated with subsequent development of hyperactivity and impulsivity.[97] In another cross-sectional study with 594 adults with ADHD and 719 control subjects, asthma diagnosis was associated with an increased prevalence of mood and anxiety disorders, highlighting a comorbidity between ADHD and asthma.[98] Proposed theories regarding the association between asthma and mental conditions include (1) somatic effects of hyperventilation, (2) hypersensitivity of carbon dioxide receptors in the brain, (3) the effects of asthma medications, and (4) mutual genetic or environmental predisposing factors, such as maladaptation to stress, for asthma and panic or anxiety disorders.[88]

Rhinosinusitis can cause various neuropsychiatric symptoms as well as persistent facial pain, discomfort, or fullness which may impact daily activity. Reports of neuropsychiatric symptoms associated with RS have been scant; however, several previously published reports on CRS highlight the impact of RS on neuropsychiatric symptoms. In a study of 143 patients with CRS (mean age 43.4 years), psychiatric comorbidity (mainly anxiety and depression) was reported to be associated with increased CRS symptoms.[99] In a study of 76 adults with CRS, 25% of patients scored in the moderate-to-severe depression range on the Patient Health Questionnaire-9, and depression severity improved with improvement of sinus symptoms following endoscopic sinus surgery.[100] Another study with 207 patients with CRS or recurrent acute RS reported that 28% of the patients had probable or possible anxiety or depressive disorder when assessed by the Hospital Anxiety and Depression Scale.[101]

Studies addressing the impact of CRS on children, especially children with limited expressive language, are scant; however, given the above-described study results in adults, it is likely that symptoms associated with anxiety and depression may be observed in pediatric populations as well. Anxiety symptoms can manifest as worsening behavioral symptoms in children with ASDs, in addition to behavioral symptoms associated with pain and discomfort.

Children with antibody deficiency syndrome are at risk for recurrent sinopulmonary infections associated with persistent pain and discomfort including sinus headaches. Anxiety symptoms caused by CRS may also manifest as changes in behavioral symptoms in children with ASDs. In children with recurrent sinopulmonary infections, infection-induced asthma and airway hyper-responsiveness are common complications. Anxiety-associated symptoms may be frequently seen in these subjects if asthma is not properly controlled. In addition, these patients are often treated with a prolonged course of antibiotics which, in turn, can cause a disruption of the natural bacteria colonization in the intestine, resulting in chronic GI symptoms. Preventative use of probiotics may be helpful in these cases. When managing children with ASDs and Ab deficiency syndrome, we should remember that their behavioral symptoms can be affected by chronic infection with secondary pain and discomfort as well as common comorbid conditions such as asthma.

Since PANDAS and PANS are behaviorally defined syndromes which are characterized by acute onset of behavioral symptoms (especially OCD), it is difficult to determine whether a child with an ASD also has PANDAS or PANS. In our experience, there appears to be a subset of children with ASDs who exhibit fluctuating behavioral symptoms and repeated loss of cognitive skills. In these patients, triggering events causing acute exacerbation are typically immune insults, mainly microbial infection.[102] These individuals also have persistent GI symptoms and some of them demonstrate progressive decline of specific antibody responses.[70] While some of their clinical features overlap with PANS criteria, these individuals appear to have distinct blood-monocyte genetic profiles.[102] Further studies are required to address the controversial roles of PANDAS and PANS in ASDs.

TAKEAWAY POINTS

- Food allergies (FAs) can be mediated by both IgE- and non-IgE-mediated immune reactions and diagnosis of FA should be based on the clinical presentation, since no definitive laboratory measures are currently available for either type of FA.

- Clinical diagnosis of FA is more difficult in individuals with limited expressive language. In addition, GI discomfort and pain associated with FAs likely worsen behavioral symptoms in these individuals, which makes the clinical picture more confusing.

- Aeroallergen allergy (AA) is prevalent in the general population and is expected to be as prevalent in children with ASDs. Under-treated AAs can cause or aggravate neuropsychiatric symptoms.

- Anaphylaxis is likely to be under-diagnosed or delayed in being diagnosed in individuals with minimal expressive language, including children with ASDs. In addition, behavioral and neuropsychiatric symptoms that may be triggered by an anaphylactic reaction can also be confusing and may cause delay in treatment for anaphylaxis.

- Drug allergy (DA) is caused by multiple immune mechanisms, and a detailed history is an essential component in diagnosing DA; therefore, diagnosis of DAs is more challenging in children with ASDs.

- Atopic dermatitis (AD) can affect neuropsychiatric symptoms, and controlling AD symptoms should be integrated into the general care of children with ASDs.

- Asthma is often under-diagnosed and under-treated in children with ASDs. In addition, treatment of asthma can also be challenging for these children, since they are often not able to use meter-dose inhalers effectively.

- Asthma, if not well controlled, can affect neuropsychiatric symptoms including anxiety, irritability, and hyperactivity.

- As described in allergic rhinitis, chronic rhinosinusitis can cause significant neuropsychiatric symptoms partly due to chronic pain (sinus headache) and discomfort. Since diagnosis of sinusitis is generally harder in children with limited expressive language, extra effort may be required for assessing the relationship between behavioral symptoms and sinusitis-associated symptoms.

- Primary and secondary antibody deficiency syndromes can be seen in children with ASDs; secondary antibody deficiency can be associated with use of certain medications. Better control of recurrent infections that occur as a result of antibody deficiency likely leads to improvement in the quality of life in children with or without ASDs who have an antibody deficiency syndrome.

- Pediatric autoimmune neuropsychiatric disorders associated with streptococci (PANDAS) and pediatric acute-onset neuropsychiatric syndrome (PANS) are behaviorally defined syndromes that may be difficult to diagnose in children with ASDs. At this time, a role of PANDAS and PANS is not clearly defined in these children, and individualized approaches are required for managing children with ASDs who have fluctuating behavioral symptoms.

Acknowledgment

This work was partly supported by Jontay Foundation, St. Paul, Minnesota, and Autism Research Institute, San Diego, California.

Chapter 6

Oral and Dental Issues for Individuals with Autism Spectrum Disorders

Evan Spivack, DDS, Mark D. Robinson, DMD, and Tomas J. Ballesteros, DMD

Introduction

Oral and dental care is a critical, yet sometimes overlooked, component in the overall health of the child and adult with an autism spectrum disorder (ASD). In many cases, it is difficult to find dentists familiar with the issues faced by persons with ASDs and comfortable enough to work with this patient population.

The mouth is a sensitive and personal space that, when encroached upon, may lead to significant and even aggressive reactions on the part of the patient. This can lead to enormous challenges on the part of caregivers to provide even the most basic home care and may make routine dental office visits impossible.

This chapter discusses common oral and dental problems noted in the child and adult with an ASD, home-care issues, how to find dentists that will provide appropriate care for this patient population, and how to interact with the professional dental community to achieve the best outcomes.

Dental concerns for the person with an ASD

Dental caries and periodontal disease are two of the major disease entities of dentistry. Children and adults with these conditions suffer from significant pain, infection, and loss of teeth. As a result, they may suffer from a decreased ability to chew and swallow food, nutritional imbalances, difficulties speaking, and social liabilities related to bad breath and an unwillingness to smile.

Other consequences that may often be overlooked are the costs of the hours and days missed from school and work as a result of oral pain, both for the sufferer and for those in caregiver roles.

Dental caries

Dental caries (Figure 6.1), also known as tooth decay or cavities, is the most common chronic disease of childhood.[1] It is a bacterial disease that causes demineralization (weakening) and destruction of the hard tissues of the teeth. If left untreated, caries may also affect the tooth's nerve and blood supply (the pulp). Tooth decay is caused by an attack on the tooth from strong acids produced by oral bacteria that feed on food debris accumulating on tooth surfaces. In the early stages, dental decay appears as a chalky white spot on the tooth; over time, this spot takes on a brown stain and the surface of the tooth breaks down (cavitation).

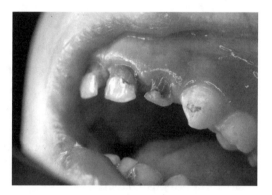

Figure 6.1 Dental caries

In some instances carious tooth changes may be readily visible, while in others dental radiographs may be needed to determine the extent of tooth destruction. Similarly, while dental caries may cause severe pain for some people, others may experience little or no discomfort or other symptoms. Too often, the quiet nature of dental caries makes people defer care, leading to worsening tooth conditions and the need for treatment that is more invasive and expensive than that which might have been needed earlier.

The question of whether persons with ASDs have a higher incidence of dental caries than those without ASDs has been the subject of numerous studies since the 1960s. To date, no definite answer has been reached in this regard, but the evidence seems to lean towards the belief that persons with ASDs actually have a *lower* incidence of dental caries than do their peers without ASDs.[2] Given the factors that are known to lead to carious tooth destruction, this is a somewhat surprising finding.

Numerous studies over the years have shown that a high incidence of caries is linked to the presence of dental plaque around the teeth.[3] Plaque is the sticky mass of bacteria that breaks down food debris into carbohydrates and produces the tooth-destroying acids. The majority of plaque is located in the occlusal pits and fissures (the grooves found on the biting surfaces of the tooth) and along the inner- and outer-facing tooth surfaces at the gumline. Due to behavioral concerns, children and adults with ASDs often have difficulty in performing toothbrushing or other oral hygiene tasks, which leads to an increase in plaque accumulation.

A second issue related to caries formation is the individual's diet.[4] A diet high in carbohydrates, particularly sticky and/or sweet foods, is more likely to contribute towards the development of tooth decay. Often, children with ASDs are very selective in what they eat, and their food choices seldom include tooth-friendly fruits and vegetables. Additionally, many children with ASDs receive sweets as rewards both at school and at home, further contributing to an oral environment that would seem to encourage an increased incidence of dental caries.

Prevention is clearly preferable to treatment of dental caries in terms of time, effort, and cost for tooth restoration. Dental caries prevention is also important in limiting the loss of natural tooth structure. A three-pronged approach towards dental caries prevention is recommended by all major dental organizations. First is a commitment to regular dental checkups, with the first dental examination scheduled at age 1 year, or when the first tooth begins to erupt. The second preventive approach is the use of fluoride, be it in the public water supply, as oral supplements, or in toothpastes and mouth rinses. The third component of the prevention plan is the most important and yet often the most difficult to implement: the establishment and maintenance of a good program of home oral hygiene combined with the avoidance of a caries-friendly diet. Each aspect of this prevention program is discussed at greater length later in this chapter.

If dental caries do occur, it is important that they be treated as soon as possible to avoid further destruction of tooth structure and possible tooth loss. Generally, treatment goals are the conservative removal of decayed tooth structure, with restorations making use of amalgam, glass ionomer, or composite materials. Greater structural loss may require the placement of crowns on the teeth to preserve their integrity (Figure 6.2a and 6.2b). Root canal treatment may be considered if the pulp of the tooth (nerve and blood supply) is compromised.

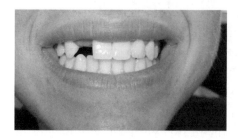
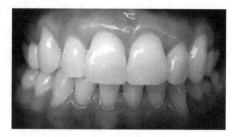

Figure 6.2a and 6.2b Replacement of a missing tooth

Dental amalgam is a restorative material composed of a number of elements including mercury. Although the silver color of the filling itself is not esthetic, amalgam provides superior strength and versatility in placement compared with other material choices. While some have questioned the safety of dental amalgam, all major medical and dental scientific organizations (including the World Health Organization, Centers for Disease Control, Food and Drug Administration, American Dental Association, Academy of General Dentistry, American Academy of Pediatrics, and American Academy of Pediatric Dentistry) have repeatedly supported the use of dental amalgam as effective and without known risk.[5]

Composite restorations are the most esthetic of the dental materials used in caries restoration. These materials also bond to tooth structure, adding to their versatility; however, they lack some of the strength of amalgam and are more susceptible to decay.

Glass ionomers are a third class of dental restorative materials with a wide range of applications. The great advantage of this material is its ability to bond to tooth structure much like composites, but in addition the glass ionomers contain fluoride which they continually release, limiting damage from dental caries.[6] For patients with poor oral hygiene or poor diet, these are often the restorations of choice.

Periodontal disease

Whereas dental caries affects the teeth, periodontal disease affects the structures of the mouth supporting those teeth. These structures, together termed the periodontium, are the gingiva (gums), the alveolar bone, and the periodontal ligaments (fibers attaching the tooth to the bone). While there are several diseases that affect the periodontium, periodontal disease is divided into two primary categories, gingivitis and periodontitis (Figure 6.3a–6.3c).

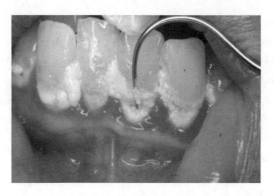

Figure 6.3a Gingivitis caused by plaque accumulation

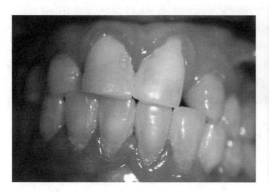 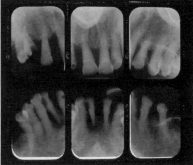

Figure 6.3b and 6.3c Periodontitis
The amount of loss of gingiva and bone support is shown. The dental X-rays
demonstrate severe bone loss from periodontitis in another patient.

Gingivitis is the most common form of periodontal disease, affecting between 50 and 90% of adults worldwide.[7] While most have a mild form of this inflammatory disease, gingivitis can often become severe, causing redness, swelling, and irritation of the gingival tissues that can be unsightly and painful. In more severe cases of gingivitis, there is often bleeding from the inflamed gum tissues. Gingivitis may also contribute to halitosis (bad breath).

Gingivitis is caused by an accumulation of dental plaque in the sulcus (the space between the tooth and the gums) and between the teeth. Chemicals released from the bacteria in the plaque cause an inflammatory response leading to enlargement of, and damage to, the gingiva. As plaque is the primary cause of most forms of gingivitis, oral hygiene is the key to both prevention and treatment of this dental disease. Effective toothbrushing and flossing, as well as the appropriate use of mouth rinses, is the mainstay of a preventive program. This is combined with regularly scheduled professional dental maintenance, including scaling and prophylaxis.

Gingivitis may be more severe in persons with a weakened immune system, including those with diabetes and other medical conditions. Several medications may also lead to an increase in tissue inflammation. This response, often referred to as gingival hypertrophy or gingival hyperplasia, is most commonly seen in children and adults taking the antiepileptic medication phenytoin and calcium channel blockers, most notably nifedipine.[8] Especially in the presence of poor oral hygiene, the gingiva may become extremely inflamed (Figure 6.4a and 6.4b). While physicians are aware of this side effect, it may not be practical to change medications. Treatment of drug-induced gingival inflammation therefore centers on maintaining good oral hygiene and in some cases surgically removing excess tissue. After surgical treatment, proper home care can minimize gingival regrowth and decrease the need for future surgical interventions.

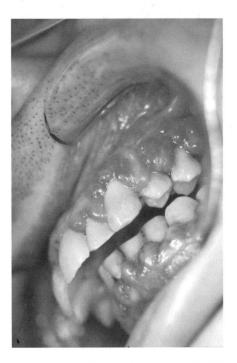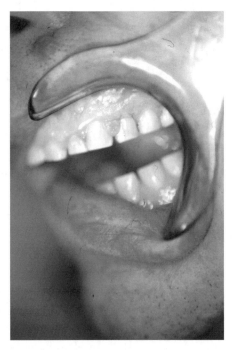

Figure 6.4a and 6.4b Gingival condition of a patient
on phenytoin, before and after surgical treatment

If left untreated, the infection in the gum tissues caused by gingivitis can spread to the periodontal ligaments and bone, causing periodontitis. As this disease progresses, there is continued destruction of the structures supporting the teeth, resulting in eventual tooth loss. Although it is seldom seen in children, the incidence of periodontitis increases during adolescence and becomes the leading cause of tooth loss in adults.[9]

In its earliest stages, it is difficult to distinguish periodontitis from gingivitis; however, as plaque hardens into calculus (tartar), these deposits on the tooth surfaces and at the base of the sulcus cause an increase in inflammation. The infected sulcus deepens and becomes a periodontal pocket, which deepens over time. The periodontal ligaments are destroyed as calculus builds in the pockets and the cementum (the outer surface of the tooth root) becomes rough with attached calculus. Over time, the bone supporting the teeth is destroyed and the teeth begin to loosen. The gingival tissues bleed easily and it is not uncommon for the person with periodontitis to awaken with blood from the gums on their pillow. As the infection deepens, periodontal abscesses may develop, characterized by pain, swelling, and purulence (pus) oozing from the gum tissues (Figure 6.5). Antibiotics are often needed to treat infections that have reached this stage.[10]

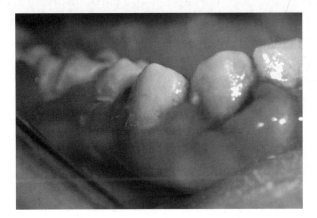

Figure 6.5 Severe inflammation and periodontal
infection due to poor oral hygiene

As with gingivitis, periodontitis is addressed through the implementation of a rigorous program of prevention and treatment. To remove calculus buildups and smooth the roughened cementum surfaces, scaling and root planing must be accomplished before dental prophylaxis. This may require multiple visits, and local anesthetics may be used to relieve discomfort during the procedure. In some cases, the extent of the periodontal destruction is such that surgery on the gingiva and underlying bone is required. Rigorous home oral hygiene efforts must be followed to prevent calculus reformation and reinfection of the pockets, and regular professional dental maintenance is critical. Antimicrobials, chlorhexidine rinses, and low-dose doxycycline can be prescribed to supplement in-office scaling and root planing.[11]

It is important to understand that once periodontitis begins, it cannot be reversed; only managed. The goal of treatment is to slow or stop the destructive inflammatory forces and maintain the remaining periodontium. Once lost, alveolar bone will not return unless it is replaced through complex bone grafting procedures.

Dental and oral injuries

Children and adults with autism are generally not any more likely to suffer from oral injuries as a result of external traumatic events than are those without autism; however, caregivers should be aware of several types of oral and dental injuries that are commonly seen in persons with ASDs.

Seizure disorders are commonly diagnosed in individuals with ASDs. Those persons with ASDs who also have a seizure disorder may suffer oral injuries during or after a seizure resulting in a fall or involving a tongue biting. Generally, the upper front teeth (maxillary incisors) sustain the most damage, sometimes chipping or fracturing more severely (Figure 6.6). Damage may require fillings or even crowns to restore the teeth to health and function, and root canal therapy may be indicated if the nerve has sustained sufficient trauma. The oral soft tissues, particularly the lips and the tongue, may also be cut or bruised as a result of a fall. Any dental or oral trauma observed as a result of a fall should be immediately evaluated by a dentist, who may recommend X-rays to better determine the extent of any damage. In some cases, the effects of a fall on oral tissues may not be immediately apparent, and may only come to light weeks or even months later.

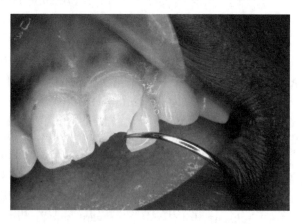

Figure 6.6 Tooth fractured in a fall

Another form of dental damage is the significant wearing down of the biting and chewing surfaces resulting from bruxism (parafunctional grinding and clenching of the teeth; Figure 6.7). In some people, damage to the teeth may take years to become evident, while in others a sudden onset or increase in bruxism may cause rapid and dramatic loss of tooth structure. Soreness in the teeth, jaw, and temporomandibular joint is another effect of excessive grinding and clenching. Many people with bruxism also suffer from gastroesophageal reflux disorder. In addition to teeth sustaining damage from the physical effects of parafunctional forces, the gastric acids can cause significant chemical damage to the teeth as well.[12]

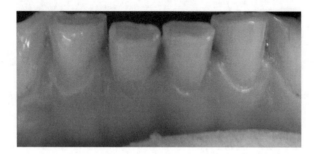

Figure 6.7 Tooth wear resulting from bruxism

The exact cause of bruxism is unknown and likely is multifactorial. Bruxism in those children and adults with ASDs may result from frustration stemming from inability to communicate, as well as from other neurological triggers. Pain, sometimes from toothache, earache or other sources, may also cause an increase in bruxism behavior. If there is a sudden onset or a dramatic increase in bruxism, a dentist should be consulted to rule out dental pain and consider appropriate intervention. Studies have shown, however, that typical interventions are seldom successful. In some cases, mouth guards may be constructed to protect the teeth from harmful forces, but these can only be considered for those patients able to tolerate fabrication and wearing of such an apparatus.[13]

Self-injurious behaviors are another cause of orally related trauma for persons with ASDs. Self-injury presents in several forms, many of which involve the mouth, and can be both severe and difficult to manage. Hitting or punching the face and mouth is not uncommon; in some cases, the force may be enough to fracture teeth or cause lacerations of the lips or other soft tissues. Picking behaviors may be seen as well, and may manifest in the use of fingernails to abrade the gingiva. Often more troubling is the use of the teeth to cause self-injury, presenting as biting of the hands and arms or, less frequently, the lips (Figure 6.8), tongue, and inside of the cheeks. As with bruxism, these behaviors are difficult to manage and often require combined efforts on the part of the dentist and other members of the medical team.

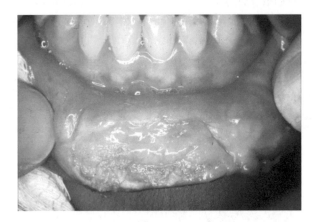

Figure 6.8 Self-injurious behavior: chronic lip biting

The effect of medications

Children and adults with ASDs often take medications having side effects that can complicate the presentation and severity of dental caries and periodontal disease. One of the most common of these side effects is xerostomia (dry mouth). Over 400 commonly used medications have xerostomia as a potential side effect, including antidepressants, antipsychotics, sedatives, antihypertensives, antianxiety medications, antihistamines, bronchodilators, and analgesics.[14] The reduction in saliva flow is often more than just a nuisance, because saliva has a number of properties that make it very valuable to oral comfort and overall health.

Saliva plays a major role in digestion, mixing with food and moistening it to allow the food to be more easily swallowed. A decrease in saliva may lead to choking on foods and require significant modifications in diet. Often, a regular diet may be replaced by a soft or even pureed diet, resulting in the oral health concerns noted earlier.

As an oral lubricant, saliva protects the soft tissues of the mouth from small cuts or scrapes and has both antibacterial and antifungal properties that protect the mouth from infection. These oral infections can be painful and often spread beyond the mouth to affect other body systems. Although it is beyond the scope of this chapter, it is noteworthy that oral infections have been linked to a number of systemic diseases, increasing the importance of proper oral hygiene and the need for vigilant professional dental oversight.

In addition to xerostomia, medications may have other negative effects on the mouth and oral function. These effects, notably seen with many of the medication classes mentioned above, include inflammation of the gingiva and other oral soft tissues (mucositis), discoloration or swelling of the tongue (glossitis), salivary gland inflammation (sialadenitis), and changes in the taste of foods (dysgeusia). When made aware of these problems, the prescribing physician may be able to modify the drug regimens to reduce or eliminate these side effects.

The role of diet

The mouth is a dynamic environment that can be significantly affected by changes in diet and nutritional status. Many children and adults with ASDs maintain specific diets calling for the eliminations or additions of certain nutrients, and these dietary modifications must be considered in an assessment of risk for dental caries and periodontal diseases. Treatment recommendations made by the dentist will also often be influenced by dietary patterns, particularly in those instances where increased exposure to sugars is anticipated.

Diets commonly followed by persons with ASDs may include increases in fiber, healthy oils, vitamins, and protein. Specifically, the gluten-free, casein-free (GFCF) diet and the ketogenic diet offer many food choices which contain short-chain sugars. Although naturally sourced, these sugars present the same risks for dental disease as do other food choices. Fiber is made up of long-chain sugars, which are less readily available to bacteria and therefore less likely to contribute to the dental disease process. Protein, oils, and vitamins are not fermentable by bacteria: foods rich in these substances meet specific dietary requirements and at the same time contribute to a healthier oral environment. It is recommended that people interested in using the GFCF diet consult their primary physicians or pediatricians in order to ensure that proper nutritional requirements are met.[15]

Adequate water intake offers a number of health benefits. From a dental perspective, water plays a critical role in cleansing the mouth, with frequent rinsing one of the easiest ways to remove food debris. The mouth's anatomy allows for fluids to travel in places that most tooth brushes cannot reach, and such rinsing is particularly beneficial for those individuals who are more prone to developing very thick plaque and calculus.

Many people with ASDs consume beverages high in sugar content. These drinks are acidic and over time may place teeth at risk for acid erosion and demineralization. It is recommended that low-sugar drinks be substituted for drinks high in sugar. If it is not possible to eliminate these drinks from the diet, diluting the drinks with water can reduce the effects of the sugar.[16]

Behavior prompting is a commonly used technique meant to elicit specific responses through verbal, auditory, and tactile stimuli. In some cases, food is used as a prompt in order to keep the individual's focus and attention. While highly acidic or high-sugar-content candies, soda, or coffee are often used as prompts for specific behaviors, different food groups should be encouraged that can provide the same benefits in behavior prompting while also serving as a source for proper nutritional health;[16] for example, sugar-free flavored waters or seltzer (replacing soda, iced tea, or coffee), vegetables (in place of candy), and pretzels (in place of cookies or chips).

Developing a proper home-care regimen

The development of a proper regimen of oral home care is the cornerstone of dental and oral health, and it has significant ramifications for overall systemic wellness. The specific needs and challenges faced in developing such a regimen are as unique as the particular person for whom such a regimen is being prepared, and as such, there is no "cookbook" approach to preparing a home oral health plan. This section discusses concepts in oral hygiene that may be applied in a given situation; the reader is encouraged to work with a dentist or dental hygienist to craft these ideas into a usable regimen that fits the specific needs of the adult or child with an ASD. The successful home-care program will be effective in removing plaque, maintaining the health of the hard and soft tissues of the mouth, and will not prove so onerous that it cannot be maintained.

The standard oral hygiene maintenance program recommended by dental professionals is the mechanical removal of food particles through toothbrushing, flossing, and rinsing. Many individuals with ASDs and other special needs require modifications of this standard. If the child or adult with an ASD cannot maintain an attention span sufficient to allow for all three components of this regimen, the focus should be on proper and effective toothbrushing.

The classic method of toothbrushing recommended by most dental professionals is known as the modified Bass technique (Figure 6.9a and 6.9b). This approach to plaque and debris removal calls for the toothbrush bristles to angle towards the gumline, effectively cleaning both the teeth and gingival tissues. While the American Dental Association (ADA) recommendation is to brush twice daily, patients with special needs who are at higher risk for oral disease may benefit from brushing after each meal.[17]

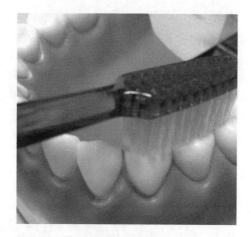

Figure 6.9a and 6.9b The Bass technique for proper toothbrushing

There is a broad variety of toothbrush types easily available for purchase in pharmacies, supermarkets, and other venues. Studies have demonstrated the superiority of powered toothbrushes over manual brushes.[18] The vibrations caused by power brushes, however, may be unsettling to people with ASDs. For those who require or prefer manual brushes, it is important to note that the brush purchased should have soft nylon bristles. These bristles are the most gentle when contacting oral hard and soft tissues, and are least likely to produce damage. To maintain the bristles at their most effective, brushes should be changed every few months, or when the bristles begin to fray (Figure 6.9c). The toothbrush should also be changed after an illness.

Figure 6.9c The top toothbrush is frayed
after 3 months of use and should be replaced

Dental flossing is critical in removing food and plaque from between the teeth and from the gum tissues. The ADA recommends flossing once per day.[17] While dental floss is commonly wrapped around the fingers for use in the mouth (Figure 6.10), there are a wide variety of flossing aids available for purchase. These devices hold the floss in place and provide handles that make the floss easier to manipulate, whether it is done by oneself or by someone else. To prevent injuring the gum tissues, it is important that the person whose teeth are being flossed remain cooperative and still throughout the procedure. If this is not possible, it may be better to forgo flossing and devote greater attention to toothbrushing and the use of mouth rinses.

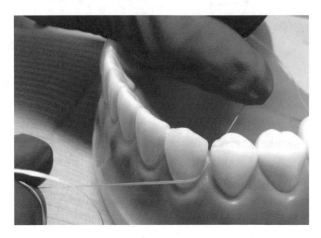

Figure 6.10 Correct flossing technique
The floss hugs the tooth surface and is moved in an up-down motion.

The surface area of the mouth far exceeds that of the teeth, and a proper oral care regimen will assure that the entire area is maintained. Mouth rinses offer a way to reach those areas of the mouth that are not cleaned with brushing and flossing alone.[19] There are many mouth-rinse products available, each having their own directions for use. Alcohol-containing mouth rinses have dominated the marketplace for decades, and while the alcohol content of these rinses is safe when used appropriately, illness can occur when large quantities of these products are swallowed against manufacturer recommendation. Many suitable non-alcoholic mouth rinses have been developed that provide comparable benefits to alcohol-containing rinses.[20] For those individuals who cannot use the mouth rinses in the typical "swish and spit" manner, a positive effect may still be obtained by applying the mouth rinse to the gums with a toothbrush, oral sponge, or even a towel.

Most mouth rinses on the market are sold as over-the-counter products, and these are effectively used for the vast majority of individuals. For patients with advanced periodontal conditions, a prescription-strength mouth rinse may prove necessary. In these cases, chlorhexidine gluconate 0.12% rinse is prescribed for its antibacterial properties. Despite a minimal and mild side-effect profile, when using chlorhexidine it is important to adhere to the directions for use and not use it for longer than the period prescribed.[20]

Fluoride and toothpastes

For decades, fluoride has been acknowledged as an important weapon in the fight against dental caries. Fluoride is a mineral commonly found in nature that helps to reduce the damage caused by the bacterial acids that are the cause of dental caries. In addition to its antibacterial effects, fluoride can also help to remineralize areas of the tooth that are weaker and prone to damage and cavitation.[17]

There are many available sources of fluoride. A large number of communities in the United States have access to fluoridated water; a local dentist as well as resources on the Internet can assist in locating nearby fluoridated areas. Dentists and hygienists also use topical fluoride gels and varnishes after dental cleaning to help strengthen and protect the teeth.[17] Many toothpastes, mouth rinses, and dental products contain fluoride. These products should be used for individuals who are at risk for dental decay. Those individuals who are at a severe risk of dental decay, due to either medical issues or poor oral hygiene, may be prescribed toothpastes which have a much higher concentration of fluoride. When using these prescription-strength toothpastes, be sure to follow directions so as not to exceed the recommended dosage of fluoride.[17]

The dental office visit

Finding the right dentist

Selecting a dentist to care for the patient with an ASD can be a very difficult task. While there is no shortage of dentists in highly populated areas of the United States, there may be a limited number of providers in the more rural areas. Living in a more sparsely populated area often requires the patient or patient's family to seek care longer distances from home. As the dental needs of children with ASDs are often more complex, it is frequently challenging to find dentists prepared to treat these patients.

When selecting a dentist, it may be advantageous to first speak with the caregivers of others with ASDs in your area. They may be very happy with their dentist and offer that dentist as an immediate referral. Local networks of caregivers and providers who work with adults and children with ASDs may also yield the name of a qualified dentist. Online research may prove helpful as well, but it is often difficult to sort out who is comfortable working with this patient population, and there are many dentists in the community with varying degrees of training and experience in caring for those with ASDs.

When looking for an oral health care provider, most people first look to the general dentist. General dentists may have some training in the care of patients with special needs, but this training may be minimal or suboptimal. If general dentists advertise that they care for patients with special needs, however, often they have had some form of advanced training in treating patients with ASDs and other complex concerns. The general dentist with experience in caring for those with ASDs will help create a "dental home" for his or her patients, and will be able to coordinate care for any needed dental services outside the scope of general practice.

Pediatric dentists treat patients from infancy through the adolescent years and have training in providing care to those with special needs. Some pediatric dentists may continue to care for their existing patients through adulthood if behaviors can be managed in the office without disruption of the office's daily routine and if the complexity of the dental procedures remains within the pediatric dentist's scope of practice.

While the general dentist or pediatric dentist serves as the primary dental care provider, it often becomes necessary to refer a patient to a dental specialist. Such referrals are dictated by the type of treatment deemed necessary by the referring or primary dentist. The more commonly referred-to specialists, with a description of their areas of expertise, are discussed below.

Oral and maxillofacial surgeons treat diseases of the hard and soft tissues of the mouth. They extract severely decayed teeth as well as teeth that may be malpositioned, "crooked," or severely infected. The oral surgeon can also treat deformities of the mouth and facial structures as well as place dental implants. Due to the complexity of the care they provide, oral surgeons often treat patients while they are under sedation or general anesthesia.

Periodontists treat diseases of the periodontium, and may be called upon to provide extensive scaling or "deep cleaning" of the teeth. These specialists may also place dental implants. The periodontist also performs surgery on the gingiva and bone supporting the teeth. One common surgery is a gingivectomy, in which excessively overgrown gum tissue is removed, as may be noted with phenytoin use.

Endodontists specialize in treating the pulp tissue that is inside the tooth. When infected, this small amount of nerve and vascular tissue may cause significant pain. Root canal procedures remove this pulpal tissue, often from teeth with very narrow or severely curved roots. In most cases the patients referred to endodontists have infected teeth that require such treatment to avoid extraction.

Special care dentists are general dentists that have extensive training in providing comprehensive dental treatment to patients of all ages with a variety of special needs. Most of these dentists have privileges in local hospitals, allowing them to treat medically and behaviorally complex patients in a safe manner. In utilizing a hospital for treatment, the more complex patients with ASDs may receive needed dental care while under sedation or general anesthesia provided by a trained anesthesiologist.

Preparing for the initial office visit

The American Academy of Pediatric Dentistry and the American Academy of Pediatrics agree that a child's first dental visit should be scheduled by age 1 year, or by the time the first tooth has begun to erupt. At this early age, the focus is on discussions of oral home care, nutritional issues, and potential future developments that might require specific dental intervention. Early intervention, particularly for children with special health needs, often makes a significant difference in the years to come.

For older patients who have not had prior dental care, it is important to arrange the initial visit as soon as possible. The initial visit would consist of a dental examination, X-rays, and review of all findings by the dentist with the caregiver. The visit would also include a thorough review by the dentist of the patient's medical history, dental history, home-care routine and behavioral issues, as well as a diet analysis. This information impacts the dentist's final plan of treatment for the patient. It is recommended that the following information be available at the first visit to a new dentist:

- The names and telephone numbers of all of the patient's current health care providers, primary as well as specialists. This is necessary since the dentist may need to contact other members of the patient's health care team to gather important information that may impact the final plan for dental treatment.

- Prior medical records from a pediatrician, primary care physician, and/or neurologist. These records can be very helpful for the medical history review.

- List of previous surgeries and records. This information can also impact the final plan of dental treatment.

- List of current medications and a list of any drug, food, or environmental allergies. Over-the-counter medications, vitamins, and herbal supplements should be included.

- Record of past dental encounters, treatments provided in dental offices or in the hospital setting, along with any X-rays taken at the time, either in printed or digital format.

The first dental visit

The first encounter with a new dentist may range anywhere from a comfortable experience to a very frightful one. Patients with ASDs, particularly those with more severe behavioral difficulties or those who are strongly ingrained in their own habits or routines, may benefit from some degree of preparation prior to this first visit.

Before the initial appointment, it would be best to prepare by describing the dental visit to the patient. They should be told where they will be going and what to expect when they get to the office. Showing pictures of the dental office and, if possible, pictures of the actual dentist they will be seeing may help to limit first-visit surprises. The dental office that you are visiting may be able to provide this to you, and may be willing to give both caregiver and patient a quick tour of the office before the appointment date. Other online resources from dental organizations may also be helpful, particularly those showing images of dental equipment, instruments, toothbrushes, and dental home-care devices.

The caregiver should consider behavioral issues when scheduling the initial dental visit. Thorough familiarity with the patient's behaviors and daily routine may increase the chances for a successful appointment. If the patient seems to be calmer in the morning, for example, then that may be the best time to schedule the dental visit. While some patients do well at their dental visit, others may have greater difficulty in acclimating to the new surroundings and cooperating for care. When possible, let the dental office staff know in advance what behaviors to expect and what they can do to help make the visit a more comfortable one. If the patient has a favorite toy, that should be brought to the office. The same is true if there is a favorite video or music selection that has a calming effect. If the patient works with a behavioral therapist, that person may be invited to accompany the patient to dental visits to provide a "friendly face" and another point of familiarity. Some dental offices may allow several desensitization visits before actual care is initiated to increase patient comfort.[19]

If anxiety-reducing routines prove ineffective, oral sedation may be considered. Short-acting, mildly sedating medications are used to slightly reduce the patient's level of consciousness so that there is a minimal reaction to the dental treatment. Often, when patients are sedated, they need to stay in the dental office for some period after treatment so that they can recover from the effects of the medication.[21]

Nitrous oxide analgesia, or "laughing gas," is a form of sedation that has been successfully used in dental practices for over 100 years. A mixture of nitrous oxide and pure oxygen is breathed in through a mask fitted over the nose, calming the patient and allowing the performance of the planned dental treatment. Recovery from nitrous oxide analgesia is almost immediate, so the patient can leave the office after treatment is completed. One caveat is that the patient must allow the nasal mask to be kept in place, and must be able to cooperate to some extent by breathing the gas in through the nose for the entire procedure. The more fearful or combative patient usually does not allow this.[22]

In situations where oral medications or nitrous oxide sedation will not work, it may be necessary to consider the use of intravenous sedation or general anesthesia. These modalities of treatment are generally reserved for use with patients who will not sit in a dental chair or allow treatment, who may be combative, and those who may exhibit severe self-injurious behaviors as a result of the anxiety they experience in the dental office environment.

General anesthesia is administered by an anesthesiologist or another highly trained health care provider in either the dental office, an outpatient surgical center, or in the hospital operating room setting. The significant advantages of providing care under general anesthesia include patient safety and comfort, as well as the ability for the dentist to complete all necessary dental treatment in one session.[23] While a very safe modality of care, the possibility of side effects and treatment complications does exist; for this reason, the use of general anesthesia is considered only after other treatment modalities have been determined to be ineffective or untenable.

Scheduling follow-up care

After treatment has been rendered over the course of one or more visits, the dentist will recommend that the patient return for a recall or checkup visit. These visits most often are scheduled anywhere from 3 to 6 months from the date of the last checkup and/or cleaning. By maintaining appropriate professional vigilance, dental concerns can be addressed early, before multiple problems have time to develop and worsen.

If the patient has required oral premedication or the use of nitrous oxide in the past, this may be utilized at the recall visit as well. Those patients who require general anesthesia for treatment often are brought to the office for a brief examination only and scheduled for treatment under general anesthesia on an as-needed basis. In many instances, patient behavior will improve over time as familiarity with the dental setting and routine increases.

Paying for dental care

Depending on the needed treatment, the cost of dental care may be quite significant. The majority of dental offices accept payment in all forms, including cash, check, or credit card. While many offices require payment in full at the time of treatment, many others are flexible and offer payment plans with several payment options.

Some offices participate in private insurance plans, while others do not accept insurance payments but will help the caregiver in completing forms to obtain some degree of reimbursement for their expenses. In many states, dental treatment is covered to some extent by Medicaid. Such coverage varies widely by state, and not all offices accept Medicaid payments. The caregiver should determine, in advance of the first visit, how payment will proceed. The dental office staff will be very knowledgeable in this area and can be an excellent resource for information and assistance.

TAKEAWAY POINTS

- Dental caries and periodontal disease both have real and significant consequences, including pain, infection, tooth loss, nutritional imbalances, and social concerns.

- Prevention is the key to a good oral health program: regular dental checkups, use of fluoride, appropriate and effective oral home care, and a diet that promotes oral health are all key components.

- Many people with ASDs take medications that can dry out the mouth, which may worsen dental caries and periodontal disease. A decrease in saliva may also make it harder to swallow foods.

- The most important part of a good home-care program is effective toothbrushing done at least twice daily. Mouth rinses, used as a rinse or swabbed on the gums, are effective supplements.

- For patients who have difficulty tolerating dental care, options include medications to reduce anxiety, oral sedatives, intravenous sedation, and treatment in the operating room setting under general anesthesia.

Chapter 7

Genetic Considerations for Individuals with Autism Spectrum Disorders

Beth A. Pletcher, MD

Introduction

Although it is clear that most individuals with an autism spectrum disorder (ASD) do not have a specific genetic condition that underlies their ASD diagnosis, many children and young adults are referred for genetic evaluation or have some type of genetic testing along the way. Knowing a definitive genetic diagnosis may be helpful to patients and their families by providing medical information and educational strategies specific to that particular condition, as well as guidance for future family planning. In this chapter we discuss some of the genetic tests that may be recommended, the meaning of a positive test, what a genetic consultation usually entails, and what questions you may want to ask as part of the genetic encounter. As with any interventions or potential consultations, you will want to discuss the risks and benefits of genetic testing and/or genetic evaluation with your primary care provider and ASD specialists before proceeding.

Genetics 101

Chromosomes are the large structures made up of DNA that contain most of our vital genetic information. The actual genetic elements which we refer to as genes reside on our 46 chromosomes (which come in 23 pairs). There are approximately 23,000 genes that determine aspects of our growth, development, and daily function. At birth we receive one copy of each chromosome pair from our parents. These chromosomes are numbered 1 through 22 (autosomes), with the final pair representing our sex chromosomes, which are named the X and Y chromosomes. Males typically have one X and one Y chromosome, and females have two X chromosomes. It is therefore the contribution of the sex chromosome from the father that determines a child's gender: if the sperm that fertilizes the egg contains an X, the child will be a girl, and if the sperm has a Y, the child will be a boy. Whereas the X chromosome contains many genes, the Y chromosome has a much smaller number of genes that are responsible for male sexual development and growth. This is an important concept when we consider genes that reside only on the X chromosome and how having a Y instead of a second X chromosome (i.e., being a boy rather than a girl) may impact the expression of certain genetic conditions. At conception when the egg and sperm come together to create a new life, each contains 23 individual chromosomes that represent our blueprint that will control how we develop and grow both before and after birth. Variations in our genetic material (either too much or too little) can significantly impact not only how we physically grow but also how our brains grow or how the cells in our brain interact with each other.

Genes inherited from our parents on chromosomes are the instructions that direct our cells how to function. Chromosomes and genes are made up of DNA, which is built from four building blocks called bases. These bases, which we can simply refer to as A, T, C, and G, are the entire genetic alphabet. All of the information contained within our genetic makeup is spelled with just these four bases. It is the order of these bases and their interactions with each other that create the double-helix DNA that is wound into chromosome structures. If we think of a chromosome as a skyscraper, the genes on chromosomes are like the thousands of rooms inside that building. Genetic testing and technologies focus on examining the chromosome structure itself or identifying a genetic "typo" (gene mutation) that may be responsible for a particular problem or condition.

Some genes direct the formation of structural proteins like scaffolding and guide the production of tissue building blocks, such as collagens, that make up cartilage, bones, and skin. Other genes direct the production of proteins called enzymes that are responsible for facilitating key steps in cellular metabolism, which enable our cells to take in and utilize nutrients and break down waste products. Still other genes are responsible for production of cellular energy, regulating cell growth, promoting cellular communication, and so forth. Cells in different organs in our bodies have very different patterns of gene expression, so that the genes that are active or "turned on" at any given time in a kidney cell, for instance, are quite different from the genes that are active in a neuron or brain cell. One can imagine that slight changes in gene expression within certain cells in the body may impact how that organ and person functions. In ASDs we are most often focused on how brain or neuronal function differs from that of typically developing children, and in some cases genetic changes may be responsible for these functional differences.

Within our genetic makeup each of us harbors a number of harmful or dysfunctional genes along with many healthy, normal ones. Some of these non-working genes are hidden or recessive genes that will not cause a problem unless by chance we receive a double dose or two mutated genes, one from each of our parents. Other genes that are not working properly may predispose us to certain conditions such as heart disease, diabetes, hypertension, or even an ASD. In many cases, a genetic predisposition requires other genetic or environmental factors to also be present before a problem develops. In other cases, a number of genetic changes in many different genes coming from both sides of the family may result in a condition in a child that is not present in the parents or other family members. Changes or mutations in individual genes result in conditions which we call single-gene disorders. In genetics we also use the term *syndrome* to define a specific collection of physical and/or developmental features that fits a pattern; therefore, many single-gene disorders that may be seen in children with ASDs are given a specific name followed by the word syndrome (i.e., Rett syndrome, Smith–Lemli–Opitz syndrome, or Fragile X syndrome). Other single-gene disorders will have a designation that does not include the word syndrome (i.e., tuberous sclerosis or CHARGE association). Although most children with an ASD do not have a single-gene disorder, it is important as part of a genetic evaluation to assess whether this is or is not the case. How these types of genetic conditions are passed on in a family is referred to as the mode of inheritance. For our purposes we briefly discuss the four most common modes of inheritance.

Autosomal dominant inheritance

In autosomal dominant inheritance, one needs only to have a single gene that is not working properly for the condition to be present. In this case the same gene on the other chromosome that was passed down from the other parent is perfectly fine. With autosomal dominant inheritance, the parent that passes on the non-working gene is affected with the condition and there is a 50% chance for each child to also inherit the genetic condition. It would be like flipping a coin with each pregnancy and getting heads (the child has the condition) or tails (the child is unaffected). Autosomal dominant inheritance is not the most likely form of inheritance when one examines families with more than one member with an ASD, although if a parent was mildly affected with an ASD, this could certainly be possible. For many autosomal dominant conditions there is great variability in how the condition manifests, so some people in the family may have more serious problems and others may have mild signs of the condition. For some autosomal dominant conditions, an individual may harbor a gene change that was not present in either parent. This is referred to as a de novo (new) mutation and is believed to arise during egg or sperm formation prior to cell division. Once a person has a mutated gene within their genetic makeup, even if it is a new event, they can pass this down to their children. When assessing a family history for autosomal dominant inheritance, you would typically see the condition affecting equal numbers of males and females in multiple generations, with approximately half of children born to an affected parent also being affected.

Autosomal recessive inheritance

In autosomal recessive inheritance, one needs to have both copies of a gene not working properly for the condition to be present. With this type of inheritance, each parent passes down one copy of the non-working gene and the affected child has a "double dose" of the non-working gene (i.e., no working gene on either chromosome). For a couple where both parents silently carry one copy of the non-working gene, there is a 25% chance for each child to manifest the genetic condition. It would be like flipping two coins with each pregnancy and getting double heads (the child has the condition), heads and tails or tails and heads (the child is an unaffected carrier), or double tails (the child is an unaffected non-carrier). Autosomal recessive inheritance is a more likely form of inheritance, especially when more than one child in a sibship (brothers or sisters) are diagnosed with an ASD. In this case, one would not expect to see other affected family members such as aunts, uncles, or cousins. Once a person has a mutated gene within their genetic makeup, as a carrier, or two mutated genes, as an affected person, they can pass this down to their children. When assessing a family history for autosomal recessive inheritance, you would typically see the condition affecting equal numbers of males and females in a single generation, with approximately 25% of children born to carrier parents being affected.

X-linked recessive inheritance

In X-linked recessive inheritance, mostly boys would be affected because the non-working gene is carried on the X chromosome. Because boys only have a single X chromosome, they cannot compensate for a non-working gene on their X chromosome, whereas girls, who have two X chromosomes, have a "back-up" copy of the gene on their second X chromosome that can offset the effects of a single non-working gene on the other X chromosome. Although there are rare situations where a girl may manifest an X-linked recessive condition, this is not usually the case; very rarely girls who carry a single copy of an X-linked gene may have very mild or minor manifestations of a genetic condition. Because there are many genes on the X chromosome that are associated with cognitive function, X-linked recessive inheritance may partially explain the excess of males with profound or severe intellectual disabilities. It does not, however, necessarily explain the preponderance of males with ASDs, since there could be any number of other reasons for this skewed ratio of affected boys. When assessing a family history for X-linked recessive inheritance, you would see the condition affecting only males who are related through unaffected carrier females. Mothers who are carriers have a 50% chance of having an affected son with each pregnancy and about half of their daughters would be expected to be carriers. Because the condition is passed down on the X chromosome, we would never see a father pass an X-linked condition to a son because he only passes a Y chromosome to a son.

Mitochondrial inheritance

In mitochondrial inheritance, genetic information is transmitted to a child through the egg cell alone. This genetic information does not reside inside of a cell's nucleus, but instead is present in many copies in the cellular cytoplasm. The mitochondrial DNA structure is much simpler than nuclear DNA, but mitochondrial DNA is essential to cellular metabolism. When a mother passes on mitochondrial DNA to her children through the egg cell, children may receive all healthy or normal mitochondrial DNAs or may receive a percentage of abnormal DNAs. If a child receives a significant number of abnormal mitochondrial DNAs, he or she is likely to exhibit signs of a mitochondrial condition. Because mitochondria are important to cellular metabolism and help produce fuel to boost cellular energy, symptoms of a mitochondrial condition are more often present in tissues that have a high energy requirement. These body systems include the brain, skeletal muscles, heart, nerves, retina of the eye, and sometimes even the kidney and digestive tract. Typical symptoms of a mitochondrial disorder include seizures (especially myoclonic epilepsy), cognitive delays, myopathy or weak muscles, neuropathy or nerve dysfunction, visual changes due to retinal dysfunction, and/or laboratory finding of lactic acidosis (elevated lactic acid in the bloodstream). Mitochondrial conditions fall into the category of metabolic conditions because they impact cellular function by disrupting an important cellular pathway, and are characterized by accumulation of harmful biochemical by-products. Because only mothers pass on this DNA, we often see multiple children affected in a single generation. Brothers and sisters may exhibit milder or more severe symptoms depending on the percentage of abnormal mitochondrial DNAs inherited at the moment of conception. In some families we can see a mitochondrial condition in multiple generations, especially if the condition is mild enough that it does not impact a mother's ability to reproduce. Since the mitochondria are contained only in the egg cell, fathers cannot transmit a mitochondrial disorder to their sons or daughters. Mitochondrial conditions are not especially common in children with an ASD, but some individuals with a mitochondrial disorder may exhibit behavioral features of an ASD.

For single-gene or mitochondrial disorders that are associated with an ASD, genetic evaluation and counseling may be critical parts of overall health care. For many of these disorders, although autism may be the initial manifestation, there may be other health concerns that need to be addressed over time. If the diagnosis of a specific condition is made, it is helpful for parents and other family members to know the mode of inheritance, if there is carrier testing for at-risk family members, and if prenatal or other testing is feasible for future pregnancies.

Despite the advances in genetic technologies, we are only able to uncover a clear genetic diagnosis in children with ASDs between 6 and 15% of the time.[1-3] Genetic evaluation generally includes a physical examination for signs of a genetic "syndrome" as well as more routine genetic testing (described in the next section). For children with a single-gene disorder, parents can be provided very specific information regarding that particular condition including other potential health issues and long-term outlook (prognosis) based on a certain diagnosis. For other individuals, a less clear diagnosis may be uncovered with a variation in genetic information that is of uncertain significance or that poses perhaps a predisposition to the development of an ASD.

When genetic testing and examination fails to uncover a diagnosis, we often turn to empiric recurrence risks to describe potential occurrence of an ASD in subsequent children or relatives. Unlike single-gene disorders where risks are solely determined by the inheritance or non-inheritance of a gene, the majority of individuals with an ASD either have no family history of another affected relative, or even if there is an affected relative, the pattern does not fit a clear mode of inheritance. Because the brain is a complex organ and many factors influence how our brains grow and develop and how our neurons undergo maturation and communicate with each other, it makes sense that there is not a single causative gene, exposure, or event uncovered for most individuals with an ASD. With empiric risk assessment, we depend upon large numbers of individuals in the general population to help us define the risks for a condition. By looking at hundreds of other couples with a single child with an ASD with no known cause and then looking at their subsequent children, it is estimated that recurrence risks for a full brother or sister to be affected with an ASD if the first affected child is a girl is 7% and if the first affected child is a boy is 4%.[4] This means that there is a 93–96% chance for the next child to be unaffected with an ASD. For the approximately 2–3% of families who have more than one child affected with an ASD, risks for recurrence jump significantly in subsequent pregnancies to between 25 and 35%.[4] The best explanation for these risks for recurrence for an ASD is that the majority of children diagnosed with an ASD have it as a result of a combination of factors including potentially some predisposing gene changes, environmental factors before or after birth, and even a gender influence, with three to four times more boys affected with an ASD than girls. Newer genetic technologies looking at minor gene variations (polymorphisms) that are present in the population at large have enabled us to identify predisposition genes for many common conditions, including ASDs. Unlike a true gene mutation that has a known pathogenic effect and is directly responsible for a condition, these common polymorphisms individually do not seem to cause discrete conditions. Genome wide association studies, however, allow us to look at many unrelated individuals to see what minor gene variations are seen with increased frequency or decreased frequency in the general population for any given condition. For some individuals with an ASD, they may have three, four, or five predisposing gene variants inherited from both sides of the family that together allow for the appearance of an ASD. An unaffected brother may have some of the same predisposing genes but also a protective polymorphism; an unaffected sister may have the same predisposing gene variations, but because she is a girl, she has a slight protective advantage and does not exhibit signs of an ASD. Only with time and more broad-based population testing will we be able to sort out what polymorphisms and what environmental factors seem to come together to explain the occurrence of most ASDs, which appears to be a much more common cause of ASDs than single-gene, mitochondrial, or chromosomal disorders altogether.

Specific genetic tests

The range of genetic tests available today continues to grow, and while some tests have been utilized for decades, the majority of tests are quite new. As with any new test, we need to assess the relative value in performing a genetic test compared with any downside of testing such as uncertain or confusing results, potential risks to the patient, and cost of testing. In this section we describe the most common types of tests that may be offered as part of a genetic evaluation, recognizing that no one would advise performing all of these tests on all patients. Instead, we feel that it is essential to take an individualized approach to testing based on the physical exam findings as well as family and medical histories. In recent times many thoughtful clinicians have tried to develop strategies or algorithms for genetic testing based on solid medical evidence of benefit.

A cytogenetic or chromosome analysis involves the examination of the genetic material within the nucleus of cells. This represents the largest segments of genetic material (chromosomes) that carry our genes. This type of study can identify major alterations or changes in genetic material. Most of the time, cytogenetic analyses are performed on a sample of blood where the white blood cells are analyzed, or prenatally on the amniocytes (fetal cells floating in the fluid surrounding the baby); however, there are certain circumstances when a chromosome study is best done on another tissue such as a skin sample. Some chromosome changes, such as Down syndrome (which is caused by the presence of a whole extra chromosome 21), or even a condition where a substantial bit of genetic material is missing, such as velocardiofacial syndrome (caused by a missing piece of genetic material on chromosome 22), are quite easily seen on routine analysis. For partial deletions or duplications of genetic material, chromosome analysis may or may not detect variations. Chromosomes are divided into two "arms" with the upper arm called the "p arm" and the lower arm called the "q arm." Each chromosome is also divided into sections with specific numbers denoting different regions based on the appearance of the chromosomal architecture, which we see as stripes or bands under the microscope. These landmarks help the doctors and other providers to pinpoint the exact location of a genetic change that is observed under the microscope. Chromosome analysis is one of the older tests, and for many diagnoses, this test is slowly being replaced by more sophisticated chromosomal analyses; however, a routine chromosome analysis is often one of the first tests offered in the evaluation of a child with a developmental disability or ASD, and it may not only uncover large extra or missing bits of genetic material but can sometimes uncover a rearrangement of genetic material called a balanced translocation, which may not be seen with more sophisticated technologies. A balanced translocation occurs when two pieces of genetic material break off their respective chromosomes and exchange places, but no important genetic material is lost in the exchange. Since this rearrangement might not be seen on a more high-tech study known as a chromosomal microarray (CMA), and it is possible that an important gene may have been disrupted during the exchange of material which could potentially cause a genetic condition or developmental problem, a chromosome analysis still has a place for now in the evaluation of some children with an ASD. In addition, since many cells are analyzed during a routine cytogenetic analysis, this test may also uncover a situation where there are chromosomally normal cells as well as some cells with a chromosome variation (called chromosomal mosaicism). Chromosomal mosaicism, if the number of abnormal cells is small, may also be missed on CMA.

If a chromosome analysis is like studying skyscrapers from a street perspective, chromosomal microarray (CMA) would be akin to walking down the corridors of each of these chromosomes/buildings looking for changes in structure. Whereas there are many CMA technologies, each with their advantages and disadvantages, most information that can be gleaned from a CMA is whether there is a significant loss or gain of genetic material on a specific chromosome, compared with a control or the "normal person's" DNA. In some cases we are able to identify a definitive condition or chromosomal syndrome strongly associated with an ASD on a CMA analysis done on a blood sample, and in other cases we may uncover a small genetic change that simply is seen in more children with an ASD than in the general population (what we would call a known predisposing variation), or we may uncover a variant of uncertain significance with a few extra or missing genes not known for sure to be associated with an ASD. Even though this type of testing is relatively new, we have already identified a few variations on CMA that clearly are associated with ASDs or a high likelihood of developing an ASD. These abnormalities which geneticists call "copy number variants" (CNVs) include small extra or missing pieces of genetic material that may not be detected on routine cytogenetic testing. CMA changes clearly known at this time to be associated with ASDs include: a duplication or extra copy of a genetic material in chromosomal region 15q11-q13, a deletion or loss of genetic material in chromosomal region 7q21, and either a deletion or duplication of genetic material in chromosomal region 16p11.2. Other possible associated regions include CNVs on chromosomes 1q21.1, 2q37, 7q11.23, 15q13.3, 17p11, 22q11.2, and 22q13. In the future it is anticipated that many more small chromosomal deletions or duplications will be identified that pose a risk for developing an ASD. In approximately 5% of the CMA studies we perform on children with an ASD, we find instead less clear-cut variants. In such cases we often turn to the parents to provide blood samples to determine if this genetic variation is inherited or something that arose for the first time in the affected child; however, even when we determine that one of the parents has the exact same variation, we may not be able to say with absolute certainty that this is a harmless variation versus a possible genetic change that predisposes to the development of an ASD. It is the uncertainty coming from some of these studies that causes the most problems for physicians and families, who are anxious to better define whether or not the ASD has a genetic underpinning. Over time, as more and more patients undergo CMA analyses, we will establish a much better database and determine with certainty the meaning of these test results.

Chromosome abnormalities may be detected in up to 5% of children and adults with an ASD.[5] The chances of finding an abnormality on routine chromosome analysis (also called a karyotype) are greater if the patient has some subtle changes in physical or facial features (dysmorphisms), has a more significant degree of intellectual disabilities, has one or more birth defects, or has differences in growth such as short stature, failure to thrive, or a small head size (microcephaly). When children with ASDs undergo a CMA, the chances of finding a subtle change in the amount of genetic material (i.e., CNV) increase significantly (somewhere between 10 and 35%).[5] For children with ASDs who have normal chromosome studies and normal CMAs, the chances of uncovering a mutation in a single gene today are less than 5%,[5] but this may be a low number because we can only test for individual genes when we have a very good idea from the history and exam which of the 23,000 genes may be responsible. Over time, as technologies improve and the cost of genetic testing becomes more affordable, we may find that many individuals with ASDs have minor gene mutations in one or more genes that predispose to developing the condition.

Metabolic or biochemical testing is not routinely recommended by most experts for a child with uncomplicated autism. Because the majority of otherwise healthy children with an ASD do not have a metabolic derangement, the cost and difficulty of doing this testing may outweigh the benefits of doing these studies. Metabolic testing frequently involves very specialized studies on blood, urine, or other tissues. In some instances we are measuring a specific compound or metabolite that is in the blood or urine that could point to a defect in cellular metabolism, and in other cases we may be measuring a specific enzyme or protein that may be important in carrying out a step in a cellular metabolic pathway. The testing is quite difficult to do at times, because the blood or urine sample needs to be processed or prepared in a special way or kept frozen, testing can only be performed in specialized laboratories, and testing requires expertise in interpretation. As a result, many "abnormalities" found on complex metabolic testing turn out to be false alarms and may require additional samples to be sent. This can also cause upset and needless worry for providers and parents. That being said, there are a number of circumstances where metabolic or biochemical testing may be warranted. Interestingly, all infants born in the United States undergo metabolic screening shortly after birth through their state's newborn screening program. These tests are designed to identify children born with the most severe or life-threatening metabolic conditions that are amenable to treatment. One of these conditions is called phenylketonuria (PKU), which results from a deficiency in the enzyme phenylalanine hydroxylase. Undiagnosed or untreated infants and children with PKU are at risk for severe intellectual disabilities and may also exhibit signs of autism. Because of newborn screening programs, very few children affected with PKU are missed at birth. Several very rare metabolic conditions may occur in children with an ASD, including (1) a disorder of purine metabolism called adenylosuccinate lyase (ADSL) deficiency, (2) a disorder affecting neuron function called succinic semialdehyde dehydrogenase (SSADH) deficiency, and (3) several disorders of creatine function, especially one called creatine transport 1 (CT1) deficiency.[6] Children with ADSL deficiency typically have seizures, intellectual disabilities, and low muscle tone, in addition to features of autism. Children with SSADH deficiency may have an abnormal pattern of by-products on urine organic acid testing and usually have intellectual disabilities, low muscle tone, an unsteady gait, and seizures as clinical findings. Children with CT1 often have developmental delays early, with later recognition of intellectual disabilities, autistic behaviors, seizures, and low muscle tone. Based on the rarity of these conditions, limited treatment options, and difficulty in testing, it would seem prudent to only perform metabolic studies on children who have other features suggestive of a metabolic condition in addition to the diagnosis of an ASD. Some of the clues that doctors may recognize that might suggest a possible metabolic disorder are:

- failure to gain weight

- recurrent episodes of vomiting not related to reflux

- recurrent episodes of acidosis (extra acids in the bloodstream)

- developmental regression including more than just speech regression

- enlargement of the liver and/or spleen

- cataracts

- seizures

- significant abnormalities in muscle tone (hypertonia, i.e., increased tone; or hypotonia, i.e., decreased tone).

In at least one published paradigm for stepwise diagnostic evaluation for children with an ASD, simpler metabolic screening is offered in the third and final tier of testing—measurement of both serum (blood) and urine uric acid. Additional metabolic tests would then be done only if these screening tests are outside of the normal ranges.[4] The bottom line is that only your providers can determine if and when metabolic testing makes sense for your child. Although metabolic conditions are rarely associated with birth defects, there is one notable exception: a recognized inborn error of metabolism that is seen in children with changes in facial features, poor head growth, multiple birth defects, and ASDs. This condition is called Smith–Lemli–Opitz syndrome and results from an inability to make enough cholesterol before and after birth to support adequate growth and development. Because these individuals have a deficiency in the enzyme that is necessary in the final step to produce cholesterol, they are at risk for many problems. This diagnosis is often made based on recognizing a specific collection of physical features and patterns of birth defects, with confirmation coming from measurement of the compound just preceding cholesterol in the metabolic pathway. It is not, however, detected on newborn screening panels at present and, even though it can be treated with dietary cholesterol supplements, this change in diet is not considered a cure for the condition.

Gene sequencing looking for a "spelling error" or mutation in an individual gene is costly, time-consuming, and often difficult to do. It is best done when there are clinical signs or features of one of the known single-gene disorders that may be associated with ASDs. Metabolic conditions are also single-gene disorders, but the testing is usually not done on the DNA itself but instead examines the metabolic by-products as outlined above, when clinically indicated. There is a growing list of single-gene disorders that may be associated with autism, but for most children, performing tests on many genes at once (or even one gene) is cost prohibitive. For some single-gene disorders that may cause autism, we see other clinical features in addition to the ASD that help us establish the diagnosis of a specific syndrome. Syndromes with known ASD associations include Rett syndrome (girls only), tuberous sclerosis, Cowden syndrome, and Fragile X syndrome, as well as many others. Physical examinations as well as the medical and family histories may be very helpful in guiding your providers, who can decide if testing for one of these may be indicated. For girls with an ASD, providers can usually get gene testing done for mutations in the MECP2 gene responsible for Rett syndrome and atypical autism. For boys with an ASD associated with intellectual disabilities, testing for Fragile X syndrome is readily available through most commercial laboratories. Fragile X testing is routinely offered to these boys and selected girls with milder features of developmental disabilities. Making this diagnosis has a number of medical and reproductive implications. For children with autism and a very large head size (macrocephaly), testing for a PTEN gene mutation is suggested, although at this time this gene test is not usually available through the major commercial laboratories. In some cases, doctors may be able to establish the diagnosis of a specific syndrome without doing gene sequencing or mutation analysis; however, in the past few years there have been increasing numbers of genes that have been identified that are associated with non-syndromic ASDs (autism without any other physical signs or symptoms). Some laboratories have set up autism diagnostic "panels" that include a number of these genes that account for a small proportion of genetic causes of autism. Once again, the expense of doing gene sequencing panels can be a huge barrier to diagnostic testing and may not be paid for by insurers unless there is an identifiable medical benefit emerging from a positive test. That being said, some of the genes that have been shown to confer an increased risk for developing an ASD include *NRXN1*, *SHANK2*, and *SHANK3* on the non-sex chromosomes (autosomes), and *PTCHD1*, *NLGN3*, and *NLGN4X* on the X chromosome.

Whole-exome and whole-genome sequencing are the newest, emerging technologies that take genetic "spell-checking" to a whole new level. In the case of whole-exome sequencing, instead of just looking at a few genes on a panel and checking base by base for a mutation or spelling error, this technology does spell-checking on every known gene in the patient's DNA! Although still quite expensive, it is often less costly than looking at a panel of even four or five individual genes. Since this test is very new, and quite time- and labor-intensive, it is still uncertain how this can be used in the diagnostic evaluation of individuals with an ASD. For now, this test is typically requested for patients with a complex combination of developmental and physical findings that defy clinical diagnosis. Until thousands of individuals (healthy and those with signs of a genetic condition) undergo whole-exome sequencing, we will have difficulty interpreting the massive amount of genetic information coming from such studies. Whether this testing will be routinely covered by health insurance companies, and how to identify the patients who are most likely to benefit from this testing, remains unanswered at this time. Until we have many more data and experience with whole-exome sequencing, and the technology advances to the point that the time required to do the test and the cost of doing it comes down substantially, it is unlikely to be widely applied in clinical testing for any groups of patients. Whole-genome sequencing is even more detailed testing that includes spell-checking of the entire genetic sequence, including even the parts of the DNA in between genes. This will be a potential diagnostic tool once we have established the value and utility of whole-exome sequencing.

The genetic evaluation

Whether to pursue a genetic evaluation is a personal decision and is best made in consultation with your primary care physician or ASD specialists. In many instances, first-line genetic testing may be ordered by a pediatrician, family physician, or other specialist such as a neurologist or developmental pediatrician; however, many children who are diagnosed with an ASD are never offered genetic testing or decline a genetic evaluation when it is offered. Although having a diagnosis of a specific genetic condition may be helpful in terms of medical, educational, or family planning, not everyone is ready for what the genetic testing may uncover. Possible outcomes as well as risks and benefits of testing should be considered before proceeding. Although nobody can control what chromosomes and genes are passed to a child, human nature sometimes influences how a person reacts when that person learns that he or she has passed on a potentially harmful gene. In the case of a predisposition gene, a parent may learn through testing that they were the parent that passed on the ASD susceptibility gene to their child. In the case of an autosomal recessive gene, both parents share equally in the "blame" since each passed on one copy of the gene to the child. In the case of a chromosomal translocation, one parent may carry this genetic variation and a child receives an unbalanced chromosomal complement. In the case of an X-linked condition, such as Fragile X, the mother and not the father passes on the gene to a son. It is important to do whatever we can to take away the personal stigma that "genetic guilt" can create and instead focus on the benefits of getting a precise diagnosis.

So who can benefit the most from genetic testing and perhaps a genetic evaluation? For couples who are considering having more children, genetic testing may more clearly define their reproductive risks for recurrence. If the child with an ASD is found to have a single-gene disorder, then specific risks for an ASD in future children can be defined, and at-risk couples can consider their reproductive options. In addition to prenatal testing after becoming pregnant, newer reproductive technologies can help couples avoid having another affected child prior to conception. If the genetic change occurred for the first time in the affected child, then parents may be reassured that their risks for having another child affected with an ASD are quite small. If genetic testing and genetic evaluation is unremarkable (in other words, no genetic condition is identified), then the risks for recurrence can be estimated using the empiric recurrence risks discussed under the Genetics 101 heading. In light of the varying modes of inheritance, positive genetic test result may provide critical information for other relatives such as brothers, sisters, aunts, and uncles. If a specific genetic diagnosis is made, parents may find themselves in the position of needing to explain the results to other interested parties such as close relatives. In the case of a family who has had the opportunity to seek consultation with a genetic professional, such as a geneticist and/or genetic counselor, the parents may get some guidance on how to relay this information to appropriate family members, which may include information on genetic centers close to their relatives and/or sending relevant reports to these individuals; however, it is the parent and patient who decide whether and how best to share this information with family members. One survey of parents who have one child with an ASD suggests that the majority of parents (80%) would be interested in doing genetic testing on their affected child if the test result would provide ASD risk information for younger brothers or sisters.[7]

The genetic office appointment

Most individuals referred for a genetic evaluation for autism are seen and examined by a geneticist and are interviewed and counseled by both the geneticist and a genetic counselor. During or before the visit, medical records may be reviewed, and a detailed prenatal, birth, medical, and developmental history are recorded. If prior genetic testing has already been performed, these test results are reviewed by the genetic team. A three-generation family history will likely be reviewed and should include both medical and developmental histories of the patient's brothers and sisters, parents, aunts, uncles, cousins, and grandparents.

Following the initial interview, the patient generally undergoes a physical examination looking carefully for any subtle variations in facial and physical features, including a careful examination of the skin, and looking for physical changes or findings, such as liver enlargement or a heart murmur, as well as assessment of muscle tone, strength, coordination, and general neurologic function. The patient is assessed as well for speech output, ability to follow directions, and behavioral features.

Based on the history and exam, the genetic team then makes recommendations regarding appropriate testing, which could include some of the genetic tests described above as well as imaging studies, such as X-ray, computed tomography (CT), or magnetic resonance imaging (MRI), eye exams, or other specialty evaluations. A plan for follow-up should be established prior to concluding the visit depending on whether or not a test is diagnostic. In some cases a family or patient need not return for another visit to the genetic office unless a test comes back with a positive result suggestive of a specific genetic condition or genetic risk.

An algorithm for possible genetic testing for an individual with an ASD

Although a number of thoughtful clinicians have developed a possible plan for genetic testing, each child undergoing evaluation is a unique individual and each family's needs may be different; therefore, it is important to establish what information would be helpful and the reasons for seeking a possible genetic diagnosis at the time of the genetic visit. Below is an amended program of evaluation and testing recommended by the Professional Practice and Guidelines Committee of the American College of Genetics and Genomics for individuals with an ASD.[4]

- Before testing consider:

  ○ confirmation of the ASD diagnosis by a trained professional

  ○ hearing testing with an audiogram to rule out a hearing loss

  ○ electroencephalogram if seizures are suspected

  ○ cognitive or IQ testing

  ○ reviewing the results of the newborn screening test.

- First-line testing:

  ○ Conduct an examination by a trained expert looking for subtle features or physical findings that might be suggestive of a specific genetic condition or syndrome. This might include a careful look at the skin for birthmarks and light spots with a special light.

  ○ If the exam suggests a specific condition, then testing for that condition should be done instead of other more general genetic tests. In some cases a diagnosis can be made on the exam alone and may not require any specific genetic tests. Genetic testing in some instances may include metabolic studies if the exam and history point in that direction.

○ For those individuals without a specific genetic concern, a high-resolution chromosome analysis with reflex to a chromosomal microarray as well as DNA testing for Fragile X should be strongly considered. (More recent studies have suggested that chromosomal microarray should be part of the first-line genetic testing for patients with an ASD, although it had been initially assigned to the second line of testing.[8,9])

- Second-line testing if the first-line testing is unremarkable:

○ Chromosome analysis on a skin sample if the blood karyotype is normal and there are some irregular changes in skin pigmentation that suggest chromosomal mosaicism.

○ DNA testing of the MECP2 (Rett) gene for girls.

○ DNA testing of the PTEN gene if the head size is significantly increased.

- Third-line testing if the first two are unremarkable:

○ Consider MRI of the brain. (We would generally consider doing this in a child with a very large or very small head, seizures, or prominent neurologic symptoms.)

○ Analyze serum and urine uric acid (looking for those rare causes of ASDs).

To put this in perspective, preliminary studies have suggested that in an unselected group of individuals with ASDs, the chances of finding an abnormality on a chromosome analysis are a little more than 2%, on Fragile X testing close to 0.5%, and on chromosomal microarray about 18% (although only 7% had variations that were known to cause cognitive disabilities or likely associated with an ASD).[10] This means that with evaluation and testing at present, we may be able to identify a likely causative genetic factor for about 9.5% of individuals with an ASD.

Preparing for the genetic visit

Prior to a genetic evaluation, it is helpful to collect key medical and other records that may assist the genetic team. Because the genetic team will be taking a detailed history, it is important to know (when possible) details about the pregnancy and birth history, medical history including any major illnesses, hospitalizations and surgeries, developmental history, and family history. You will be asked to provide information about the child's brothers and sisters, parents, aunts, uncles, cousins, and grandparents, including major medical conditions, developmental concerns and diagnoses, behavioral issues and age(s), and cause(s) of death, if applicable. Medical and developmental records may be reviewed by the genetic team. Things that are especially helpful during or before the genetic encounter include:

- reports from any imaging studies such as CT, MRI, X-ray, or sonogram

- results of any genetic tests

- results of any recent routine blood tests

- summaries from any developmental testing, including therapy evaluations, cognitive testing, results of ASD screening tests, and early intervention or child study team reports

- reports from other medical or surgical subspecialists.

It is important for you to be comfortable sharing detailed medical and developmental information with the genetic team in order for them to be able to come up with an individualized diagnostic plan. In cases where a specific genetic condition is identified, it may have implications for future children as well as other family members. The value in making a genetic diagnosis is also dependent upon your current family situation and plans for the future. Possible information that may come from having a genetic diagnosis in a child or adult with an ASD includes:

- identification of additional medical or developmental issues

- for metabolic conditions, specific dietary or medical management recommendations

- fine-tuning of an individual education plan based on what is known about a particular genetic condition

- risk estimation for an ASD diagnosis in future children (in some cases genetic testing for at-risk family members may be offered to determine if they do or do not carry a specific genetic trait)

- whether prenatal genetic testing or even testing prior to conception is feasible for couples who are at increased risk

- prognostic information based on knowledge about outcomes in other children or adults with a specific genetic condition.

Clearly, which pieces of this genetic information are beneficial to someone is quite individual and many people would not, for instance, consider prenatal testing but may make family planning decisions based on their new knowledge about risks. In some cases couples may learn that the genetic change occurred for the first time in their child with an ASD, and therefore risks for future children or other concerned family members are actually quite low. If a specific genetic diagnosis is made and if it has implications for other family members, decisions about how or whether to tell other family members are quite personal, and speaking to the genetic team about your preferences and concerns may be critical for you and your family. The genetic team members would not ever take it upon themselves to reach out to family members without input and consent from the patient and/or guardians. Genetic information, unlike other general medical information, has an even more stringent set of restrictions in regard to privacy and confidentiality as the result of laws such as the Genetic Information Nondiscrimination Act of 2008 (also known as GINA).

Families are encouraged to develop a list of questions for their genetic health care professional that will help guide the genetic evaluation and genetic counseling process. Below are examples of some questions that you may consider asking as part of your genetic encounter:

- If we make a specific genetic diagnosis, how will this help us assess risks for an ASD to occur in future children?

- If we do not make a specific diagnosis, how will this help us assess risks for an ASD to occur in future children?

- Based on your exam and the results of genetic testing, are there any additional services or interventions that you would recommend for our child?

- Is there any value in screening or testing any other family members based on the test results and our family history?

- As new genetic technologies come online, how can we best ensure that we are able to take advantage of this, if we have no specific diagnosis right now?

- Do we need to come back to see you at any specific intervals, or do we just need to contact you again if something new comes up through our other health care providers?

TAKEAWAY POINTS

- Children with ASDs may benefit from a genetic evaluation.

- If you are considering a genetic evaluation for your child, you might wish to discuss the goals and value of this visit with your primary care provider.

- Come prepared to the genetic visit with a list of questions, the best family history information you have, and be ready for a lengthy office visit.

- In some cases the diagnosis of a genetic condition, such as a metabolic disorder, may lead to specific dietary treatment; in other cases having a diagnosis may not drastically alter medical management but instead provide useful information for the child and family for the future.

- As new genetic technologies become available, we may be able to uncover more and more underlying causes for ASDs, but there are in fact many different causes, some of which may not be genetic in nature.

- Current genetic testing along with a careful examination may provide up to a 25% detection rate for a genetic variation or genetic "answer" for selected children and young adults with an ASD.

- Chromosome changes and mutations in specific genes may be associated with a well-described genetic condition (syndrome) or only a predisposition to developing an ASD. Interpretation of genetic test results may require the expertise of a genetic professional.

Chapter 8

Traditional Treatment Options for Individuals with Autism Spectrum Disorders

Caroline Hayes-Rosen, MD

Introduction

Each child with an autism spectrum disorder (ASD) is unique and therefore requires an individualized approach to care. Treatment may consist of a variety of therapies and possibly medications. Therapies are geared toward improving communication and socialization skills, improving behavior and compliance, easing anxiety, and overcoming sensory issues. We explore various forms of therapy in this chapter, including speech therapy, occupational therapy, physical therapy, behavioral therapy, and sensory integration therapy. In addition to the therapies and education, some children with ASDs may require medications. There are no specific medications for autism. Medical management focuses on targeting specific problematic symptoms associated with an ASD, as opposed to targeting the core features of autism: communication impairment, social issues, and repetitive behaviors. In this chapter we discuss medications used for managing comorbid diagnoses or symptoms, such as attention deficit hyperactivity disorder (ADHD), mood disorder, anxiety, irritability, seizure disorders (epilepsy), and sleep disorders, in the child with an ASD. Addressing comorbid symptoms can help to improve mood, comfort, and attention, and may therefore make the child more available for learning and positive interactions.

There is great variability in the presentation of an ASD. Even among the core features of the disorder there are varying degrees of impairment. For instance, some children with an ASD may not speak, while others may progress to the point of having conversational speech. Some children have disabling repetitive behaviors and routines, while others can be fairly flexible and easygoing. In addition to variability among the core features, comorbid symptoms and diagnoses can differ from child to child. There is a group of children with ASDs who seem to have sensory integration issues; some seek out sensory stimulation, while others are distressed by overstimulation. Some children on the autism spectrum have no sensory problems at all. Other symptoms that may or may not be seen in children with ASDs are sleep problems, seizures, motor incoordination, agitation, and anxiety. Children with an ASD can have very uneven skills, excelling in some areas while having deficits in other areas. Because each child with an ASD has their own unique personality and symptom complex, it is essential to have an individualized approach to treatment. The most problematic symptoms should be targeted first.

The mainstay of treatment over the years has been, and continues to be, special education services and therapies. There have been great advances made in educating parents, teachers, and doctors on early identification of signs and symptoms of ASDs. Earlier recognition leads to earlier treatments. This process usually involves statewide programs referred to as early intervention. These programs are geared toward providing a wide variety of therapies to children under the age of 3 years. The sooner the therapies are started, the better the outcome. Once a child reaches 3 years of age, they become eligible for therapeutic services through the public school system.

Studies of interventions have methodological problems that prevent coming up with definitive conclusions about efficacy. Although many psychosocial interventions have some positive evidence, suggesting that some form of treatment is preferable to no treatment, the methodological quality of systematic reviews of these studies has generally been poor, their clinical results are mostly tentative, and there is little evidence for the relative effectiveness of treatment options. Intensive, sustained special education programs and behavior therapy early in life can help children with ASDs acquire self-care, social skills, job skills, and may help to improve functioning, as well as decrease symptom severity and maladaptive behaviors.

Speech therapy

For most children, deficits in communication skills are noted and addressed first. The vast majority of children with an ASD receive speech therapy, as communication difficulties are one of the core features of the disorder. Speech therapy should be instituted at a very young age when speech delays are first noted, and should be tailored to fit the individual child's speech and language needs. Each child should be evaluated by a speech pathologist or a speech therapist. Depending on the child's needs, the focus may be on expressive language, receptive language, pronunciation, or pragmatic language (social language). Difficulties with expressive language (speaking) are much more common than receptive language problems (understanding spoken language) in children on the autism spectrum.

Speech therapy can be started through early intervention, the board of education, or privately through hospitals or centers. Speech therapy is usually given two to five times per week depending on the child. It can be given in an individual or group setting. For some children there is a focus on learning to communicate. This communication may be by any means (e.g., pointing, gesturing, signing, or using a picture board, computer, or other electronic communication device). Communicating with other devices is called augmentative communication. A common method used for children who are not verbal is the Picture Exchange Communication System. Children learn to request things by exchanging the picture for the actual item. Teaching a child to use an augmentative communication device does not mean that we have given up on verbal communication. It will not prevent them from learning to speak. There is some evidence to show that learning to communicate nonverbally may actually stimulate speech. Learning to communicate may also help to alleviate frustration and thereby improve behavior. Children who are able to communicate verbally may benefit from group speech therapy so that they can focus on social speech and communication. In a group setting they are able to learn about the give-and-take of a conversation.

Occupational therapy

Some children with an ASD have deficits in fine motor skills. This can impact self-care skills, play skills, and academic skills. Children may have difficulty with buttons and zippers, using utensils, and brushing their teeth. Playful activities like doing a puzzle or using beads can be very difficult. Once of school age, fine motor deficits can affect a child's ability to use scissors and write or draw. An occupational therapist evaluates the child's fine motor skills and sensory processing. They develop an individualized plan for the child. Like speech therapy, occupational therapy services can be obtained through early intervention, the school system, or privately through insurance. Families should help children practice fine motor skills at home through play with peg boards, beads, clay, drawing, and other creative activities.

Sensory integration therapy

Some children with an ASD have difficulties with sensory processing. Children can be hyper- or hyposensitive to sensory stimulation. Some of these children seek out sensory stimulation by spinning, rocking, mouthing objects, looking out of the corner of their eye, rubbing things, or looking for deep pressure, while others have difficulty with sensory overload and may cover their ears or close their eyes. Children with sensory integration deficits may have difficulty with motor skills, balance, and hand–eye coordination. Sensory integration therapy, first developed by an occupational therapist, has remained a component of the occupational therapy evaluation. Therapy involves exposing the child to certain sensory stimuli through the use of swings, slides, trampolines, skin brushing, and weighted vests. Therapy is thought to increase the child's threshold for sensory input thereby allowing them to function better in stimulating environments. Studies show that sensory processing deficits are more common in children with an ASD. Conclusions about the effectiveness of sensory integration therapy are limited and inconclusive.

Physical therapy

The exact pattern of motor deficits in ASDs has not been clearly described. Some children with an ASD have problems with motor planning (dyspraxia), while others have been described to have postural instability. Some believe that motor deficits are a result of sensory integration issues. Gross motor delays and deficits should be treated with physical therapy. There is no evidence to suggest that treating motor deficits in children with an ASD, however, has any effect on the comorbid or core symptoms of autism.

Behavioral therapy

It is not uncommon for children with an ASD to have behavioral difficulties at some point during their childhood. Behavioral issues can vary widely. Behavioral therapy seeks to help children on the spectrum learn more socially appropriate behaviors.

Many of the well-known therapies for individuals with an ASD use a method known as applied behavioral analysis (ABA). ABA-based techniques have demonstrated effectiveness in several controlled studies; children receiving ABA therapy have been shown to make sustained gains in academic performance, adaptive behavior, and language. ABA-based interventions focus on teaching tasks one-on-one using the principles of stimulus, response, and reward. A skilled behavioral therapist conducts a functional behavioral analysis to target behaviors that need to be addressed. This process identifies the antecedent or trigger and the consequence of a particular behavior. The goal of ABA therapy is to increase desired behaviors and decrease troublesome behaviors. Desired behaviors are then taught using repeated trials with positive rewards being given for the desired behavior. There is wide variation in the professional practice of ABA and among the assessments and interventions used in school-based ABA programs. Moreover, ABA has become a new generic term for behavior modification, but it is important to note that not all behavior therapy is ABA.

Discrete trial teaching (DTT) is one of the most widely used ABA therapies. Many behavioral interventions rely heavily on DTT methods, which use stimulus–response–reward techniques to teach foundational skills such as attention, compliance, and imitation. Sessions are conducted one on one with a therapist and focus on a single task. Critics of DTT feel that it is difficult for the child to transfer learned skills to spontaneous use in a natural environment.

Pivotal response treatment (PRT) is a naturalistic intervention derived from ABA principles. Instead of targeting individual behaviors, it targets pivotal areas of a child's development, such as motivation, responsivity to multiple cues, self-management, and social communication initiation. By improving broad areas of function, it indirectly improves self-control, social behaviors and play skills. PRT is child directed; they determine the activities and objects that will be used in a PRT exchange. Intended attempts at the target behavior are rewarded with a natural reinforcer. For example, if a child attempts a request for a toy, the child receives the toy, not a piece of candy or other unrelated reinforcer.

Behavioral therapies that focus more on relationships

Some experts in the field believe that we should not merely focus on changing behaviors, but should instead strengthen relationships in an effort to overcome the challenges that a child with an ASD faces. There is less scientific evidence about the efficacy of these programs. Two common types of behavioral therapy employing this theory are the developmental, individual differences-based, relationship-based (DIR)/Floortime model and relationship development intervention (RDI).

The DIR/Floortime model approach is a developmental intervention for ASDs. The DIR model is based on a theory of emotional development created by Wieder and Greenspan.[1] They describe six developmental milestones that must be achieved in order to develop a foundation for learning. These developmental stages are as follows:

1. Regulation and interest in the world: being aware of their environment, regulating their response to sensory stimulation, and staying calm.

2. Engagement and relating: showing interest in people and engaging and relating to them in an intimate way; distinguishing inanimate objects from people.

3. Two-way intentional communication: simple back-and-forth interactions between child and caregiver (e.g., smiles, anticipatory play, peek-a-boo).

4. Social problem solving: using gestures, interactions, and so forth to indicate needs and wants in an effort to get a caregiver to help with a problem.

5. Symbolic play: using words, pictures, or symbols to communicate an intention or idea; communicate ideas and thoughts, not just wants and needs.

6. Bridging ideas: the foundation stage of logic, reasoning, emotional thinking, and a sense of reality.

Typically developing children naturally proceed through these milestones. The child on the autism spectrum may require discrete therapies to progress through these stages. The core principle is to understand the child's sensory differences, follow the child's lead, and use these to encourage children with an ASD to "climb up" the developmental ladder. Floortime is the most common therapeutic technique used in the DIR model. In this type of therapy the therapist, teacher, or parent gets down on the floor to meet the child at his or her level. Treatment is very individualized and follows the child's interests and emotions. The idea is to follow the child's lead, but to engage him or her and help them relate to their therapist through meaningful play. The goal is to help the child learn to regulate their behaviors, engage with others, and communicate effectively.

Relationship development intervention is a family-based treatment program for children with an ASD. This program is based on the belief that the development of dynamic intelligence (the ability to think flexibly, take different perspectives, cope with change, and process information simultaneously) is key to improving the quality of life of children with an ASD. RDI targets six main deficits:

1. Emotional referencing: ability to learn from others' experiences.

2. Social coordination: ability to observe and regulate one's behavior to engage in meaningful relationships.

3. Declarative language: ability to use verbal and nonverbal language to interact with people.

4. Flexible thinking: ability to quickly adapt.

5. Relational information processing: ability to obtain meaning from a larger context; solving problems with no right or wrong answer.

6. Foresight and hindsight: ability to reflect on the past and anticipate the future in a helpful way.

RDI usually involves the parents but may be used by teachers and therapists. In the early stages, the child works one on one with a parent on daily activities. The program relies on visual cues, such as eye contact and facial expression, to encourage nonverbal communication during joint tasks. As the child progresses, lessons become more challenging and start to involve academic learning and real-world problem solving.

The SCERTS (social communication, emotional regulation, and transactional support) model is an educational model for working with children with ASDs. It was designed to help families, educators, and therapists work cooperatively together to maximize progress in supporting the child. It borrows ideas from many of the aforementioned approaches. In an effort to promote social communication, this model emphasizes joint attention and symbolic behavior. This model tries to help the child cope with changes and challenges. Transactional support involves the implementation of supports to help families, educators, and therapists respond to children's needs, adapt the environment, and provide tools to enhance learning. This program is semi-structured but flexible. It is not as rigid as ABA but is more regimented than child-driven approaches such as DIR. This model is usually implemented in a school setting. One theory used in this approach is that children learn better from modeling and interacting with other children. Many children receive a combination of different types of behavioral therapy.

Social skills training

Social skills treatment focuses on increasing social and communicative skills of individuals with an ASD, thereby addressing a core deficit. Social skills training should involve joint attention training in which children learn to share experiences. Symbolic play skills are a second important part of social skills. Children are taught how to respond to others and how to initiate interaction. A wide range of interventional approaches is available, including modeling and reinforcement, adult and peer mediation strategies, peer tutoring, social games and stories, self-management, pivotal response therapy, video modeling, direct instruction, visual cuing, Circle of Friends, and social skills groups. A 2007 meta-analysis of 55 studies of school-based social skills intervention found that they were minimally effective for children and adolescents with an ASD, and a 2007 review found that social skills training has minimal empirical support for children with Asperger syndrome or high-functioning autism.[2]

Medications

For some children, despite the best therapies, difficulty continues in one area or another. When symptoms continue to interfere with daily life function, medications may be helpful. There is no cure for autism, but medications can help to improve problematic symptoms and therefore help to improve function. To date, there are no medications effective in treating the core features of an autistic disorder. Some medications are used for comorbid medical diagnoses such as sleep disorders, tic disorders, or epilepsy. Children with an ASD may have behavioral issues such as irritability, self-injurious behaviors, mood swings, obsessive–compulsive tendencies, and ADHD symptoms. It is often more difficult for parents to make decisions about medications geared toward improving behaviors. Parents sometimes fear side effects and do not view behavioral medications as essential. Medication decisions are made more difficult by the fact that many medications are not as well studied in children as they are in adults. Many medications used are not specifically approved by the Food and Drug Administration (FDA) for use in individuals with ASDs or in children in general. Pediatric specialists rely on their own experiences and the experiences of other professionals in the field to decide on the best management for their pediatric patients. Similar to a therapeutic treatment plan, choosing a medication requires an individualized approach. There is no standardized treatment for ASD; therefore, an experienced physician must take into account many factors before choosing a medication. Individuals may respond differently to the same medication. To a certain degree, medication management is done by trial and error. You try something and see how it works. Depending on the outcome, you can manipulate the dosage or the timing, or discontinue the medication if debilitating side effects are noted.

Epilepsy treatment

Epilepsy is defined as recurrent unprovoked seizures. Epilepsy is more common in children with ASDs than in the general population. Approximately 7–40%

of children with an ASD have epilepsy.[3-5] A seizure is caused by excess electrical activity from the brain cells (neurons). There are numerous types of seizures. The most common type of seizure is one in which a person loses consciousness and the whole body shakes. Some seizures involve the whole body, while others involve only part of the body. Some seizures, however, are very subtle and present as "staring off into space" or unresponsiveness. If your child has a seizure, the doctor will probably recommend an electroencephalogram. Once a child has had two unprovoked seizures, medications are usually recommended. Treating children with an ASD and epilepsy is no different than treating any child with epilepsy. There are many medications that can be used to prevent seizures. A medication appropriate for their seizure type should be chosen. Potential side effects and potential secondary benefits may come into consideration when deciding on a medication.

All medications have potential side effects. Some medications require periodic blood tests to monitor for side effects. Levetiracetam is a good choice because it has few side effects and does not interfere or interact with other medications. Blood work does not need to be done. One small study showed that levetiracetam may be useful in reducing hyperactivity, impulsivity, aggression, and emotional lability in children with an ASD.[6] Another small study showed no behavioral improvements.[7] There is a case report of a child with autism who had a regression of her skills with the start of levetiracetam that was fully reversible with cessation of the medication.[8]

Valproic acid, lamotrigine, and topiramate are antiseizure medications that have actually been studied in children for their behavioral effects. In a study on intractable epilepsy, parents of children on the spectrum reported improved behavior with the use of lamotrigine.[9] Lamotrigine is thought to decrease autistic symptoms in patients who have used it for epilepsy; however, one study comparing lamotrigine to a placebo (no active medication) showed no significant difference in behavior among children with autism.[10] Valproic acid has been studied for its effects on the behavior of children with autism. It may help to improve mood and aggression. One study showed a significant effect on irritability.[11] Another small study gives preliminary evidence of its effectiveness for treating repetitive behaviors.[12] The effects of topiramate on weight in patients with ASDs on risperidone was studied. Risperidone is an antipsychotic medication used for treatment of irritability in children with ASDs. Risperidone can cause significant weight gain, while topiramate can cause weight loss. Results for patients on both medications were inconsistent with weight loss in some patients but weight gain in others.[13] Another small retrospective study showed no difference in autistic behaviors in children with ASDs on topiramate.[14] A study of topiramate and risperidone suggested that the combination of these medications may be superior to risperidone alone for its treatment of irritability, hyperactivity, stereotypies, and noncompliance.[15]

Tics: to treat or not

It is estimated that 20–30% of people with ASDs are affected by vocal or motor tics, Tourette syndrome, or involuntary movement disorder. These issues can occur in conjunction with obsessive–compulsive disorder (OCD). Tics are brief, involuntary movements or noises. These movements can be simple, such as eye blinking or face twitching. Some movements can be more complex involving more than one part of the body. Sometimes unprovoked, repetitive, self-injurious behaviors can be tics. Some vocal tics can be throat-clearing noises, sniffing, coughing, or humming. For the most part, tics are benign. They become more pronounced when people are nervous, anxious, tired, sick, or have a fever. Tics should ideally be ignored. Most times the tics do not bother the person who is having them. There are medications that can help to decrease the number of tics. Medications are usually not recommended unless the tics are interfering with daily function or causing social problems.

There are several medications that can be used for tics. Clonidine, an alpha-2-agonist medication, is FDA approved for use in children with tic disorders and Tourette syndrome. It has not been investigated regarding its use in decreasing tics or repetitive behaviors specifically in children with an ASD. It is a good medication to start with because of its relatively benign side-effect profile. For some individuals it can be sedating and is therefore used for sleep disturbances (discussed below). Potential side effects include a dry mouth and constipation. Haloperidol and pimozide are also used for treatment of tics. These medications are considered "typical" antipsychotics. They work on the dopamine system. The typical antipsychotic medications can have significant side effects such as sedation and dyskinesias (abnormal movements). Haloperidol has been studied in children with ASDs, but not regarding its effects on tics. It has been shown to decrease stereotypies, which are different from tics.[16,17]

Stereotypies are behaviors that involve repetition, rigidity, and invariance. They tend to be inappropriate in nature. Common examples of repetitive behaviors would be hand flapping, body rocking, toe walking, spinning objects, echolalia, and running objects across one's peripheral vision. Some stereotypies involve restricted and stereotyped patterns of interest or the demand for sameness. These forms may involve a persistent fixation on parts of objects or an inflexible adherence to specific, nonfunctional routines or rituals. This may be evident during play with a child who is only interested in the wheels on the toy car or a child who insists on lining up blocks in identical rows repetitively. Although haloperidol may decrease stereotypies, there is concern about side effects of dyskinesias. Thirty-four percent of autistic children on haloperidol developed dyskinesias in one long-term treatment study.[18] There are very few reports on the use of pimozide in ASD. It has the same potential side effects as haloperidol. Risperidone and aripiprazole are two "atypical" antipsychotic medications that are discussed in more detail later. The atypical antipsychotics have less potential for side effects such as dyskinesias. Both risperidone and aripiprazole have been shown to be effective in treating stereotypies in children with an ASD.[19,20] Reports on other medications, that is, citalopram, levetiracetam, guanfacine, and atomoxetine, suggest that they are not helpful in reducing stereotypies in individuals with ASDs.

Treatment of sleep disturbances

Research has shown that anywhere between 44 and 83% of children with ASD have sleep disturbances.[21,22] This is higher than what is seen in typically developing children, which is in the 25–50% range.[23] Children with an ASD can have difficulty initiating sleep and/or maintaining sleep. Some children may take a long time to fall asleep; others fall asleep readily but awaken multiple times in the night or very early in the morning and are unable to go back asleep. Similar to typically developing children with sleep disturbances, children on the autism spectrum with sleep disturbances are prone to more severe behavioral symptoms. Treating the sleep disturbance may help to improve problematic daytime behaviors. It is very important for physicians to discuss and address sleep issues. Behavioral strategies and improved sleep hygiene techniques should always be tried prior to medications. One small study showed improvement in the time to fall asleep, bedtime resistance, and anxiety with initiation of parental education and behavioral interventions; however, in this study there was no decrease in nighttime awakenings or early-morning awakenings.[24]

The most evidence exists regarding the use of melatonin for sleeping issues. Melatonin is a natural compound found in our bodies. Melatonin is categorized by the FDA as a dietary supplement, not a drug. Circulating levels of melatonin vary in a daily cycle, thereby allowing the body to follow circadian rhythms (day/night, wake/sleep cycles). Some individuals with ASDs may have lower-than-normal levels of melatonin.[25] Many studies have looked at the use of melatonin for sleep issues in the autistic population. Multiple small studies have demonstrated that 2–10 mg of melatonin may benefit children with an ASD who have trouble falling asleep and/or maintaining sleep.[26–29] Various studies have shown improvement in sleep latency (time to fall asleep) and total sleep time. The effects on nighttime awakening have been variable, showing improvement in some studies and no change in others.[30] One study on melatonin also looked at daytime behaviors and reported improvement.[28] Melatonin was found to be safe and well tolerated.

Clonidine is currently approved for use in treating ADHD and tic disorders. Because of its sedating side effects, it has been studied for the treatment of sleep disorders as well. One small study has shown that clonidine can be helpful for sleep initiation and maintenance in children with an ASD.[31]

Treatment of general irritability

Many children on the autistic spectrum can be aggressive, self-abusive, and easily agitated. Antipsychotic medications are the most efficacious drugs for the treatment of irritability in autism. Risperidone and aripiprazole, perhaps the two best-studied antipsychotic medications, are the only medications specifically approved for children with autism. They are FDA approved for treatment of irritability in children with ASDs, which are not thought to be secondary to psychosis. Antipsychotics (a term which can have a negative connotation) prevent the brain chemical dopamine from attaching to certain receptors in the brain.

The older or "typical" antipsychotic medications (e.g., haloperidol and pimozide) have more significant side-effect profiles and have not been as well studied as the newer or "atypical" antipsychotic medications. Abnormal movements called extrapyramidal side effects were a serious concern with the typical antipsychotics but are rarely a possibility with the newer atypical antipsychotic medications. In addition to their effects on the dopamine system, atypical antipsychotic medications have some effects on serotonin receptors in the brain much like those of antidepressant medications.

Risperidone has been well studied in children with ASDs. It was approved by the FDA in 2007 for use in children with ASDs. There have been two large studies showing the efficacy of this medication in treating irritability in children with ASDs.[19,32] A few of these studies have shown improvement in hyperactive symptoms as well.[33,34] Potential side effects of risperidone are weight gain, sedation, and elevated levels of a hormone called prolactin. Weight must be monitored carefully as weight gain can become a serious medical issue if excessive, since it has the potential to lead to diabetes. Elevated prolactin levels can lead to an increase in breast tissue.

Aripiprazole has been shown to be efficacious in the treatment of irritability in children and adolescents with autism in two large studies and has also been approved for use in this population by the FDA.[20,35] Improvement in hyperactivity was also noted in these studies. Side effects, such as sedation and weight gain, are similar to those of risperidone.

Other related medications, such as olazepine, ziprasidone, and quetiapine, have a similar mechanism of action but have not yet been widely studied or approved for use in children with ASDs. Nevertheless, they are being used by experienced professionals with reports of improvement in children with ASDs. Adverse effects of increased appetite, weight gain, and sedation are common with these medications too.

Haloperidol, a typical antipsychotic, has been studied in children with autism and is efficacious. It has been shown to be helpful for irritability, emotional lability, anger, uncooperativeness, and in reducing stereotypies. Adverse effects of sedation and dyskinesias have limited its use since the development of the atypical antispsychotics.

Although no studies have been done involving the use of the alpha-2-agonists, such as clonidine and guanfacine, for irritability in children with ASDs, they can be used to control aggression, explosive outbursts, and self-injurious behaviors in addition to their usefulness for hyperactivity, impulsiveness, tics, and sleep issues.

Treatment of ADHD symptoms

Attention deficit hyperactivity disorder is caused by a chemical imbalance in the dopamine system of the brain. People with ADHD have symptoms of inattention and easy distractibility that can impede learning. They may be hyperactive and impulsive. Hyperactive and impulsive behaviors can cause problems ranging from physical safety issues to inappropriate behaviors. There are several types of medications that can address these symptoms. Many children with an ASD have difficulty staying on task. It is unclear whether the child with autism truly has difficulty paying attention or whether their apparent inattentiveness is secondary to perseveration or persistent focus on something else. Children on the autistism spectrum can be hyperactive and impulsive.

First-line treatment for ADHD is with a stimulant medication. There are two main types of stimulant medications: the methylphenidate derivatives and the amphetamine derivatives. Medications with a form of methylphenidate as the active ingredient include Ritalin, Focalin, Methylin, Metadate, Daytrana, and Concerta. These medications increase dopamine in the brain. Medications in which the active ingredient is a form of amphetamine serve to increase both dopamine and norepinephrine. These medications include Adderall, Dexedrine, Vyvanse, and Procentra. Eighty percent of children with ADHD respond favorably to the first stimulant medication they try. This is not the case for children with an ASD and ADHD symptoms. There have been three well-designed studies looking at the effects of methylphenidate on children with ASDs.[36-38] There are currently no studies looking at the amphetamine medications in this population. While evidence shows that these medications are helpful for treating inattention, hyperactivity, and impulsivity, the response does not seem to be as strong as in those with ADHD alone. Children with an ASD also seem to have more side effects from the medications. The most common side effect with the stimulant medications is a decrease in appetite. For children with an ASD there can be complaints of irritability, agitation, and emotionality.[39]

Atomoxetine is a nonstimulant medication that increases norepinephrine in the brain. In children with ADHD it has been shown to be as effective as the stimulant medications. At present there is only one small study looking at its use in children on the autism spectrum. This study showed atomoxetine to be helpful in treating ADHD symptoms while causing infrequent side effects.[40] Although only limited evidence from a couple of small studies is available, in my experience a group of medications called the alpha-agonists seem to be helpful for ADHD symptoms, as well as sleep issues, tics, and possibly mild anxiety.

Clonidine can be used in a pill form or a skin patch. There is a long-acting pill form of clonidine called Kapvay (Concordia Pharmaceuticals, Bridgetown, Barbados). Clonidine has been shown to be effective for treatment of hyperactivity and irritability in a study conducted in children with ASDs.[41] Guanfacine is available in a long-acting pill form called Intuniv (Shire, Wayne, PA). Most evidence for the use of the alpha-agonists in children with ASDs comes from numerous case reports in which children showed improvement. In addition to being helpful for several different symptoms, there are no serious side effects. These medications are usually well tolerated. Potential side effects are constipation, dry mouth, sedation, and irritability. For some children the use of these medications in the daytime for ADHD symptoms is limited by sedation. Some studies support the use of the aforementioned antipsychotic medications, risperidone and aripiprazole, in the treatment of ADHD symptoms in the child with an ASD.

Treatment for anxiety and/or obsessive–compulsive tendencies

Children with ASDs are prone to anxiety. Because of their rigid character, changes and transitions can easily lead to anxiety and upset. Anxiety may manifest as nervousness, hyperactivity, whining, screaming, tantrums, and aggression. In addition to anxiety, many children with an ASD may have obsessive or repetitive behaviors. They may want things a certain way. They may have specific routines and rituals to which they feel they need to adhere. When these routines or rituals are disrupted, this leads to anxiety and inappropriate behaviors. At times it is unclear whether the repetitive and ritualistic behaviors seen in children on the autistic spectrum are more closely related to tics or obsessive–compulsive tendencies.

A group of medications called selective serotonin reuptake inhibitors (SSRIs) are used for anxiety, OCD, and depression. They are currently the most widely used antidepressant medications. These medications increase available serotonin in the brain. The following medications are part of the group of SSRIs: fluoxetine, sertraline, citalopram, fluvoxamine, paroxetine, and escitalopram. The SSRIs have been studied in children with ASDs, but evidence for their effectiveness seems to be insufficient. Most studies have focused on their effects on repetitive behaviors. A large, well-designed study involving 149 children with autism on citalopram showed no effect of the medication on repetitive behaviors and restricted interests in children with autism.[42] There are two small studies on the use of fluoxetine: one involving children with ASDs and the other looking at its effects on adults with ASDs. For children with ASDs there seemed to be no clinically significant improvement in repetitive behaviors.[43] A study conducted in adults with an ASD, however, showed significant improvement.[44] Fluvoxamine was found to be effective in decreasing repetitive thoughts and behaviors in a study of adults with autism.[45] A recent study in children, however, showed it to be minimally effective and poorly tolerated.[46]

Although data from well-controlled studies suggest that the SSRIs are not effective in the treatment of children with autism, there are uncontrolled studies and case reports that do support their use. These medications can be useful for anxious behaviors in some children with an ASD. More investigation of these medications is necessary. The SSRIs are indeed less efficacious and more poorly tolerated in children with ASDs as compared with adults. These medications may trigger manic or agitated states in some children with ASDs. Other adverse effects include decreased sleep, diarrhea, and dry or itchy skin.

Tricyclic antidepressant medications are an older type of antidepressants. These medications increase norepinephrine levels. They can be sedating. They do not address anxiety the way the SSRIs do. They have been shown to be helpful for children with ADHD but have not really been used broadly because of their side-effect profile. Of this class of medication, clomipramine has been shown to be efficacious in the treatment of repetitive behaviors and stereotypies in children with an ASD in one study.[47] It may also be helpful with aggression and hyperactivity. Additional studies looking at clomipramine have had mixed results regarding effect. Many patients, particularly children and adolescents, have significant side effects precluding its use.

New investigations

Memantine is an N-methyl-D-aspartate (NMDA) receptor antagonist that is FDA approved for treatment of dementia in Alzheimer disease. There are no robust studies providing controlled data to date, but there are several reports of its use being helpful for OCD symptoms and social interaction. Reports of side effects have been variable. Further research is needed.

Other medications used in treatment for schizophrenia and Alzheimer disease are undergoing preliminary investigations in the population of individuals with ASDs. These medications include acetylcholinesterase inhibitors, such as donepezil and tacrine, as well as amantadine, an NMDA glutamate receptor antagonist. Oxytocin, a neuropeptide involved in social and emotional development, is also being studied.

Conclusion

In conclusion, there are many reports of various classes of medications being helpful for some of the symptoms of ASDs. There is a lack of controlled data available, however, in children with an ASD. More research needs to be done looking specifically at this population of children. Although there is not a wealth of evidence supporting medications other than risperidone and aripiprazole, many of these medications can be helpful for an individual child. Response to any given medication varies from child to child. Sometimes a trial of a particular medication is necessary to determine if it may be helpful in your child. Most medications do not have serious, life-threatening side effects, and any adverse effect can usually be reversed upon stopping a medication. It is important to speak with your physician about the possible benefits and potential side effects before initiating a medication.

TAKEAWAY POINTS

- All children with autism are unique and therefore deserve an individualized approach to treatment.

- The mainstay of treatment for children with ASDs has been therapies and special education.

- Many types of medications have been used to target various symptoms in children with autism.

- There are two medications which are currently approved for use in treating irritability in ASDs: risperidone and aripiprazole.

- Many medications are used off label in pediatric patients as medication research studies are conducted more often in the adult population.

Complementary and Alternative Therapies for Individuals with Autism Spectrum Disorders

Jeffrey Kornitzer, MD

Introduction

While conventional medicine has offered treatments for some symptoms of autism spectrum disorders (ASDs), there are still symptoms and systemic disorders seen in individuals with an ASD that require a multi-modal approach. Parents, physicians, and researchers have been increasingly looking toward complementary and alternative medicine (CAM) and off-label uses of medications hoping to find a novel treatment approach for ASDs. Indeed, CAM offers a plethora of treatment options. As its name implies, CAM is an umbrella term that includes all those modalities that offer alternatives and complementary therapies to conventional medicine. While the benefits of a number of these therapies have not been clearly and reliably demonstrated, many have demonstrated, through scientific research, clear benefits in some children with ASDs. This chapter presents some of the numerous CAM therapies for ASDs, what current research shows regarding risks and benefits of these treatments and therapies, and how parents, if they so desire, can choose an appropriate CAM therapy and provider for their child under the guidance of their physicians.

Specific therapies

Dietary therapies

Dietary therapies are not unique to ASDs. The cornerstone of treatment for a number of diseases, including celiac disease and diabetes mellitus, is dietary modification. Although an ASD is not specifically a gastrointestinal disease, children with ASDs suffer from high rates of gastrointestinal reflux, chronic constipation, lactose intolerance, diarrhea, and abdominal pain (see Chapter 4).[1-7] A growing body of research showing intrinsic abnormalities in intestinal anatomy[8] and the intestinal bacterial "profile" has supported the link between ASDs and gastrointestinal disturbances.[9-16] Since children with ASDs have increased rates of gastrointestinal ailments, much attention has been given to diet as a modifiable variable for children with ASDs. In fact, therapies that involve dietary modifications are the most common form of CAM used by families in the treatment of ASDs.[17] Among the most popular dietary therapies for children with ASDs are organic diets, gluten-free/casein-free diets, and ketogenic diets.

ORGANIC DIET

Having been marketed as being healthier, more natural, and more nutritious, organic food has experienced a tremendous upswing in popularity. In the United States, any food labeled as "organic" must fit strict criteria set by the National Organic Program. Organic crops are those grown without artificial pesticides, herbicides, or fertilizers on land that has been free of these chemicals for at least 3 years. Additionally, any crops grown with artificial pesticides, herbicides, or fertilizers must be sufficiently far away from the organic crops such that there will be no cross-contamination. In order for livestock to be organic, it must never have received antibiotics or growth hormones. Besides these strict regulations, there are a host of other details that allow a food to be legally labeled as organic. Whether these foods devoid of pesticides are in fact healthier has been the subject of much debate.

A comprehensive analysis of organic foods by the American Academy of Pediatrics observed that, although no nutritional difference between organic and non-organic food was found, organic food was noted to reduce human exposure to chemical pesticides.[18] Similarly, a small study found that eating a fresh organic diet reduced levels of bisphenol A and bis(2-ethylhexyl)phthalate, two toxins found in plastics and food packaging.[19] These reductions may be especially relevant in children with ASDs. Given that children with ASDs have abnormal detoxification pathways,[20-23] they may be more susceptible to environmental toxins (see Chapter 10). A study in California showed that maternal residence near agricultural pesticides increased the rate of autism in their children.[24] As such, reducing pesticide and other toxic exposure should theoretically improve the child's health; however, there is not yet convincing clinical research demonstrating this.

Organic food tends to be more expensive than non-organic food. If a family decides to follow an organic diet, it is important to read the labels carefully to ensure that, for the higher cost, they are actually receiving food that is certified as organic. Foods labeled as "natural" may or may not be actually organic. Overall, an organic diet is a very low-risk treatment that can be tried, though there is no prospective evidence showing utility in managing ASDs.

GLUTEN-FREE/CASEIN-FREE DIET

Food allergies and sensitivities among children with ASDs have been heavily researched as possible contributors to the spectrum of gastrointestinal ailments seen with ASDs. A subset of children with ASD has antibodies (a targeted immune response) to gliadin and casein.[25–28] Gliadin is one of the two components of gluten, a protein found in most grains (e.g., wheat, barley, spelt, and rye). Casein is a protein found in all mammalian milk. As a result of the increased rates of gliadin/gluten and casein sensitivity in some children with ASDs, many parents have sought to eliminate sources of gluten and casein from their children's diets. As a result, a diet that is devoid of both gluten- and casein-containing foods, known as the gluten-free/casein-free (GFCF) diet, has become one of the most attempted interventions for children with ASDs.[29]

Numerous interventional studies have examined the effect of the GFCF diet on children with ASDs. The GFCF diet was noted by parents to improve both gastrointestinal symptoms, such as nausea and abdominal pain, and behavioral symptoms, such as communication and adaptation to change.[30] Another study showed that those with more severe pre-treatment gastrointestinal symptoms had more impressive post-treatment behavioral improvement.[31] Two randomized, controlled studies found that children with ASDs treated with a GFCF diet showed significant improvements in communication, linguistic ability, and abnormal behaviors;[32,33] however, due to a reported lack of large-scale, randomized studies, a meta-analysis (a large-scale analysis of all previously performed research on a topic) did not find sufficient evidence to uniformly recommend the GFCF diet for all children with ASDs.[34] Nevertheless, a subset of children with ASDs, especially those with gastrointestinal problems, may benefit from being on a GFCF diet.

Some families may want to attempt a GFCF diet. Currently, GFCF alternatives for nearly every food exist, from cookies and ice cream to pizza and even bagels. Like organic foods, however, GFCF foods can be quite expensive. In addition, children with ASDs tend to have an uncanny ability to taste a fraud; if pizza is one of the few foods a child eats and he or she is given a GFCF pizza, there is a good chance that the "new pizza" may go uneaten. Of course, the GFCF diet can be attempted for a relatively short time (usually at least 6 months in order to see full results[31]) and then abandoned if it proves too difficult to sustain.

KETOGENIC DIETS

A far more restrictive diet that has been investigated is the ketogenic diet. This diet has been used for decades to treat epilepsy and has now been suggested as a CAM treatment for ASDs. With the ketogenic diet, children take in the vast majority of their calories in the form of fat, with 80% of calories from fat being the ideal. Typically, children need to consume a ratio of 4 grams of fat to every 1 gram of carbohydrates and proteins combined.[35] Although the exact mechanism for the effect is unknown, we know that a high-fat and low-carbohydrate diet shifts the body's energy metabolism from a sugar-based (glycolytic) to a fat-based (ketotic) system. With ketosis, fatty acids are broken down into ketone bodies, which may then interact with various neurons and channels within the brain. In children with epilepsy, these interactions may decrease the likelihood of seizures.

The mechanism of action of the ketogenic diet in a child with an ASD may or may not be similar. Interestingly, even without being on a ketogenic diet, children with ASD naturally produce elevated levels of ketones after receiving glucose.[36] Hypothesizing that these high levels of ketones reflect an abnormality in mitochondrial function, it has been suggested that a ketogenic diet could bypass this defect by providing ketones as a fuel to the body in a more direct way: among 30 children with ASDs placed on a ketogenic diet for 6 months, over half had variable improvements in autistic behavior.[36]

Despite these findings, at this point the ketogenic diet is only investigational for children with ASD. The diet is often initiated in hospital settings and requires high levels of medical supervision. As such, it is not a diet that can be initiated by a family without close participation by a physician; however, research has begun to focus on several other "milder" low-carbohydrate diets, such as the Atkins diet, as alternatives to the ketogenic diet. Although these diets have not been investigated formally in ASDs, they have been researched in children with epilepsy and have shown great promise.[37–40] In these diets, the emphasis is still on switching from a sugar-based to a fat-based energy production system; however, the rules are less rigid and the diet can be initiated at home. The potential risks of a high-fat diet, such as cardiovascular disease, may be less with a more flexible diet. Nonetheless, even a low-carbohydrate diet may be too restrictive for a child with an ASD and may not be a practical option.

Nutritional supplements

The use of nutritional supplements is popular in CAM. Because supplements are available without prescription and are generally regarded as safer than medications, many people prefer to use nutritional supplements to treat an ailment even when conventional medicine offers proven therapeutic options. All the more so, when there are few proven therapeutic options (such as in ASDs), nutritional supplements are frequently used in an attempt to manage symptoms.

In ASD specifically, supplementation with vitamins and minerals has been aggressively investigated by researchers. Supplementation may be especially relevant in this population, as children with ASDs have been found to be deficient in a number of nutrients.[41] Because vitamins and minerals are necessary for the proper formation of neurotransmitters (the chemical signals that allow the brain to properly function), correcting a deficiency could improve neurologic function.

Vitamin B6

Vitamin B6, also known as pyridoxine, is essential in neurotransmitter formation. It has been studied as a possible treatment for a number of neurologic and psychiatric disorders ranging from epilepsy to schizophrenia to ASDs.[42] In much of the research, large doses (i.e., megadoses) of vitamin B6 are given.[43] At such high doses, several side effects, such as irritability and inability to control urination, can occur. For this reason, magnesium is often given alongside the vitamin B6 since it has been shown to alleviate these adverse effects. A number of studies found that supplementation with vitamin B6 and magnesium was beneficial to children with ASDs.[44–46] One study of children given vitamin B6 and magnesium showed a significant improvement in both IQ and social skills;[47] however, due to lack of sufficient large-scale, randomized studies, a meta-analysis that explored the use of vitamin B6 and magnesium for ASDs found insufficient evidence to support its routine use.[48] While vitamin B6 together with magnesium cannot be uniformly recommended at this time, it does appear to offer benefits in some children with ASDs. Caution should be exercised, though, as high doses of vitamin B6 have been known to cause reversible nerve damage, leading to symptoms such as numbness and muscle weakness.[49]

VITAMIN B12

Vitamin B12, also known as cobalamin, is likewise essential in the production of DNA and neurotransmitters. Children with ASDs have been shown to have abnormalities in these metabolic pathways, and supplementation with injectable vitamin B12 has been shown to, at least partially, "correct" these pathways;[50,51] however, little research has been done investigating whether supplementation with vitamin B12 leads to clinical improvement. In one small study, the majority of children with ASDs treated with vitamin B12 by injection had no clinical improvements despite improved vitamin levels.[51] While supplementation with vitamin B12 is relatively benign and may improve metabolic pathways, there is little evidence that it offers symptomatic relief. A practical obstacle is that vitamin B12 is most commonly injected intramuscularly,[52] though recent evidence has clearly demonstrated that oral vitamin B12 is at least as effective as intramuscular vitamin B12 in increasing blood levels of the vitamin.[53,54] A transdermal patch has been developed that may be similarly effective at delivering vitamin B12.[55]

VITAMIN C

Vitamin C, also known as ascorbic acid, is necessary for the formation of the neurotransmitter norepinephrine. Its antioxidant properties have also been well documented.[56] Some children with ASDs have low levels of vitamin C,[57] which suggests a possible role for vitamin C supplementation. One trial of 18 children with ASDs found a significant improvement in autistic behavior among those supplemented with high doses of vitamin C.[58] No side effects were noted, and vitamin C supplementation is generally benign. Supplementation with vitamin C may be a treatment to consider, as it may lead to improvement in some children with ASDs.

FOLIC ACID

Folic acid, also known as folate, is a form of vitamin B9. It is essential in a vast array of biologic processes, including DNA production. For decades, prenatal use of folic acid has been known to prevent the neural tube defect known as spina bifida. Folic acid supplementation during pregnancy also reduces the rate of childhood ASDs by around 60%.[59] In light of this, folic acid is not only recommended for prevention of spina bifida but also for prevention of ASDs. Research has already noted that children with ASDs have defective folic acid metabolism pathways.[60,61] In some children with ASDs, high levels of folic acid may be required for proper functioning of certain metabolic pathways. Giving children with ASDs a combination of vitamin B12 and folinic acid (a derivative of folate) may improve oxidation pathways.[50,61] Supplementation with folic acid derivatives can correct abnormally low levels of folate in the cerebrospinal fluid (CSF).[62] In a small subset of children with ASDs, cerebral folate deficiency may be due to the presence of antifolate transporter antibodies.[63] In these children, supplementation with the active form of folate, folinic acid, is required. At this time, though, there is no evidence to suggest that giving folic acid outside of the prenatal window alters the clinical course of ASDs. Nonetheless, folic acid is a well-tolerated and generally benign vitamin that could be given on a trial basis with little risk of adverse effects.

TETRAHYDROBIOPTERIN

Tetrahydrobiopterin, abbreviated as BH4, is a biochemical cofactor that binds to proteins to permit neurotransmitter formation. Due to this central role, tetrahydrobiopterin is crucial to proper brain function.[64] Interestingly, the CSF of some children with ASDs has lower levels of tetrahydrobiopterin than the CSF of children without ASDs.[65] Supplementing children with low tetrahydrobiopterin levels can improve social interactions and communication/language abilities with few side effects.[66,67] While these findings are certainly encouraging, the only reliable way to measure levels of tetrahydrobiopterin is in the CSF obtained through a spinal tap, which requires sedation in most children with ASDs. Nonetheless, tetrahydrobiopterin supplementation remains a reasonable therapeutic option even without a documented CSF BH4 level.

CARNITINE

Mitochondria, the "energy factories" of the body's cells, play a crucial role in the function of all cells, including the neurons in the brain. Up to 5% of children with ASDs may have mitochondrial dysfunction,[68] leading to abnormal biochemical profiles.[69] Such dysfunction could lead to a host of the clinical abnormalities associated with ASDs. Since the active form of carnitine (L-carnitine) plays a pivotal role in the production of energy from fatty acids in the mitochondria, its potential role in mitochondrial dysfunction has been investigated. Children with ASDs have significantly lower levels of carnitine as compared with children without ASDs.[70] Supplementing children with ASDs with carnitine over the course of several months may improve autistic behavior in some children.[71,72] Carnitine supplementation has few side effects and may provide symptomatic improvement in a subset of children with ASDs.

CARNOSINE

Carnosine is an amino acid complex that has both antioxidant and neuroprotective properties. As with many other antioxidants, carnosine levels are markedly reduced in children with ASDs.[15] In one double-blind, placebo-controlled study, children supplemented with L-carnosine (the active form of carnosine) for 8 weeks showed significant improvements in autistic behaviors, socialization, and communication.[73] The authors suggested as a possible mechanism the neuroprotective role of carnosine, especially in the frontal lobe. The frontal lobe of the brain is especially hard hit in ASDs and, given the low levels of carnosine in children with ASDs, supplementation with carnosine may allow for improved frontal lobe functioning. Carnosine is generally well tolerated and supplementation may provide improvement in a number of domains in some children with ASDs.

MULTIVITAMINS

Multivitamins, which allow for a broad-based supplementation of numerous vitamins and minerals with a single medication, have been investigated as a possible intervention for children with ASDs. Since children with ASDs tend to be picky eaters, some researchers have suggested that they may have myriad vitamin deficiencies.[74] In addition, due to the high prevalence of gastrointestinal symptoms in this population, absorption of the vitamins might also be impaired, further exacerbating the deficiencies. The idea of using a multivitamin is also founded upon the positive results of research which describe the therapeutic benefit of supplementing with individual vitamins, such as B6 with magnesium, B12, and C. In one double-blind, placebo-controlled study of 141 children with ASDs, those who received multivitamins for 3 months had significant improvement in parent-reported autistic behaviors.[75] In addition, biomarkers for numerous metabolic pathways that had previously been noted to be abnormal were significantly improved. As a result, the authors hypothesized that continued progress in areas such as language could be expected as biochemical pathways assumed normal function.

Multivitamins appear to provide a win-win treatment option. Pediatricians uniformly recommend the use of multivitamins for all children, and there is evidence that multivitamins may improve abnormal biochemical pathways and reduce autistic behavior. Families should note, though, that multivitamin doses often do not contain the megadoses of vitamins that may be needed to correct specific deficiencies. If a family is supplementing a specific vitamin or nutrient, the dosing should be carefully discussed with a physician and/or nutritionist.

MELATONIN

Melatonin is a hormone produced in the brain's pineal gland that regulates circadian (wake/sleep) cycles. Melatonin allows for the natural biochemical variations that establish the body's sleep cycle. In children with ASDs, sleep is often an issue. It has been hypothesized that melatonin abnormalities play a role in this sleep disturbance. Research in the past decade has shed light on this correlation. Melatonin is formed through a complex series of biochemical reactions. One of the enzymes necessary for the reaction is encoded by the gene *ASMT*. Interestingly, children with ASD were found to have a higher incidence of errors in this *ASMT* gene and, as a result, to have lower levels of melatonin.[76]

Melatonin can be given as an oral supplement at bedtime. Melatonin supplementation has been shown to significantly shorten the time it takes to fall asleep and to lengthen total sleep time in children with ASDs.[77-79] There is even evidence that, along with improving sleep quality, melatonin can improve stereotyped behaviors and hyperactivity during the day.[80] Melatonin has few side effects and is generally well tolerated. For children with ASDs who have problems with sleep, melatonin is a reasonable therapeutic option.[81]

OMEGA-3 FATTY ACIDS

Omega-3 fatty acids are essential fatty acids necessary for normal metabolism, including in the nervous system. In the context of nutrients, the term "essential" refers to the fact that they cannot be made by the body and must be ingested. Omega-3 fatty acids are actually a complex of two components: eicosapentaenoic acid and docosahexaenoic acid (DHA).[82] DHA plays a pivotal role in the proper development of the brain,[83,84] and low levels of DHA have been associated with cognitive behavioral impairments.[85] In fact, children with ASDs have significantly lower levels of DHA than children their age without ASDs.[86] Studies analyzing omega-3 supplementation in children with ASDs have shown mixed results. One small study showed that supplementation provided no benefit,[87] and a meta-analysis exploring the use of omega-3 fatty acids in the treatment of ASDs could not find sufficient evidence to support its routine use.[88] Other small studies found a beneficial effect in some children. In one study, omega-3 fatty acid supplementation over 6 weeks led to a marked decrease in hyperactivity and stereotyped movements.[89] In another study, children with ASDs treated with omega-3 fatty acids over 12 weeks had significant improvements in hyperactivity.[90] Since omega-3 fatty acids are generally well tolerated and there is evidence to suggest that they may provide benefit in some children with ASDs, supplementation may be reasonable in an attempt to improve autistic behaviors, especially hyperactivity.

PROBIOTICS

As has been noted above, children with ASDs tend to have a host of gastrointestinal problems, including gastrointestinal reflux, chronic constipation, lactose intolerance, diarrhea, and abdominal pain.[1-7] Several theories have been proposed to explain the high rate of gastrointestinal ailments in children with ASDs. One interesting theory implicates the gastrointestinal bacteria. The gastrointestinal system is lined with billions of bacteria that maintain a healthy gut ecosystem. Changes in this ecosystem can lead to problems, such as diarrhea, that often follow antibiotic treatment which, in addition to treating a specific infection, also kills off many of the bacteria that normally inhabit the gut. Children with ASDs have been noted to have gut bacteria profiles (populations) that are significantly different from those of other children their age without ASD.[9,11,12,14-16] The guts of children with ASDs may have higher levels of toxin-producing bacteria, such as *Clostridium histolyticum*,[10] and lower levels of beneficial bacteria, such as *Bifidobacteria* species and *Akkermansia muciniphila*.[13] There may be an association between these abnormal bacteria levels and gastrointestinal problems. It is further hypothesized that this abnormal gut ecosystem could cause of host of neurologic ailments through a gastrointestinal–brain link.[14,91-93]

One common approach to correct the abnormal gastrointestinal ecosystem is to introduce "good" bacteria back into the gut. Probiotics are oral formulations of these bacteria that, when taken as dietary supplements, may improve the gut flora profile. Probiotics are widely used today in conventional pediatric practice to treat a range of gastrointestinal maladies.[94] Studies with probiotics in children have demonstrated its efficacy in preventing gastrointestinal disease in premature infants,[95] preventing and shortening the course of diarrhea,[96] and treating abdominal pain.[97] Little research, though, has been done to determine whether probiotics improve neurologic systems in patients with ASDs; thus, probiotics remain an uninvestigated treatment approach.

Off-label uses of medications and therapies

In order for medications to be approved for use in the United States, the drug must undergo rigorous scientific and clinic testing in the population for which it seeks to be used. In addition, the drug must be approved for a specific indication or usage. Testing in the pediatric population (because of a host of ethical and legal complexities) is often lacking. As a result, many medications approved only for adults are routinely used for non-indicated or off-label uses. In the search for treatment options for ASDs, researchers have also looked at the large arsenal of approved medications and have sought to use them in innovative ways. The off-label use of medications (i.e., the use of medications for indications and populations other than its approved indication) has provided some interesting management options for a number of ASD symptoms.

NALTREXONE

Naltrexone is an opioid receptor antagonist that blocks (or antagonizes) the protein structures to which opioids bind, leading to a decrease in the action of opioids. The binding of opioids at the opioid receptors leads to the classic effects of sedation, euphoria, and constipation. In addition, animals treated with excessive opioids seem to exhibit autistic behavior. Several trials have investigated blocking opioids to see if they may diminish autistic behaviors.

A number of studies have shown improvement of autistic behaviors with naltrexone,[98–101] and self-injurious behavior seems to be particularly responsive to naltrexone.[102] This improvement, though, is not seen in adults with ASDs.[103] In addition, it has been suggested that stereotyped behavior might actually worsen with naltrexone, though further research is needed to substantiate this.[104] Still, naltrexone may provide relief for self-injurious behavior in a subset of children with ASDs.[105]

INTRAVENOUS IMMUNOGLOBULIN

Intravenous immunoglobulin (IVIG) is an intravenous formulation of antibodies that are extracted and processed from the blood of healthy human donors. IVIG is used to treat a host of autoimmune and neurologic disorders. Autoimmune disorders are those in which the immune system becomes overactive and begins attacking the body. Although the exact mechanism of an IVIG effect is not completely understood, it appears that these "new" foreign antibodies overwhelm the overactive immune system, leading to a temporary but relatively rapid relief of symptoms.

A growing body of research has suggested an autoimmune component of ASDs.[25–28,63,106] IVIG has been investigated for the treatment of ASDs. One study found improvement in behavior after a minimum of 6 months of IVIG treatment;[107] however, another study of seven children with ASDs found no significant behavioral improvements after treatment with IVIG.[108] It has been suggested that IVIG works on a very narrow group of children with ASD, namely, younger children with abnormal immunologic profiles.[109] Aside from the conflicting results, given that IVIG must be administered in a specialized setting and is very expensive, it is not currently a practical therapeutic intervention for most children with ASDs.

ACETYLCHOLINESTERASE INHIBITORS: DONEPEZIL, RIVASTIGMINE, AND GALANTAMINE

Donepezil, rivastigmine, and galantamine are acetylcholinesterase inhibitors (medications that block the enzyme acetycholinesterase from breaking down the neurotransmitter acetylcholine). In essence, then, the acetylcholinesterase inhibitors increase the level of acetylcholine. This class of drugs has been used with success in Alzheimer disease.[110] There has been interest in determining if using these medications will improve symptoms in individuals with ASDs.

In a study of donepezil use in children with ASDs, no significant behavioral improvements were noted;[111] however, galantamine was found to produce significant improvement in irritability[112] and aggression.[113] Rivastigmine use led to improved language and overall behavior.[114] From these studies, it appears that rivastigmine and galantamine may be useful in helping to alleviate irritability and unwanted behaviors in some children with ASDs.

SECRETIN

Secretin is a hormone produced in the intestines that regulates gastric and pancreatic secretions. Secretin may also act as a neurotransmitter.[115] There was much enthusiasm when secretin was shown in a small study to improve social and language skills in children with ASDs;[116] however, numerous subsequent studies failed to show any similarly encouraging results.[117–123] Although at first an exciting prospect, secretin appears to have now become a footnote as opposed to a useful therapeutic option.[124]

ANTIBIOTICS

As discussed previously, there is evidence to suggest that the gastrointestinal tract of children with an ASD has a different bacterial composition than that of children without ASDs.[9–16] In theory, there are several approaches in trying to re-establish a normal gastrointestinal "ecosystem." The first approach, as mentioned previously, would be to provide probiotic supplementation that could support the growth of "good" bacteria. An alternate method would be to use antibiotics to kill off the "bad" bacteria and, in turn, allow the "good" bacteria to thrive. In one small study of children with regressive ASDs who received the antibiotic vancomycin, there were improvements in a host of autistic behaviors;[125] however, these improvements were lost soon after stopping the antibiotic. In another study, children with ASDs given the antibiotic D-cycloserine showed improvements in autistic behaviors;[126] however, there have been no large-scale, well-controlled studies looking at the use of antibiotics to treat ASDs. Due to the risks involved in the prolonged use of antibiotics (including causing bacterial resistance and further alterations in the gastrointestinal flora), treatment of ASDs with antibiotics is not common practice and requires further study.

OTHER MEDICATIONS

The list of medications that are being investigated for use in ASDs is continuously growing. Mamentine is used primarily to treat moderate-to-severe Alzheimer disease.[127] In some children with ASDs, mamentine has been shown to improve inattention, self-stimulatory behaviors, and social skills.[128–131] N-acetylcysteine, used primarily for acetaminophen overdoses,[132] has antioxidant properties.[133] One study showed an improvement in irritability when N-acetylcysteine was given to children with ASDs.[134] Propranolol is a beta-blocker, a class of drugs primarily used to treat hypertension.[135] Besides treating hypertension, propranolol may improve language abilities in some children with ASDs.[136–139]

CHELATION THERAPY

In the search for the causes of ASDs, there have been many theories. It has been suggested that high levels of metallic elements in the body are at least partly responsible for ASDs. There is, in fact, evidence that the urine of children with ASDs has higher-than-normal levels of metallic elements such as cadmium, mercury, and lead;[140–142] however, studies comparing levels of metallic elements in the hair[143] and levels of mercury in both the hair and blood failed to show such a consistent trend.[144] The proposed correlation between metallic elements and ASDs has led to fear of receiving thimerosal-containing vaccinations, since thimerosal contains mercury. Although current research has not demonstrated a link between ASDs in general and thimerosal-containing vaccinations,[145] the Food and Drug Administration moved to eliminate or bring to a trace level thimerosal in vaccines.[146]

Researchers have examined attempts to lower the levels of metallic elements in children with ASDs through chelation. Chelation uses medications to remove elements from the body. In the setting of lead poisoning in children, chelation is used to remove lead from the body. Chelation is usually given intravenously, though oral formulations exist, and requires extremely careful monitoring since electrolyte imbalances and other side effects commonly occur. When given to children with ASDs, chelation has been demonstrated to decrease the urine levels of heavy metals.[142,147] Compared with other children their age, children with ASDs treated with oral chelation therapy have been found to excrete higher levels of mercury.[148] In children with both ASDs and lead poisoning, chelation has been shown to improve autistic behaviors;[149,150] however, for children with ASDs without lead poisoning, there have not been well-controlled studies examining clinical benefits of chelation. Although planned, two large chelation trials were halted by the Food and Drug Administration due to safety concerns.[151] Chelation does have prominent risks associated with it, including electrolyte abnormalities and liver toxicity. One child with an ASD was reported to have died after receiving chelation therapy.[152] Until there are further studies examining the effects of chelation on children with ASDs, it is difficult to draw conclusions regarding its potential therapeutic role outside of reducing heavy metal levels.

Hyperbaric oxygen therapy

Hyperbaric oxygen therapy (HBOT) is a treatment in which the patient is placed into a chamber and receives oxygen at levels higher than naturally occur in the atmosphere. Whereas normal air is only 21% oxygen, the chamber used in HBOT can deliver from 21 to 100% oxygen. In addition, the chambers can be pressurized, allowing the patient to receive oxygen at a higher pressure. Currently, HBOT is routinely used to treat carbon monoxide poisoning, chronic bone infections (osteomyelitis), serious soft tissue infections (necrotizing fasciitis), thermal burns, and numerous other acute conditions. By providing oxygen at a high pressure, HBOT increases the amount of oxygen in the blood, leading to dilation of blood vessels and therefore increased perfusion to organs, including the brain.[153–155] HBOT may also exercise potent anti-inflammatory and antioxidant properties,[156–161] and may activate stem cells.[162] Based on this, it has been hypothesized that HBOT may improve certain symptoms of ASDs.[163]

Cerebral blood flow has been noted to be decreased in children with ASDs.[164,165] Since HBOT leads to increased blood flow, it might improve cerebral blood flow and therefore symptoms in ASDs.[166] Based on the concept that there may be mitochondrial and energy abnormalities in children with ASDs, it has been suggested that HBOT could deliver enough oxygen to the mitochondria to overcome the dysfunction.[167] The anti-inflammatory and antioxidant properties of HBOT may reduce inflammation and oxidative stress that have been shown in ASDs.[26,106,168,169] If, indeed, HBOT rallies stem cells to injured parts of the body, it could theoretically lead to new neuron growth in children with ASDs.

In one study of children with ASDs, C-reactive protein (a marker of inflammation in the blood) decreased significantly after extensive HBOT. In addition, parents reported improvement in autistic behavior.[170] Other studies of HBOT have noted improvements in social skills and motor skills,[171] in parent-reported behaviors,[172] and in eye contact, communication, and overall functioning.[173] Other studies, though, found no significant behavioral improvements following HBOT.[174,175] Although there are conflicting results, most of the studies examining HBOT showed generally positive outcomes with minimal side effects,[176] making HBOT an appealing CAM option for some families. Side effects to keep in mind include pressure-related trauma to the ear, sinus injury, rashes, and asthma exacerbation. HBOT can be expensive and requires numerous sessions. If a hyperbaric oxygen chamber is placed in the basement, it poses a potential explosion/fire hazard; therefore, families should carefully consider these risks and the cost (both in time and money) when deciding on HBOT.

Vision therapies

While it is generally assumed that simply having 20/20 vision in both eyes corresponds to "good" vision, the growing and increasingly popular field of behavioral optometry would likely find this assessment incomplete. In behavioral optometry, visual health is seen not just as a product of good visual acuity (20/20 vision in both eyes), but of the entire integrative process in which visual input is processed by the brain and then informs the body's actions. Among emerging modalities in the field of visual therapy is the use of prisms on glasses. For several years now, prism lenses have been used in an attempt to alter brain pathways and improve function in people with neurologic deficits.[177] Among children with ASDs, it has been noted that they often tilt their heads to the side, suggesting an abnormal visual-perceptual system.[178] There is very limited research into this hypothesis, though one study of children with ASDs found that visual therapy with prism lenses improved posture and hand–eye coordination.[179] Although there is currently no evidence of improvement in autistic behaviors with visual therapies, this is an increasingly popular field that will likely see more research.

Auditory and sensory therapies

Auditory integration therapy is a sensory-based treatment employed in the management of ASD. In this therapy, children are given headphones with a carefully arranged spectrum of sounds. Typically, children listen to two 30-minute sessions per day for 10 days. According to the hypothesis underlying this therapy, children with ASDs have abnormalities in the way sensory material (including sound) is integrated, thus affecting behavior. Some studies of auditory integration therapy in children with ASDs demonstrated mildly improved sensitivity to sound,[180,181] whereas others showed no benefit.[182,183] If families choose to attempt a trial of auditory or sensory integration therapy (see Chapter 8), they should discuss goals of treatment with the therapist,[184] as the therapy could become quite expensive and time-consuming if no goals are set early.

Acupuncture

According to traditional Chinese medicine, the body contains lines along which energy flows, known as meridians. Obstruction along these meridians leads to most common ailments and diseases. In order to relieve this obstruction, acupuncture needles are placed at strategic points along the meridians. Energy flow can therefore be restored, allowing the body to heal itself. In one placebo-controlled study of 50 children with ASDs, those who received authentic acupuncture, as opposed to sham acupuncture, had significant improvements in self-care and cognition.[185] Variants of traditional acupuncture, including electroacupuncture (in which the acupuncture needles are attached to an electric current)[186,187] and scalp acupuncture,[188] have likewise been found to improve autistic features, especially communication; however, due to a reported lack of large-scale studies, a meta-analysis reviewing the use of acupuncture in ASDs found insufficient evidence to recommend its routine use in ASDs.[189] Families should also be aware that needling time may be difficult for some children with ASDs to tolerate, though general tolerability of acupuncture by children with ASDs has been noted.[190] Most certified acupuncturists therefore offer acupressure, a reasonable alternative to acupuncture in which tiny metal beads provide pressure at the acupoint. Both acupuncture and acupressure require multiple treatment courses to consolidate any effect.

Choosing a complementary and alternative therapy

Deciding on a treatment course for a child with an ASD can be a daunting task. Unlike treating illnesses such as an ear infection where there is a proven cure with limited side effects, treating autism offers no similarly clear directive. Some CAM methods have been shown in rigorous scientific studies to alleviate symptoms of autism; many, though, have unclear benefits and do have potential risks. Currently, no single management technique has been discovered that can cure or even drastically alter the course of ASDs permanently. When such a treatment modality is discovered, it will surely rise to the forefront of public awareness and become the standard of care. Until that time, there are important questions that need to be asked before attempting a treatment approach, and especially before attempting CAM. The benefits of a given treatment, the risks of that treatment, and the goals of treatment all need to be considered before embarking on a course of action.

The first step in investigating a therapy is to assess whether there is any benefit to it. Many parents look into CAM because they have heard that a therapy may offer beneficial results,[17] but it is crucial to investigate the validity of these claims. Ask health care providers, talk to friends who have tried the therapy, search the Internet, and read current scientific assessments of the therapy. While previous research may have shown a treatment to be relatively useless, new research may demonstrate that a treatment leads to profound improvements in a different domain, or vice versa. When examining whether a therapy may be beneficial, it is important to look at what the newest research shows. Another important point to consider when looking at a therapy's reported benefits is to carefully examine the specific results. Did the treatment improve language abilities? Did the treatment reduce aggressive behavior? Did the treatment decrease stereotyped movements? Also, when looking at benefit, the magnitude (that is, the size and scale) of the improvement needs to be noted. Did stereotyped movements decrease by 5% or 75%? Although possible, improvement more than that seen in research should not be expected, and it should not be the basis upon which treatment is started.

Every treatment modality has some inherent risk. Although these risks may be small or almost negligible, they are still ubiquitous. Even vitamins, minerals, and supplements can lead to adverse effects if taken in toxic doses. Furthermore, all interventions carry the risk of pain, discomfort, and emotional stress in the child. The possibility also exists that a therapy can have the opposite of a desired effect. For example, after starting a GFCF, it has anecdotally been noted that a subset of children with ASDs can actually become more aggressive.

Besides the biologic risks, most therapies require a financial commitment. Many CAM therapies are quite expensive and may not be covered by insurance. In addition, there is a strong emotional commitment required. All therapies require the dedication of caregivers to comply with a treatment regimen that may be extremely cumbersome, as in the GFCF diet. All of these risks and commitments need to be carefully considered and then balanced against the potential benefits of the therapy.

Once potential benefits and risks are clearly understood, the goals of treatment need to be established. Goals should be realistic and objective—realistic in the sense that the outcome has been demonstrated in research and objective in the sense that the outcome is measurable. For example, a child with an ASD may have particular difficulty with tantrums. A realistic goal might be to reduce tantrums; an objective way to measure this might be to ask the child's teacher to make a tally of how many tantrums the child has per day over the course of several weeks and for the parents to do the same. A reduction in the total number of tantrums would be an objective measure of the treatment goal. Whether the reduction is due to the therapy or merely to chance variation may be difficult to ascertain. In formal research, this is borne out through statistical analysis that confirms whether or not the reduction is statistically "significant." In the case of non-research treatment of a single child, though, whether or not a result is "significant" is ultimately the decision of the parents. In general, it may be useful to observe the following guideline: the magnitude of the goal should be proportional to the "cost" of the treatment. In other words, more tedious, costly, or risky treatments should produce more pronounced, long-lasting, and functionally relevant benefits. Using the previous example, a parent may set a goal of a 50% reduction in tantrums for a burdensome treatment such as the GFCF diet but a goal of a 15% reduction in tantrums for a relatively undemanding treatment such as multivitamin supplementation. By setting realistic and objective goals before starting treatment, parents can feel confident that they are approaching a treatment modality rationally.

Before starting any therapy, it is important to ask the appropriate provider how long the treatment needs to be given before clinical results should be expected. Since every child is different, it is reasonable to extend this time frame somewhat before expecting results. If a treatment modality professes to lead to clinical improvements within several months, it is reasonable to establish 6 months as an end point by which results are expected. Using the example above, before starting a child with an ASD on a GFCF diet, a goal could be set that a 50% reduction in tantrums is expected within 6 months. If that does not occur within the established time frame, parents may consider discontinuing the diet. Establishing a time frame for the treatment goals gives parents the comfort of knowing that they have given the treatment a "fighting chance" before discontinuing it. Furthermore, time frames prevent parents from unnecessarily maintaining therapies that are not producing significant clinical improvement in their child.

Choosing a practitioner

The next step in initiating a therapy is to select a practitioner who can assist in executing the therapy and in evaluating the outcome. In the context of starting a multivitamin or vitamin supplement, this might be a therapy that could be started in conjunction with the child's primary pediatrician, neurologist, or developmental pediatrician; however, for any specialized diets or more complex CAM, parents should work in tandem with a practitioner who has advanced training and ample experience in that specific treatment modality. For example, if starting a GFCF diet, parents might want to work with a nutritionist to ensure that the diet is being properly followed and that the child is still meeting all nutritional requirements. For acupuncture, parents should select an acupuncturist who has experience working with children with ASD.

All practitioners, whether of conventional medicine or CAM, should be licensed by their respective accreditation board. Usually, that information is easily accessible on the Internet. If the licensure information is not available there, insurance companies may have this information. Of course, if no amount of investigation can produce this information, it is well within the parents' right to ask the practitioner or his or her office staff for information regarding licensure. Recommendations from physicians or other parents of children with ASDs are also useful.

When meeting the practitioner for the first time, it is important to remember that there is absolutely no obligation to continue seeing the practitioner or to comply with recommended therapies. The first meeting with a practitioner is the best time to see whether he or she is the right person with whom to form a therapeutic alliance. There needs to be trust that the practitioner is providing true information and has the best interests of the child in mind. Any practitioner who promises to "cure" the child's ASD is highly suspect. Similarly, claims such as "all children who use this therapy always do better" are highly dubious. Other claims that should raise a red flag are that (1) a single treatment can actually treat numerous and unrelated disorders, (2) a treatment has no risks or side effects, (3) the treatment is untested, or (4) research into a treatment is unnecessary.[191] Although there are certainly many treatments which offer some reprieve from the symptoms of ASDs, a therapy that seems too good to be true is likely just that.

Regardless of which therapy a family decides to employ and whom the family chooses as a practitioner to guide them, proper medical supervision of the child is necessary. The child's primary care physician (usually a pediatrician) and the child's autism specialist (usually a child psychiatrist, a child neurologist, or a developmental pediatrician) need to closely follow the child. The physician(s) must be aware of which CAM therapies are being attempted, as well as any changes (positive or negative) that the family has noticed in the child. The physician should be a part of the therapeutic alliance, establishing a network with the child, the family, and the CAM practitioner. When all members of the therapeutic alliance work together and are on the same page, there is the greatest chance of success.

TAKEAWAY POINTS

- Complementary and alternative medicine (CAM) offers a wealth of therapeutic options for children with ASDs.

- Dietary modifications (namely, the gluten-free/casein-free diet) may improve behavior, especially in children with gastrointestinal symptoms.

- Vitamin supplementation, for example with vitamin B6, vitamin B12, vitamin C, and folic acid, may lead to improved behaviors in a subset of children with ASDs.

- Off-label use of medications or therapies for ASDs may be helpful in some children with an ASD but should only be done under the close supervision of a physician.

- When choosing to employ any CAM therapy, families should discuss it with their health care provider, carefully balance risks and benefits, set realistic goals, and routinely re-evaluate the treatment's efficacy.

Chapter 10

Environmental Risk Factors and Autism Spectrum Disorders

Sue X. Ming, MD, PhD

Introduction

It is recognized that certain environmental factors may contribute to the occurrence of an autism spectrum disorder (ASD), or may exacerbate symptoms in a child with an ASD, including the occurrence of associated medical disorders. While there has been no single toxin or group of toxins scientifically proven to be specifically causative of an ASD, scientists believe that certain children with ASDs may have reduced detoxification mechanisms that render them more susceptible to environmental toxins. This chapter discusses what we currently know about environmental factors that have been reported to be associated with ASDs and what parents can do to minimize the impact of environmental toxins on their child.

The hypothesis of gene and environmental toxin interaction as a cause of ASDs

It has long been hypothesized that occurrence of an ASD is associated with risk factors related to gene and environment interactions. The prevalence of ASDs is increasing, independent of broadened diagnostic criteria. It is not clear that ASDs are a direct consequence of an infectious agent. We no longer believe that ASDs are man-made disorders, caused by the emotional frigidity of mothers (so-called refrigerator mothers). Experts also believe that the prevalence of ASDs far exceeds any disorders predicted to result from gene alterations alone. Studies of ASDs in twins showed concordance in identical twins of less than 90%,[1-3] and a significantly lower concordance in fraternal twins (20–31%),[1-3] suggesting that factors other than genetics also play a role. Coinciding with the increasing incidence of ASD worldwide, there has been a worldwide trend towards industrialization that introduces large quantities of chemicals into the environment and causes disturbances in our ecosystems. Furthermore, many comorbidities in ASDs can be explained by changes in environmental factors. For example, environmental or ecosystem changes are known to trigger new allergies. A new or altered species of plant could introduce new allergens. A new type of detergent, even a household detergent, may introduce new allergens, especially to young children. Allergies are recognized to be more common in children with ASDs.[4–6] Chemicals can sometimes interfere with endocrine (hormone) function. Research has shown that prenatal exposure to endocrine disruptors or events that lead to fetal endocrine disruption are associated with ASDs.[7] It is proposed that ASDs are associated with endocrine abnormalities.[6,8,9] Prenatal exposure to chemicals that disrupt thyroid function has been reported in mothers of children with ASDs;[10] however, an earlier study found no significant association of low neonatal thyroid hormones in children with ASDs as compared with healthy controls.[11] We observe in our clinical practice that a higher percentage of children with ASDs compared with typical children have hyperarousal to sensory stimulus and precocious puberty that are consistent with literature reports of enhanced cortisol response or hyperarousal to stress and disturbances of hypothalamic pituitary adrenocortical function.[12–14] Furthermore, a subpopulation of individuals with ASDs have a history of in utero exposure to toxins such as valproic acid (VPA), thalidomide, hazardous air pollutants, pesticides, and bisphenol A. Many of these toxins are known endocrine disruptors.[7,15–17] We know from the twin studies cited previously that genetic factors clearly play a role. Although the evidence may not be as strong, we can also reasonably assume that exposure to certain toxins, directly or indirectly, may contribute to the occurrence of an ASD. As a result of epidemiological information collected thus far, the hypothesis of gene and environmental interactions in the development of an ASD has emerged and has been held to be the main hypothesis to be tested by many scientists.

Studies of environmental toxins and ASDs

In the past decade, studies of environmental toxins and ASDs were supported by many major funding agencies, including the National Institutes of Health, the Department of Defense, Autism Speaks, and many smaller not-for-profit organizations. An increasing number of articles related to environmental factors and ASDs have been, and continue to be, published.

Prenatal exposure

Exposure to toxins can begin in utero. Such a claim is supported by the finding that a significant quantity of various toxins were detected in Philipino newborns' meconium (first stool collected from a newborn), including lead, cadmium, mercury, chlordane, chlorpyrifos, diazinon, DDT, lindane, malathion, parathion, and pentachlorophenol.[18] Prenatal toxin exposure has been documented in a subset of children with autism including thalidomide embryopathy (birth defects recognized to be caused by prenatal exposure to this medication) as well as Moebius sequence (facial and eye paralysis with or without certain limb defects) associated with misoprostol use during pregnancy.[16] A very high percentage of offspring born to pregnant women who took thalidomide for morning sickness were diagnosed to have an ASD. Likewise, some pregnant women who were exposed to misoprostol gave birth to children with Moebius sequence and autism.[19] Maternal use of the anticonvulsant VPA during gestation was reported by several investigators to be linked to offspring with autism.[17,20–24] Exposure early in pregnancy to thalidomide, misoprostol, VPA, and organophosphate insecticides have also been shown in other studies to be associated with ASDs.[25,26] A study in New York City found a relationship between increased maternal prenatal exposure to phthalates and behavioral problems in the children some years later.[27,28] Although autism per se was not documented in this study on phthalate exposure, "behavioral problems" which might include ASDs were increased in children whose mothers were exposed to high levels of this chemical. Phthalate exposure was estimated from maternal urine phthalate metabolite levels. In addition, indoor dust samples were also found to be contaminated by phthalates.[29]

In support of human data, many animal studies demonstrate a link between toxin exposure and autistic behaviors and/or brain pathology. Exposure of mouse cerebellar Purkinje cells to hydroxy-polychlorinated biphenyl (PCB) and estrogenic chemicals shows significant inhibition of thyroid hormone-dependent dendritic (cell process) development of these cells, which are responsible for motor coordination in this region of the brain,[30] a finding consistent with autopsy results in individuals with autism. This study suggests that exposure to PCBs and other environmental chemicals may disrupt normal neuronal development and cause developmental brain disorders, such as autism. Prenatal and postnatal exposure to VPA has long been used as a means of developing a mouse model of autism (experimentally created autism in mice, in an effort to identify causes of, and treatment for, autism).[31–33] (I had the good fortune to work with the great animal psychologist, Dr. George C.

Wagner, at Rutgers University in 2004 and witnessed firsthand the dramatic autistic behaviors in these VPA-exposed mice.)

Postnatal exposure

A study of mercury exposure conducted in Texas, the fourth highest mercury-release state in the United States, found that the association of mercury exposure and special education rates was mediated by an increase in autism rates. This study examined the level of mercury release into air, water, and land by industrial facilities in each county and correlated the rate of special education students and the rate of autism in the corresponding county. On average, for each 1000 lbs of environmentally released mercury, there was a 43% increase in the rate of special education services and a 61% increase in the rate of autism.[34] Usually, an industrial facility releases waste that contains a multitude of toxins, including other heavy metals such as arsenic and lead, organic and inorganic solvents, pesticides, and other toxins. While not examined by the investigators, other chemical exposures may have also contributed to the increase in special education and autism rates in these Texas counties. The same group of investigators subsequently evaluated the distance from industrial mercury release or power plants and autism rates. Proximity to industrial release or power plants was associated with an increase in autism rates. For every 10 miles away from industrial or power plant sources, there was an associated decrease in autism rates.[35] Although these studies could not directly link the mercury exposures to autism, the positive association is intriguing and raises the question of whether toxin exposure at a critical time of development in a genetically vulnerable child renders them susceptible to abnormal brain development, which in some cases may manifest as an ASD.

Our own observation of environmental toxin exposure and ASDs in the state of New Jersey suggests a potential link. We reported a considerable overlap of identified toxic landfills and the residence of an ASD cohort, as well as a correlation between the identified toxic superfund sites in each U.S. state and the total number of diagnosed cases of ASDs in those states. The residence of 495 patients with ASDs in New Jersey were sorted by postal codes along with the toxic landfill sites and were plotted on a map of northern New Jersey. The areas with the highest numbers of ASD cases coincide with the highest density of toxic landfill sites, whereas the areas with lowest numbers of ASD cases have the lowest density of toxic landfill sites. Furthermore, the number of toxic superfund sites and autism rates across the 50 states shows a statistically significant correlation between the number of identified superfund sites and the rate of ASDs per 1000 residents in 49 of the 50 states (the exception being the state of Oregon). This observation does not directly tie superfund sites to the development of ASDs, but it does support the general hypothesis of environmental risk factors contributing to the increased prevalence of ASDs.[36]

Further evidence of the association between ASDs and toxin exposure is summarized as follows:

- A study suggested a potential association between autism and estimated metal concentrations, and possibly solvents in ambient air, in children who were born in the San Francisco Bay area in 1994.[37]

- A study of body burden of toxins in children with ASDs revealed that the body burden of multiple toxins, including industrial solvents, pesticides, and heavy metals, in 20 children with ASDs far exceeds the limit of an adult burden.[38,39]

- A group of widespread environmental pollutants and brominated flame retardants, including polybrominated diphenyl ethers (PBDEs), have been used at increasing levels in home furnishings and electronics over the past 25 years. High PBDE levels are found in food, household dust, and indoor air. These compounds mimic thyroid hormone, and the long-term neurological effects of exposure to PBDEs during development has been implicated as an autism risk factor.[40]

- Maternal smoking, condensation on windows (low ventilation rate in homes), and polyvinyl chloride flooring (especially in the parents' bedroom) during early childhood were associated with an ASD diagnosis 5 years later in Swedish children.[41]

- A study found that perinatal exposure to the mixture of air pollutants containing phthalates was associated with ASDs in children evaluated at the age of 8 years.[42]

We have highlighted studies supporting the hypothesis of environmental risk factors in contributing to autism or autism symptoms. Readers are also encouraged to do their own research to find more studies on this topic and to keep abreast of new studies as they are published. It is important to note that there is no single toxin consistently reported to be associated with ASDs across studies. Furthermore, the studies discussed did not include any sudden, catastrophic exposures to toxins. All the postnatal studies involved insidious, chronic exposure, either indoors or outdoors.

Some children with an ASD have reduced detoxification capabilities

By now, readers may appreciate that while increased exposure to toxins in children with ASDs is plausible, siblings or neighbor children may also be exposed to similar toxins and do not have features of an ASD. Then the question becomes, "Why is my child the one who developed autism?"

There is evidence from the literature suggesting that detoxification abilities are different in some individuals with an ASD. Our body has a fine-tuned mechanism to metabolize chemicals produced by our own body or ingested. These chemicals could include certain food additives, medications, or toxins. Our detoxification system converts primary chemicals into innocuous chemicals (by-products) which are excreted either by the kidneys (in urine) or by the gastrointestinal tract (in stool). A defect or inefficiency in the detoxification mechanisms may allow toxins additional time to exert their toxic effects on our cells and organs. One study found that 90% of children with autism who also had a known food or chemical intolerance were deficient in phenosulfotransferase, a liver enzyme involved in detoxification.[43,44] A study by Edelson and Cantor reported an increase in urinary glucaric acid, a biomarker for chemical/toxin contamination, in children with ASDs together with the abnormal liver detoxification profiles.[45] Another study found decreased acetaminophen conjugation (sulfation) by the liver in 20 low-functioning children with ASDs.[46] James et al. reported DNA hypomethylation in children with autism and their parents.[47] Glutathione S-transferases (GSTs) are enzymes that catalyze the conjugation of glutathione to toxicants which serves a detoxification role. Genetic polymorphisms (minor genetic variations) of GSTs (GST M1 and GST P1) resulting in reduced or absent GST enzyme function have been described in families with children with autism.[47–51] Another major cellular glutathione enzyme involved in detoxification, glutathione peroxidase, is more likely to contain a genetic variant and/or be functionally different in families with children who have autism.[52]

Oxidative stress is a circumstance that reflects the body's burden of adversity caused by toxins, infections, inflammation, and so forth. Oxidative stress can lead to cell death, and endogenous (inside the body) or exogenous (from outside the body) antioxidants work to quench the free oxygen species which we associate with oxidative stress, in order to prevent cell death. Both increased oxidative stress and individuals' ability to deal with oxidative stress have been shown to be perturbed in individuals with autism. We and others have demonstrated an association between high levels of oxidative stress and autism. We reported an increase in a biomarker of oxidative stress (15-F2t-isoprostane) in urine of individuals with an ASD,[53] a finding later confirmed by others.[54] In a follow-up study we found that a double dose of the GST mutation (*GST M1 null allele*) is associated with a greater increase of 15-F2t-isoprostane excretion in individuals with autism, suggesting more directly that the GST mutation is a contributor to oxidative stress in autism (unpublished data).

We investigated the metabolism of plastic toxins, known as phthalates, in autism. Phthalates are a group of chemicals used in making plastic more malleable. As such, phthalates are present in all plastic-containing products, which are so widespread that it is impossible to avoid them in daily life. From the moment a child is born, he or she is exposed to plastic products in the hospital (e.g., pacifiers, feeding bottles, medical devices). A child has ample circumstances in which to be exposed to a variety of plasticware later in life.[55,56] Because phthalates are known to be endocrine disruptors,[57] we thought that investigating phthalates exposure and metabolism in children with autism and comparing them with typically developing children (controls) might shed light on their potential toxic effects in the development of autism. We found that total phthalate metabolites (phthalates and their converted inactive chemicals) are similar in children with ASDs and controls; however, the percentage of metabolized phthalates is significantly lower in children with ASDs. In another words, at least some of the children with ASDs in our study had significantly lower capacity to detoxify phthalates.[58] Another group of investigators found that children with ASDs had a higher exposure to phthalates.[57]

I found that some children with ASDs have either paradoxical or unusually heightened responses to some medications compared with the general population. It is my general practice to start a medicine at 25% to even 10% of the recommended dose, because of the hypersensitivity some children with ASDs experience with medications. Although this is merely a clinical observation, if it is confirmed by a systematic research study, it might suggest that some children with ASDs have altered metabolism of medications (detoxification mechanism).

At this point, it is reasonable to assume that at least some children with ASDs have impaired or reduced detoxification mechanisms. This altered detoxification mechanism could in part explain why only some children developed ASDs even when raised in the same environment with others who do not develop an ASD. Another plausible hypothesis is that exposure to toxins or environmental risk factors is most harmful at certain critical points in development in the susceptible individual. In general, early childhood (the first 3 years of life) is the period when the brain and body systems, such as the immune system, undergo rapid growth and maturation. For a susceptible, at-risk individual, adversity during this critical period for brain development could result in developmental disorders including autism.

General practices to reduce the impact of environmental toxins

Environmental toxins are virtually in every dimension of our living space. The following passage is quoted directly from the abstract of an article by Rudel and Perovich:

> The past 50 years have seen rapid development of new building materials, furnishings, and consumer products and a corresponding explosion in new chemicals in the built environment. While exposure levels are largely undocumented, they are likely to have increased as a wider variety of chemicals came into use, people began spending more time indoors, and air exchange rates decreased to improve energy efficiency. As a result of weak regulatory requirements for chemical safety testing, only limited toxicity data are available for these chemicals. Over the past 15 years, some chemical classes commonly used in building materials, furnishings, and consumer products have been shown to be endocrine disrupting chemicals—that is they interfere with the action of endogenous hormones. These include PCBs, used in electrical equipment, caulking, paints and surface coatings; chlorinated and brominated flame retardants, used in electronics, furniture, and textiles; pesticides, used to control insects, weeds, and other pests in agriculture, lawn maintenance, and the built environment; phthalates, used in vinyl, plastics, fragrances, and other products; alkylphenols, used in detergents, pesticide formulations, and polystyrene plastics; and parabens, used to preserve products like lotions and sunscreens.[59]

It appears impossible to escape exposure to toxins in today's life.

Of the many toxins listed above, I chose to focus on phthalates. My collaborators and I have data on phthalates in children with ASDs,[58] and phthalates are important toxins that children are being exposed to during early childhood. In a 2006 article, Schettler stated the following:

> Many consumer products contain phthalates, including building materials, household furnishings, clothing, cosmetics, pharmaceuticals, nutritional supplements, medical devices, dentures, children's toys, glow

sticks, modeling clay, food packaging, automobiles, lubricants, waxes, cleaning materials and insecticides. Consumer products containing phthalates can result in human exposure through direct contact and use, indirectly through leaching into other products, or general environmental contamination. Phthalates are in the air particles.[55]

One could conclude that ingestion, inhalation, and skin absorption are potential pathways of phthalate exposure. Dietary intake from contaminated food is likely to be the largest single source of phthalate exposure in the general population.[60] As you can see, phthalates are a group of important toxins to avoid, and it is possible to reduce phthalates exposure by exercising plastics-conscious measures.[61]

Some of the recommendations below are not from any published literature or established practice guidelines, nor supported by sound scientific evidence. Readers should therefore bear this in mind when using the information to make decisions about lifestyle and life choices. Reducing toxin exposure does no harm, and although these practices may be inconvenient and initially more expensive, in the long run they are cheaper by keeping your family healthier.

While it is not possible to completely avoid exposure to plastic toxins, it is possible to reduce the *level* of exposure. Since ingestion is one of the major exposure routes, one can control how food is prepared, stored, and ingested. Plasticware is light weight, durable, convenient to use, and inexpensive. If you walk through a grocery store, you will see that more than 90% of items have plastics or Styrofoam either in the containers or wrappers. Particles of plastic toxins are in the air, furniture, flooring, countertops, plastic bottles, plastic wrapper, computer keyboards, and cell phone covers. How can you reduce exposure to toxins? Reducing exposure time to the plasticizers of dietary origin is feasible. A study showed that just avoiding food wrapped in plastic could reduce exposure to the plasticizers by more than 50%.[61] Boiling food contained in a plastic bag or heating this in a microwave may introduce your food to an extra dose of the plastic toxins. So, do not use plastic ware in the microwave, even though it is labeled with the microwave-safe insignia. Heating food in the microwave changes its structure, as well as the structure of preservatives in food. Although preservatives permitted in food products may not be recognized carcinogens (thanks to the FDA), who knows what the microwave-produced by-products of these preservatives can do to the human body? Also chemicals in polystyrene (Styrofoam) containers can leach into food when they are heated in a microwave oven. Polystyrene cups for hot beverages are discouraged. Use glass products whenever possible.

When purchasing groceries, one may want to avoid pre-packaged goods, especially food shipped from overseas. Use eco-friendly reusable bags instead of plastic bags. Wash your food to remove the residues of phthalates on the surface of food, whether it was wrapped in plastics, foil, or paper. Wash your vegetables again even though the bags may be labeled "triple washed, ready to use." Phthalates have even been found in sugar packed in paper bags, with these chemicals leaking from the adhesives used to seal the paper bags.[60] Avoid plasticware as much as possible and use aluminum foil instead of plastic film to wrap food. Beverages in tin cans or glass bottles may have less phthalates, although they may not contain fewer toxins. Even with glass bottles, if the bottles are capped with a plastic cap, then the cap may serve as a source of phthalates. While I cannot find information on whether cardboard cartons contain less phthalates than plastic jars, my educated guess is that the former have less phthalates. The longer food is stored in plastic or cardboard containers, the higher quantity of phthalates migrate into food; therefore, you are better off buying smaller quantities and fresh foods. Avoid products that require many layers of wrappers. If possible, use metal or glass water bottles when traveling, and avoid food or drinks with dietary dyes. Fresh fruits may still have pesticides on the surface, so wash them prior to consuming. Canning is a good way to preserve food, but many canned foods contain preservatives such as bisphenol A. Another recommendation is to use uncoated cookware made of stainless steel, raw cast iron, or glass for your cooking or baking. Avoid polytetrafluoroethylene (Teflon) non-stick coatings (which contain perfluroctanoic acid).

I would like to share with readers the following information to further substantiate my support for plastics-conscious practice: In 2005, the European Food Safety Authority established the tolerable daily intakes with legislative limits for phthalates in both plastic and food simulants,[62] and the limits have been enforced by European Union plastics legislation since 2008. Danish food inspectors analyzed phthalates in a sample of food-contact materials and found the following objects to have higher than the daily tolerable limit: conveyor belts (6 of 6 tested), lids from packed foodstuffs in glasses (8 of 28 tested), tubes for liquid foodstuffs (4 of 5 tested), and gloves (4 of 14 tested).[62] We hope the Food and Drug Administration, and Environmental Protection Agency, will follow the Europeans' footsteps to make food safer for its citizens.

Other practices to reduce toxin exposure should also be considered. Household detergents (scented or unscented) contain chemicals that may be toxic to young children. Similarly, wipes soaked in detergents could have chemicals you wish your child not to be exposed to, even though they make your life much easier. Indoor air quality is another focus of attention. Poor ventilation, as noted above, was one of the factors found to be associated with autism in a Swedish study.[41] So, open windows and let chemicals out. Household pets may become "reservoirs" for chemicals, especially airborne chemicals that get trapped in fur. Leave new furniture, toys, and other household products in an open, ventilated, non-living space to allow solvents or chemicals to evaporate prior to moving them into a space where your child will come in contact. Indoor air purifiers may reduce chemical residues in the air.

No doubt there are many more measures one can take to further reduce toxin exposures. It is beyond the scope of this book to list all the practices. It is not our intention to recommend radical or extreme measures to create a life in a vacuum. We hope that by changing your daily routines to a degree that is suitable to your family's lifestyle you can reduce your child's toxin exposure significantly.

TAKEAWAY POINTS

- Environmental toxins are believed to play a role in the causation of ASDs.
- Increased toxin exposure and/or reduced detoxification have been reported to be associated with ASDs.
- Be aware of phthalates, a group of toxins in plastics and many household products.
- Reducing toxin exposure is possible. Plastics-conscious practice can reduce, but not eliminate, phthalate exposure.

Tests for Individuals with Autism Spectrum Disorders and Their Associated Medical or Behavioral Conditions

Devorah Segal, MD, PhD

Introduction

Autism spectrum disorders (ASDs) are increasingly the subject of much scientific research. Though our recognition and understanding of ASDs continue to grow, there is still no single test that can be used to diagnose an ASD; instead, practitioners making a diagnosis of an ASD rely on clinical observation and information gleaned from family members. Although there is no definitive diagnostic test for ASDs, many children with an ASD undergo various tests that help confirm the diagnosis by ruling out alternative diagnoses, as well as tests for other medical or behavioral conditions that may occur more frequently in individuals with an ASD. This chapter discusses the utility of some of the common tests physicians order for children with an ASD, why a specific test may be ordered for a particular child, what preparations and procedures the tests entail, how to interpret results, and what further studies or diagnoses may be recommended as a result of these tests.

Electroencephalography

What is an electroencephalogram?

An electroencephalogram (EEG) is a test used to measure the electrical activity of the brain. It is a non-invasive test that requires usually about 20 metal electrodes to be placed on the scalp using special glue or paste. The electrodes are connected via wires to a recording device that may be hooked directly to a computer or may send signals wirelessly to a computer that records and displays the data. Often, initial EEGs are performed in an outpatient setting. Most EEGs are recorded for 20–30 minutes, with additional time needed to place the electrodes and then remove them afterward. Prolonged EEGs can last from 24 to 72 hours and may be performed in a hospital or in your home. Dense-array EEG is a method of performing EEGs that uses a specialized net or cap with either 128 or 256 electrodes embedded directly in the net. There are no gels or glues involved, and the net is simply placed on the child's head. This technology is not as widely available as conventional EEG.

Why would an EEG be ordered?

An EEG may be ordered by a doctor to differentiate between normal and abnormal brain activity, in particular to identify activity patterns associated with seizures. Seizures are more common in children with an ASD than in the general population, with up to 30% of children with an ASD diagnosed with epilepsy. Risks for seizures depend to some degree on the characteristics of the child, such as sex, intelligence, and associated known disorders. A person may be diagnosed with epilepsy if they have had at least two clinical seizures. Children with ASDs who also have intellectual disabilities or cerebral palsy are at increased risk for developing epilepsy,[1] as are children with loss of milestones.[2] Any child with an ASD who has an event that may be a seizure should have an EEG. These events may occur while awake or asleep and can look like staring episodes, unresponsiveness, shaking of all limbs, or repetitive purposeless movements.[2] Many children with an ASD have stereotyped behaviors that can mimic seizures, but any concern for a seizure warrants performing an EEG. In addition, an EEG may be performed in any child with an ASD who initially had language skills but then lost them.[3] There are other disorders, such as Landau–Kleffner syndrome, that have features similar to those of ASDs but present with a loss of previously attained language milestones that begins after 3 years of age. This disorder has characteristic findings on EEG during sleep and can be diagnosed with the help of an EEG.[4] Many have argued that every child with an ASD should have an EEG as part of their routine workup, regardless of whether they have had a clinical seizure,[4] though there is no solid evidence to support this.[5] (See Chapter 2 for more information on epilepsy.)

What to expect if your child has an EEG

If your child is having a conventional EEG, electrodes are placed on the scalp to measure electrical brain activity. The scalp is lightly scraped with alcohol pads, and the electrodes are attached using special glue or gel. Gauze is often wrapped around the head to keep the electrodes in place. These outpatient EEGs are generally performed as a screening measure and only record 20–30 minutes of information. If additional information is required, your physician may recommend a prolonged EEG that can last between 24 and 72 hours. These EEGs are often performed in the hospital, requiring overnight stay and monitoring with a video camera to try to record the suspicious episodes. Sometimes the electrodes (leads) can be placed in an outpatient setting and the child can be recorded at home. This is often a more viable option if video recording is not necessary. Most children can tolerate application of the EEG leads with distraction, such as a favorite video. Some children with ASDs become agitated and upset by the unfamiliar sensation and require sedation in order to apply the leads. For these children, short outpatient recordings may not be an option, as the child should be monitored in an inpatient setting while sedated. Some children find the leads itchy; diphenhydramine is often given to alleviate this itching. For centers that offer dense-array EEG, this is often preferred over conventional EEG. The leads are embedded in a cap that takes only a few minutes to apply and requires no gel or glue. Children tend to tolerate this well and generally do not require any sedation.

How to interpret results

In some studies, up to 60% of children with an ASD, but without any clinical evidence of seizures, were found to have abnormal patterns on EEG, particularly during sleep,[2,3] making interpretation quite difficult. These findings may consist of abnormal spikes of electrical activity that can occur at various times and over various brain regions, called epileptiform discharges or epileptiform activity, and do not represent clear seizure activity. Slowing or asymmetry of the usual brain activity may be seen as well.[2] These EEG abnormalities are more commonly observed in children who experience the loss of previously mastered skills but may be observed in children with an ASD even in the absence of developmental regression.[3] It can be difficult to interpret abnormal EEG findings in a child who has no clinical seizures. These findings probably do not reflect a predisposition to seizures but may be a measure of abnormalities in brain activity related to the ASD itself.

The next step if the EEG is abnormal

If clear seizures are seen on an EEG in a child with episodes suspicious for seizures, a neurologist or epileptologist will likely recommend starting an anti-epileptic medication to control the seizures. The choice of which particular medication to start depends on the type of seizure as well as any other medical problems the child may have. In children without obvious seizures, however, the decision of whether or not to treat the abnormal EEG is less clear. Some physicians who treat children with ASDs feel that abnormal patterns on EEG, though not causing seizures, may have an adverse effect on the child's language or behavior. They theorize that treating these epileptiform discharges will help improve behavior and language development. There are several published case studies that report such improvement, but these results have not been demonstrated consistently.[2] As of this writing, there have been no carefully done studies that support using anti-epileptic drugs in the absence of seizures. The general practice is therefore not to start medication unless a child has seizures, but this may change as further research is performed.[2]

Imaging studies

Imaging studies that may be ordered and their risks and benefits

Several different technologies exist for imaging the structure of the brain. The most common technologies used in clinical medicine are computerized tomography (CT) and magnetic resonance imaging (MRI). Both technologies involve the child lying on a cotlike platform that slides through the opening of a donut-shaped machine, which gathers the information used by computers to compile images. CT is a much faster process, with a typical CT scan of the brain taking only about 2 minutes, and provides good-quality images of the bones, overall structure of the brain, and whether there is bleeding or excess pressure in the brain. It is therefore usually the imaging method of choice in the emergency department when rapid assessments are necessary, as when trauma is suspected. MRI scans, on the other hand, can take 20–45 minutes to complete a single study and can be more difficult to schedule due to equipment availability and whether there is a need for sedation to enable the patient to lie still for an extended period of time. Unlike CT scans, however, MRI scans do not use radiation to obtain images and instead operate with specialized powerful magnets. MRI provides far better resolution of brain structures, resulting in high-quality images of brain matter that are far more detailed than those of CT. In imaging of children with ASDs, MRI is a significantly more valuable test and more likely to provide useful information.

Positron emission tomography and functional MRI are methods of imaging the brain that can provide information about brain *function*, as opposed to merely brain structure. These studies capture images of the brain while a child is performing a specific task, such as reading a series of words projected on a screen. These studies are used primarily in research settings with scientists trying to pinpoint regional brain differences in how children with ASDs process and use information as compared with typical children.

Why an imaging study may be ordered

Many ongoing research studies involve obtaining images of the brain, often using MRI, to try to identify a structural abnormality that may be responsible for autism. Though studies have published various results showing individual brain areas to be affected in ASDs,[6,7] it is not clear whether these findings have any direct clinical relevance. The vast majority of children with ASDs have completely normal brain MRIs,[4] and imaging results play no role in making the diagnosis or determining the management of an ASD. At present, brain imaging is not part of the routine assessment of a child with an ASD. If a child has localized abnormalities on EEG or localized neurologic deficits, an imaging test may be recommended to look for structural problems that may cause these findings and perhaps be related to the ASD symptoms. Large head size alone in a child with an ASD may not require imaging, as this finding is common in the disorder.[5]

What to expect if your child is having brain imaging

If your child does require brain imaging, it will likely be performed in either a hospital or in a specialized imaging facility. Many children with an ASD have difficulty staying perfectly still during the scan, which is necessary for good-quality images. Some children are frightened or anxious when they slide into the CT or MRI scanner, and some have difficulty tolerating the loud noises emitted by the MRI machine during the study. If brain imaging is required, your physician may recommend sedation to ensure the results are of good quality. This is usually done as an outpatient in a hospital setting with some time for observation afterward, but the child does not typically require admission to the hospital.

How to interpret results

Minor variations in brain anatomy and size are common in children with or without an ASD and generally require no special follow-up. To date, no studies have found a direct correlation between specific brain abnormalities and specific behaviors or symptoms of autism. Most of the abnormalities found on MRI require no specific intervention or treatment.

The next step if the imaging is abnormal

If an abnormality is found on brain imaging, the next step depends on the nature of the abnormality. Most variations are benign and of no medical consequence and therefore require no special follow-up. Sometimes repeat imaging is recommended within months or a year to monitor for signs of change or worsening. In very rare instances, a structural problem is found that requires surgical intervention, and the child is referred to an appropriate pediatric neurosurgeon.

Sleep studies

What is a sleep study?

Sleep studies are designed to measure characteristics of sleep and sleep patterns. The simplest sleep study consists of actigraphy. Actigraphy is a non-invasive, home-based study in which the child wears a device shaped similar to a wristwatch. The device can be worn for multiple days at a time and records different levels of movement. This, in turn, provides information about time spent asleep and awake.[8] If more information is required, official polysomnography may be recommended. These studies are typically performed at specialized sleep centers and require an overnight stay. In polysomnography, monitors record brain activity, eye movement, breathing patterns, heart rate, and muscle activity. When these data are combined, they can provide a good picture of the child's sleep patterns.

Why a sleep study may be ordered

Sleep disturbances are very common in children with ASDs and may occur in as many as 83% of these children,[9] starting as early as 2 years of age[5] or even in infancy. The high incidence of sleep problems in children with ASDs may be related to abnormalities in GABA and melatonin, two natural chemicals in the brain that help regulate sleep and which appear to be affected in ASDs.[9] Several other conditions that are more common in children with ASDs, such as anxiety and reflux, can affect sleep as well. The sleep problems seen in children with ASDs can include difficulty falling asleep, waking during the night or very early in the morning, disruption of breathing patterns during sleep, and talking or moving abnormally during sleep. Problems with sleep can have a profound impact on a child's behavior during the day, resulting in hyperactivity, disruptive behavior, and difficulties with social skills.[9] In addition, all members of a family are affected when a child has disordered sleep, as the child may interrupt the sleep of caregivers and siblings during the night. Since sleep is such a common problem in children with ASDs, many physicians provide a screening questionnaire to parents of these children to look for sleep difficulties. If sleep disruptions are suggested by a questionnaire or by a family member's concerns, a sleep study may be recommended to clarify the nature of the sleep problem and look for underlying abnormalities. Sleep studies are not necessary if the child's sleep problems are exclusively due to difficulty in falling asleep or maintaining sleep. Some children with ASDs have sudden night awakening and crying that are suspicious for parasomnia or seizures. Parasomnia refers to sleep walking, sleep terror, confusional arousal (in which a child appears to be awake, yet the brainwaves show a state of sleep), nightmares, or acting out of a dream. All of these types of parasomnia have been reported in ASDs.[10] Polysomnography may be necessary when a doctor cannot clearly differentiate a parasomnia from a seizure.

What to expect if your child has a sleep study

Actigraphy can be easily performed at home. The actigraph is usually placed on a wrist, and the child continues his or her regular activities at home while the actigraph is recording. Some children with an ASD may dislike having the actigraph around their wrist, but it is generally well tolerated. Polysomnograpy is usually conducted at specialized sleep centers and requires an overnight stay. Most centers are arranged to look like comfortable hotel rooms. Wire leads are placed on the scalp to measure brainwaves, on the face to measure eye activity, and around the nose, the chest, and the abdomen to measure breathing. A paper electrode is placed on the shin of leg and an oxygen detector on a finger. Bringing a favorite toy or book can help your child tolerate setting up the leads and spending a night away from home in a sleep center. A parent or guardian is required to stay with the child in the same room, but in a different bed, during the sleep study.

How to interpret results

Both actigraphy and polysomnography can provide information about the amount of time a child spends asleep and how often he or she wakes up at night. Taking a long time to fall asleep and multiple nighttime awakenings suggests insomnia; however, polysomnography is not routinely performed for insomnia only. Polysomnography can also look for signs of parasomnia or sleep apnea, in which a child can stop breathing for brief periods of time. The results of the sleep study can help you and your doctor tailor treatment to address the particular sleep problem and determine whether a child needs to be referred to specialists such as a neurologist or pulmonologist.

The next step if a sleep study is abnormal

Insomnia is the most common sleep problem reported in children with an ASD. As in the general population, insomnia has a very strong behavioral component, and behavioral methods are often tried first in managing insomnia. You can work with your child's doctor to establish a bedtime routine that allows your child to develop self-calming techniques. These behavioral techniques can help greatly in reducing the amount of time it takes your child to fall asleep.[3] If this alone is not effective, melatonin may be recommended. Melatonin is a naturally present hormone that helps regulate our innate sleep/wake cycle and can help induce sleep when taken before bedtime.[5] If this is still not effective, your child's doctor may recommend other medications to help induce sleep. Sleep problems may be found to be a result of another medical problem, such as seizures, anxiety, or gastroesophageal reflux. In those cases, treating the underlying cause often helps with sleep, as well. Some medications used to treat seizures or anxiety can causes sleepiness, so the choice of medication can be made with both problems in mind. (For more information on treatment, see Chapter 8 on traditional treatment and Chapter 9 on complementary and alternative medicine.)

Occasionally, very specific sleep problems are found during a sleep study, such as deficits in restorative rapid eye movement sleep, frequent movements, or obstructive sleep apnea causing breathing problems during sleep.[9] Medications, such as clonazepam, may be recommended if your child is found to have abnormal movements during sleep that are frequent and disruptive, including sleepwalking or shaking of a limb. A child who is found to walk in his or her sleep may need safety measures, including locks or alarms on the bedroom door. Disordered breathing during sleep may trigger a referral to an ear, nose, and throat specialist to assess whether removing your child's tonsils and adenoids may be advisable, or whether assistance is needed with breathing at night, such as with a continuous positive airway pressure machine that blows in air using a facemask during sleep. Your child may be referred to an allergist to treat congestion related to allergies if this appears to be impacting his or her sleep.

Endoscopy and colonoscopy

What are endoscopy and colonoscopy?

Endoscopy and colonoscopy are procedures that allow physicians to directly examine the gastrointestinal system. In endoscopy, a thin, flexible tube with a light and video camera on the end is inserted into a patient's mouth. The tube is then passed into the esophagus, the stomach, and the initial segment of the small intestine to get direct visualization of these organs. Specialized instruments can be passed through the endoscope, as well, to allow biopsies to be taken from tissue inside the intestinal system. In colonoscopy, the same type of instrument is passed through the rectum and into the large intestine to visualize and biopsy the large intestine (if necessary).

Why endoscopy or colonoscopy may be ordered

Chronic gastrointestinal symptoms, including abdominal pain, diarrhea, reflux, bloating, and constipation, are common in children with an ASD; however, because these symptoms are common in all children, it remains controversial as to whether they are more common in children with an ASD.[3,11] Many children with an ASD show feeding preferences, refusing to eat certain foods or only eating a limited variety of foods. This can be a result of reflux or food intolerances and can lead to constipation or vitamin deficiencies, though this is rare.[5] Gastrointestinal symptoms in children with an ASD can be vague and difficult to characterize, particularly in children who have limited communication abilities. Many children with an ASD cannot fully explain their symptoms, so endoscopy or colonoscopy may be necessary to rule out serious gastrointestinal problems.

What to expect if your child has endoscopy or colonoscopy

Before a colonoscopy, your child's doctor may prescribe a laxative to help empty the colon of stool, which can interfere with the study. Your child may temporarily have larger or more frequent loose or even watery bowel movements because of the laxative. Children should not eat after midnight on the night before the procedure in preparation for sedation and to enable the doctor to see the gut without food getting in the way, so they are usually scheduled for early morning appointments. Both of these tests are typically performed by gastroenterologists in special procedure suites within hospitals. Children are sedated with intravenous medication for the procedure, though medication given through a facemask can be given first so that the child is already asleep when the IV is placed. After the procedure, children are monitored in a recovery area until the sedation wears off, which can take a few hours. The sleepiness and mild confusion that may remain after sedation can last up to a full day. Children sometimes experience a mild sore throat due to the placement of the endoscope. This can be treated with acetaminophen or other mild pain medications and typically resolves in about a day. After colonoscopy, your child may experience abdominal bloating or flatulence over the next day, which then resolves.

How to interpret results

Endoscopy may show inflammation in the esophagus, which can be a sign of gastroesophageal reflux disease. Ulcers may be noted in the stomach or first part of the small intestine. Biopsy results can indicate inflammatory diseases of the esophagus or stomach and can diagnose celiac disease, which results from sensitivity to gluten in foods. Colonoscopy and biopsy may detect inflammation in the colon, which may explain some of the bowel problems seen in ASDs.

The next step if endoscopy or colonoscopy are abnormal

The gastrointestinal symptoms seen in children with ASDs are common in all children and are usually benign and resolve with no intervention. Children with ASDs are particularly prone to food selectivity, which can be extremely restricting and can itself cause gastrointestinal problems such as constipation.[11] Depending on the findings of these tests, specific treatments may be recommended. This can include dietary changes and medication for gastroesophageal reflux or ulcers. Biopsy results can help diagnose celiac disease, eosinophilic esophagitis, or colitis, rare disorders that require dietary modification and treatment by a gastroenterologist.

Lab tests

Typical blood and urine tests

As mentioned above, there is no lab test that can diagnose an ASD. Lab tests, including tests of blood and urine, can help diagnose conditions that may be present in children with an ASD and conditions that may look similar to ASDs. Genetic tests are described in Chapter 7. Some of the blood tests commonly ordered are a complete blood count (CBC), which looks at the number of different kinds of blood cells in the body; basic metabolic panel to look at levels of important electrolytes in the blood; and levels of trace metals, vitamins, and hormones (particularly thyroid hormones). Urine tests may be performed to look for specific proteins, and stool tests may be ordered to look for infection or signs of problems with digestion.

Why lab tests may be ordered

The CBC is a basic blood test that is performed on nearly all young children as a screening tool. A CBC measures the levels of specific blood cells and can detect anemia, signs of infection, and decreases in platelets that may cause problems clotting blood. Anemia can lead to learning and behavior problems, so all children with a suspected ASD should have a CBC to rule out anemia. In addition, some medications used in ASDs to help with behavior can affect blood counts, so a CBC should be checked before starting these medications in order to establish a baseline for comparison, and then checked periodically afterward.[4] Some studies have suggested that there may be an increase in incidence of mitochondrial disorders in children with an ASD.[12] (This is discussed in more detail in Chapter 7.) Basic metabolic testing can serve as a screening tool for some mitochondrial and metabolic disorders by looking at levels of bicarbonate, sodium, or liver enzymes that may be affected. Some other lab tests used to detect mitochondrial dysfunction look at the levels of lactate, pyruvate, carnitine, and ammonia in the blood. Your child's doctor may request these tests if your child has features that suggest a metabolic disorder, such as poor growth, lethargy, and differences in facial features.

Children with an ASD may also have pica, a tendency to eat non-food substances such as paint chips or soil. Children with pica should have screening for lead levels, as lead may be ingested with the foreign substances. Iron and zinc should be checked as well, as these can be low in individuals with pica and may present as developmental delays.[5] Other metals, such as copper, can be checked if there is a history suggestive of toxic exposure. Vitamin deficiencies, including B12 and folic acid, can sometimes present with developmental delay, so these should be checked, too. Amino acid levels can be checked and may suggest a metabolic disorder if abnormal. Common metabolic disorders, such as phenylketonuria (PKU), are tested on routine newborn screening and typically do not need to be checked again.

Some hormonal deficiencies may cause developmental delay, particularly thyroid problems. This is checked through newborn screening to detect any problems present at birth, but it may need to be rechecked later in childhood if other signs suggest a thyroid problem or if a child's mother has a thyroid problem.[4] Researchers are increasingly studying the role of inflammation and the immune system in ASDs. Very specialized immune tests can be performed, but they should only be ordered if there are particular concerns for an immune dysfunction, such as frequent or unusual infections. These tests are usually ordered by immunologists who are trained to interpret results that can be ambiguous.

Urine tests for amino acids may be performed in select children if there is suspicion for a metabolic process that would affect how the body processes proteins. Similarly, stool studies are useful to look for signs of parasite infections or nutrient malabsorption in select children, but these studies may not be a useful screening tool in the evaluation of an ASD without a gastrointestinal disorder.

What to expect if your child has lab tests

Lab tests may be performed in your doctor's office or in a lab collection center. If getting blood drawn at a lab collection center, it is helpful to make an appointment and call ahead to ensure they have a nurse or phlebotomist available who is experienced in drawing blood from children. Some metabolic tests are valid only when drawn early in the day or before your child eats, so you should get this information from your doctor when arranging blood tests. Blood drawing for children, especially children with an ASD, can be challenging. Anxiety or fear tends to be the problem in most of the children who experience difficulty. Preparing your child psychologically ahead of time may be helpful for some children with ASDs.

How to interpret results

Interpreting blood test results can be tricky, because many healthy children could have minor variations in lab values. It is the pattern of abnormalities that is often more important than any single number; certain patterns may suggest an underlying genetic or metabolic disorder. Specialized blood tests, such as metabolic or genetic testing, should be interpreted by physicians experienced with those tests.

The next step if lab tests are abnormal

If lab tests are abnormal, the first step is often to repeat the test to ensure that results are not spurious. If anemia is present, iron supplements can be given. Vitamins can be used to treat vitamin deficiency, and medications that decrease blood counts can be stopped if this problem is detected. Mitochondrial disorders have no curative treatment, but symptoms (mitochondrial dysfunction) may improve with certain supplements such as carnitine, coenzyme Q, and B vitamins. Children with an immune deficiency should be referred to an immunologist for specialized management, and hormone deficiencies should be treated by an endocrinologist.

Audiology testing

What is audiology testing?

Audiology testing includes several different methods for testing hearing ability. All infants born in the United States have their hearing tested before they are discharged from the nursery after birth. Even if a child passed his or her newborn screening exam, however, he or she should be tested again if new concerns arise about the child's ability to hear. A screening test is usually performed first, most commonly the pure-tone test in which sounds are played through headphones or speakers and the child raises a hand or claps to indicate that the tone was heard. For infants or children who cannot participate in pure-tone testing, auditory brainstem response testing may be used. Several electrodes are pasted to the head, as in EEG, and tones are played in the ears. A characteristic brain activity can be seen in response to tones that are heard, and the child does not have to voluntarily respond. Children can be asleep during this test or resting quietly. If a deficit is found, more detailed audiology testing may be necessary in order to clarify the exact nature and extent of the hearing problem.

Why audiology testing may be ordered

All children with a language delay should have their hearing assessed, even if the newborn screening test was normal. Similarly, all toddlers newly diagnosed with an ASD should have their hearing tested. Hearing deficits can significantly affect language development, as children learn language by imitating what they hear. Hearing deficits can also cause behavior problems, as the child uses his or her behavior as a form of communication and to express frustration.

What to expect if your child has audiology testing

Standard audiology screening consists of raising a hand in response to a sound through headphones, as described above. Many children with an ASD cannot tolerate headphones and must have the tones presented via speakers. This kind of testing can miss hearing loss that is present in only one ear. The American Speech-Language-Hearing Association (www.asha.org) provides a number of helpful suggestions for testing the hearing of children with an ASD. For example, pure-tone testing can be performed by rewarding the child with something he or she enjoys each time he or she completes a round of testing. Practicing the task can help a child with an ASD understand what is being asked in the test and can ease the anxiety associated with this new experience. If your child is referred for hearing testing, call the audiologists first to find one who is experienced in testing children with ASDs. Even with these special methods, it may be difficult for children with an ASD to cooperate with the task or even understand what is required of them. The auditory brainstem response test can be used instead, as it is not dependent on a child's cooperation; however, some children with an ASD have difficulty tolerating the electrode placement for this test, as well, and require sedation.

How to interpret results

The results of an audiology screening test are usually reported as a simple pass or fail notation for each ear. Any child who fails a screening test needs more detailed testing, using the same testing methods but testing a variety of tones and loudness levels. Any hearing loss is charted on a graph called an audiogram that displays the frequency, or pitch, of the sounds heard along with the intensity, or loudness, which is measured in decibels. Ordinary conversation is usually at the 60-decibel level and consists of frequencies between 400 and 5000 Hz. A child who has hearing loss in that frequency range is likely to have difficulty understanding speech.

The next step if audiology testing is abnormal

If audiology evaluation is abnormal, your pediatrician and audiologist will recommend different options for your child. These options may include hearing aids, assistive technologies, such as specialized microphones used by teachers, cochlear implants, American Sign Language instruction, and hearing rehabilitation. Your doctor may also want to reassess your child after his or her hearing deficit is addressed appropriately and possibly revisit the ASD diagnosis.

TAKEAWAY POINTS

- There are many conditions that may accompany an ASD and may require specialized testing.

- Special considerations and challenges are present when obtaining tests in a child with an ASD.

- Parents can help ensure that a test will be successful by adequately preparing their child and bringing along items the child will find comforting, such as a favorite toy or video.

- Interpretation of the results of some of these tests can be unclear.

- You and your child's doctor should discuss the results and the appropriate next steps after performing any test.

Chapter 12

The Medical Home for Individuals with Autism Spectrum Disorders

Jennifer Bain, MD, PhD

Introduction

The family of a child with an autism spectrum disorder (ASD) will undoubtedly encounter a number of clinicians over the years to achieve a healthy, successful quality of life for their child. Parents will arrange for many visits with these specialists throughout the years and may struggle to keep all of these medical professionals up to speed with their child's specific needs. The many resources available to children with special needs should not be overwhelming, and with a little help and planning, care for a child with an ASD can be coordinated. The goal of this chapter is to delineate the team members that families may encounter during their child's health care journey. Moreover, we hope to advise parents on how the many players on the health care team can work together to become an asset, rather than serve a divisive role in their child's life.

The patient-centered medical home

The patient-centered medical home model is a team-based health care delivery system led by a primary health care provider, whether this be a physician, physician assistant, or nurse practitioner, who coordinates medical care to ensure that an individual patient receives the necessary care when and where they need it, in a manner they can understand. The American Academy of Pediatrics (AAP) was one of the forerunners in defining the concept of a medical home, initially referring to a central location for archiving a child's medical record in 1967. The AAP subsequently published a policy statement in 2002 further conceptualizing the medical home in pediatric care.[1] There have been other professional associations that have also incorporated a patient-centered medical home model into their practices, including the American Academy of Family Physicians, American College of Physicians, and the American Osteopathic Association.[2] In a patient-centered medical home model, a patient and his or her family should develop a partnership with their primary health care provider that is based on trust and mutual responsibility. Some of the key characteristics of the medical home include:

- sharing clear and unbiased information with the family about the child's medical care and management

- providing families with information about or connections to specialty and community services and organizations they can access

- assurance that a child will have access to health care 24 hours each day, 7 days a week, whether this be at a clinic or in a hospital

- smooth transitions and coordination of care between health care providers

- identification of the need for consultation and providing appropriate referral to pediatric medical subspecialists or surgical specialists.

These basic principles are just some of the important functions carried out in the medical home. Theoretically, the medical home should strengthen patient care and streamline health care resources; however, recent studies have shown that this model has encountered obstacles in a number of circumstances. Notably, children with an ASD, depression, anxiety, or behavior or conduct problems have been less likely to receive care in true medical homes compared with children without these conditions.[3] Analysis of this study suggests that families coping with these diagnoses require more subspecialty care and, as a result, their needs are less likely to be met, making coordinated subspecialty care a major barrier in the medical home model. Similarly, a retrospective study found that the majority of children with ASDs who were evaluated by a pediatric neurologist came to care through parent-initiated referrals and not through their primary care provider.[4] With this knowledge, it is important for those parents and caregivers reading this book to recognize potential barriers and have an open discussion regarding subspecialist involvement with their primary care provider (PCP).

An individual's medical home is not a small circle but instead should—and does—extend into other aspects of day-to-day life. For example, a large portion of a child's everyday life is spent in educational activities, whether this be in daycare, school, after-school, or other educational environments. The school system has undoubtedly become one of the mainstays in providing opportunities to advance developmental, social, and cognitive skills for a child with an ASD. There is an inherent need for the medical home to be in contact with the educational providers for your child. (An in-depth discussion of this topic is provided in Chapters 12 and 13, which highlight information on working with outside providers, most notably within the educational system.)

Medical home providers

There are many trained specialists that may be involved with your child's care within and outside of the medical home over the years. First, let's discuss the many potential providers that may be involved with your family. Then, we will present recommendations on how to best utilize your relationships with these providers to facilitate optimal health and developmental outcomes for your child. Bear in mind that some clinicians will play a more transient role, while others may be involved for several years or more in caring for your child. In this section, a brief description of each of these clinicians is provided, as well as the typical training program each of these individuals has completed.

One of the earliest clinicians who plays a role in your child's health care is the general pediatrician or family practitioner. This individual has likely been involved with caring for your child since birth or a very young age and therefore plays a major role in the medical home for your child. General pediatricians and family practitioners typically spend 4 years in medical or osteopathic school. Basic science studies and extensive clinical experience are the foundation for both medical and osteopathic training programs. Both MDs and DOs can legally and professionally practice medicine, prescribe medications, and perform surgery. Medical physicians are typically described as "allopathic," as opposed to osteopaths who are more "holistic" or "homeopathic." While medical school has been the traditional model for training physicians in the United States, an osteopathic training program provides more emphasis on complementary and alterative therapeutics for the mind–body–spirit. For example, osteopaths are specially trained in manipulation of the muscles and skeleton of the body, similar to massage therapy. Regardless of graduate training program, after completing either training period (typically over 4 years), the individual receives a doctorate degree in medicine (MD) or osteopathic medicine (DO).

Medical or osteopathic school is followed by specialized training called a residency program. Residency is a postgraduate training program that specializes in a certain field, such as general pediatrics or family practice. A general pediatric residency program is typically 3 years and trains an individual extensively in all areas of pediatrics, from neonatology (caring for newborns and premature infants), to adolescent medicine, to emergency pediatrics, and exposes them to a spectrum of pediatric medical subspecialties. On the other hand, family practitioners, also known as family doctors, typically are trained over 3–4 years to gain more diverse knowledge about comprehensive health care from childhood through adulthood, including gynecologic and obstetric services. The oversight of many of these residency training programs is by a board of experts in that area, and upon completion of such a program, an individual can achieve the prestige of being "board certified" in that specialty after passing a rigorous exam.

Alternative providers, such as physician assistants (PAs) and nurse practitioners (NPs), are also playing a larger role in primary care. To become a PA, an individual must earn a bachelor's degree and then complete a 2- or 3-year graduate program leading to the award of a master's degree or higher. Professional licensure is regulated by the medical boards of the individual states, and these providers are usually required to work under the supervision of a physician.

An NP, also referred to as an advanced practice registered nurse (APN or APRN), is trained in the field of nursing. He or she receives a bachelor's degree and then continues graduate education and obtains a master's degree. Similar to PAs, APNs are licensed by individual states, and in certain states they may not be required to have MD or DO oversight. For each of these primary care providers, MDs, DOs, PAs, and APNs, there are specific requirements to be licensed to practice and, after initial certification, requirements for continuing education programs to keep them abreast of new knowledge and advancements in their respective fields.

Whereas the abovementioned health care providers typically play a more central role in your child's medical home, there are many other providers, such as specialists, that may participate as well. In certain circumstances, the specialists described below may actually take on the major role in overseeing or coordinating the medical home. Importantly, a child with an ASD is an individual, with different needs and resource requirements critical to their health care, and thus under some circumstances a certain specialist may become the key player over a PCP in a child's medical home.

A number of pediatric specialists, including developmental pediatricians, neurodevelopmental pediatricians, pediatric neurologists, and psychiatrists, have emerged as frequent point-of-care providers for children with an ASD. Each of these specialists have been expertly trained to treat the child with an ASD; however, they have different training experiences. Some confusion often arises when parents ask, "What experts should I bring my child to?" Despite decades of intense research, health care professionals have yet to clearly elucidate the entire autism spectrum with all of the subsets of patients and underlying causes. As a result of the uncertainty and variable presentations, there have been several groups of experts that have studied and cared for children with ASDs over the years. Each of these groups has developed their own special relationship with the diagnosis and its implications, and each may offer a different perspective on the care of an individual with an ASD. Given their diversity of training, each group may bring different views on the etiology, diagnosis, and management of your child with an ASD. The decision about which provider to call on to evaluate your child with an ASD is best done on a case-by-case basis depending on what specialists are available to patients in your area, who has the most expertise in working with children with ASDs, and which providers are a good "fit" for the entire family. Below we provide the basic training track for each of these specialists.

A general pediatrician may continue their training after the initial residency with 2 or 3 years of fellowship training that focuses on a narrow area of expertise. For example, a developmental pediatrician is specially trained in typical and atypical development of a child. Developmental pediatricians are often essential in differentiating developmental delay from behavioral disorders. Given that the etiology and pathology of ASDs have not been clearly elucidated, these specialists have played a major role in evaluating children with concerns for possible ASD. Similarly, doctors may be trained in specialized neurobehavioral or neurodevelopmental programs with emphasis on the neurologic aspects of development and behavior. These professionals may also be evaluating your child at some point in their care.

Many children with an ASD are also evaluated by a pediatric neurologist (also known as child neurologist) at some point in their medical journey. This specialist is trained primarily in the field of neurology with special emphasis on pediatric neurology. There are several tracks of study that can bring this individual to be trained under this umbrella. The traditional training includes 2–3 years of pediatric training followed by 3 years of neurology training in both adult and pediatric neurology. This specialist is often board certified in both neurology and pediatrics and may have additional subspecialty training in areas such as epilepsy, headache, or neuromuscular disorders. While every child with an ASD may not be evaluated by a pediatric neurologist, parents should be aware that all physicians are trained to perform complete general neurologic exams and will likely incorporate these exam findings in their evaluation of the child.

A large proportion of children with an ASD also have a mental health disorder such as anxiety, depression, problems with aggression, and/or attention deficit hyperactivity disorder. These children often benefit from the expertise of psychiatrists and psychologists. Psychiatrists are MDs that have approximately 1 year of general medicine residency followed by 3 years of psychiatry training beyond medical school. Many psychiatrists also continue their training with a fellowship in child psychiatry. A psychologist, on the other hand, has a doctorate of philosophy (PhD) or doctorate of psychology (PsychD). In a similar fashion, a PhD may attain more extensive training in child psychology as well. These specialists may play some role in your child's medical home depending on the child's individual needs.

With the many scientific advances, such as in genome sequencing and microarray technology, your child may encounter a geneticist during his or her medical care. A geneticist typically has a doctorate degree in either medicine (MD) or in philosophy (PhD) with specialized training in genetics. Medical geneticists are MDs or DOs who receive residency training in a general field of medicine such as pediatrics, internal medicine, or obstetrics and gynecology, followed by 2 or 3 years of fellowship training in medical genetics.

Coury *et al.* highlighted the high prevalence of gastrointestinal (GI) problems, including constipation, diarrhea, and abdominal pain, in children with ASDs.[5] A child with an ASD who has GI symptoms may be referred for an evaluation by a gastroenterologist. The training to become a gastroenterologist typically involves 3 years of medicine or pediatric residency followed by an additional 3 years of specialty training in gastroenterology.

Another specialist that your child may encounter is an allergist and/or immunologist. For reasons unknown at this time, some children with an ASD have alterations in their immune system or may have allergies to foods or environmental substances. In some situations, allergies may make behavioral symptoms worse for children with ASDs. If your child has signs of an immune problem or allergies, he or she may be referred to an allergist/immunologist. This MD completes a residency in internal medicine or general pediatrics, followed by another 3 years of fellowship training in allergy and immunology. This specialist is trained to treat both children and adults.

Although children and adults with an ASD may be cared for by a general or pediatric dentist, individuals with an ASD may benefit from referral to a special care dentist. These practitioners are general dentists who have expanded training in providing dental treatment to patients of all ages and with a variety of special needs, including ASDs. In some cases they treat medically and behaviorally complex patients in a hospital setting to decrease risks for complications and for the comfort of the anxious or uncooperative patient.

Some non-physician providers may include speech, occupational, or physical therapists, nutritionists or dieticians, and even holistic or complementary and alternative medicine specialists. These providers have specialized training in their own fields, which may offer your child certain resources not directly available through your medical providers. It is imperative for a parent to inform their PCP of all professionals that are providing services to their child so that they be aware of all interventions, medications, and therapies in place. This is the foundation of the medical home, and enables the head of the medical home and other providers to know everything about the child's care in and outside of the medical setting.

Aside from the abovementioned providers and specialists who have completed specific training requirements, parents may encounter other "self-proclaimed autism specialists" that have not been formally trained through standardized programs. Parents should be wary of these individuals who may recommend unrecognized or unproven treatments that lack any scientific basis or solid medical evidence to support their use. There are many complementary and/or alternative medicine experts that parents may encounter in caring for their child. In this book we provide some of the scientific evidence in support of some alternative or holistic management of children with ASDs. Most importantly, it is crucial for parents and caregivers to inform their primary providers of the involvement of other non-traditional providers in the medical care of their son or daughter.

The parent's role in the medical home

As discussed earlier, any of the abovementioned providers should be incorporated into your child's medical home when appropriate. Parents or caregivers can play a major role in shaping this medical home and should feel empowered to do so if they feel they can; this is most appropriate for the majority of pediatric patients. Parents and caregivers are encouraged to ask each of these providers where they trained and whether they are certified by their respective entities. They are encouraged to delineate *who* the major players are in the medical home and *what* will be the roles of each of these players in caring for their son or daughter. Moreover, a parent or family member should continue to remain the primary advocate for their child, asking questions and being an interactive member of the medical home, rather than becoming a passive bystander who merely abides by a provider's plan. An interactive parent should ask questions such as, "What is your assessment of my child?" or "What do you recommend to help my child, and why have you chosen these specific interventions?" or "If these interventions are unsuccessful, when will I know and how will we proceed?"

Each health care provider will have their own assessment and recommendations after evaluating your child, and a parent is likely the only person who will have direct contact with every one of these providers. A parent should use these opportunities to address concerns about conflicting reports or opinions from each of these individuals.

The medical home is an interactive environment for all participants to share ideas, discuss successes and remaining problems, and to brainstorm together about how best to proceed; however, problems can arise if parents and the coordinator of the medical home are overwhelmed by a dozen "expert opinions," especially if there is no coordination of care or interactions between providers. The PCP, such as a pediatrician or family practitioner, should be willing to discuss with the parent each of these providers' recommendations and help the parent and/or family put together a cohesive plan that incorporates all of the ideas and management strategies that make sense at any given time. Importantly, a parent may come to realize that not all expert opinions are applicable simultaneously, but these resources may be useful in the future depending on certain circumstances that may arise. While there are many resources available to individual patients with ASDs, the parents, in consultation with the leader of their child's medical home, need to identify the ones that are most appropriate for a given moment and resist the urge to access all services simultaneously. A trusting and open relationship between families and PCPs should help delineate which resources to utilize and under what circumstances. Moreover, circumstances will change and individuals will change; therefore, some flexibility and fluidity is needed because each way station along the journey may require parents and providers to embrace new ways of thinking and devise new plans in a proactive and thoughtful way. Parents and families must understand that a medical home should remain a stable foundation for a patient and his or her family, but the goals embodied by the home for the individual child or young adult may well change over time. Keeping an open mind will make transitions easier for the caregiver as well as for the child with an ASD.

Another common concern for parents is how to find the right provider for their child. The term "doctor shopping" may have a negative connotation; however, there may be some legitimacy to aspects of this practice. It is imperative that an individual build an open and trusting relationship with their health care provider. Just as every patient is different, so is every physician.

The relationship between a patient (and their family, in the case of pediatric patients) and a physician is unique. While patients or parents who "shop" for physicians who are in sync with their goals and approach to care are often criticized, it is essential that a patient develop a strong relationship with a physician that will play a major role in their medical home; therefore, contrary to the negative implications of "doctor shopping," finding the right provider for an individual should be regarded as proactive in a positive manner. Of note, there may be PCPs in your area that are more in tune with your child's specific needs. For example, some providers may have a higher proportion of patients with complex special needs and may be more comfortable interacting with multiple specialists and coordinating care. There are many ways a parent can find the "right" PCP for their child, and it is clearly an individual decision. Finding a physician who is a good fit for your child may require talking with other parents of children with ASDs or even asking the specialists themselves which pediatricians they have had good relationships with in coordinating care. Parents may also speak with advocacy groups in their area or seek online reviews of PCPs that may be more appropriate. A parent is encouraged to ask PCPs directly if they feel comfortable caring for their child who will undoubtedly have a number of specialists with whom they will coordinate care. If the PCP does not feel confident in this role, or a parent feels the PCP has not been able to adequately provide care for their child, they should not feel obligated to continue their care with that PCP. In this instance, finding the right PCP may necessitate a change in PCPs.

What are the responsibilities of the caregiver in the medical home model? While the parent or caregiver may not carry around a detailed file outlining their child's entire past medical history or medical reports, there are some things that a parent may provide to new participants in their child's health care journey that are especially helpful. For example, it is very important for a parent or caregiver to have a list of all medications, including dosages, to provide to other health care providers, both during scheduled visits and unanticipated emergency or hospital visits. It may also be important to keep a record of other key providers' contact information, for example the pediatrician and other physician specialists that are core members of a child's health care team. This information will be useful for coordination of care between these specialists. Some parents find it useful to keep a home health file on all family members, including their child with an ASD, which may include summary reports from the school and Child Study Team, therapists' evaluations, results of cognitive testing, results of blood tests or radiology studies (such as MRIs or sonograms), and reports from specialists. When seeking advice from a medical subspecialist or other provider, it is especially important to request that a summary of the visit be sent if at all possible to the coordinator of the child's medical home as well as the parents.

We fully support and encourage parents to be proactive about medical care for their child, and consequently it is in your child's best interest for *all* treatments to be discussed with the child's medical providers. As previously discussed, the Internet and many self-proclaimed autism experts may offer parents provocative, novel, and "successful" treatment options to "cure" autism. These regimens may seem promising for families who are naturally anxious to help their children; however, parents must be aware that many of these alternative treatments may not be scientifically proven to be effective or—more importantly—to be *safe*. We highly encourage discussing treatment plans with doctors *before* initiating any treatments for your child.

Altogether, the medical home for a child with an ASD should provide the entire family with a support structure for years to come. While there will likely be many health care providers your child will encounter over time, this model can help streamline these resources and ensure that they are utilized in the most appropriate manner. There are many experts available, especially with the growing World Wide Web and advances in science, and we hope that the use of a medical home model will provide the best coordination of care for a child with an ASD.

 ## TAKEAWAY POINTS

- Children with an ASD will likely have evaluations and interactions with several health care providers over many years.

- The patient-centered medical home can provide a child with an ASD and his or her family a streamlined approach for integrating health care providers.

- A primary care provider to help manage all involved in a patient's medical home will likely be a pediatrician, family practitioner, nurse practitioner, or physician assistant. Other specialists, such as a pediatric neurologist, developmental pediatrician, or psychiatrist, may play a major role in the medical home as well.

- A child with an ASD and their family should feel comfortable and be proactive about asking potential health care providers what their training and credentials are in their area of expertise. Furthermore, the recommendations of these specialists should be openly discussed with the primary care provider to keep everyone abreast of potential action plans and interventions for the child.

Chapter 13

Working with Non-Physician Members of the Treatment Team for Individuals with Autism Spectrum Disorders

Caroline Hayes-Rosen, MD

Introduction

If your child has been diagnosed with an autism spectrum disorder (ASD), you will want to begin seeking treatment for your child. In addition to working with your pediatrician and other physician specialists (e.g., developmental pediatrician, child neurologist, child psychiatrist), you will be meeting and working with many other experts. In order to appropriately address your child's needs, a number of therapists, educators, and counselors will work with you and your child. Because so many individuals will be involved in your child's care, you will need a team approach. As the parent, it is your duty to lead the team and advocate for your child. This chapter focuses on coordinating treatment and care outside of the physician's office for your child with an ASD.

Your child's rights

The Individuals with Disabilities Education Act (IDEA) was first enacted in 1975. It was revised and renamed the Individuals with Disabilities Education Improvement Act in 2004. IDEA specifies that young children with developmental delays, or young children in danger of developing developmental delays, are eligible for early intervention services. This law mandates that the state provide all eligible children a "free and appropriate education." This education must meet each individual's specific needs. It is up to you to work with the school to determine what an "appropriate" education is for your child. IDEA legislation provides you as the parent the right to be treated as an equal partner with the school district in creating an educational plan for your child. This allows you to advocate for your child. Parents should be informed, active participants in the planning and monitoring of their child's education.

Early intervention

Early intervention is a system of coordinated services that promotes the child's age-appropriate growth and development and supports families during the critical early years. Infants and toddlers, from birth to age 3 years, with any type of developmental delay or disability can receive assistance through the early intervention program. In the United States, early intervention services are federally mandated through the IDEA. This act mandates a statewide, comprehensive, multidisciplinary service system to address the needs of infants and toddlers who are experiencing developmental delays or are diagnosed with a physical or mental condition with a high probability of an associated developmental disability in cognitive development, physical development, language and speech development, psychosocial development, and/or self-help skills. Early intervention is available in every state and territory of the United States.

Early intervention programs can provide many different types of services. Available services may include assistive technology, audiology or hearing services, behavioral therapy, speech and language services, counseling and training for families, medical services, nursing services, nutrition services, occupational therapy, physical therapy, psychological services, and educational services.

Children with developmental delays, or children who are at risk of developmental delays, are eligible for early intervention. If your young child has been diagnosed with an ASD, he or she will likely qualify for services through early intervention. Your child's pediatrician should be familiar with this program and will refer you there for services if your child has signs of developmental delays; however, *a referral from a physician is not necessary*. Parents can reach out to early intervention on behalf of their child. Once connected with the early intervention program, you will be assigned a service coordinator who will explain the early intervention process and help you through all the steps. The service coordinator will be your initial contact person.

Your child will then be evaluated by the program free of charge. Eligibility for services is determined after a comprehensive evaluation. You must provide your written consent before an evaluation can take place. The evaluation group will be made up of qualified people who have different areas of training and experience. Your child may be evaluated by a speech pathologist, physical therapist, occupational therapist, educator, and neuropsychologist. Together as a team, they know about children's speech and language skills, physical abilities, hearing and vision, and other important areas of development. As part of the evaluation, the team will observe your child, play with your child, and talk to you and your child in an effort to gather information.

Your child's development will be assessed on five domains: cognitive, physical, communication, social–emotional, and adaptive. The cognitive domain includes learning, remembering, and thinking. A child's cognitive skills are reflected in the ways in which he or she plays and solves problems. This domain is assessed by a special education evaluator. The physical domain consists of evaluation of the motor system. This includes both fine motor and gross motor skills. Gross motor skills refer to those tasks that require use of the large muscles for skills such as sitting, walking, and jumping. These skills are evaluated by a physical therapist. Fine motor skills are used for tasks that require use of smaller muscle groups, such as the muscles in the hand which allow us to pick up small items, hold a pencil, or zip a zipper. Fine motor skills are assessed by an occupational therapist. Your child's communication skills will be evaluated by a speech-language pathologist. This domain includes assessment of receptive language skills (what the child understands) and expressive language skills (how they make their needs and wants known). Communication is not always a verbal skill. The social–emotional component refers to a child's ability to interact and relate to other people including parents, friends, and other family members. Social–emotional assessment is conducted through observation and analysis of the child's interaction with his or her family, caregivers, and the evaluators. A special education evaluator assesses the social–emotional development. The adaptive domain refers to self-help skills that we use for functional daily living. Activities of daily living would include eating, drinking, brushing your teeth, and getting dressed. Both an occupational therapist and special education evaluator include the adaptive domain in their evaluations.

If a developmental problem is identified, the early intervention team will help develop an individualized family service plan (IFSP). The premise of this plan is that the family is the child's greatest resource. This plan therefore involves the family as a whole. As part of the early intervention team you will take part in developing this plan. An IFSP will describe your child's current levels of function and set goals for the treatment team to follow. It will also list the specific services he or she will receive, as well as where and how often these services will be provided. This process, from referral to IFSP, must be completed within 45 days. Parental consent is required in order for services to be instituted. Therapy at this point focuses on the child's development as a whole. The IFSP contains global goals that you and your team have decided are best for your child. It is the plan which everyone on the team references when working with your child. It should be tailored to the individual needs of your child. The IFSP will be an evolving document. Sometimes it will be necessary to make changes as goals are re-evaluated or new challenges present themselves. Any changes to the plan must be communicated to all members of the team. You, as the parent, play a crucial role in developing the IFSP and communicating with all members of the team. The IFSP is reviewed every 6 months and is updated at least once a year. This takes into account that children can learn, grow, and change quickly in just a short period of time.

All evaluations and assessments through early intervention are free of charge. In some areas services are free of charge as well. Some programs do charge fees for services based on a sliding scale depending on the family's income. All children must receive services if warranted regardless of their family's ability to pay. In some cases early intervention services may be provided and paid for through the child's health insurance. Parental consent is necessary for this option.

A child with an ASD may receive multiple services. Given the varied presentation of ASDs, you may find that you need some professionals but not others. At baseline, a child with an ASD may receive behavioral therapy, speech therapy, occupational therapy, and educational or play therapy services. If your child has additional delays, he or she may require additional services. This means that you and your child will be working with multiple therapists. Team members have specific roles in your child's therapy and each specializes in certain areas. The behavioral therapist works with your child to develop appropriate behaviors and eliminate undesirable behaviors. The therapist's approach to your child may vary depending on your child's level of function and the goals set forth in your IFSP. At times the behavioral therapist may work with the family to impart necessary skills to them for managing their child's behavior and affecting change. The speech and language therapist will work with your child to improve their communication skills. The occupational therapist may work with your child on fine motor activities in an effort to help him or her develop self-help skills (such as personal hygiene, feeding, and dressing) and school readiness tasks (such as writing and cutting). They may also provide coping strategies for sensory issues through sensory integration therapy. Physical therapists will work with your child on gross motor activities such as sitting, standing, walking, and balance. It is extremely important for you to know what therapies your child is receiving and exactly how often they receive them. It is essential for you to know who your child's therapists are and what they do. All members of your team must be willing to work together for the benefit of your child. Teams may meet periodically to discuss and re-examine the progress and goals of your child's therapy. It is important that you attend these meetings.

Therapy services through early intervention can be conducted almost anywhere. Often these services are provided in the child's home, as the natural environment is preferred. Services can also be administered at a child care facility. If your child is receiving early intervention services in the home, it is encouraged that you observe and at times participate in your child's therapy sessions. By watching and working with the therapists you will be able to continue stimulating and engaging your child in a similar way. With therapy sessions conducted in the home you can monitor your child's progress firsthand and discuss any concerns or ideas with your child's therapists promptly.

Transitioning to special education services

Children with developmental delays or disabilities who are 3 years of age or older can receive therapies and assistance through school-based programs. Special education services in your child's local school district will continue providing services for your child when they age out of early intervention. In most instances the providers from early intervention guide parents through this transition process. Although therapists and physicians can recommend special education services, their referral is not necessary. Parents of children with developmental disabilities can contact their local school district to request special education services. Children with demonstrated developmental issues are eligible for special education services after they turn 3 years of age. Parents should reach out to the school system prior to this, as the initial evaluation process can take up to 90 days. Your child will be evaluated by a team sometimes referred to as the child study team or the individualized educational plan (IEP) team.

Evaluation

Any parent of a school-aged child can request an evaluation for their child if they have concerns. Evaluations should be requested in writing. The school can recommend an evaluation if they have concerns about a child. Parental consent is required prior to an evaluation. If the school recommends an evaluation, it is suggested that the parent consent as it is likely in the best interest of the child to identify a potential learning issue and address it. An evaluation must be completed 60 days after consent is obtained.

Evaluators will use objective tests to assess your child's skills. Standard parts of the evaluation usually include a psychological evaluation, educational assessment, speech and language evaluation, and social assessment. Additional evaluations, such as an occupational therapy evaluation, physical therapy evaluation, or behavioral assessment, may or may not be warranted. The specific tests done in each component may vary depending on your child's age and abilities. The psychological evaluation usually includes IQ testing and behavioral screening tools. These tests are usually conducted by a neuropsychologist. The speech and language evaluation assesses your child's articulation, as well as his or her expressive and receptive language skills. This portion of the evaluation is conducted by a speech-language pathologist. Educational assessment assesses and compares your child's academic skills to those of their typically functioning peers. A behavioral assessment conducted by a behavioral psychologist identifies problematic behaviors and their potential triggers. Fine motor skills are assessed by an occupational therapist and gross motor skills are assessed by a physical therapist. An evaluation also includes teacher reports and classroom observations, parent reports, evaluations by experts, physicians, counselors, and therapists, evidence of school performance, and prior evaluations and assessments. At the end of an evaluation it is determined whether your child is eligible for special education and/or related services. Parents may request an independent or private evaluation if they are dissatisfied with the school district's evaluation.

Initial IEP meeting

Once your child's evaluation is complete, the school will contact you and set up a meeting to discuss your child's evaluation results and develop a plan of action. It is crucial that you be involved in the IEP process from start to finish. Prior to the initial IEP meeting, parents should research programs, placement options, related services, and supplementary aids that may benefit their child. Have an idea of what you think your child's goals should be and what services you think he or she may need. Think about your child's strengths and weaknesses. What behaviors are most problematic? What skills is your child lacking? How does your child learn best? Which approach has worked before, and which has not worked? What does your child enjoy and how can that be incorporated into his or her learning plan? This meeting is your opportunity to educate the team about your child. Gather and bring with you any additional information that you feel may be helpful to share with the team. This may include reports from physicians, letters from teachers, private evaluations, and so forth.

Again, there will be a team approach with many specialists in attendance at this meeting. Participants in this meeting will include you, your child's teacher, a representative from the school district, and several specialists. Specialists may vary depending on your child's needs. It is likely that the speech and language therapist, psychologist, occupational therapist, physical therapist, and behavioral therapist will be there. Parents have the right to invite anyone they choose to attend this meeting with them. Parents may choose to bring a relative, physician, independent evaluator, parent advocate, or lawyer. Parents must advocate for their children. It is imperative that you voice any concerns that you have at this meeting.

The initial IEP meeting should result in a written plan. Based on your child's evaluation and discussions at this meeting, an IEP will be developed.

Individualized educational plan

An IEP outlines educational goals for your child for the school year. There may be academic goals, social goals, behavioral goals, functional goals, and possibly motor goals, depending on the needs of your child. In addition, the IEP describes the special services or therapies that will be provided to your child. All services, including counseling, occupational therapy, speech therapy, physical therapy, and so forth should be delineated in this document. It should include information about the frequency of these services, the setting in which these services will take place, and the name and title of the individual who will be administering the service. Both you and a representative of the school district must sign the IEP in order for it to be implemented. Your child's IEP should begin promptly after it is signed. You are not obligated to sign the IEP at the IEP meeting. You should sign the attendance page and consent to further evaluations if necessary, but if you do not agree with the plan delineated in the IEP, you should not sign off on the actual IEP. You may propose modifications to the plan. If your modifications are rejected, you may write a letter to the special education administrator explaining your proposed revisions. If you reject the IEP, send a written letter to the school district explaining why.

Once your team is in agreement and your child's IEP has been implemented, it is up to you to monitor your child's progress and ensure that all facets of the IEP are being honored. You should keep in touch with your child's teacher. Review your child's work regularly. Identify your child's strengths and weaknesses. Make sure that related services are being carried out with the same frequency called for in the IEP. Reach out to your child's therapist. View your child's education as a partnership or team effort. Reinforce skills and routines that are being worked on at school in the home. Reach out to your fellow team members for advice. If you are having a particular behavioral issue with your child at home, ask the teacher what she is doing in the classroom to combat similar issues. Communicate with other members of your team on a regular basis. Warn them if your child is having a particularly bad morning. Teachers and therapists should be communicating with you as well, making you aware of your child's accomplishments and difficulties. Often a communication notebook is used so that parents, teachers, and therapists can communicate on a daily basis.

Annual IEP meeting

IEPs must be updated on a yearly basis. You will be scheduled to meet with the IEP or child study team around the same time each year. These meetings must occur on a yearly basis but may occur more frequently. At any time, you can request an IEP review if you feel that your child's goals have changed or your child's needs are not being met with the current plan. Your child's IEP will likely be modified at your annual meeting as your child may have attained previous goals and you may have discovered new challenges. Decisions regarding goals and services will be based on prior evaluations and assessments as well as input from parents, teachers, physicians, and therapists. Under the IDEA, a re-evaluation is required at least once every 3 years. A re-evaluation would include new formalized testing in the form of a psychological evaluation, educational assessment, and speech and language evaluation.

Extended school year services

If there is evidence that your child experiences substantial regression of skills during time away from school, he or she may qualify for an extended school year program. These services provide schooling over summer vacation. Children with ASDs can benefit from this service, as some children on the spectrum can be prone to developmental regression with relatively minor changes in routine or schedule.

Least restrictive environment

As noted in IDEA, your child's education should be experienced in the "least restrictive environment." This means that your child should have the best possible opportunity to participate in the general education curriculum and interact with typically developing children. The school district must first consider "mainstreaming" or including your child in the general education environment before deciding on a more specialized educational setting. Mainstreaming generally means that your child is placed in a general education classroom with minimal support or accommodations. Your child would be expected to follow classroom routines and behave appropriately in a large class size, attend to the teacher, and produce near grade-level work. This type of class may be appropriate for a child with high-functioning ASD and moderate social abilities. An inclusion class is similar, but the child usually requires more support. Children with ASDs are included in the general education class with typically developing peers, but with significant support systems. Supports may include a personal aide, a modified curriculum, social groups, and pull-out supplementary services. This type of classroom may have two teachers: one with a general education background and one with special education training. Obvious benefits to this type of setting include the opportunity to socialize with typically developing peers. Potential concerns can include bullying. If the child's curriculum is significantly modified, your child may not be fully included in all classroom activities. The aide may be teaching them the adapted curriculum. It may be determined that your child would benefit more from a specialized environment.

Many children with ASDs can be placed in the general special needs classroom. This could be a class for children with mixed types of disabilities or maybe a class specifically for children with speech and language deficits or communication impairment. The benefits of this type of classroom include smaller class size, higher teacher-to-student ratio, and the use of multiple teaching modalities. Children in the special needs classroom are still included in school activities and events. Most children in this setting have academic needs but normal social skills. This setting can be helpful for the child with an ASD as long as the teacher has some experience in teaching children with ASDs. Social deficits and rigid character can cause behavioral difficulties in the classroom. The teacher must be experienced in dealing with these concerns.

Some children with an ASD may require a specialized autistic support class. These are classes that are specifically set up to accommodate the needs of the child with autism. Here the teachers and aides are all trained in working with children with ASDs. These are small classes with high teacher-to-student ratios. Intensive behavioral, speech, and social skills training may be incorporated into the daily curriculum. Children who are nonverbal or who have more difficult behaviors may benefit from this type of class setting. There is less exposure to the typically developing child in this setting, however. Other than being included in school activities, children in an autistic class interact primarily with other autistic children. There may also be concern about the level of academics being taught in this setting. In general, you want your child to be in a classroom where there are some children who are higher functioning than they are. For example, you do not want your child to be the only verbal child in a classroom with nonverbal children. Ideally you want your child to have other children with whom he or she can talk and play. You want your child to have good role models in their class.

If your school district does not have an appropriate class for your child, they will need to pay for your child to attend a special needs private school. Not all special needs private schools are prepared for teaching children with ASDs. Some of these schools are geared more towards teaching children with learning disabilities and typical social skills. There are many special needs private schools that are exclusively for children with ASDs. Advantages of this type of school include a well-trained staff, in which all personnel know how to work with children with an ASD. There may also be a wide range of therapeutic resources available in this type of setting. The greatest disadvantage to this type of program is that there is no exposure to typically developing peers. This is the most restrictive type of educational setting. Children with more severe forms of ASD may benefit from this type of setting.

Developing a successful school–parent partnership

Remember that parents and other team members share a common goal: to develop a program that will be appropriate for your child and allow him or her to grow and accomplish their goals. Be optimistic about developing a partnership with the school. Try not to be adversarial or demanding. Educate yourself and advocate for your child. Reach out to the school to learn about the evaluation process and obtain the help your child needs. Know what you and your child are entitled to by law. Do not waste time arguing for services that are not indicated. View IEP meetings as a time for both you and the school to share information and knowledge that will lead to improving your child's education. Get to know your team members. Be willing to educate team members about your child and about autism in general. Be willing to take advice and work with the team. Consider all your options. Learn how to negotiate. Remember that this is a collaborative effort.

Additional therapists or programs for your child

Many parents opt to look for additional services outside of school. Some children with an ASD may have additional speech therapy sessions with a speech pathologist. Some children join social skills training groups. Some families require the help of a behavioral therapist in the home. Be sure to find programs that encourage you to be involved. Be wary of programs that do not include you. You will be the one to coordinate your child's care, and therefore you need to be aware of goals and techniques set forth in private therapy sessions. Outside therapists need to be interested in being part of your child's treatment team. Ideally they should communicate not only with you but with their therapeutic counterparts in your child's school. It makes sense for therapists from the same discipline to be working together with similar approaches to help your child attain his or her goals.

Research a particular therapy or program. Ask what evidence there is for that treatment's effectiveness. How will your child's progress be measured? Who will be working with your child? When choosing a therapist for your child, be sure to check references. Ask about their educational background. Ask about their experience working with children with ASDs. Meet with them in person. Have them meet with your child and observe their interactions. If you find that a particular therapist is not working out and that the quality of your child's therapy is suffering because of it, you must find a new therapist.

Team leader

Nobody knows your child as well as you do. When it comes to making decisions that affect your child, you have the final say. You are the leader of the team and it is up to you, with the advice of your team members, to set the priorities and goals for your child's therapies. Although you are the expert on your child, it is essential that you call on other experts on your team to advise you in developing a treatment plan for your child. Each team member may have their own expertise or unique perspective on autism. Collaborating and sharing ideas will ensure that a comprehensive, well-rounded treatment plan is developed. You will be the one to make sure that your team members are serving the needs and interests of your child. Although you are the team leader, you must also be part of the team. Participate in team meetings. Participate in training. You cannot lead the team and advocate for your child appropriately if you are not aware of your child's goals or the techniques being used to achieve those goals. By educating yourself about your child's program you will be able to carry over some techniques in the home, further reinforcing your child's learning. You will also be able to oversee the team more accurately and be able to tell if the strategies implemented are helpful in achieving your child's goals. Make sure that all team members are aware of areas of difficulty, approaches that are working, and any changes that will need to be made. Educate team members about your child. Make sure your plan targets your child's weaknesses and takes advantage of their strengths. When parents educate themselves, coordinate their child's care, and work with the team, appropriate, individualized programs can be developed and children can make progress.

It is also essential that you help bridge any gaps between your team of physicians and your team of therapists and educators. It is very important for therapists, teachers, and counselors to communicate any concerns, challenges, or accomplishments with your child's physicians. This is particularly important if your child is taking a medication. There is no better way for the neurologist or psychiatrist to know that your child's medication is helping him or her to focus better in school than by hearing firsthand from the teacher. Does the effect of the medication last all day or does he or she have difficulty focusing again after lunch? Should the physician consider adjusting the medication? The behavioral therapist should be communicating closely with the physician who is prescribing behavioral medications. Has the medication made it easier to work with your child? Is a new medication making your child more agitated or too sleepy to work? Does the physical therapist have concerns for your child? Perhaps the therapist feels that your child should have an increase in their physical therapy services. Maybe the speech therapist believes that your child would benefit from an augmentative communication device. The therapist and physician can work together to try to obtain approval from the insurance company for said device. The more information your child's physician is given, the more educated decisions he or she can make regarding your child's care and management.

Children attend school for the majority of the day. Your child's teacher and therapists spend a good amount of time with your child. It is important for them to let you and your child's physician know if there has been a change in their behavior or any other changes that may signify a medical issue or medication side effect. We are all (parents, therapists, educators, and physicians) working towards the same common goal: to help your child be successful. We all have our own niche on the team, but we need to work together to allow your child to achieve his or her goals. Communication is the key.

TAKEAWAY POINTS

- It takes a team to provide appropriate care to a child with an ASD.

- You are the leader of your child's treatment team.

- The team needs to communicate and work together to develop and implement individualized plans for your child.

- The Individuals with Disabilities Education Act (IDEA) ensures that young children with developmental disabilities receive early intervention services and that school-aged children are entitled to a free and appropriate education.

- Early intervention provides therapies and services to children of age up to 3 years old and their families.

- An individualized family service plan describes your child's current levels of function and sets goals for the treatment team to follow. It also lists the specific services he or she will receive through early intervention, as well as where and how often these services will be provided.

- An individualized educational plan outlines educational goals for your child for the upcoming year, as well as lists his or her educational setting and related services.

- IDEA mandates that your child be placed in the least restrictive environment.

- You must be involved and advocate for your child.

Chapter 14

Puberty and Sexuality for Individuals with Autism Spectrum Disorders

Susan R. Brill, MD, Tishi Shah, MD, and Barbie Zimmerman-Bier, MD

Introduction

This chapter provides an overview of the sexual development in females and males with an autism spectrum disorder (ASD), including pubertal changes, sexual behavior, and common medical conditions that may require treatment. In addition, the authors review sexual diversity, gender identity, and methods for education on this topic. Inappropriate sexual behavior and treatment strategies are discussed.

Puberty

Puberty is a time of both physical changes in the body as well as emotional experiences and social relationships. While children with ASDs may be delayed in social or cognitive skills, their bodies often pass through pubertal changes at expected times. The physical changes of puberty are centered on the development of secondary sexual characteristics and the onset of menstruation (in girls) and ejaculation (in boys). Parents of children with ASDs have the challenge of helping their child understand these changes in the most developmentally appropriate way.

The physical changes that occur during puberty are the effects of hormones produced by the endocrine system. The three main axes of the endocrine system are the (1) hypothalamic–pituitary–gonadal axis, (2) hypothalamic–pituitary–adrenal axis, and (3) growth-hormone axis, which are involved in pubertal changes. These hormone systems produce normal variations in the timing of puberty[1] and can be affected by medical conditions and treatments.

The hypothalamic–pituitary–gonadal axis

The hypothalamic–pituitary–gonadal axis is mediated by the release of two gonadal hormones: luteinizing hormone (LH) and follicle stimulating hormone (FSH). LH and FSH are known as gonadotropins and act on the ovary to produce estrogen and progesterone in females, and on testes in males to produce testosterone. In girls the first change in puberty is usually the onset of breast-bud development, called thelarche. In boys the first sign is usually testicular enlargement. As puberty progresses, the hormones continue to cause maturation of the breasts, uterus, and ovaries in girls which leads to onset of menses, or periods, known as menarche. In boys the testes and penis grow and develop, leading to an increase in sperm production and nocturnal emissions (also known as "wet dreams").

The hypothalamic–pituitary–adrenal axis

Hormones secreted by the adrenal gland that are involved in pubertal changes are called androgens and include dehydroepiandrosterone (DHEA) and DHEA sulfate. A second component of puberty, called adrenarche, is controlled by the hypothalamic–pituitary–adrenal axis. A major manifestation includes pubarche, which means growth of pubic hair. Other changes occurring as part of adrenarche include development of axillary (armpit) hair, body odor, and acne.

The growth-hormone axis

Growth hormone is secreted by the pituitary gland and acts via insulinlike growth factors. It is responsible for growth of long bones and the subsequent growth spurt in both boys and girls. The physical changes that occur during puberty as a result of the endocrine system lead to a predictable sequence of changes in secondary sexual characteristics referred to as "Tanner stages," as described below.[2] This includes external genitialia changes in boys, thelarche (breast development) in girls, and pubarche (development of pubic hair) in both boys and girls.

Tanner stages

In boys puberty is evaluated by development of external genitalia and is defined by the following stages:

- Tanner stage 1: pre-pubertal.

- Tanner stage 2: enlargement of scrotum and testes; scrotum skin reddens and changes in texture.

- Tanner stage 3: enlargement of penis (length, then breadth); further growth of testes.

- Tanner stage 4: increased size of the penis and development of the glans; testes and scrotum are larger, scrotum skin becomes darker.

- Tanner stage 5: adult genitalia.

In girls, puberty is evaluated by breast development in the following stages:

- Tanner stage 1: pre-pubertal.

- Tanner stage 2: breast bud; elevation of breast and papilla (nipple), with enlargement of areola (tissue surrounding the nipple).

- Tanner stage 3: further enlargement of breast and areola; no separation of their contour.

- Tanner stage 4: areola and papilla form a secondary mound above contour of the breast.

- Tanner stage 5: mature stage, with projection of papilla only, related to regression of areola.

In both boys and girls, puberty is also assessed by progression of growth of pubic hair. This process is known as pubarche and is defined as follows:

- Tanner stage 1: can see velus (soft and downy) hair similar to hair on abdominal wall.

- Tanner stage 2: sparse growth of long, slightly pigmented hair, straight or curled, at base of penis in boys or along mons in girls.

- Tanner stage 3: darker, coarser, and more curly hair, spread sparsely over the base of penis or mons.

- Tanner stage 4: hair is adult in type but covers smaller area than in adult; no hair on medial (inside) surface of thighs.

- Tanner stage 5: adult distribution in type and quantity.

Variations in timing of puberty in boys and girls

Pubertal changes in girls occur for a period of 3–4 years, beginning at an average age of 10 years with thelarche (age of onset may vary with ethnicity). The growth spurt occurs next, followed by menarche. In the majority of girls, menarche is achieved at Tanner stages 3–4. Factors that may influence this include nutrition, ethnicity, and genetics. After girls get their period, they continue to grow about 4–6 cm (about 1.5–2.4 inches), but the majority of their growth has already occurred. The body continues to change in the years following menarche. There is a decrease in lean-body-mass percentage due to increase in adipose (fat) mass. The pelvis becomes more rounded and fat is deposited on the hips.

Pubertal changes in males occur for a period of 2–5 years. In a majority of boys increase in testicular volume greater than 4 milliliters is the first noticeable sign, but growth of pubic hair may be noted first. The growth spurt in boys occurs in mid to late puberty at approximately Tanner stage 4. Other changes during the same period include changes in voice and development of facial and axillary hair. Acne is often noted at this stage. In late puberty boys continue to gain muscle mass and strength.

Teaching your child about the physical changes of puberty

Parents of children with ASDs have the challenge of helping their child understand their changes in the most developmentally appropriate way. When discussing puberty with a child with ASD it is important to teach to the child's level of understanding. It is generally recommended to keep the information factual. For example, use medical terminology when talking about boy and girl body parts (i.e., penis, testicle, and pubic hair for boys, and vagina, breasts, and menstruation for girls). If the child has a limited understanding and poor verbal communication skills, parents might want to focus on key points such as privacy, appropriate touch, safety, and hygiene. For children that are more verbal or with more understanding, it is important to begin with what the child already knows and tailor your discussions. It is important to check for understanding of the topic by asking questions or having the child repeat in their own words what you have said. Sometimes you may need to have repeated conversations before the concepts are learned. Parents should utilize teaching strategies that have been used to teach their children other skills when discussing such things as menstruation and nocturnal emissions. Some strategies may include visual graphics, videos, books, pictures of what is happening to their bodies, and social stories about, or modeling of, correct behavior.

Achieving independence in personal hygiene skills is important for all children. Poor hygiene can negatively impact peer relationships and affect self-esteem. Children in late childhood usually are independent in their basic self-care tasks such as toileting and maintaining body hygiene. Children with ASDs often need more frequent cues and supervision to achieve these developmental milestones.[3] Parents can use visual schedules, videos, and modeling to facilitate independence. It is useful to think of puberty as another stage of development with specific sets of skills to learn. (There are a number of resources available to assist parents listed at the end of this chapter.)

Common medical concerns during puberty

Gynecomastia

Transient increase in glandular and stromal breast tissue in boys during puberty is called gynecomastia. Breast tissue development in males depends on a balance between estrogen and testosterone levels during puberty. It can be of concern for boys and their caregivers[4] especially if the breast growth is unilateral. In most cases, only reassurance is needed. The problem usually resolves within a year. It is important to keep in mind and possibly eliminate or correct other causes of gynecomastia, including medications, nutritional status, and certain medical conditions such as liver and kidney disease. Obesity is also a common contributing factor.

Scoliosis

Scoliosis or curvature of the spine is a condition frequently seen in adolescents and occurs more commonly in girls. Adolescent idiopathic scoliosis occurs from age 10 years to skeletal maturation and should be differentiated from scoliosis occurring due to neuromuscular or skeletal abnormalities. Scoliosis implies a lateral (side to side) curvature of the spine, with 10 degrees or more curvature on frontal X-ray. A curvature of more than 10 degrees occurs in 2–3% of adolescents. Based on the degree of scoliosis, initial management options often include clinical monitoring with regular imaging. Sometimes children are referred to pediatric orthopedists for close observation. If the curvature occurs in a skeletally immature child, he or she will need to be monitored for possible treatment.

Acne

Acne is prevalent among adolescents, appearing from pre-pubertal age and increasing in severity with puberty. Peak ages are 14–17 years in females and 16–19 years in males, but it may persist until age 30 years. Increased androgens stimulate oil glands in the skin resulting in additional sebum production. Coupled with abnormalities in keratinization (skin cell shedding) and the presence of a bacteria known as *Propionibacterium acnes*, adolescents develop whiteheads, blackheads, and papules commonly known as pimples. Acne can cause significant consequences in the quality of life of an adolescent, particularly if it is severe. Children with developmental disabilities may have poor skin hygiene or pick at their skin excessively, which can exacerbate the condition. In addition, acne may flare up with particular medications such as oral steroids. The condition is very responsive to treatment that can be initiated either by primary care providers or dermatologists. Various treatment options include topical medications such as benzyl peroxide, topical antibiotics, and topical tretinoin. For more severe cases, oral medications that are offered include oral antibiotics, oral contraceptives in females only, or oral isotretinoin.

Sleep changes

Normal sleep can be divided into alternating cycles of rapid eye movement (REM) sleep and non-rapid eye movement (NREM) sleep, with NREM sleep further divided into three stages. A normal night's sleep has approximately 90 minutes of NREM sleep, followed by increasing REM sleep with each cycle. During puberty, typical adolescents display a decrease in deep sleep and an increase in light sleep stages with changes in circadian rhythm, which may delay bedtime and rising time which cause sleep disturbances if a set wake and sleep schedule is demanded.

Children and adolescents with ASDs suffer from sleep problems, particularly insomnia, at a higher rate than typically developing children, ranging from 40 to 80%.[5] Identifying and treating sleep problems with behavioral and/or psychopharmacologic interventions can improve daytime behavior and family functioning.

For children with new sleep problems during puberty, it is important to look for new environmental as well as medical causes for sleep disturbance. For example, children with ASDs are more prone to epilepsy during the adolescent years, which can present as sleep seizures. These seizures occur during NREM sleep and slow-wave sleep, and result in more awakenings, less sleep, and lighter sleep. Often the child experiences increased daytime sleepiness. Medications used to treat epilepsy, if this is diagnosed, can also cause daytime sleepiness or sleep difficulties.

Other medications, particularly stimulant medications, can delay sleep onset and cause disrupted sleep. These medications may cause more difficulty during the adolescent years. It may be necessary to work with the child's physician to adjust the dosages and types of medications that the child receives. Psychiatric conditions, such as anxiety or depression, are common causes of sleep disturbances in adolescents and should be considered in adolescents with ASDs who display changes in behavioral functioning and new onset of sleep problems.

Menstrual problems

A significant percentage of girls experience problems with their periods. The most common condition that affects teen girls includes painful periods, or dysmenorrhea. Dysmenorrhea is reported to occur with increasing frequency in adolescent girls, affecting up to 72% by the fifth year after menarche.[6] This is due to the increase in percentage of ovulatory cycles as the hypothalamic–pituitary–ovarian axis matures. Ovulatory cycles cause an increase in secretion of prostaglandins with menstrual flow which causes painful "contractions" of the uterus, especially within the first few days of bleeding.

Conversely, for girls in their early to mid teens, many do not ovulate regularly which can lead to excessive or irregular bleeding. This may put girls at risk for iron-deficiency anemia. There may be other health issues, such as thyroid disorders, pituitary growths, or significant shifts in body weight, that cause irregular periods. Girls who lose weight due to high-intensity exercise and/or limitation of caloric intake often have complete cessation of their periods until the root cause is identified and treated. The most common cause of irregular periods that begins in adolescence, often presenting with long gaps between periods or amenorrhea (no menstrual periods), is polycystic ovary syndrome, the most common endocrine disorder in females.[6] This condition appears soon after menarche with irregular or absent periods, often accompanied by acne, extra body hair, and, in many girls, additional weight gain. Other metabolic conditions, such as insulin resistance (a pre-diabetic condition), and high cholesterol, may accompany the clinical presentation.

In girls with developmental delays, particularly for girls who have limited verbal abilities, there may be a worsening of behavior either before or during the menstrual cycle. Therefore clinicians who treat girls with developmental concerns need to be aware of subtle behavioral changes that can be a manifestation of dysmenorrhea or premenstrual syndrome. Caregivers should be instructed to keep a detailed menstrual calendar to identify possible correlations between behavior changes and menstrual cycles. Nonsteroidal anti-inflammatory medications (over-the-counter painkillers such as ibuprofen) are a mainstay of therapy for dysmenorrhea and can be very useful in treating these conditions. For patients who do not respond to these medications, hormonal treatment has been very helpful in allowing lighter, more predictable periods with concomitant improvement in behavior. Oral contraceptives have been used very successfully in teen girls, either taken monthly for regular periods or taken for extended cycles to minimize bleeding and accompanying symptoms. Girls who are taking certain medications such as anticonvulsants may need particular dosing regimens to minimize interactions of these medications. Other medications recommended for teen girls may include medroxyprogesterone (Depo-Prover) (Pfizer, New York, NY), an injectable progestin that may allow suppression of menstruation, or even an intrauterine device for long-term treatment in select cases. Consultation with a clinician familiar with the risks and benefits of these medications is crucial to obtaining proper care for adolescent women.

Sexuality

Sexuality, as defined by the World Health Organization, is a central aspect of being human throughout life and encompasses sex, gender identities and roles, sexual orientation, eroticism, pleasure, intimacy, and reproduction. The process is influenced by social, cultural, ethical, legal, religious, and spiritual factors. Sexual development is a process that is often thought of in terms of typical development; however, individuals with developmental disabilities also go through these stages as they physically mature. The process begins with gender awareness. At this point children know they are a male or female and can understand the difference between boys and girls. This is commonly referred to as gender identity. Most children achieve this awareness by 2–3 years of age.

Once their identity is established, children behave in ways that are in sync with this identity. For example, boys may begin to prefer playing with cars and trucks, and girls enjoy dolls and playing dress up. These activities establish a gender role. As children head to preschool, they have a strong sense of identity and begin exploring their bodies, and "playing doctor" is common at this age. They develop friendships and learn how to act to maintain these relationships. By elementary school age, children want more information about sex and reproduction. They may be exposed to a great deal of information from peers and/or media. As children mature and experience puberty, there is further maturation of their gender roles. Often children become aware of their sexual orientation, or to which gender they sense attraction (including emotional, romantic, sexual, and behavioral), regardless of whether they act on this attraction.

All children face the task of moving through these developmental milestones. For children with ASDs their core social communication problems often confound the process. For example, delays in gender identity reflect delays in communication. Sexual identity (which normally develops in adolescence) may develop later in individuals with ASDs who have difficulty expressing and interpreting these feelings. Individuals with ASDs may also lack social judgment, flexibility, decision-making skills, and may have limited peer relationships. This can limit the opportunities and availability for romantic and intimate relationships.

Inappropriate sexual behavior

Individuals with ASDs may have difficulty determining what and where sexual behaviors are permitted due to inability to read and interpret social cues. These inappropriate behaviors include masturbation in public, removing clothing in public, inappropriate touching, stalking, inappropriate comments, lack of regard for privacy (e.g., not knocking on doors), or obsessive interest in someone. These behaviors can have negative legal implications or social consequences. It is therefore important to begin early with behavioral and educational interventions to teach privacy behaviors and skills. Teens need to know when and where they can touch themselves, and they must learn to respect the need for privacy.

Potential for abuse

For all children with disabilities, including those with ASDs, there is an increased incidence of physical and sexual abuse.[7] Early on parents should begin teaching about circles of comfort (who may touch you or ask you to undress) and basic bathroom and locker safety. Children should specifically be taught about inappropriate or unwanted sexual touching (good touch/bad touch), and about possible harassment and victimization that may occur via the Internet or social media. In particular, teens with ASDs may have a difficult time distinguishing between Internet "friends" and true friends who have their best interests in mind. Teens can be taught about sexually transmitted diseases, the importance of using condoms in limiting exposure to these conditions, and basic contraceptive counseling. Modifications, such as using anatomically correct dolls or role playing, may be helpful for children who have difficulty grasping abstract concepts.[3]

Medication concerns

Medications can cause significant distress in an adolescent or adult with an ASD by interfering with sexual desire or sexual potency. For example, SSRI medications (selective serotonin reuptake inhibitors) are frequently prescribed to help with anxiety or repetitive behaviors in this population. This group of medications can negatively affect one's sexual desire or the ability to achieve an orgasm. Unintentional self-injury may result from prolonged attempts at masturbation.

Sexual education

Sexual education for children with ASDs should start early and continue with reinforcement during the teen and adult years. Parents may begin by helping the child learn about his or her body, safety, hygiene, and privacy, but they may need the support of a formal sexual education program in the school system. Education about sexuality is most effective when adapted to the individual's cognitive and social–emotional functioning and is highly individualized. Several models for sexuality education for those with ASDs have been published. We acknowledge that individuals with ASDs have a right to a sexual life with guidance, support, and assistance in expressing sexuality in an acceptable way.

TAKEAWAY POINTS

- Puberty occurs in a stepwise fashion and is directed by hormones that are released sequentially over a period of years.

- Individuals with an ASD usually experience puberty at the same time and in the same order as typically developing children and teens, but they may face more hurdles if they are unable to communicate their symptoms or feelings.

- Like typically developed teens, adolescents with ASDs are likely to experience the medical problems common in adolescence and need appropriate medical surveillance for management of problems such as gynecomastia, scoliosis, acne, sleep changes, and menstrual problems.

- Medications may impact pubertal development and concomitant medical problems.

- Children, teens, and adolescents need the opportunity to learn about appropriate sexual behaviors, privacy, and ways to protect themselves from sexual abuse.

Resources for parents on puberty and sexual education

American Girl Library (1998) *The Care & Keeping of You: The Body Book for Girls*. Middleton, WI: Pleasant Company Publications.

Davies, C. and Dubie, M. (2012) *Intimate Relationships and Sexual Health: A Curriculum for Teaching Adolescents/Adults with High-Functioning Autism Spectrum Disorders and Other Social Challenges*. Shawnee Mission, KS: AAPC Publishing.

Hartman, D. (2013) *Sexuality and Relationship Education for Children and Adolescents with Autism Spectrum Disorders. A Professional's Guide to Understanding, Preventing Issues, Supporting Sexuality and Responding to Inappropriate Behaviours*. London: Jessica Kingsley Publishers.

Loulan, J. and Worthen, B. (2001) *Period: A Girl's Guide*. Minnetonka, MN: Book Peddlers (also available in Spanish).

Madaras, L. and Madaras, A. (2000) *The What's Happening to My Body? Books for Boys: A Growing-up Guide for Parents and Sons*. New York, NY: W.W. Norton & Company.

Planned Parenthood (2004) Sexuality & disability: A resource list for those who work with, live with, or care for people with disabilities. New York, NY: Planned Parenthood Federation of America, Inc.

Planned Parenthood. Topics on puberty. Available at www.plannedparenthood.org/info-for-teens/our-bodies-33795.htm.

Specher, J. (Producer) (1999) "Body Parts and Grooming." Milwaukee, WI: Anything's Possible, Inc. [Videotape]. TMW Media Group. OSI: 709629040304.

Stanfield, J. (Producer) (1996) "Hygiene for Females." First Impressions, Hygiene Part 1. Available at www.stanfield.com/products/social-life-skills/first-impressions/module-1-hygiene.

Stanfield, J. (Producer) (1996) "Hygiene for Males." First Impressions, Hygiene Part 1. Available at www.stanfield.com/products/social-life-skills/first-impressions/module-1-hygiene.

Strong, B., DeVault, C., Sayad, B.W., and Yarber, W.L. (2005) *Human Sexuality: Diversity in Contemporary America* (5th Ed.). New York, NY: McGraw-Hill.

Wrobel, M. (2003) *Taking Care of Myself: A Hygiene, Puberty and Personal Curriculum for Young People with Autism*. Arlington, TX: Future Horizons, Inc.

Chapter 15

Bridging the Gap to Adulthood
Navigating the Transition for Individuals with Autism Spectrum Disorders to Their Futures

Susan L. Connors, MD, and
Julie M. O'Brien, MEd, LMHC

Introduction

Transition is defined as the movement from one set of activities to another, or from one life stage to another. For adolescents with autism spectrum disorders (ASDs) transition refers to the move from the school years to adulthood. For parents, this period can be confusing and anxiety provoking, and the preparation involved can appear to be an overwhelming task. Parents who have worked hard to obtain appropriate services and supports since their child was diagnosed are now faced with more learning, navigating, and planning for the future.

Transition is preparation for life. Experts who work in the field of ASDs caution that transitioning to adulthood is a process that cannot occur overnight, and that it is never too early to begin. There is much to learn and do during the transition years, and planning must relate to key domains in the child's life such as medical, educational and vocational planning, safety, social skills and recreation, housing, transportation, legal and financial planning, and accessing public benefits. This period is a crucial time for preparation and should be person centered and unique to the child. Transition involves teaching the young adult with an ASD about self-determination,[1] coming to a better understanding of his or her interests, strengths and needs in all domains of life, and carefully planning for a successful future. Although the adolescent is still a student, he or she should not only continue to develop academic abilities during the transition years, but also, and perhaps more importantly, should acquire life skills so that he or she will be able to live as independently as possible during adult life.

The entire transition process can span from age 14 years through adulthood, and it is best if parents begin early, are proactive, and create a vision for their child. It is important to organize, plan, learn, and *keep* learning: work with professionals in the field, attend workshops, research options, network, advocate, know your rights, and voice your needs throughout the process.

We realize that this is a time of anxiety and anticipation. Our goal is to help parents become prepared and confident so that they are better able to provide a bridge to a successful future for their sons and daughters. In this chapter we provide information, guidelines, and resources so that parents understand transition and how to plan during this critical time in the life of the young adult with ASD. Although we are sharing this information as professionals who are most familiar with the laws and resources in our state of Massachusetts, much of the information provided is translatable to all 50 states of the United States. We hope that we not only provide helpful guidance and support but also communicate to parents of adolescents with ASDs that they are not alone, and that parent and child can successfully cross the bridge to adulthood.

Accessing medical care

For an individual with an ASD, the goal of transition is not only successful movement from secondary school to post-secondary programs and into the workplace, but also the transition to adult medical care providers. This includes successful development of self-advocacy and responsibility for the young adult's own appointments and prescriptions, if possible.

Primary care providers

Transitioning to adult medical care is just one facet of a child's journey to adult life. Like other aspects of development, it is a gradual process, not a one-time event, and consists of steps that overlap and build on each other. The American Academy of Pediatrics (AAP) currently suggests six core elements in the model of transitioning youth with complex medical needs (including developmental disabilities) from pediatric to adult medical care. These elements include (1) transition policy, (2) transitioning youth registry, (3) transition preparation, (4) transition planning, (5) transition and transfer, and (6) transition completion. This is a national guideline that was first published in 2011.[2] It requires that certain preparations be made by pediatricians and families, and that the receiving physicians-for-adults become active participants. Parents may want to ask their children's pediatricians whether they plan to follow the AAP recommendations on the transition of medical care for their child.

Finding a primary care physician (PCP) or nurse practitioner (NP) is the first step in the journey from pediatric to adult medical care. This can actually be a difficult process for several reasons. In virtually all 50 states there is a shortage of PCPs, even for typically developed adults. When one adds the extra time necessary to care for an adult with significant problems in communication, social interaction, sensory processing, and behavioral differences, the task can become challenging. In addition, the extra time required for our young adults is not compensated by insurance companies. Finally, it is important to understand that although parents would like their adult children with ASDs to be cared for by a "provider who specializes in autism," no such specialty training exists yet. There is no residency or fellowship in the United States that is specific for providing medical care to adults with ASDs.

When parents need to find a new PCP for their young adult with ASD, they should ask the child's pediatrician for a referral. The age of a physician can matter. A younger physician may have more familiarity with ASDs since autism awareness has permeated most medical school curricula in recent years. Some parents ask their own PCPs to accept their child with autism as a new patient. This often works, as long as the provider is willing to learn about the child, become familiar with ASDs through the parent, and allow extra time at visits.

There are several options when choosing a PCP for medical care. Internists are "doctors for adults" trained to care for adults only, and their training is focused on diagnosis and treatment of adult diseases as well as the maintenance of health and prevention of disease. Family medicine physicians have been trained to provide continuing and comprehensive health care for the individual from birth to death within the context of family and community. Because of this, they may adopt a more developmental approach to their patients. They are familiar with much of the same basic knowledge of adult diseases as internists. Graduates of medicine-pediatrics (med-peds) residencies study longer than doctors specializing in internal medicine, pediatrics, or family medicine. Their training usually lasts 4 years compared with 3 years for the other specialties mentioned, because they need to have extensive knowledge of both adult medicine and pediatrics. There are fewer med-peds physicians practicing in the United States than internists or those in family medicine.

In Massachusetts, as in many other states, nurse practitioners (NPs) and physician assistants (PAs) can also be PCPs. Their training typically consists of 2 years (for PAs) or 3 years (for NPs) of full-time graduate study and clinical training. Nurse practitioners and PAs can be trained in either pediatric or adult medicine; if trained to see adults, both have enough education in adult medicine to care for our young adults, and both can write prescriptions and provide direct care. Nurse practitioners and PAs may have more time available to spend with each patient and may be more accessible than internists, family medicine physicians, and med-peds physicians. In many internal medicine, family medicine, and med-peds practices, it is the NP or PA who attends patients with acute illnesses and injuries, simply due to availability; thus, adults new to these practices might be seen more often and become more familiar with NPs and PAs. It is good to clarify who will attend patients for acute visits when calling a medical practice to inquire about becoming a new patient.

It is important to make sure the new primary care practice accepts the insurance carried by the individual in transition, and this should be clarified during the first phone call when making an appointment. Not every primary care practice accepts patients who have only Medicaid for health insurance (rules for physicians accepting Medicaid insurance can vary from one state to another), and a desired practice may not be open to new patients simply due to large volume. In general, Medicaid reimbursements to physicians for health care visits are lower than those paid by private insurance. The difference can be a factor that causes many practices to limit the percentage of Medicaid patients they care for, in order to assure the practice's financial stability and ability to pay its employees.

Specialists

Should a young adult with an ASD need a subspecialist, finding one may not be as challenging as finding a PCP. For example, if the individual has a seizure disorder, he or she will need an adult neurologist; for gastrointestinal concerns a gastroenterologist is needed; and seasonal allergies might require an allergist. Virtually all subspecialists take new patients into their practices (subspecialists are not expected to provide primary care), but not all accept Medicaid and Medicare. Finding an adult medical subspecialist who is familiar with, and understands, autism may be a goal for many parents, but it is not always necessary or possible, depending on the specialty area. It might be more important that the specialist listen to parents and be open to learning about ASDs from them and other resources. The young adult who has comorbid mental health diagnoses, however, may need an adult psychiatrist who is familiar with ASDs, since indications, dosing, and efficacy of many drug treatments may be unique to ASDs. Parents can engage the help of the child and adolescent psychiatrist for transition to an adult psychiatric provider who may be a good fit and who could rely on the child psychiatrist for historical information as the transfer of care progresses.

Insurance

Many parents ask whether it will benefit a child to have him or her remain on the parents' private insurance until at least age 26 years, compared with enrolling in only Medicaid or Medicare. In Massachusetts there is an autism insurance law (known as ARICA) signed in 2011 that mandates that private insurance pay for medically necessary therapies for patients with ASDs, and it includes *no age limit*. Since this law applies only to private insurance (at the time of this writing), obtaining home behavior programs, ongoing speech and communication therapies, physical therapy, and occupational therapy is easier if the adult with an ASD has commercial insurance as primary coverage, whether or not he or she has Medicaid as secondary coverage. Many other states have insurance laws providing coverage for autism-related therapies, and parents are encouraged to investigate the options in their home state (or country).

Planning medical visits

Because new experiences and changes in routine are often difficult for individuals with ASDs, there are some pre-visit preparations that can be helpful before an office appointment with a new medical provider. The patient's method of communication is important for the office staff to know: Does the young adult use spoken language, sign language, pictures, or an electronic device? Depending on the patient, it may be important for office personnel to know if there are sensory difficulties or triggers for anxiety and maladaptive behaviors. If there are difficult parts of the physical exam, if the patient has specific fears, or if the patient may need to be in a quiet room or leave the waiting room and take a break, these concerns should be communicated as well.

The hospital experience

We all know that emergency room visits, outpatient tests and procedures, as well as overnight admissions to the hospital can be problematic for young adults with ASDs. The environment is unfamiliar; there are bright lights, many strangers, busy waiting rooms, and loud noises. The young adult does not know what to expect. It would be helpful if knowledge of an individual's communication method, sensory difficulties, dietary habits, anxiety triggers, and safety concerns could be easily accessed in a commonly used format, such as an electronic medical record. We have created the Acute Care Plan for Autism, which records this information as an online survey completed by parents or guardians and patients themselves (if able). The survey is accessible from the Lurie Center website (www.LurieCenter.org) under the Support and Wellness tab or directly at http://j.mp/15AJOGS. The completed form can be printed, and then it is uploaded as a note in the Massachusetts General Hospital's electronic medical record and becomes available to nurses, physicians, therapists, and other providers in the hospital. This type of information is currently being studied for improvement in the quality of medical care delivery and as a method to decrease anxiety on the part of the patients.

Educational planning

It is important for parents of adolescents with an ASD to realize that there are both federal and state laws that provide protection for the child and mandate transition planning and services. Autism spectrum disorder is considered a disability under special education law. The Individuals with Disabilities Education Act (IDEA) 2004 requires that transition goals be integrated into the individual education plan (IEP) at age 16 years, but the process can begin as early as age 14 years (in Massachusetts). The IEP should be developed with the student's individual vision in mind, what he or she wants to do with his or her life in adulthood, and should support his or her preferences, strengths, and interests. The intent of the transition planning is to prepare the young adult with an ASD for life as he or she moves from school (being a student) to adulthood and "post-school activities" such as community college, employment, volunteering, independent living, social and recreational opportunities, and community participation.

Parents may not realize that under IDEA, the school system is obligated to provide formal and informal assessments and related services that support the goal of success for the student in adult life. These assessments should be student specific and must be completed similar to the usual cognitive, academic, language/communication, and other related assessments that are required every 3 years. Parents are strongly encouraged to seek independent evaluations related to transition, including vocational assessments, if the school system is unable to do so. There is no standardized template for a transition evaluation; however, categories that are usually included are:

- intelligence

- school performance

- post-secondary education readiness and training

- self-determination and advocacy

- emotional/behavioral considerations

- social skills

- personality/preferences

- functional/life skills

- community participation and travel

- leisure/recreation

- vocational/career interests

- work readiness

- situational vocational assessment.

The choice for which of these types of assessments to include should be unique to the student's needs. It is important that parents learn about the federal (and relevant state) laws related to transition in order to most effectively advocate for their young adult with an ASD.

School districts in some states have expanded special education programs to include more formal transition or "bridge" programs for ages 18–22 years. With support from the IDEA transition-specific law, young adults (and their parents) can more often remain enrolled in special education and have more time to work on post-secondary school-related goals. Young adults with ASDs and their parents need to realize that colleges and universities have disability support offices and programs to serve students with disabilities. Some colleges have staff who specialize in working with individuals with ASDs. Whether the interest is in community college or a 4-year college, it is good to know that today there are more college-based services, private consultants, and general resources for those students with ASDs interested in pursuing post-secondary education.

Legal and financial planning and accessing public benefits

Parents who have a child with an ASD have important questions about how best to provide for the future well-being and quality of life for their son or daughter. A parent or caregiver of a person with an ASD faces unique and difficult planning decisions for their loved one's future well-being. The most important question is how to provide for future care and services after the parent or caregiver is no longer able to do so, or dies. As one parent of an adult with an ASD stated, "As a parent of a young man with autism, the question of what will happen to my son after my wife and I are gone is never very far from my mind."

Estate planning

Estate planning is an important part of transition because it allows parents to organize legal and financial information and document their wishes as they develop a long-term plan for financial and personal care of their child across the lifespan. Estate planning is a critical safeguard for the child with special needs and should involve updating or creating wills, applying for government benefits and services, creating special needs trusts (SNTs), and petitioning for guardianship.

Along with developing wills and special needs trusts, parents need to write down all the important information about the child with special needs, along with their personal plans and wishes for him or her. This document becomes a critical one-stop-shop for all future caregivers to reference. It is commonly known as a letter of intent (LOI) and should be a comprehensive and well-written narrative that includes all pertinent information about the child, including provision of care, medical and financial information, housing services, and current needs. Parents should begin to develop an LOI during adolescence and work with attorneys who specialize in financial planning and creating SNTs.

An SNT is a legal entity created by the parents of a child with a developmental disability so that funds and other assets can be protected. In order for an adult with a developmental disability to receive public benefits, such as supplemental security income (SSI), his or her assets must not exceed $2000. Funds and property held in an SNT cannot be counted toward the maximum government-allowed assets of the child, and can be used for, and only for, the benefit of the child whose name is on the trust. An SNT provides a reliable, legal way to safeguard the child's eligibility for public benefits while simultaneously providing for additional needs in adult life. It enables a designated trustee to pay expenses for items or services that enhance the quality of life of a disabled adult beyond that provided by public benefits. Special needs trusts should be developed with a lawyer who specializes in this field to avoid jeopardizing the child's eligibility for public benefits.

It is important that parents of adolescent children with ASDs become educated about accessing federal and state government resources. Public benefits, such as SSI, social security disability insurance, Medicaid (waivers), and long- and short-term adult disability services can provide long-term access to, and funding for, specialized day programs, day services, medical insurance, and employment and housing options that are not mandated or prioritized for adults with ASDs. It is rare that a family has the financial resources to care for an adult with an ASD across the lifespan.[3]

Sibling considerations

For many families who have a child (or children) with ASDs, the typically developing sibling may naturally assume some or all of the responsibility for decision making and care after the parents die. Planning for this responsibility can produce an assortment of feelings and certainly requires much planning, open communication, and frequent discussions about the future. Individuals with an ASD can have a normal lifespan, and information about aging and long-term health in this population is currently unknown. Adult siblings enter into their own lives and have families of their own, and may naturally feel that the responsibility of a sibling with an ASD is a burden. As the prevalence of ASDs increases, more awareness about the experiences of siblings has been generated. Siblings can access support by joining local networks or online groups. Resources such as the Autism Society and the Sibling Support Project are available for children, teens, and adult siblings of individuals with ASDs. (See the list of resources at the end of this chapter.)

Guardianship and alternatives to guardianship

Once a child reaches the age of majority (which varies by state), in the eyes of the law, he or she is considered "emancipated," or presumed competent to make informed decisions about his or her life. In other words, when a child with an ASD turns eighteen (or twenty-one in some states), parents are no longer the legal guardians of the young adult, and can no longer automatically make decisions concerning medical care, finances, education, housing, and other important choices in life. This is true even though the child has a documented disability and his or her parents have always made these decisions.

Emancipation means that parents are *no longer* entitled to obtain personal or legal information about their child from professionals including those in education and health care; thus, the "newly adult" individual can direct his or her own health care (or refuse to do so), handle his or her own finances, and sign legal contracts and other documents without parental permission or involvement. Educational decisions can be made either solely by the child or by the child and parents together. There are strict medical privacy laws (according to HIPAA, the Health Insurance Portability and Accountability Act of 1996; see www.hhs.gov) that prevent a medical provider from disclosing private medical information without consent of the patient.

Guardianship is an important option to consider if an adult child is incapable of making informed decisions in some or all areas of life. It is decided by the court and gives a parent (or parents) the legal right to make decisions on behalf of the young adult, and to access his or her financial, educational, and health care information beyond the age of majority. Guardianship laws and processes differ nationwide and require evidence of disability and incapacity from a licensed professional or team.

There are less restrictive alternatives to guardianship that can provide some legal and medical protection for the young adult with ASD. A health care proxy is a legal document that allows a competent person to designate another person to make health care decisions should this become necessary. A durable power of attorney is created when a person with mild or moderate disability appoints another person to handle his or her affairs and gives that person the legal authority to do so. In many states, conservatorship can be considered for an adult child who has assets, such as property or bank accounts, but who is unable to make informed financial decisions that are necessary to protect those assets.

Parents should educate themselves by obtaining updated information about guardianship laws and related processes that apply in their own state and by seeking consultation with legal professionals who focus on special needs law. They can also access resources online such as Autism Speaks, National Guardianship Association, and Autism After 16 (see the "Useful resources" section at the end of the chapter).

Lead agency for adult services

Deciding which agency will provide long-term supports for an adult child with an ASD is an important part of transition planning. Many states are more committed to providing lifetime services and supports to individuals with an ASD than has been true in the past. Each state has its own service agencies or divisions that provide services for adults with disabilities, including those with an ASD. Typically, services and supports are provided through a combination of federal, state, county, and local government services and contracts. Private businesses, support groups, and volunteers are also widely utilized.

Each state differs with regard to agency name, eligibility criteria for services, funding streams, and method of service delivery; however, most agencies generally provide one or more of the following short- or long-term services, depending on the agency mission: family support, case management, respite, day programs, residential, employment, and crisis supports.

There are usually strict eligibility criteria that must be met in order for adults to receive services. These requirements differ from those that apply to a young child with an ASD and usually focus on intellectual capacity and level of adaptive functioning. Unlike programs and supports that are provided during the school years through an IEP and IDEA, services for adults with ASDs are not mandated by law and are available only through prioritization. Parents should investigate their options for a lead agency and research the agency providers, learn the related eligibility criteria, as well as attend workshops and talks by known experts and agency providers in the field.

In some states, specific special education laws ensure adequate time for transition planning and also have transition coordinators whose job is to assist the family with a smooth and well-planned transition. Other states may not offer formal assistance with transition planning, so the task is left up to the parents of children with an ASD. At this time, no state has developed a single agency dedicated to providing lifelong benefits, supports, and services for adults diagnosed with an ASD. Given the increasing number of individuals diagnosed with ASDs, the longer survival rates, and the extremely low employment rates among persons with disabilities, there is a critical need for developing such an agency.

Life and vocational skills

An important part of the transition process is evaluating the developmental and functional level of an adolescent in areas of independent living and employment. This encompasses his or her social awareness as well as understanding of, and ability to perform, self-care, problem solving, and decision making, all of which influence the young adult's independence in life and work. It is critical for parents to understand the broad scope of skills needed to maximize independence in everyday life.

Life skills

For parents of children with an ASD, there are many concerns to address during the early years, such as maximizing educational services and teaching communication, academics, and social skills; however, compared with childhood, trying to teach and maximize all of the skills necessary for adult life in a young adult with an ASD can be overwhelming.

Every young adult needs to develop life and vocational skills in order to become independent. Not only are individuals with an ASD less likely to spontaneously learn skills by "osmosis," they also take much longer to learn (some) skills, regardless of their level of cognitive functioning. No matter how capable an individual is academically, if he or she cannot choose clothing, get dressed, make a simple meal, do laundry or other chores around the house, save money to buy preferred items, or manage leisure time, then that young adult must rely on a parent or other caregiver for everyday living skills. This reliance on caregivers can foster dependence on others, not independence. In addition, for individuals with an ASD, learning how to problem solve, manage feelings, and develop and maintain social relationships are often as crucial for success in adult life as the ability to read and write.

Parents can support the adult child by making sure independent living skills are assessed as early as middle school, so that related goals are developed and closely monitored through the IEP. Adolescents and young adults with an ASD can set short- and long-term goals at home to develop life skills, such as learning to make doctor's appointments, keeping a budget, making social and recreational schedules, and doing chores, in order to foster generalization of skills (being able to maintain and implement the skill in real life after the instruction is completed). Important life-skill domains that need to be targeted during middle and high school include safety (physical, personal, and Internet), activities of daily living, time management, social skills, health management, money management, community navigation, and travel training. Self-advocacy should be encouraged as much as possible. Support and encouragement are important as the child gradually experiences increased responsibility.[4]

Life skills are just as important for young adults with an ASD who have intellectual disabilities. These skills should be explicitly taught to individuals who are cognitively challenged, less able to communicate, and who may have maladaptive behaviors, because they need to learn basic self-care skills such as dressing, toileting, and bathing.

Success is defined differently for each individual. Teaching and learning different life skills is a process that involves many steps such as assessment, instruction, training, and practice. The ultimate goal for life-skills acquisition is generalization, that is, the ability to perform a skill in situations beyond the training session, and maintenance of the skill over time.[5] Parents can expect life-skills training to be part of IEP goals, and they can request that the school work on these skills at home and in the community.

Vocational options and employment

Employment is an important part of life for everyone. Finding a meaningful job is especially satisfying. Benefits from working include financial independence and security, self-confidence, skill development, and possible development of a social life. Individuals with an ASD do not do well when they have unstructured time without goals and routines. For individuals with an ASD who struggle with communication, social interactions, the ability to be flexible, and sensory regulation, finding and keeping employment can be challenging. It takes careful thought, information gathering, creativity, access to community resources, and ample time for planning and specialized training. Although IDEA mandates services and programs while the young adult is still in school, there are no state or federally mandated services, including vocational services, for adults after graduation.

One of the most important areas of transition to adult life involves deciding what type of employment would be best for a young adult with an ASD, based on interest, experience, cognition, language and social capability, and other factors. The "job match" is important. Parent and child must consider the social navigation of the job, the physical components, job expectations, and the grooming requirements as well as communication demands.

Adolescents with an ASD and/or intellectual disabilities should be encouraged to obtain vocational experience and participate in "career development" as much as possible. They can begin early, learning to do chores around the home. Parents should make the most out of the transition years during school to have the adult child develop life skills and prepare to enter the world of employment. He or she should learn as much as possible about various vocations, participate in training programs, identify transportation options, work at voluntary internships, and participate in summer job experiences to develop pre-vocational skills and practice them.

Often the best employment outcomes for an adult with an ASD who remains in the family home occurs when he or she can be employed close to home with "natural supports" at the worksite, meaning that people who work there understand the challenges of ASDs and are willing to help. Often this type of community employment is developed by parents themselves. It is important for parents to realize that this part of transition involves much more than simply identifying that the child has an area of special interest. Although a child's focus can be a starting point for successful employment, parents may need to be creative and think "out of the box." An adult who is preoccupied with vacuums could become a successful member of the housekeeping staff at a local hotel, and for another young adult with an ASD an interest in pipes and drains could develop into a career in plumbing or heating.

Some young adults with ASDs graduate from high school and go on to various post-secondary education opportunities at colleges or trade schools, and others require more structure with job coaching or supported employment through agencies. Regardless of the type of employment, the planning and steps involved are generally similar. While the adolescent is still in school, it is important to obtain comprehensive functional vocational assessments as well as explore interests, strengths, and options, and obtain training to develop job skills and encourage self-advocacy. If appropriate for the individual, a young adult with an ASD should be taught to prepare a résumé and learn how to participate in interviews.

Once a young adult enters the adult service system at age 18, 21, or 22 years, he or she may work with different types and levels of supports, including a job coach and vocational counselor, with the goal of becoming employed. For some adults with an ASD who have more needs, a realistic objective is to have a balance which may include some days of work and other days doing volunteer work, while also accessing public benefits to supplement low income. Depending on the agency, vendor, and funding source(s), different types of employment can include competitive (full or part time, paid) community-based employment, individual job coaching, supported employment based in a day program, or volunteering. Support models include employer-based supervision, job coaching, or agency-based supervision, all with the goal to develop increased independence as support gradually decreases.

Individuals with ASDs and their parents need to realize that employment options in adulthood are available, but that preparation must start early with the development of life skills such as communication, social and daily living skills, as well as identification of the young adult's long-term goals for adult life. There are local and national agencies that provide support, information, and guidance. Some good resources include "Life Journey Through Autism: A Guide for Transition to Adulthood" from ResearchAutism.org, and the Autism Speaks transition toolkit (see "Useful resources").

Social and recreational activities

Like everyone else, individuals with an ASD deserve to have access to meaningful social and recreational activities. Life is more satisfying when people have life-enriching opportunities such as developing friendships, pursuing interests and talents, and participating in other leisure interests that promote health and happiness. Because individuals with ASDs struggle with social interaction and communication, it may be challenging to accomplish such important life goals. Even so, that is not to say adults with ASDs do not desire a social life; the opposite is usually true, and does not change with transition to adulthood.

Individuals and families can consider and explore specialized programs such as sports leagues, social skills groups, summer camps, adaptive swimming, expressive art or music, karate, horseback riding, gardening, and mentoring, among many others. Such group or individual activities may be offered through local community-based YMCAs, ARCs (Association(s) for Retarded Citizens), Best Buddies, Special Olympics, and many other local and national organizations.

Housing

Parents of young adults with an ASD need to consider (and perhaps create) a housing arrangement that will realistically meet the needs of their individual child during the adult years, satisfy the child's desires as much as possible, and foster his or her happiness. Finding and securing appropriate supports and housing can be challenging and might seem overwhelming. Many questions arise in starting this process, and parents want and need to know about different models of housing available in their local community or state (or country), what legal rights apply, and where to find resources to help in the process.

There are many more options for housing for adults with ASDs than in the past, mostly due to parent-led initiatives, family creativity, and parent advocacy. The availability of each model depends on the locale (town, city, county, state, country), funding streams, and private resources. Parents are much more involved today in the decision-making process to develop housing for young adults with an ASD due to the popularity and dissemination of person-centered planning.[6]

As is true in every other area of transition planning, parents should do their research as well as network with other families who have previously weathered the process and with some who are at the same point in the journey. They can obtain help from professionals knowledgeable about the types of housing available and possible funding sources. Finding the "best fit" involves identifying the level of support a young adult needs, envisioning the ideal living environment, and figuring ongoing expenses including staffing, costs related to the young person's interests and preferences, and figuring out federal and state funding. Most families cannot afford to privately support an adult with an ASD across the lifespan. Since adult services are not an entitlement (i.e., are not mandated by law), parents may need to constantly advocate with their state lead agency and vendor agencies, and network in the community, in order to access the best options for their child.

Community-based housing options include group homes, supported or supervised (shared) living, adult foster care (which is Medicaid funded), and farming communities. Farm-based programs are becoming very popular with parents who envision them as providing rich, varied, and abundant opportunities for physical and distraction-free activities that are productive and meaningful.

Some helpful resources include the book *Moving Out* by Dafna Krouk-Gordon and Barbara D. Jackins, Autism Housing Pathways, the Autism Speaks housing toolkit, and two farmstead programs, Sage Crossing Foundation and Bittersweet Farms (see "Useful resources").

Transportation

Being able to get from one place to another in a community as an adult is a major part of becoming independent and successful. For this reason, exploring the most appropriate and accessible means of transportation for an adolescent with an ASD during the school years is important. A young adult's ability to safely navigate his or her community should be assessed, and goals unique to that individual's skills in this area should be developed as part of the IEP.

Travel training is a critical part of transition planning and services because it maximizes the ability to go to work, access post-secondary education, and participate in social and recreational opportunities. Whether an adolescent is going to be capable of driving a car or will need to rely on public transportation, with or without support, are basic considerations. Young adults with an ASD and their parents can explore what realistic options exist in their own communities. Many states have developed adaptive driving programs, and federal- and state-supported transportation options are often available. A helpful resource is the National Dissemination Center for Children with Disabilities Transition Summary "Travel Training for Youth with Disabilities."

Sexuality

Sexuality is a normal, healthy part of life, and at some point the subject of sexuality comes up for everyone. Many individuals with an ASD lack even a basic knowledge of sexuality, and many do not know whom to ask or when to ask questions. There are very few programs that teach people with ASDs about love, sex, intimacy, and sexuality. Because people with ASDs are often unaware of social cues and peer expectations, clear, direct education is often crucial. While typically developing individuals learn about sexuality through their natural environment, individuals with ASDs require direct instruction. The majority of the time it is the parents who take on this challenge. (Parents are directed to the "Useful resources" section for a list of resources, such as Newport *et al.* (2002) *Autism–Asperger's and Sexuality: Puberty and Beyond*, that provide frank discussions and clear instruction, as well as Chapter 14, which discusses puberty and sexuality in greater detail.)

Communication

As nearly all parents of a child with an ASD know, deficits in communication are included as criteria for the diagnosis. This will most likely continue to be a challenge in one form or another for the child through adolescence and into adulthood, especially for those who are nonverbal or minimally verbal with little functional language. Ideally, communication supports in place during the school years and leading up to transition should continue to be part of a young adult's program later on; however, this is often not the case with adult services.

It is important, however, that individuals with an ASD have a method of functional communication because, as is true in children, behaviors in adolescents and young adults might improve once they are able to communicate their needs and desires.[7] For this reason, we strongly support as much direct communication therapy as possible for young adults with an ASD during the transition years, and that this be continued in day programs, housing, and job sites in adulthood. Augmentative and alternative communication methods, such as picture schedules and electronic devices with or without speech output, are becoming increasingly useful, and the technology supporting them is more accessible, affordable, and creative than ever.

Behavior plans

Increased frustration and aggression can develop in young adults with ASDs, and new or increased obsessions, perseverations, rituals, anxiety, and self-injury can result from having unstructured time and with exposure to new environments. Maladaptive behavior can be viewed as a form of communication when a child or adult is unable to share his or her needs. When the young adult with an ASD leaves a familiar school environment, some or all of these problems can occur because services for the adult will be less intensive than before transition. Usually there is a decrease in the level of support between the school years and adulthood. Also, challenging behaviors can occur when an individual with an ASD feels unhappy or is ill, and may worsen due to less structure in the adult environment.

Maximizing intensive, consistent behavioral programs for those who need them, especially for the home and community, are important during the transition years. Parents are strongly encouraged to inform the human services agency, employer, and direct care staff (who will be involved with their child during adulthood) about the behavior plans that have been most effective. Independent consultations from clinicians who have expertise in working with individuals with ASDs in fields such as psychiatry, psychology, neurology, speech therapy, and applied behavior analysis are helpful. Communication and collaboration among team members, and continuing strong advocacy throughout the transition process, can help all involved to better cope with challenging behaviors.

 ## TAKEAWAY POINTS

- Individuals with ASDs and their families have much to consider, starting in early adolescence, in order to best prepare for a successful transition to life as an adult.

- The transition process can be daunting since there is much to plan and do. Developing a comprehensive and detailed transition plan is the key and, by definition, facilitates the movement from school to the world of adult work, living, and community participation.

- The most important areas of transition that need attention are special education, life skills, social skills and recreation, state and federal benefits, legal and financial planning, housing, and employment.

- Effective transition planning involves much thought, effort, time, and planning on the part of many people. Families, the individual with an ASD, and his or her team need to gather information, plan, network, collaborate, and constantly advocate. There are countless resources with up-to-date information consisting of books, articles, and websites (some of which are listed below).

- Timelines and checklists can be helpful in maintaining organization throughout the transition process. Parents need to realize that transition planning is not about what is probable but what is *possible* for their child with an ASD.

Useful resources

Books

Gerhardt, P. and Crimmins, D. (2013) *Social Skills and Adaptive Behavior in Learners with Autism Spectrum Disorders.* Baltimore, MD: Brookes Publishing.

Krouk-Gordon, D. and Jackins, B. (2013) *Moving Out: A Family Guide to Residential Planning for Adults with Disabilities.* Bethesda, MD: Woodbine House.

Lawson, W. and Jones, G. (2005) *Sex, Sexuality and the Autism Spectrum.* London: Jessica Kingsley Publishing.

Newport, J., Newport, M., and Bolick, T. (2002) *Autism–Asperger's and Sexuality: Puberty and Beyond.* Arlington, TX: Future Horizons.

Robinson, R.G. (2011) *Autism Solutions: How to Create a Healthy and Meaningful Life for Your Child* (pp. 307–325, 343–353, 354–366). Ontario: Harlequin.

Shore, S. (2004) *Ask and Tell: Self Advocacy with Disclosure for People on the Autism Spectrum.* Shawnee Mission, KS: Autism Asperger Publishing Co.

Wrobel, M. (2003) *Taking Care of Myself: A Hygiene, Puberty and Personal Curriculum for Young People with Autism.* Arlington, TX: Future Horizons.

Online

Act Relevant to Insurance Coverage for Autism (ARICA)

www.disabilityinfo.org/arica

Asperger's Association of New England

www.aane.org

Autism After 16

www.autismafter16.com

Autism Consortium (Boston) Transition Manual (Transitioning teens with autism spectrum disorders: Resources for timeline planning and adult living)

www.autismconsortium.org/families/transitioning-to-adulthood

Autism Housing Pathways

www.autismhousingpathways.net

Autism Society of America

   www.autism-society.org

Autism Speaks toolkits (Transition, Employment, Postsecondary Educational Opportunities Guide, Housing and Residential Supports, Challenging Behaviors)

   www.autismspeaks.org/family-services/tool-kits

Autism Today

   www.autismtoday.com/articles/Special_Needs_Trusts_Estate_Planning.htm

AutismAsperger's.net

   www.autismasperger.net/writings_self_advocacy.htm

Best Buddies

   www.bestbuddies.org

Bittersweet Farms

   www.bittersweetfarms.org

College Autism Spectrum

   www.collegeautismspectrum.com

Forward Motion Coaching

   www.forwardmotion.info

The McCarton Foundation (Sexuality & Sexuality Instruction with Learners with Autism Spectrum Disorders and Other Developmental Disabilities)

   www.howard-autism.org/docs/Workshops/Gerhardt.pdf

Got Transition?

   www.gottransition.org

Indiana University, Center for Disability Information and Referral (Sexuality and People with Disabilities Resource Guide)

   www.iidc.indiana.edu/index.php?pageId=2457

Individuals with Disabilities Education Act (IDEA 2004)

   www.idea.ed.gov

Institute for Community Inclusion

   www.communityinclusion.org

Massachusetts Autism Insurance Resource Center

   www.disabilityinfo.org/arica

McLean Hospital College Mental Health Program

   www.mclean.harvard.edu/education/cmhp/consult.php

National Dissemination Center for Children with Disabilities (NICHCY) Transition Summary Travel Training for Youth with Disabilities, volume 9, June 1996

   http://nichcy.org/wp-content/uploads/docs/ts9.pdf

National Guardianship Association

    www.guardianship.org

Neuropsychological and Educational Services for Children and Adolescents

    www.nesca-newton.com

Organization for Autism Research (2006) Life Journey Through Autism: A Guide for Transition to Adulthood

    www.researchautism.org/resources/reading/documents/transitionguide.pdf

Sage Crossing Foundation

    www.sagecrossingfoundation.org/SagePress/?p=316

Sibling Support Project

    www.siblingsupport.org

Social Security Administration

    www.ssa.gov/ssi

Special Olympics

    www.specialolympics.org

Transition from School to Life Timeline (a Guide or Map)

    www.arcmass.org

The United Arc

    www.unitedarc.org

Chapter 16

Autism Spectrum Disorders and the Law

Gary McAbee, DO, JD

Introduction

For parents of children with special needs, including autism spectrum disorders (ASDs), legal issues may arise under a variety of circumstances and at different points in time. In this chapter we review legal issues surrounding diagnosis, educational services, vocational and residential planning, as well as when you may need to consult with an attorney. We also discuss federal and state laws pertaining to disabilities as well as those specific to ASDs.

Legal ramifications of changes in the definition of autism and related disorders in the fifth edition of the *Diagnostic and Statistical Manual of Mental Disorders*

The *Diagnostic and Statistical Manual of Mental Disorders* (DSM) is a major reference book used to assist in diagnosis, treatment, research, and communication about mental disorders. The intent of the DSM is to provide uniformity in how practitioners diagnose certain diseases of the brain. Autism and other pervasive developmental disorders (PDDs) are included in the DSM. The most recent edition (fifth), the DSM-5, released in May 2013, has triggered controversy about the diagnosis of these disorders.[1] Historically, some insurance companies have relied on the DSM for diagnoses they decide to cover or exclude from coverage in their health insurance plans.

The DSM-5 has changes from the previous version, DSM-IV (revised in 2000),[2] with regard to the diagnosis of PDD. It has stricter criteria for the diagnosis of these disorders and eliminates Asperger syndrome as a separate diagnosis. Autism, Asperger syndrome, pervasive developmental disorder—not otherwise specified (PDD-NOS), and childhood disintegrative disorder had previously been categorized as separate diagnoses in the DSM-IV. Now the four separate diagnoses are combined together to form one single diagnosis called "autism spectrum disorder." Previously, many practitioners had included the first three diagnoses (autism, Asperger, and PDD-NOS) under the rubric ASD but had utilized different criteria to reach the three diagnoses; for example, patients with Asperger syndrome typically had normal language development. Additional distinctions under the DSM-5 will be based on the level of severity of symptoms. Some of the most important changes in the DSM-5 criteria are that language delay is no longer necessary for diagnosis, and more symptoms are required for the criteria of fixated interests and repetitive behaviors. The rationale for the changes in the DSM-5 included a concern for health care professionals to be more precise in the diagnosis, rather than changing the diagnosis from year to year, and the need to identify a disorder with common behaviors by a single name yet maintaining the ability for the diagnosis to be further differentiated according to the severity of symptoms.

Controversy revolves around the concern that some patients with a prior diagnosis of a PDD will no longer fulfill the criteria for diagnosis. It has not yet been established whether the DSM-IV diagnostic criteria for ASD was too "loose" or whether the DSM-5 diagnostic criteria will be too "strict." A change or loss of a diagnosis poses obvious concern for the potential loss of services (educational, medical, insurance, financial, and so forth). Persons at risk of losing the diagnosis are some who had previously been diagnosed with Asperger syndrome, high-functioning autism, and PDD-NOS. Also of concern is the change in an individual's diagnosis of PDD-NOS or Asperger syndrome to one of "social communication disorder," which may not qualify an individual for the same services. According to the DSM-5, a diagnosis of "social communication disorder" may be given to a child with communication problems that adversely affect socialization but who does not have the restricted, repetitive patterns of behavior, interests, or activities seen in children with ASDs.

Although it is difficult to predict whether the diagnostic changes will dramatically impact the delivery of educational and health related services, there is some protection for individuals diagnosed with these conditions. For example, to be eligible for educational services under the federal law called the Individuals with Disabilities Education Act (see the following section), school districts had to rely on one of the categories of disability impairment specified by the law. One such category of disability impairment is autism. Even if a prior diagnosis of Asperger disorder or PDD-NOS could no longer be applied to the individual via the DSM-5, educational services can still be provided, if needed, under another category of "other health impairment." Also, a medical diagnosis is not the only way for a child to receive special education services. For instance, a "specific learning disability" is a common disability category used to provide services; it is usually diagnosed via a learning evaluation provided by the school's educational consultants.

Specific legal issues

Education and employment

Since the primary modality of treatment of a child with an ASD is in the form of education and related therapies, it is not surprising that many of the legal cases related to persons with ASDs involve a denial of educational services.[3] There are federal and state laws that protect a child with developmental or learning delays by ensuring that the child receive educational and therapy interventions to help improve these delays. For example, a child with speech delay that meets a certain threshold would be eligible for speech therapy. These laws, which are discussed below, should protect persons with ASDs; however, parents should be aware that these laws are not specific as to exactly what type of educational and other therapy services must be provided to a specific child, and devising the appropriate educational placement typically is determined by the school with guidelines established by the state. Parents should also be aware that a physician who is knowledgeable about ASDs can be of great help in guiding the parent to establish a working relationship with the school to attain the ideal or optimal educational interventions for their child. There are various laws that protect individuals from discrimination based on their disability. The primary ones related to education and employment are the Individuals with Disabilities Education Act (referred to as IDEA), Section 504 of the Rehabilitation Act of 1973, and the Americans with Disabilities Act of 1990 (ADA). The National Dissemination Center for Children with Disabilities website can be a valuable resource for parents who want further information about these laws in English or Spanish.[4]

INDIVIDUALS WITH DISABILITIES EDUCATION ACT

The Individuals with Disabilities Education Act is a federal law that mandates how states and localities provide education and related services to children with disabilities, from birth to age 21 years. It is a consolidation of several prior laws dating back to 1975. It mandates that a school district provide a "free and appropriate public education" to an individual qualified with a disability. The law determines how special education is provided to children with disabilities such as ASDs. The intent of the law focuses on the individual needs of the child and is not used to shift all of the costs related to the disability of the child to the public school district.[5] The law is complicated but is briefly summarized in the next paragraph.

Anyone (including a parent) suspecting an infant or toddler of having any type of developmental delay (such as delay in walking or talking) should arrange for the child to be evaluated by the state to determine if specialized services are required through the "early intervention" process. If the infant or toddler is determined to have the minimum disability that is required to be entitled to services, they will be provided. States set their own eligibility requirements, but they must have a minimum requirement for what fulfills the definition of "developmental delay." Early intervention services (e.g., speech, occupational or physical therapy) are provided in as natural an environment as possible (e.g., the home). An individualized family service plan (IFSP), similar to an individualized education plan (IEP) discussed below for school-age children, outlines the type, frequency, and location of the services provided and also notes the needs of the family in assisting the child to attain the appropriate developmental goals. A service coordinator monitors the activities outlined in the IFSP. If intervention is still required upon the child reaching their third birthday, the state may, but is not required to, continue to provide services until the child reaches school age. The school district supervises the continued provision of these services after age 3 years.

For school-aged children, IDEA mandates special services that apply to public schools. The intent is for the child to remain in the neighborhood school, with appropriate modifications, rather than attend a special school. The request to evaluate a child for a disability can come from a parent, school, or state agency. Parents are asked for their consent to the evaluation. IDEA requires the evaluation to take place within 60 days following the granting of parental consent, but if the state has a different time window, the state's time frame is used. The purpose of the evaluation is to determine if the child has a disability and then to determine the child's educational needs. Besides educational services, the services can include other services, for example, transportation as well as psychological, speech, occupational, or physical therapy (20 U.S.C. section 1401 (3) (A)). Schools cannot require parents to place their child on medication as a condition to receiving services (20 U.S.C. 1412 (a) (25)). A child is determined to have a disability if the evaluation finds one or more of the following categories of disability:

- autism

- specific learning disability (defined as a disorder in one or more of the basic psychological processes involved in understanding or in using language, spoken or written, and the disorder causes difficulty with the ability to listen, think, speak, read, write, spell, or do mathematic calculations)

- intellectual disability

- hearing impairment including deafness

- speech or language impairment

- visual impairment including blindness

- serious emotional disturbance

- orthopedic impairment

- traumatic brain injury

- developmental delays (as defined by the state) in one or more of the following areas: physical, cognitive, communication, social or emotional, or adaptive

- multiple disabilities

- other health impairment, which is a classification for a child who has "…limited strength, vitality or alertness, including a heightened alertness to environmental stimuli that result in limited alertness with respect to the educational environment" that is due to a chronic or acute health problem which adversely affects a child's academic performance (e.g., attention deficit disorder or attention deficit hyperactivity disorder).

An IEP is devised to place modifications in the school program to accommodate the disability. The IEP is a written document that is reviewed and revised accordingly and must include the student's current academic performance, the type and frequency of the services to be provided, and the annual goals for the child with the modifications that will be in place to assist the child in attaining those goals. The IEP should focus on the individual student rather than the medical condition that causes the disability. The team that monitors the IEP typically consists of a regular education teacher of the student (if applicable), a special education teacher, one who can interpret the educational testing (such as a psychologist), a school administrator who has knowledge of the services available and the authority to provide the required services, and the parents. The law mandates that the child be reassessed once every 3 years, but the reassessment can occur annually, unless the parent and the educational agency agree that a reevaluation is unnecessary. The IEP must also include a transitioning strategy for appropriate employment and living objectives as the child reaches adulthood. Parents have a right to a hearing if they disagree with the IEP. Children with disabilities who are protected by IDEA are also automatically protected by the Rehabilitation Act of 1973 and the ADA. Children who do not qualify for services under IDEA may still qualify for accommodations and modifications under the Rehabilitation Act of 1973 or the ADA.

SECTION 504 OF THE REHABILITATION ACT OF 1993

Section 504 of the Rehabilitation Act of 1993 provides for an individual with a disability to have access to any program benefits and services of any employer or other organization that receives any financial assistance from any federal agency (such as the U.S. Department of Education). A person is determined to have a disability according to the criteria of the Americans with Disabilities Act Amendment Act (ADAAA) discussed below. Because the term "disability" is much broader under Section 504 and the ADAAA, more children are entitled to services from these laws than under IDEA. Modifications in a school program for a child with a disability under the Rehabilitation Act of 1993 are often referred to as a "504 plan." A 504 plan is similar to an IEP but is usually not as extensive, and it generally provides a lower level of protection. It differs from an IEP because the IEP is provided to a child who has one of the specific diagnoses listed under the IDEA law. An advantage of Section 504 is that it also affords protection from discrimination during extracurricular activities such as school sports. It also applies to private schools that receive federal monies as well as to postsecondary schools (e.g., state colleges and vocational training schools).

AMERICANS WITH DISABILITIES ACT OF 1990

The Americans with Disabilities Act (ADA) was enacted by Congress in 1990. It was later amended in 2008 as the ADA Amendment Act of 2008 (ADAAA). This law is a civil rights law that broadly prohibits discrimination of individuals with disabilities in the area of employment, prohibits discrimination by public entities at the local and state governmental levels, prohibits discrimination in public accommodations which include areas such as those related to education, lodging, dining, recreation, and transportation, and prohibits discrimination in areas involving telecommunications (primarily related to hearing-impaired individuals and those with speech impairments). It applies to both public and private schools, unless the private school is affiliated with a religious organization (although these types of schools may be covered by state anti-discrimination laws). There also may be limits on the assistance the private school is required to provide under the ADA. A "disability" is defined as "a physical or mental impairment that substantially limits one or more of the 'major life activities' of such individual, a record of such impairment or being regarded as having such an impairment" (American with Disabilities Amendments Act). The ADAAA includes a list of major life activities. Examples of major life activities include learning, reading, concentrating, thinking, speaking, walking, caring for oneself, seeing, breathing, and performing manual tasks.

School-aged children tend to be protected against discrimination for their disabilities by federal laws other then the ADA (such as the IDEA and/ or Section 504 of the Rehabilitation Act of 1973). The ADA should be more protective following completion of education when the individual is attempting to enter the workforce. A person with an ASD should theoretically be protected by the ADA, but it does not necessarily equate with absolute protection from discrimination. Many aspects of an individual with an ASD could be problematic during employment opportunities despite the person being qualified for the job. Examples which could lead to discriminatory behavior include communication difficulties, social awkwardness and trouble with interacting with work peers, and difficulty with transitioning tasks throughout the day. Some useful information can be obtained from a user-friendly site explaining the ADA.[6]

FAMILY EDUCATIONAL RIGHTS AND PRIVACY ACT OF 1974

The Family Educational Rights and Privacy Act of 1974, a federal law, protects the privacy of student educational records. The law applies to all schools that receive federal funding. The right transfers to the student when he or she attains the age of 18 years or enters a school beyond high school. Parents can review the educational records and request changes if they are inaccurate or misleading. Schools can disclose the student's records only under limited circumstances.

Other relevant laws

COMBATING AUTISM ACT OF 2006 AND COMBATING AUTISM REAUTHORIZATION ACT OF 2011

The Combating Autism Act of 2006 (CAA) and the Combating Autism Reauthorization Act of 2011 (CARA) provide for federal monies for the purpose of autism education, detection, and treatment. CARA re-authorizes CAA by providing $693 million from 2011 to 2014. The law also authorizes the director of the National Institutes of Health to develop a plan for autism research based on recommendations from the Interagency Autism Coordinating Committee, a federal advisory committee related to autism research that coordinates all efforts involving ASDs with the federal Department of Health and Human Services; reauthorizes the Autism Centers for Excellence supporting basic and clinical research; provides funding for the collection and storage of data generated from public and private research partners; and establishes a program whereby tissue and genetic materials, and other biological markers, are available for research.

State laws regarding health insurance

As of 2012, 37 states and the District of Columbia had enacted laws related to autism and insurance coverage. Thirty-one states specifically require insurers to provide coverage for the treatment of autism (Alaska, Arizona, Arkansas, California, Colorado, Connecticut, Florida, Illinois, Indiana, Iowa, Kansas, Kentucky, Louisiana, Maine, Massachusetts, Michigan, Missouri, Montana, Nevada, New Hampshire, New Jersey, New Mexico, New York, Pennsylvania, Rhode Island, South Carolina, Texas, Vermont, Virginia, West Virginia, and Wisconsin). Alabama mandates limited coverage under certain circumstances. Other states may require coverage under existing state mental health laws. These laws vary from state to state, and a summary of them can be obtained from the website of the National Conference of State Legislatures (www.ncsl.org) or from a legal textbook.[3] Many of the laws have a cap on the amount the insurer must pay for services each year. This represents a significant change in philosophy. Historically, many insurers excluded coverage for ASDs by classifying them as "developmental" or "mental health" disorders which were considered disorders where the evidence for effective treatment was lacking. It is now generally accepted that a range of educational and behavioral therapies as well as medications can be effective for many children with ASDs. One potential concern about mandating insurance companies to pay for treatment relates to a potential conflict with school districts that historically were responsible for paying for needed services. Since the primary treatment of ASDs is educationally based, the concern relates to a potential "battle" over who will pay for treatment, the school districts or the insurance companies.

Vaccines and ASDs

The theory that childhood vaccines and/or the preservative thimerosal in the vaccines may cause autism has met with increasing scientific skepticism over the years. The prestigious Institute of Medicine (IOM) reviewed the scientific evidence regarding vaccines in 2011 and found no evidence that the measles, mumps, and rubella vaccine causes autism. The Centers for Disease Control and Prevention supports the position of the IOM. Additional scientific studies provide additional support for this conclusion.[7]

Several legal cases were concluded through the federal court system to determine if vaccines or thimerosal caused autism and whether children with ASDs would be compensated through the National Vaccine Injury Compensation Program, a program which provides money to persons who sustain an injury determined to be due to a vaccine. These courts concluded that there was insufficient evidence to link vaccines or thimerosal as a cause of autism.[8]

Criminal behavior and ASDs

There is no compelling evidence that individuals with an ASD are prone to criminal behavior; however, anecdotal reports exist in the published literature and, for a few specific individuals, such a relationship may exist.[9–12] Reasons for an individual with an ASD to become involved in a potentially criminal situation include a lowering of impulse control; cognitive impairment; difficulty with understanding social cues and circumstances; difficulty in understanding the mental state of another individual and being unable to put themselves in "another's shoes" (i.e., deficits in "theory of mind"); difficulty in displaying empathy; misinterpreting another person's intentions; fixating on people or interests; or overreacting to an ordinary, non-threatening physical nearness.[9] Some affected individuals may have a comorbid disorder, such as attention deficit hyperactivity disorder, anxiety, or depression, that underscores the issue. There are also concerns for manipulation during police questioning and false confession.[9]

For an individual involved in an incident with potential criminal ramifications, a diagnosis of an ASD may be a mitigating factor. One high court has reversed a criminal conviction because it determined that a diagnosis of Asperger syndrome was relevant to the defense and should not have been excluded at trial (State v. Burr 2008). Several states have laws stating that a diagnosis of an ASD may be a possible basis for finding the defendant incompetent to stand trial (California Penal Code 2010). Research in this area is in its infancy and continues to evolve. This could be a potential major public health issue as the increased number of children given this diagnosis in the past decade start to reach adolescence and adulthood. Programs to educate law enforcement personnel about persons with ASDs are increasing nationwide.[13] Models to proactively prevent the potential for precipitating violent behavior are of value.[14]

Life planning and vocational or housing issues

Determining the future of a child with an ASD after they reach an age where they are no longer eligible for educational services is a major challenge for families. Much of the federal, state, and private monies have thus far been used in diagnosis and treatment, and less on the vocational and housing needs of the population with ASDs as they reach adult years. This is especially true for those individuals who are moderately and severely affected and may have made few developmental gains. Families need to realize that this may be their responsibility, and they should prepare for it years before the child leaves the school system. Laws such as IDEA mandate a transition plan, but often the strategy used is inadequate and, in some cases, a transitioning plan is completely ignored.

Finding employment and housing opportunities for an adult with an ASD can be challenging. One should emphasize the individual's strengths and skills even if these skills were previously considered an obstacle. For example, some individuals who require rigid routine in their lives and have difficulty with transitioning may excel at performing rote activities such as data entry. Volunteering during the adolescent years can be valuable in assessing the individual's capacity to perform a job and assess how the individual will function in an employment environment.

When a child reaches the age of 18 years, most states legally recognize them as an adult regarding the ability to make health care decisions. For some young adults, their functional ability makes this impossible and the parent needs to seek guardianship of the 18-year-old. Guardianship is a legal process that varies among the states and is granted by a judge. It permits a parent to continue to make health care decisions for the child after the child's eighteenth birthday. A related concept, conservatorship, is also granted by a judge and permits the parent to make other life decisions, such as the management of social security money, after the child turns 18 years of age.

Parents should prepare a written life plan outlining their wishes for the child in the event of their death or inability to care for the child or adult with an ASD. This is important since many adults with ASDs outlive their parents.

When should a parent hire an advocate or attorney?

Although numerous situations involving children with ASDs have been settled via the legal system,[3] it is always recommended that a parent avoid this approach. It is adversarial, time-consuming, may not be successful, and can be expensive if one has to hire an attorney and the attorney fee is not reimbursable under any federal or state law. Working with the teacher and other school personnel is always the preferred way of meeting the child's educational needs. Hiring an attorney should be the decision of last resort for a parent, but do not hesitate to do so if you are convinced that your child's educational needs are not being met. Under the laws discussed above, a parent may have to go through various administrative hearings before they can seek a remedy via the legal system (C.N. v. Willmar Public Schools 2010).

Educational advocates can be valuable for a parent having difficulty negotiating with the school for services. These advocates are often psychologists in private practice. Some of them may have formerly been affiliated with the school system and may personally know some of the school personnel. They know how to talk to the school personnel in "educational" language. The Internet can be a valuable source for accessing the names of such advocates.

(Note: The information included in this chapter should not to be used for legal advice but rather for informational purposes only. If legal concerns arise, you should contact appropriate legal counsel.)

 TAKEAWAY POINTS

- It has not yet been determined whether new diagnostic criteria recommended by one authoritarian medical source (the DSM-5) will result in some children with ASDs losing educational and behavioral services.

- Children with ASDs have protected legal rights under various federal and state laws that entitle them to various educational, behavioral, and medical treatment interventions.

- Adults with ASDs have protected legal rights in the workplace.

- Currently, the major national medical organizations do not support the notion that vaccines or their ingredients cause ASDs.

- Although children and adults with ASDs are not generally prone to criminal behavior, there may be some circumstances where ASD symptoms and/or comorbid conditions can result in behavior with potential criminal ramifications.

- An ASD is a lifelong condition, and parents must prepare not only for the child's educational needs during the early years but also the child's vocational and housing needs as the child approaches adulthood.

Court cases and laws

Americans with Disabilities Amendments Act (2008), section 1630.2(g)

29 U.S.C. 701 et seq, as amended section 794, Pub Law 93-112, September 26, 1973

California Penal Code Vol 1370.1, California 2010

C.N. v. Willmar Public Schools, 591 F3d 624 (8th Cir 2010)

Combat Autism Act (2006), 42 U.S.C. section 280i, Pub Law 109-416

Combating Autism Reauthorization Act (2011), 42 U.S.C. section 280i, Pub Law 112-32

Family Educational Rights and Privacy Act (1974), 20 U.S.C. section 1232g

Individual with Disabilities Education Act (2004), 20 U.S.C. sections 1400 et seq., Pub Law 108-446

Individual with Disabilities Education Act (2004), 20 U.S.C. section 1401 (3) (A)

Richardson Independent School District v. Michael Z., 580 F3d 286 (5th Cir 2009)

State v. Burr, 948 A2d 627 (NJ 2008)

Participating in a Research Project for Individuals with Autism Spectrum Disorders

Sue X. Ming, MD, PhD

Introduction

Autism spectrum disorders (ASDs) are a group of disorders that are not fully understood. Although scientists have gathered many pieces of the autism puzzle (as discussed in previous chapters), these pieces cannot be assembled into a clear picture yet. Research is needed to find causes and effective treatments for ASDs. Research on human subjects can lead to more direct answers. Participation in some research projects may benefit your child directly, while others will instead help us to understand ASDs in general. This chapter discusses various types of human research, the pros and cons of participation, and what a parent should know prior to enrolling their child in a research project.

Why we need to perform research

If you have read most of the chapters of this book, you probably have concluded that we need to do more research on ASDs. There are many unresolved issues in ASDs, most importantly we still do not understand what causes most cases of ASDs (so-called idiopathic ASDs) or how the brain and body functions are perturbed. We still need more effective treatments for all persons with ASDs. Whereas animal studies can be helpful in providing information on basic science-related topics, such as the effect of a toxin on the brain and organ development, toxicity of a drug, or impact on behaviors or biochemical functions when a gene is deleted in mice, this does not necessarily give us direct information about these same responses or functions in humans. To translate results obtained from animal studies to humans, scientists often need to perform human-subject research, whether it involves taking samples or specimens from the human body and performing experiments on them out of the body in a test tube (in vitro), or conducting safe research directly on the human body (in vivo). When ASD research needs to be conducted on human subjects, it is more relevant if the study is actually done on subjects with ASDs. For the majority of human studies, scientists also require another comparison group of subjects (called the control group), which in the case of ASDs ideally would be composed of (1) typically developing similar-aged unrelated individuals, (2) siblings of children with ASDs, or (3) subjects with another similar disorder who do not meet the criteria for an ASD. Some studies can potentially benefit the child with an ASD directly, such as a study to find the cause of gastrointestinal (GI) dysfunction in individuals with ASDs. Other studies, such as an epidemiologic study, may not benefit persons with ASDs directly but may provide important general information about ASDs.

Issues on human-subject research and the Institutional Review Board

There are many regulations defining how human-subject research may or may not be conducted. The Institutional Review Board of the University of Virginia defines human-subject research as follows:

> Human subject research is defined as an investigator conducting research on a living human subject to obtain (1) data through intervention or interaction with the individual; or (2) identifiable private information. Intervention includes both physical procedures by which data are gathered (e.g., venipuncture) and manipulations of the subject or the subject's environment that are performed for research purposes.[1]

Every human being needs to be protected legally and ethically when he or she becomes a research subject. In the distant past there were notable ethical violations in research on human subjects, which places a tremendous moral obligation on all involved in human research today to be thoughtful, cautious, and meticulous in how we explain and conduct research. Nazi physicians conducted deadly or debilitating experiments on concentration camp prisoners toward the end of the Second World War, and the infamous Tuskegee Syphilis Experiment from the 1930s to 1940s withheld the effective treatment of penicillin to Negro (the word used at the time) men in the study of the natural history of syphilis, and the participants were not informed of the availability of the treatment. Since then, regulations and rules have been established to protect human subjects participating in research, and codes of conduct have been developed to enforce the regulations and rules.

Governing structures were created to monitor the ethical conduct of human research. One of these governing structures is an institutional review board (IRB) in the United States or ethics committees in other countries. The IRB reviews and approves all human-subject research. Members of an IRB consist of scientists and non-scientists of different ethnicity, gender, and educational backgrounds. The IRB committee must be composed of both members who are and are not affiliated with the institution under which the IRB has been established, and often includes a few members from the surrounding community.

The IRB ensures that researchers follow human-subject research guidelines and codes of conduct throughout the duration of the project. The IRB determines whether the research is scientifically sound enough to subject humans to the research proposed. The project must be approved prior to initiation of any research activities and re-approved at defined intervals (varying from 6 months to 1 year depending on the project and local IRB rules). Any deviations from the approved protocol need to be reported in a timely manner and any adverse events reported immediately. Most prospective studies (studies being done moving forward) require a consent process. During the consent process, the subject or guardian's permission is sought prior to enrolling in a research project. A consent is usually a written document. The investigators performing the study or a designee assigned by the investigator will explain the following before the consent is signed:

- the purpose of the study and whether there is an alternative to participating in the research project

- what is involved and/or what the subject is expected to do

- the sources of research funds

- the anticipated duration of research project participation

- whether the research will benefit the subject directly or not

- whether participation will incur a cost to the subject and whether the subject will be paid for their participation

- who is eligible to participate in the research project (inclusion criteria)

- who is not eligible to participate in the research project (exclusion criteria)

- what happens if the subject is harmed or injured in the course of participating in the project

- potential side effects or harm to subjects who participate in the research project

- who will be granted access to private information gathered on research subjects and how the private information will be stored and protected

- who the subject should contact if questions arise

- that the relationship between the subject and the investigator should not be affected by the decision to participate or not participate in this or any other research project

- that at any time during the course of the study, the subject may change his or her mind and withdraw from participating

- that the subject will be treated without cost to themselves if they experience side effects or if an injury occurs.

The subjects and/or guardians should be given ample opportunity to ask questions after reading through the consent. For children ages 12–17 years, an assent form also needs to be signed by the participating minor along with the parental consent. If a child is intellectually unable to take part in the assent process, as determined by the investigator in consultation with the parents or guardians, the assent may be waived. For non-English-speaking subjects, a consent in their native language should be provided, or if this is not available in their language, a trained interpreter should be used to translate exactly what is written in the consent form and then provide interpretation services to enable them to fully participate in a discussion about the research project.

The IRB is particularly cautious if studies involve children or intellectually disabled subjects because these subjects are unable to represent themselves in making the decision about participation in research; therefore, special consideration and thoughtful deliberations occur when these subjects are being considered for research participation. IRBs also caution investigators against recruitment of coworkers and their family members, students working with or under them, or their own family members, because these individuals may feel undue pressure to participate because of their relationship with the investigators.

Retrospective studies that are done by looking back over records or materials gathered from before the start of a study may or may not require informed consent from the subjects. In many cases, the records under review can be examined without specifically identifying the person or subject, so that the patient's privacy is never able to be breached and there is little or no risk to the research subject. Depending on the study, the IRB may be asked to review and approve a given retrospective study to determine if there is a need or obligation on the part of the investigators to contact or re-contact the subjects for their consent to be included in a particular retrospective study.

Types of human research

There are a few types of human-subject research in ASDs. Some research involves a one-time interview, completion of a questionnaire, or donation of specimens; other projects may require participation over a period of time. Some research compares the effectiveness of different types of therapies, for example, comparing the effect of applied behavioral analysis therapy to the Miller method. In some studies you may be allowed to choose a particular therapy, whereas in others you may be randomly assigned to one or another therapy. The investigators will observe and record your child's response over time moving forward (a prospective study). Drug trial research requires your child to take either an experimental or existing drug(s). We discuss some of the common human-subject research below.

Research studying the causes of ASDs

Research studying the causes (etiologies) of ASDs is quite broad. For instance, it could involve finding a variation in a particular gene or sets of genes or identifying a potential toxic exposure. To conduct genetic studies, genetic material, such as a DNA sample from a blood specimen, may be required and, in some cases, family members may be asked to provide a DNA sample as well. Genetic studies can, on occasion, uncover some unexpected findings, such as incorrect paternity or parental relatedness, but nothing of this nature would be revealed unless it was stated up front that this is part of the study. Some genetic studies do not involve other family members but instead focus on specific population variations of interests. An example would be a case control study comparing the presence or absence of a common variant of a specific gene in children with an ASD versus healthy unrelated children. Genetic materials are used, but only the child subject's or control subject's genes are studied. These genetic studies usually require a one-time donation of genetic materials through a cheek swab, blood draw, or saliva sample.

Etiology studies may also involve assessment of exposure of a subject to a particular toxin or proposed toxin. Determination of toxin exposures can sometimes be assessed directly by measurement of toxins or toxic compounds in body fluid, hair, nails, or baby teeth. In other instances, toxin-exposure research focuses on measuring toxins in the environment where children with ASDs live. These tests could be done by measurement of toxins in outdoor soil, air, and water, or indoor air, floor, furniture, toys, and so forth.

Studies looking to find the cause of a specific comorbidity, such as a gastrointestinal (GI) disorder (as opposed to the ASD itself), may involve a specific test, such as a stool test, to determine whether a specific species of gut bacteria may be responsible for certain GI symptoms in individuals with an ASD. Post-mortem (after-death) studies of the brains of persons with ASDs who donated their tissues for research may also fall under the heading of etiologic studies. As you can see, some of the studies may directly help the child subject as soon as the research is completed, while others contribute to a better understanding of ASDs but do not provide direct benefit to the subject.

Epidemiologic studies

Epidemiologic studies seek to examine the pattern or occurrence of a specific disorder within a larger population. These studies report the prevalence (rate) of ASDs within a specific population and may include the general population as a whole or a specific subpopulation such as an urban population, a Hispanic population, children under 5 years of age, children living near industrial-waste landfills, and so forth. Epidemiologic studies often gather in-depth information on children with ASDs including things such as their parents' ages, socioeconomic status, home environment, siblings' functioning, parents' employment, detailed medical and behavioral history, and school history. Epidemiologic studies may be helpful for identifying clustered risk factors and highlighting an increasing prevalence of ASDs. In general, epidemiologic studies involve completion of a one-time questionnaire or participating in a single interview. Sometimes subjects may be asked to repeat the procedure a few years later for a follow-up study. Although epidemiologic studies do not provide direct input about the child subject, they may have an impact on helping to change environmental or educational policies, getting more resources and services for individuals with ASDs, and ASD research funding. These indirect benefits may lead to finding a cause of or treatment for ASDs, or providing more resources locally that will help a child subject in the long run.

Pathogenesis studies

Pathogenesis studies investigate the changes in body function or structure at the level of molecules, cells, or organs. These studies focus on characterizing and understanding mechanisms leading to variations in molecules, cells, or organs noted in individuals with ASDs compared with controls (persons without an ASD). Scientists first need to establish that the function of a molecule, cell, or organ is altered in the test group (in this case, individuals with an ASD) and then try to identify what led to this alteration. For example, James et al. reported reduced levels of the antioxidant glutathione and related molecules in individuals with ASDs,[2] which may be partially related to the discovery that children with ASDs experience higher oxidative stress.[3,4] We and others reported that the function of the parasympathetic nervous system (a nervous system responsible for digestion, rest, and recovery) is reduced in children with ASDs.[5] Buie et al. reported that GI problems are more common in children with ASDs.[6] Jyonouchi et al. reported that some children with ASDs have an abnormal immunologic response to blood cell antigens.[7] As we continue searching for primary causes of ASDs, we also need to understand the underlying pathologic changes associated with these conditions so that we can continue to develop more effective treatments. Some pathogenesis studies require donation of a specimen, while other studies require a medical test, such as an electrocardiogram or a blood pressure measurement. Many of these studies may help shed light on your child's behaviors or physical symptoms.

Treatment trials

Treatment trials require the participants to receive a treatment, such as a medication (traditional or new drug), an alternative medical practice, or an interventional educational therapy. Treatment trials usually require strict adherence to outlined procedures. Most of these studies compare a test treatment with an inactive treatment such as a placebo. A stringent study design uses a double-blind placebo-controlled method. In this case, neither the participants (nor their guardians) nor the investigators know whether a specific participant receives an active or placebo treatment (so-called double blind). A computer program randomly determines who receives an active treatment or placebo. Who gets the active treatment versus the placebo treatment may be determined by the order in which your child was enrolled in the study and how many participants enrolled before your child received which treatment. By using the computer to determine the selected treatment, it is impossible to influence who receives treatment. The investigators who assess the effectiveness of the treatment have no idea which treatment the subjects received and therefore cannot be biased or influenced by this knowledge. Sometimes treatment trials may be designed for a second phase of the study to switch the subjects who received placebo to an active treatment, and vice versa. This is called a double-blind placebo-controlled crossover study. In this way, the subject can serve as his or her own control subject since each subject has an equal number of days of treatment versus placebo. Sometimes a treatment trial is designed to compare two different treatments; in this case, a participant receives one of two active treatments. This is an approach for a trial on the effectiveness of interventional therapies.

Treatment trials, as stated above, are strictly regulated and very specific about what participants can and cannot do during the study. Except under emergent circumstances where it is essential that the child receive a treatment outside of that given as part of the treatment trial, the participants in these studies are cautioned not to start another elective treatment for the duration of the study. The reason for this precaution is that if the child gets better or worse, or experiences some side effects, the investigators will not know which treatment is responsible for the effect if two new medications or treatments are given simultaneously. In the case that another new medication or treatment is started, the investigators may have to terminate your child's participation in the study. If your child develops side effects that are more than mild symptoms, for the welfare of the child, the investigators may also decide to terminate your child's participation in the study and, as indicated, treat your child's side effects. One of the benefits of participating in a treatment trial is that your child will automatically be monitored very closely and the treatment itself has been scrutinized for safety by peer scientists and the IRB committee members. After the trial, the results of the treatment are carefully analyzed to minimize bias. If your child received an active treatment and the treatment is effective, participation in the research is the best way to start the treatment (if the treatment is made available to you after completion of the study). If your child received placebo, your child could still benefit from knowing how other children who received the active treatment responded. The information could guide you in choosing to start with the active treatment after completion of the study.

Most children participating in a clinical research trial undergo detailed testing to clearly establish a diagnosis prior to enrollment. Typically, research subjects with an ASD are tested by a psychologist with tools known as the Autism Diagnostic Interview and Autism Diagnostic Observation Schedule. These tests may indicate to you the degree or severity of your child's autistic symptoms. Since these tests are costly and usually not performed routinely as a part of clinical services, participating in a research trial may provide this information to you at no cost, regardless of whether your child receives active or placebo treatment.

Natural history studies

Natural history studies are designed to collect data prospectively through observation over the long term to assess outcomes of individuals, in this case persons with ASDs. Investigators follow a cohort (set group) of children with ASDs over time and observe who improves more than others and assesses what factors may have contributed to the improvement. These studies may be carried out through a large patient registry, and individuals who agree to be a part of this registry give their permission to be contacted and make themselves available for interviews in the future. Besides being provided with the knowledge learned as a result of the study, registry participants may enjoy early or better access to enrollment in other research studies.

Studies to characterize ASDs

Some studies focus on better characterizing or delineating features of ASDs in different subsets of patients. Many of these projects investigate specific clinical phenotypes (clinically defined characteristics) of groups of individuals with ASDs. For example, some psychologists have evaluated the "theory of mind" for children with ASDs by examining their behavioral responses to scenarios that require abstract thinking.[8] Another group of investigators studied the eye-gaze patterns of children with ASDs in response to social and emotional visual images.[9] We reported motor impairment in a cohort of children with ASDs.[10] These studies are helpful in devising a plan for education and therapy by identifying specific groups of individuals who may respond to specific therapies or educational approaches.

Research to identify biomarkers for ASDs

As stated in Chapter 1, ASDs are quite variable. Our current method of diagnosis that is based primarily on behavioral criteria has significant limitations since many different disorders could have similar behavioral manifestations. Classification of disorders based instead on biologic markers may lead to identification of more homogenous groupings or patient subsets that better reflect the true nature of the disorders; thus, scientists are eager to identify biomarkers for ASDs. Biomarkers may include specific genetic variations, localized structural brain changes, specific molecular alterations, or changes in certain cell types or body systems, all of which define specified subsets of individuals with ASDs. Research projects on biomarkers could involve taking specimens from subjects with ASDs, performing clinical tests in subjects, or even giving a test agent, such as a supplement, to determine the response to the agent. These research projects could be beneficial for subjects with ASDs either immediately or some time down the road. In general, better understanding of ASDs can and should lead to better treatment. For example, a researcher who evaluates bacteria in the GI tract and gut permeability as a biomarker may discover that gut bacterial flora and permeability is significantly altered in some children with ASDs. While this started out as a focused biomarker study, the results could lead to actual clinical interventions for the child with an ASD who has these specific biomarkers.

What you need to consider before entering your child in a research study

Participating in research projects to learn more about individuals with ASDs can lead to a better understanding of the condition; however, subjects should understand that their contributions to general knowledge may or may not result in a direct benefit to them. Some research projects can benefit the participant directly, while others only can (possibly) indirectly. Before enrolling your child in a research study, you need to be aware that you and your child should follow the rules (research design) throughout the duration of the study. You may not be at liberty to choose a test or treatment, and may not initiate another treatment, or participate in another research project that may interfere with the results of the current project while remaining as a participant.

Research projects involving a one-time donation of specimens or completion of questionnaires or an interview are least restrictive. Your child's involvement is limited to the duration of donating the specimen or completion of the questionnaires or interview. Sometimes you may be contacted for future use of your child's leftover specimen for another research project, if you agreed to be re-contacted at the time of the initial consent. Research on treatment trials involves placebo and the active components, so you need to understand that your child may get a placebo. Many treatment trials may be combined with a biomarker project. For example, we are running a DHA (a component of fish oil) double-blind placebo-controlled treatment trial together with an evaluation of oxidative-stress (a type of body stress) status in these subjects.

The half of the subjects who are receiving placebo will still benefit from the results of the oxidative-stress project.

Since treatment trials are generally quite strict when it comes to initiating any practice or drug that may affect the results of the trial, you need to plan no new interventions or initiation of new medications during the course of the study. In addition, although the potential effect of the experimental treatment could be beneficial, adverse outcomes or side effects may also occur. You will have a choice to stop the participation if your child develops side effects. Your study doctor may want to stop the treatment for your child if the side effects are significant, even if you would like to continue the study. It is, however, important to comply with your study doctor's advice to end the participation. If this occurs, you may be asked to discuss the side effects or adverse events, and your child may be asked to give a specimen to clarify why the side effects occurred or how they impacted your child. Sometimes it is just as important to determine *why* your child developed side effects as it is to see if the intervention is effective. In my experience, some parents of study subjects do not comply with the instructions or contact the study doctor in time once the child develops a side effect. If the medication is discontinued without prompt notification of the study doctor, valuable information about the treatment or why your child developed a side effect is lost. Finally, some research projects require the child's cooperation. For example, a study on autonomic dysfunction requires the participant to rest and lay on a recliner, and this simple act could be very difficult for some children with ASDs. In such circumstances, your child may not be able to complete the research despite your good intentions.

 # TAKEAWAY POINTS

- Many areas and types of ASD research are still needed to fully understand the condition and to identify various subgroups of patients who may benefit from specific interventions.

- Participating in a research study could benefit your child directly or indirectly.

- Participation requires a subject's commitment in terms of following the rules set forth by a specific project protocol.

- Research subjects are protected by regulations on human-subject research and are informed about the details of project participation.

Glossary

Actigraphy: A non-invasive, home-based study in which the child wears a device shaped like a wristwatch, which records different levels of movement and provides information about time spent asleep and awake as well as how much time is required for a child to fall asleep.

Adolescent idiopathic scoliosis: Side to side curvature of the spine that begins at or after 10 years of age and is not associated with any underlying medical or genetic condition or neuromuscular disorder.

Adrenarche: Stage of pubertal development, controlled by the hypothalamic-pituitary-adrenal axis, whereby individuals develop pubic hair, grow axillary (armpit) hair, develop body odor and get acne.

Advocate: To speak or write in favor of; support or urge by argument.

Aeroallergen allergy: Allergic response to various airborne substances, such as pollen, spores or dust.

Affective disorder: A psychiatric condition that is associated with persistent changes in mood which can, in some case alter thoughts, behaviors or feelings. There are three key types of affective disorders including: depression, bipolar disorder (also known as manic-depression), and anxiety disorder.

Agoraphobia: An extreme or irrational fear of crowded or enclosed public places. It can be quite debilitating and socially isolating for individuals who are afraid to leave home or go out in public.

Allergen immunotherapy: Process of administering allergenic extracts to patients who have allergic conjunctivitis, rhinitis or asthma in an effort to decrease symptoms by reducing immunologic responses to environmental allergens such as dust, animal dander, pollen and/or mold.

Allergic conjunctivitis: Inflammation and redness of the eyes in response to airborne allergens.

Allergic rhinitis: Inflammation of the nasal mucosa in response to airborne allergens.

Allergist and/or immunologist: A medical doctor who specializes in conditions related to allergies (the body's adverse reaction to outside factors such as pollen, foods, or medications). These specialists overlap with immunologists; many subspecialists have training in both of these areas at the same time. An immunologist is also a medical doctor who treats immunologic conditions where the body has an abnormal response (overactive or underactive) to outside factors. In some cases, they treat patients whose immune system attacks the person's own cells or tissues; in other cases they treat patients whose body cannot respond appropriately to outside insults such as a virus or bacterial infection.

Amenorrhea: Cessation or stoppage of menstrual periods.

Anaphylaxis: Acute onset of severe systemic illness involving skin, mucosal tissues, or both with exposure to an allergen, often accompanied by lowering blood pressure and breathing difficulties.

Antibodies: Specialized products produced by immune system B-cells which can recognize organisms that invade the body such as bacteria, viruses, and fungi. Antibodies are able to initiate a complex chain of events designed to kill foreign invaders.

Applied Behavioral Analysis (ABA): A technique used in behavioral therapy in which triggers for undesired behaviors are identified. This behavioral therapy takes into account the child's skills, deficits, and problem behaviors in the context of their environment. By uncovering important interaction patterns, problematic interactions can be directly targeted using behavioral treatment procedures.

Apraxia: A problem with brain programming of a motor act that leads to motor incoordination.

Assent: A process for obtaining research consent for children of 12–17 years of age who have the intellectual capability of comprehending risks and benefits. The discussion is modified to be age appropriate and still also requires a signed consent from the parent or guardian.

Atopic asthma: Also known as allergic asthma, this is a form of asthma caused by exposure of the bronchial mucosa (lining of the lungs) to inhaled airborne antigens.

Atopic dermatitis: A form of eczema characterized by chronically inflamed skin and sometimes intolerable itching due to an allergic response.

Atypical antipsychotics: A newer group of medications with fewer side effects that act on the dopamine and serotonin systems; these are often used to treat psychosis.

Auditory brainstem response: Way of testing hearing by placing several electrodes on the head, playing various tones, and recording brain activity in response to these tones. Unlike pure tone testing, this method does not require the child himself or herself to respond to the sounds.

Auditory integration therapy: A sensory-based treatment employed in the management of ASDs using headphones with a carefully arranged spectrum of sounds. Typically, children listen to two 30-minute session per day for 10 days.

Augmentative communication device: A device used for communication to supplement or replace spoken language.

Autoimmune disorders: Conditions which result from the immune system becoming overactive and attacking cells or tissues, leading to damage to one's own body.

Autonomic nervous system: A non-volitional portion of the nervous system that controls organ systems of the body, including the heart, lungs, gut, and bladder.

Autosomal dominant inheritance: Results from a mutation in a single gene of a pair of genes on one of the non-sex chromosomes. Dominant conditions are typically seen in multiple generations and affect males as often as females.

Autosomal recessive inheritance: Results from a mutation in both genes of a pair of genes on one of the non-sex chromosomes. Recessive conditions are typically seen in a single generation (group of brothers and sisters) and affect males as often as females.

B-lymphocytes: Type of white blood cell that produces antibodies.

Celiac disease: An immunological disease of the intestine not caused by immunoglobulin E, but instead resulting from permanent sensitivity to gluten (a protein found in certain food products like wheat) in a genetically susceptible individual.

Cerebrospinal fluid: Fluid that surrounds and cushions the brain and spinal cord.

Chromosomal microarray: Relatively new molecular genetic technology that enables us to uncover small missing or extra bits of genetic material on one or more chromosome(s).

Chromosome analysis: More traditional genetic test that examines the large structures (chromosomes) that carry our genes.

Chromosomes: DNA structures that contain all of our genes which represents our genetic blueprint. Most humans have 46 total chromosomes that are arranged in 23 pairs with 22 pairs of non-sex chromosomes (also called autosomes) and one pair of sex chromosomes (XX for girls and XY for boys).

Chronic abdominal pain: The presence of at least three episodes of pain (constant or intermittent) occurring over a period of 3 months or more, severe enough to affect activity.

Chronic urticaria: A form of hypersensitivity reaction manifested by crops of small papules (fluid filled bumps) and wheals (welts) in which the wheals recur frequently, or persist.

Colitis: Inflammation of the large bowel or colon.

Colonoscopy: Tube with a camera (endoscope) is passed up into the anus to look at the lining of the large intestine and obtain tissue (biopsy) for microscopic evaluation.

Comorbidities: Co-occurring conditions that may or may not be directly linked to the primary disorders, in this case, ASDs.

Complete blood count: A test which measures the levels of specific blood cells (red cells, white cells and platelets) and may detect anemia (low red cells), signs of infection (elevated white cells), or potential problems with clotting (low platelets) among other things.

Complementary and alternative medicine: Medical treatment or care that includes all those modalities which offer alternatives and complementary therapies to conventional (allopathic) medicine.

Computerized tomography: A relatively fast imaging process that provides good-quality images of tissues, bones and blood, but involves some radiation exposure and does not provide the same detailed resolution as magnetic resonance imaging.

Consent: A process to obtain a subject's or guardian's permission to enroll in a research project. Usually involves reading over and signing a detailed consent form after a discussion about the specifics of the project.

Conservatorship: A legal document considered for an adult or child who has assets such as property or bank accounts, but who is unable to make informed financial decisions that are necessary to protect those assets.

Continuous positive airway pressure: Also known as CPAP, this is a way of delivering air to people under a little bit of pressure via a mask, usually during sleep, to provide better air exchange and oxygen delivery to the lungs. Often is the first line in the treatment of obstructive sleep apnea.

Copy number variants: Small changes or variation in the amount of genetic material that is found by chromosomal microarray. These small deletions or duplications (missing or extra bits of genetic material) may be benign (of no consequence), may predispose to developmental problems such as an ASD, or may be pathogenic (known to be strongly associated with an ASD).

Dental caries: Also known as tooth decay or "cavities," this is a bacterial disease that causes demineralization (weakening) and destruction of the hard tissues of the teeth.

Developmental, Individual Differences-based, Relationship-based (DIR)/ The Floortime Model: A developmental model for assessing a child's strengths and weaknesses. It emphasizes the creation of emotionally meaningful learning exchanges that encourage developmental abilities.

Developmental pediatrician: A pediatrician who has done additional training in both typical and atypical development of a child. Developmental pediatricians are often helpful in differentiating developmental delay from behavioral disorders, and may make recommendations for special therapies or prescribe medications as needed for behavioral difficulties.

Discrete Trial Teaching (DTT): A form of ABA therapy often used to teach basic skills such as paying attention, following directions and imitating instructions.

Disruptive behavioral disorder: Difficult behaviors that may cause an individual to be disruptive such as attention deficit hyperactivity disorder, oppositional defiant disorder, and conduct disorder. These disruptive behaviors can also affect others and may manifest as physical and verbal aggression or other behavior problems.

Double blind placebo controlled cross over study: A double blind placebo controlled trial with an additional phase of switching participants from placebo to active treatment and vice versa. In this way participants each get active treatment and placebo treatment for half of the study.

Double blind placebo controlled method: Research method whereby the participants (and/or their guardians) as well as the trial investigators are blinded to (unaware of) which treatment (active or placebo) a specific participant receives.

Double syndrome: Individuals with an ASD who also have a known disorder or syndrome, such as Down syndrome.

Drug-induced rhinitis: Inflammation of the nasal mucosa caused by an allergic reaction to a medication.

DSM: The Diagnostic and Statistical Manual of Mental Disorders contains sets of behavioral criteria physicians use to diagnose mental disorders. Although ASDs are biological disorders, behavioral criteria are used to make these diagnoses because of a lack of biomarkers.

Durable power of attorney: Is a document created when a person with mild or moderate disability appoints another person to handle his or her affairs; this gives that person the legal authority to do so.

Dysautonomia: Autonomic dysfunction that involves either the sympathetic (adrenaline) or parasympathetic nervous system.

Dysgeusia: Changes in the taste of food caused by external influences or medical conditions affecting the taste buds.

Dysmenorrhea: Painful menstrual periods.

Dysthymia: A mood disorder characterized by mild depression or an irritable mood. It may be accompanied by other symptoms such as loss of appetite, sleep disturbances, and/or unexplained fatigue.

Dystonia: A type of abnormal muscle activity resulting from a sustained contraction of a muscle group leading to abnormal posture of a limb, a finger, or a part of the body. It may result in twisting or arching of the body or an unusual position of a limb.

Early intensive behavioral intervention: A behavioral treatment based on the principles of applied behavioral analysis that is delivered before age 5 years and intensively (25 to 40 hours per week), usually over a span of 2–3 years.

Early intervention: The Individuals with Disabilities Education Act (IDEA) mandated, state-based program that evaluates and provides services for children under age 3 with developmental delays.

Effector cells: White blood cells (such as mast cells and basophils) that are instrumental in facilitating antigen disposal.

Electroencephalography: A non-invasive test used to measure the electrical activity of the brain.

Encopresis: Voluntary or involuntary passage of stool outside of the toilet, in individuals who have already been toilet trained; often caused by constipation or conscious withholding of bowel movements.

Endodontists: Specialists trained to treat the pulp tissue that is inside the tooth; they perform root canal procedures which can often preserve severely decayed teeth and prevent the need for dental extraction.

Endoscopic small bowel biopsy: As part of the esophagogastroduodenoscopy (see below) where tissue from the small intestine is obtained for microscopic evaluation.

Endoscopy: A procedure by which a thin, flexible tube with a light and video camera on the end is inserted into a patient's mouth and then passed into the esophagus, the stomach, and the first part of the small intestine, allowing for direct visualization of these organs. Specialized instruments can be passed through the endoscope, as well, to allow biopsies to be taken, when necessary, from tissue along the intestinal tract.

Enzyme linked immunosorbent assay: A diagnostic tool that utilizes antibodies with a color change to identify a specific substance in a blood or tissue sample.

Eosinophilc esophagitis and gastroenteritis: Inflammation of the lining (mucosa) of the esophagus or stomach characterized by the presence of specific white blood cells known as eosinophils (which are commonly associated with allergic conditions).

Epilepsy: Chronic recurrent unprovoked seizures.

Epileptiform discharges or epileptiform activity: Abnormal spikes of electrical activity noted on EEG that can occur at various times and over various brain regions, but do not necessarily represent true seizure activity.

Epileptologist: Neurologist that specializes in the diagnosis and treatment of seizures.

Esophagitis: Inflammation of the esophagus (food pipe).

Esophagogastroduodenoscopy: Procedure whereby a tube with a camera (endoscope) is passed through the mouth to look at the lining of the esophagus (food pipe), stomach and beginning of the small intestine (duodenum) and obtain tissue for microscopic evaluation.

Essential fatty acids: Fatty acids that cannot be made by the body and must be ingested.

Estate planning: A process by which parents bring together legal and financial information and document their wishes, as they develop a long term plan for financial and personal care of their child across their child's or young adult's lifespan. This activity may include but is not limited to updating or creating wills, applying for government benefits and services, creating special needs trusts, and petitioning for guardianship.

Expressive language: The "output" of language; how one expresses his or her wants and needs.

Family medicine physician: A medical doctor who is trained to provide continuing and comprehensive health care for the individual from birth to death within the context of family and community.

Fine motor skills: Tasks that require use of smaller muscle groups such as the muscles in the hand which allow us to pick up small items, hold a pencil, or zip a zipper.

Food allergy: An adverse health effect arising from a specific immune response that occurs reproducibly upon exposure to a given food.

Gastritis: Inflammation of the lining of the stomach.

Gastro-colic reflex: The presence of food in the stomach which then stimulates movement of contents within the large intestine.

Gastroenterologist: A medical doctor who specializes in the treatment of condition of the gastrointestinal tract (esophagus, stomach, intestines and liver). These subspecialists have initial training in a primary field such as internal medicine or pediatrics, followed by additional training in gastroenterology. Pediatric gastroenterologists have initial training in pediatrics and care for children and teens with gastrointestinal problems or complaints.

Gastroesophageal reflux: Also known as acid reflux, GERD and "heartburn," this condition is caused by acid moving up into the esophagus or food pipe from the stomach and can cause significant pain and sleep problems as well as irritation and inflammation of the esophagus. It may sometimes be associated with vomiting and complications such as weight loss, apnea (pauses in breathing) or pneumonia.

Gene mutation: A change in the structure of a gene that negatively impacts the function of the gene. Mutations in genes can cause the gene to make a defective protein or no protein at all, and can be passed on from parent to child. Some mutations exert their effect when present in a single copy and in other cases two mutations need to be present to cause a problem for an individual. New genetic mutations or changes can also arise at the moment of conception during egg or sperm formation, so that neither parent harbors the mutation, but the child is the first person in the family with the genetic change.

Generalization: The ability to perform a skill in situations beyond the training session, and maintenance of the skill over time.

Generalized anxiety disorder: A condition where a person has chronic feelings of excessive worry and anxiety without a specific cause. Individuals with a generalized anxiety disorder often feel tense or jittery, and may worry excessively about minor things.

General special needs classroom: Special education classroom for children with various types of learning disabilities or developmental delays.

Genes: Small units of heredity that represent our genetic code and are passed on from generation to generation. It is estimated that each of our cells contains about 23,000 genes that direct our cellular function and body functions.

Gingivitis: Inflammation of the gums, results in redness, swelling and irritation, and in more severe cases can cause bleeding from the inflamed gum tissues.

Glossitis: Inflammation, discoloration and/or swelling of the tongue.

Gross motor skills: Tasks that require use of the large muscles for skills like sitting, walking and jumping.

Growth hormone axis: Refers to the production of increasing amounts of growth hormone, which is secreted by the pituitary gland and acts via insulin-like growth factors (IGFs) to produce the preadolescent and adolescent growth spurt in both boys and girls.

Gynecomastia: Often temporary increase in breast tissue occurring in boys during adolescence due to hormonal changes.

Health care proxy: A legal document that allows a competent person to designate another person to make health care decisions, should this become necessary.

Hormonal rhinitis: Inflammation of the nasal mucosa caused by hormonal changes.

Human subject research: Research conducted on a living human subject to obtain data through intervention or interaction with the individual.

Hyperbaric oxygen therapy: A treatment modality in which the patient is placed into a chamber and receives oxygen at levels higher than naturally occur in the atmosphere. Oxygen may also be provided at a higher than usual pressure, increasing the amount of oxygen in the blood, leading to dilation of blood vessels and increasing perfusion to organs, including the brain.

Hypogammaglobulinemia: Decreased levels of immunoglobulins which can impair resistance to infection.

Hypomethylation: A decrease in the number of chemical groups (specifically methyl groups) that are attached to the DNA. Adding methyl groups shuts off or silences genes within a cell and is a regulatory mechanism that controls which genes are turned on or turned off at any given time. Under-methylation would in theory make more genes activated or turned on.

Hypothalamic-pituitary-adrenal axis: Refers to interactions between hormones released by the hypothalamus and pituitary gland located in the brain and the adrenal glands located in the abdomen just above the kidneys. In this case, hormones secreted by adrenal glands called androgens initiate the process of adrenarche in both boys and girls. This process is marked by the appearance of pubic and armpit hair as well as the development of body odor and acne.

Hypothalamic-pituitary-gonadal axis: Refers to interactions between hormones released by the hypothalamus and pituitary gland located in the brain and the ovaries in girls or testes in boys. This process begins with the release of two gonadal hormones—luteinizing hormone (LH) and follicle stimulating hormone (FSH) that act on the ovary to produce estrogen and progesterone in females, and on testes in males to produce testosterone.

Idiopathic ASDs: ASDs without an identified cause.

IgE mediated food allergy: Food allergies associated with elevated levels of immunoglobulin E.

Immunoglobulin(s): Often designated as Igs, these are antibodies produced by plasma cells (a subtype of white blood cells) that serve a critical role in fighting infection.

Inclusion class: General education classroom with two teachers (one regular education and one with special education training), typically developing children and a number of special needs children with supports.

Individualized educational plan (IEP): Educational plan for school-aged children outlining goals for the year, educational setting and related services. IEP is reserved for children with learning difficulties.

Individuals with Disabilities Education Act (IDEA): Is a law that mandates that early intervention systems be put in place to evaluate and provide services to young children under 3 years of age with developmental delays and that school age children receive a "free and appropriate education."

Individualized family service plan (IFSP): This document outlines a child's current level of function and sets goals for the treatment team to follow. It will also list the specific services he or she will receive through early intervention, as well as where and how often these services will be provided.

Inflammatory bowel disease: Inflammation of the gastrointestinal tract; Crohn's disease can involve any part of the GI tract from the mouth to the anus; ulcerative colitis involves the large intestine (colon) only.

Institutional review board: A governing structure that is developed to monitor the ethical conduct of human research and review prospective research trials.

Internist: A medical doctor trained in the care of adult patients.

Intravenous immunoglobulin: An intravenous formulation of antibodies that are extracted and processed from the blood of healthy human donors.

Intrinsic asthma: A non-seasonal, non-allergic type of asthma, typically occurring later in life than atopic asthma with a tendency to become chronic and persistent rather than occurring episodically.

Intrinsic eczema: Eczema not associated with an allergic reaction.

In vitro studies: Studies involving tissues or cells taken from a human subject. The experiments are performed on these specimens as in a test tube or culture, and not on the person themselves.

In vivo studies: Studies performed on a human subject as a whole, such as a drug trial.

Lactose intolerance: Inability to digest lactose (milk sugar) leading to symptoms like bloating, cramping and/or abdominal pain.

Landau Kleffner syndrome: An epilepsy condition that occurs in children who lose their acquired language and have abnormal EEGs while not having seizures. These children generally do not have problems with social interactions and, prior to their language regression, their language skills are usually normal for age. The cause is believed to be an abnormal immune response or inflammation within the brain because some of these children respond to immunomodulation treatment.

Letter of intent: A comprehensive, well-written narrative that includes pertinent information about the child, including provision of care, medical and financial information, housing services and current needs. Parents are encouraged to develop a letter of intent during adolescence for their child with special needs, and to work with attorneys who specialize in financial planning and creating special needs trusts.

Mainstreaming: Placing a child in the general education setting.

Medical geneticist: Also known as a clinical geneticist, is a medical doctor who has training in a primary field such as pediatrics followed by specialty training in the field of genetics. Geneticists focus their attention on hereditary components such as chromosomes and genes which may be altered in some individuals with ASDs.

Med-peds physician: A medical doctor who studies longer than doctors specializing in internal medicine, pediatrics or family medicine and who has extensive knowledge of both adult medicine and pediatrics.

Menarche: Stage of pubertal development defined by onset of menstruation.

Meta-analysis: A large-scale analysis of all previously performed research on a topic.

Mitochondrial inheritance: Results from mutations in a percentage of the mitochondrial DNAs that are inherited from a mother in an egg cell. These DNAs are not located in the nucleus, but instead are floating in the cytoplasm outside of the nucleus. Mitochondrial disorders are typically seen in a single generation of brothers and sisters. In some cases, mitochondrial conditions can be seen in multiple generations, with transmission only from mothers to their children, if the condition is not so severe in a woman to prevent her from reproducing. Men cannot pass on a mitochondrial condition because they do not contribute any mitochondrial DNAs to their offspring.

Modes of inheritance: Mechanism by which our genes or genetic traits are passed along from generation to generation.

Mucositis: Inflammation of the gums and other oral soft tissues.

Neurotransmitters: Chemical signals that allow the brain to properly function.

Non-allergic rhinitis: Inflammation of the nasal mucosa not associated with an allergic reaction.

Non-allergic rhinitis with eosinophilia syndrome: Year round inflammation of the nasal mucosa characterized by nasal congestion, profuse runny nose, sneezing spells, nasal itchiness, and occasionally loss of smell. This condition is also associated with eosinophils detected on nasal smears, negative skin test reactivity and absence of allergen-specific IgE.

Non-IgE mediated food allergy: Food allergies not associated with production of IgE specific antibodies.

Non-stimulant medication: A generic term used to describe medications for ADHD that do not fall in the commonly used category of stimulant medications.

Nurse practitioner: Also known as an advanced practice nurse or advanced practice registered nurse. A master's level trained licensed nurse who works as part of the medical team, frequently under the supervision of a physician.

Obsessive–compulsive disorder: An anxiety disorder characterized by repetitive thoughts, impulses, or images (obsessions), and repetitive behaviors or mental acts (compulsions) that cause marked distress.

Obstructive sleep apnea: Is a sleep disorder that occurs when breathing becomes partially or completely blocked again and again, and is caused by narrowing of the upper airway during sleep. Problems with daytime behavior and attention span are seen in some children with obstructive sleep apnea.

Off-label uses of medications: The use of medications for indications and populations other than its approved indication.

Oral and maxillofacial surgeons: Specialists trained in treating deformities of the mouth and facial structures as well as placing dental implants. They may be called upon to extract severely decayed or malpositioned teeth.

Panic disorder: A condition in which a person experiences debilitating anxiety and fear without reasonable cause.

Parasomnias: Unconscious behaviors that occur during sleep, such as sleep walking, sleep terrors, nightmares, etc.

Parasympathetic nervous system: One segment of the autonomic nervous system that is responsible for rest, digestion and conservation. The sympathetic and parasympathetic systems are continuously in contact with each other.

Patient-centered medical home: A team-based health care delivery system lead by a primary health care provider who coordinates medical care to ensure that an individual patient receives the necessary care when and where they need it, in a manner they can understand. Defined characteristics of the PCMH are that care is: (1) patient-centered; (2) comprehensive; (3) coordinated; (4) accessible, and (5) committed to quality and safety.

Pediatric acute-onset neuropsychiatric syndrome: Is a neurobehavioral disorder characterized by an abrupt onset of OCD or severely restricted food intake/anorexia, and at least two of seven concurrent, severe, acute neuropsychiatric symptoms (anxiety, emotional liability/depression, irritability/aggression/severe oppositional behaviors, behavioral (developmental) regression, deterioration in school performance, sensory/motor abnormalities, and somatic signs/symptoms), in the absence of another recognized neurologic or medical disorder.

Pediatric autoimmune neuropsychiatric disorders associated with streptococci: Neurobehavioral disorder occurring before puberty characterized by the presence of obsessive-compulsive disorder or a tic disorder as well as other neurologic abnormalities including hyperactivity and/or abnormal choreiform movements, with an acute onset of symptoms that are episodic and temporally associated with a group A streptococcal infection.

Pediatric dentists: Specialists trained to treat patients from infancy through the adolescent years and who have training in providing care to those with special needs.

Pediatric neurologist: Also known as a child neurologist, has training in both pediatrics and neurology. These subspecialists are trained to carefully examine the nervous system and have expertise in epilepsy, neuromuscular problems, as well as treatment of headaches and neurodevelopmental disorders including ASDs and ADHD.

Periodontal disease: Condition affecting the structures of the mouth supporting the teeth including the gingiva (gums), the alveolar bone and the periodontal ligaments (fibers attaching the tooth to the bone).

Periodontists: Specialists trained to provide extensive scaling or "deep cleaning" of the teeth and to perform surgery on the gingiva and bone supporting the teeth. These specialists may also place dental implants.

Periodontitis: Inflammation of the periodontal structures (periodontal ligaments and bone), which can ultimately result in tooth loss if left untreated. It results from untreated gingivitis with spread of the infection to adjacent structures. The incidence of periodontitis increases during adolescence and becomes the leading cause of tooth loss in adults.

Physician assistant: A master's level trained licensed provider who works as part of the medical team, most often under the supervision of a physician.

Pica: A tendency to eat largely non-nutritive substances such as clay, chalk, dirt, or sand, which can be associated with iron deficiency and lead intoxication and is seen more often in children, especially those with developmental disabilities or autism spectrum disorders.

Picture Exchange Communication System (PECS): A method that uses ABA principles to teach children with poor verbal abilities to communicate using pictures.

Pivotal Response Treatment (PRT): A child-directed form of behavior therapy which focuses on developing behaviors such as motivation, initiating communication and self-management.

Placebo: A substance containing no active medication, given to reinforce a patient's expectation to get well. Often used as a control in an experiment or test to determine the effectiveness of a medicinal drug by comparison.

Polycystic ovary syndrome: A condition that may appear soon after menarche which is associated with irregular or absent periods, with or without acne, extra body hair and additional weight gain. Other metabolic conditions, such as insulin resistance and high cholesterol, may be seen as well.

Polymorphisms: Minor variations in a gene's base sequence that may be found in more than 1% of the general population and may or may not confer increased or decreased risk for a disease, but is not in and of itself felt to be a pathogenic (disease-causing) change.

Polysomnography: An overnight sleep study which records brain activity, eye movement, breathing patterns, heart rate, and muscle activity to provide a more complete picture of a person's sleep patterns, often performed in a specialized sleep center.

Positron emission tomography and functional MRI: Much newer imaging methods that provide information about brain function as opposed to brain structure, which require the subject to perform specific tasks during the study.

Pragmatic language: Social speech; knowing what to say, how to say it, and when to say it.

Prick skin testing: Testing method where an antigen is applied to the skin in order to observe the patient's reaction; used to identify allergens producing allergic reactions.

Primary antibody deficiency syndromes: Congenital disorder of antibody production which impairs one's ability to fight bacterial infections.

Prospective studies: Studies that are designed to look forward, as in a treatment or intervention or process of following progress over time to determine whether the treatment or intervention is effective or how various factors impact outcome.

Psychiatrist: A medical doctor with training in caring for individuals with mental health disorders such as anxiety, depression or psychosis. Some psychiatrists receive additional training in child psychiatry and focus their practice on children and adolescents. Child psychiatrists may have additional expertise in medication management for children and teens with behavioral disorders such as ASDs.

Psychologist: A provider with a PhD in psychology who is trained in counseling and diagnosing psychiatric and behavioral disorders. Some psychologists may get additional training in caring for children with conditions such as ASDs.

Pubarche: Stage of pubertal development defined by the appearance of pubic hair.

Pure tone test: Initial screening test used for children to assess for hearing loss using headphones or a sound field with the child actively responding to sounds they hear.

The sounds are produced at different decibels (loudness) and pitches (frequencies) to determine if there is hearing loss in the range of spoken language.

Receptive language: The comprehension of language; listening and understanding what is communicated.

Relationship developmental intervention (RDI): A form of behavioral therapy that encourages social interaction and motivates the child to become more interested in interpersonal exchanges.

Retrospective studies: Studies that are designed to look backward over data that has already been collected or recorded; research that is performed after the occurrence of a specific event of interest.

Rhinosinusitis: Inflammation of the nose and paranasal sinuses.

Secondary antibody deficiency syndromes: Disorders of antibody production which impairs one's ability to fight bacterial infections caused by exposure to an outside agent, often a medication that decreases white blood cell (B-lymphocyte) production, and which may be reversible with discontinuation of the causative agent.

Selective Serotonin Reuptake Inhibitor (SSRI): A newer group of medications that work on the serotonin system, used to treat depression, anxiety and obsessive compulsive disorder. Studied for its potential to improve repetitive behaviors in individuals with ASDs.

Separation anxiety disorder: A condition in which a person experiences excessive anxiety over separation from people to whom the individual has a strong emotional attachment (such as parents for a child).

Sialadenitis: Inflammation of the salivary glands.

Social anxiety disorder: A condition in which a person harbors a continual fear of social situations, which may be accompanied by fear of being judged by others or feeling of unworthiness, insecurity and/or self-doubt.

Social communication, emotional regulation and transactional support (SCERTS): A form of behavior therapy or educational approach that focuses on improving social communication, emotional regulation and transactional support by emphasizing joint attention and symbolic behavior.

Special care dentists: Are general dentists that have extensive training in providing comprehensive dental treatment to patients of all ages with a variety of special needs. In some cases they treat medically and behaviorally complex patients in a hospital setting to decrease risks for complications and for the comfort of the anxious or uncooperative patient.

Specialized autistic support class: A class that is specifically set up to accommodate the needs of the child with autism.

Special needs trust: A legal document created by parents of a child with a developmental disability so that funds and other assets can be protected for the future care of that child. This trust provides a reliable, legal way to safeguard the child's eligibility for public benefits while simultaneously providing for additional needs in adult life.

Specific phobia: A persistent fear of a clearly definable object or situation, such as arachnophobia (fear of spiders), agoraphobia (fear of crowds or enclosed public spaces) or acrophobia (fear of heights). These fears are recognized by the sufferer to be irrational or out of proportion to reality.

Stereotypies: Behaviors which involve repetition, rigidity, and invariance, as well as a tendency to be inappropriate in nature. Common repetitive behaviors: hand flapping, body rocking, toe walking, spinning objects, sniffing, echolalia, running objects across one's peripheral vision. Restricted and stereotyped patterns of interest or the demand for sameness. These forms may involve a persistent fixation on parts of objects or an inflexible adherence to specific, nonfunctional routines or rituals. For example, a child who is only interested in the wheels on the toy car or a child who insists on lining blocks up in identical rows repetitively.

Stimulant medication: A class of medications that acts on the dopamine system and are used as first line medication therapy for inattention, hyperactivity and impulsivity in ADHD.

Subcutaneous allergen immunotherapy: Process of administering allergenic extracts by injection just under the surface of the skin to patients who have allergic conjunctivitis, rhinitis or asthma in an effort to decrease symptoms by reducing immunologic responses to environmental allergens.

Sympathetic nervous system: One segment of the autonomic nervous system that is responsible for the "fight or flight response."

Syndrome: Collection of physical findings or features that define a specific condition. A syndrome may be caused by an alteration in a single gene, alterations in several genes, or the presence of larger segments of extra or missing genetic material—even as much material as contained in an entire chromosome.

Thelarche: Stage of pubertal development defined by breast development in females.

T-lymphocytes: A type of white blood cell produced in the thymus gland that regulates the immune system's response to disease.

Transdermal patch: A way of delivering a medication through a drug-laden sticky patch that is placed directly on the skin and remains in place over a long period of time to allow for the medication to be gradually absorbed by the body.

Transition: Movement from one set of activities to another or from one life stage to another.

Tricyclic antidepressant medication: A class of medications used to treat depression.

Typical antipsychotic: A class of medications that act on the dopamine system and are used to treat psychosis. Studied for its effects on irritability, aggression and self-injurious behaviors in individuals with ASDs.

Xerostomia: Dry mouth, often caused by decreased production of saliva and may be a side effect of many medications.

X-linked recessive inheritance: Results from a mutation in a single gene on one of the sex chromosomes (specifically the X chromosome). X-linked recessive conditions are typically seen in multiple generations and affect males who are related through unaffected female carriers.

Contributors

Jennifer Bain, MD, PhD is child neurology fellow at Morgan Stanley Children's Hospital—Columbia University Medical Center with special interest in neurodevelopmental specialties and autism spectrum disorders. She aims to become a well-rounded pediatric neurologist and has plans to enter practice in the near future.

Tomas J. Ballesteros, DMD is a Clinical Instructor in the Special Care Treatment Center in the Department of Pediatric Dentistry at the Rutgers School of Dental Medicine. After earning his Doctorate of Dental Medicine from Tufts University School of Dental Medicine, Dr. Ballesteros completed 2 years of general practice residency in oral medicine and special care dentistry at University of Medicine and Dentistry of New Jersey.

Susan R. Brill, MD is a pediatrician and adolescent medicine specialist. She is the Chief of Adolescent Medicine at Saint Peter's University Hospital and is a Clinical Associate Professor of Pediatrics at Drexel University College of Medicine. She has over 15 years of experience working with girls with ASDs, specifically addressing gynecologic concerns.

Susan L. Connors, MD is a board-certified internist and Instructor at Harvard Medical School who works at Massachusetts General Hospital's Lurie Center for Autism coordinating care for adolescents and adults with ASDs. In addition to ongoing clinical projects that serve to improve medical care for adults with ASDs, she has conducted research into prenatal factors that contribute to abnormal brain development and developmental disabilities including ASDs, and has worked in the past in a multispecialty group practice in internal medicine. Dr. Connors is also the mother of a 22-year-old son who has autism.

Lisa Ford, MD is a pediatric neurologist who graduated from Temple University School of Medicine and subsequently undertook a pediatric internship and residency, pediatric neurology fellowship training, and a neonatal neurology research fellowship at Children's Hospital Medical Center in Cincinnati. She was an Assistant Professor of Neurology and Pediatrics at Children's Hospital Medical Center in Cincinnati and worked in the Laboratory of Neuroscience at University of Cincinnati. She was the recipient of several awards, is board certified in neurology with special competence in child neurology, and is currently an Associate Professor in the Department of Neurosciences and Neurology at Rutgers New Jersey Medical School.

Caroline Hayes-Rosen, MD is a pediatric neurologist and an Assistant Professor in the Department of Neurosciences and Neurology at Rutgers New Jersey Medical School. She has a focused clinical interest in ASDs and management of children with developmental disabilities and/or attention deficit disorder or attention deficit hyperactivity disorder. She is also Director of the Child Neurology Fellowship program and is dedicated to training the next generation of pediatric neurologists.

Harumi Jyonouchi, MD is a pediatrician, allergist–immunologist, and Associate Professor of Pediatrics at Rutgers New Jersey Medical School who has been seeing patients with ASDs for evaluation of food allergy for more than 15 years.

Jeffrey Kornitzer, MD is a child neurology fellow at Rutgers New Jersey Medical School. He has a special interest in holistic approaches for treatment of ASDs.

Gary McAbee, DO, JD is a Clinical Professor of Neuroscience at Seton Hall School of Health and Medical Sciences, South Orange, New Jersey and is a pediatric neurologist at CarePoint Health Medical Group. He has extensive clinical experience in the diagnosis and treatment of children and adolescents with ASDs. He is also an attorney with a breadth of knowledge about medico-legal principles involving patients with neurological disorders.

Sue X. Ming, MD, PhD is a pediatric neurologist and pharmacologist. She has been working with children with ASDs for more than 16 years at Rutgers New Jersey Medical School where she is currently a Professor of Neurosciences and Neurology. She received a medical degree from Fudan Medical University, and a PhD in pharmacology at Rutgers New Jersey Medical School. She completed pediatric training at SUNY Health Science Center (Syracuse, NY) and a pediatric neurology fellowship at Johns Hopkins School of Medicine.

Iona M. Monteiro, MD is an Associate Professor in the Department of Pediatrics, and Chief of Pediatric Gastroenterology, at Rutgers New Jersey Medical School. She completed her pediatric residency and pediatric gastroenterology fellowship at University of Medicine and Dentistry of New Jersey/United Children's Hospital of New Jersey program in 1996.

Julie M. O'Brien, MEd, LMHC has been working with children with ASDs and their families for over 15 years providing support, resources, and referrals. She is currently a family support clinician at Massachusetts General Hospital's Lurie Center for Autism working largely with the transition age/adult ASD population alongside Dr. Susan L. Connors. Ms. O'Brien participates on the adult service committee of Advocates for Autism Massachusetts, volunteers for the Doug Flutie Junior Foundation for Autism, and serves on the board of Bailey's Team for Autism. She is the stepparent of three young adults, two of whom have an ASD.

Beth A. Pletcher, MD is a pediatrician, medical geneticist, and an Associate Professor of Pediatrics at Rutgers New Jersey Medical School. She has worked for many years with children and families who face the challenges of ASDs.

Mark D. Robinson, DMD is a general dentist and Assistant Professor of Pediatric Dentistry in the Department of Pediatric Dentistry at the Rutgers School of Dental Medicine. His concentration is in the treatment of patients with special needs. A large percentage of his patients have ASDs as well as other developmental disabilities. In addition to direct patient care, he takes great joy in educating dental students and postgraduate residents in the care of these populations.

Devorah Segal, MD, PhD is a child neurology fellow at Rutgers New Jersey Medical School. She has a research interest in the changes in perception and attention that can be present in individuals with autism.

Tishi Shah, MD is a pediatric chief resident at Saint Peter's University Hospital. After completing her residency, she will be pursuing further training as a fellow in pediatric hematology–oncology at Westchester Medical Center in Valhalla, NY.

Evan Spivack, DDS is a Professor of Pediatric Dentistry at the Rutgers School of Dental Medicine. For more than two decades, Dr. Spivack has cared for patients with special needs in private-, hospital-, and academic-based practices. He has developed a variety of educational programming and lectures extensively on the provision of dental care to persons with developmental and other disabilities.

Barbie Zimmerman-Bier, MD is Chief of Developmental Pediatrics at Saint Peter's University Hospital. She is the mother of four children, the oldest of whom is a 24-year-old man with an ASD. Dr. Zimmerman-Bier began her career as a general pediatrician and returned for additional training in developmental and behavioral pediatrics when her son was diagnosed with ASD. She has been providing clinical care to families affected by ASDs for 20 years. Her research interests include detection of early biomarkers for autism risk and improving medical care for those affected by ASDs.

References

Chapter 1

1. Gillberg, C. and Coleman, M. (1989) *The Biology of the Autistic Syndromes*. London: Mac Keith Press.
2. Kanner, L. (1943) Autistic disturbances of affective contact. Nervous child 2, 217–250.
3. Kanner, L. (1960) The Child is father. *Time* magazine, July 25.
4. Happe, F.G. (1994) Current psychological theories of autism: the "theory of mind" account and rival theories. Journal of child psychology and psychiatry, and allied disciplines 35, 215–229.
5. American Psychiatric Association (1980) *Diagnostic and Statistical Manual of Mental Disorders*. 3rd Edition. Washington, DC: American Psychiatric Association.
6. American Psychiatric Association (2000) *Diagnostic and Statistical Manual of Mental Disorders*. 4th Edition (text rev.). Washington, DC: American Psychiatric Association.
7. American Psychiatric Association (1994) *Diagnostic and Statistical Manual of Mental Disorders*. 4th Edition. Washington, DC: American Psychiatric Association.
8. American Psychiatric Association (2013) *Diagnostic and Statistical Manual of Mental Disorders*. 5th Edition. Washington, DC: American Psychiatric Association.
9. Buie, T., Campbell, D.B., Fuchs, G.J. 3rd, Furuta, G.T. *et al.* (2010) Evaluation, diagnosis, and treatment of gastrointestinal disorders in individuals with ASDs: a consensus report. Pediatrics 125 (Suppl 1), S1–S18.
10. Buie, T., Fuchs, G.J. 3rd, Furuta, G.T., Kooros, K. *et al.* (2010) Recommendations for evaluation and treatment of common gastrointestinal problems in children with ASDs. Pediatrics 125 (Suppl 1), S19–S29.
11. Ming, X., Stein, T.P., Barnes, V., Rhodes, N., and Guo, L. (2012) Metabolic perturbance in autism spectrum disorders: a metabolomics study. Journal of proteome research 11, 5856–5862.
12. Xue, M., Brimacombe, M., Chaaban, J., Zimmerman-Bier, B., and Wagner, G.C. (2008) Autism spectrum disorders: concurrent clinical disorders. Journal of child neurology 23, 6–13.
13. Jyonouchi, H., Geng, L., Streck, D.L., and Toruner, G.A. (2011) Children with autism spectrum disorders (ASD) who exhibit chronic gastrointestinal (GI) symptoms and marked fluctuation of behavioral symptoms exhibit distinct innate immune abnormalities and transcriptional profiles of peripheral blood (PB) monocytes. Journal of neuroimmunology 238, 73–80.
14. Ashwood, P., Schauer, J., Pessah, I.N., and Van de Water, J. (2009) Preliminary evidence of the in vitro effects of BDE-47 on innate immune responses in children with autism spectrum disorders. Journal of neuroimmunology 208, 130–135.
15. Blaylock, R.L. and Strunecka, A. (2009) Immune-glutamatergic dysfunction as a central mechanism of the autism spectrum disorders. Current medicinal chemistry 16, 157–170.
16. De Andres-Garcia, S., Moya-Albiol, L., and Gonzalez-Bono, E. (2012) Salivary cortisol and immunoglobulin A: responses to stress as predictors of health complaints reported by caregivers of offspring with autistic spectrum disorder. Hormones and behavior 62, 464–474.
17. Goines, P.E. and Ashwood, P. (2013) Cytokine dysregulation in autism spectrum disorders (ASD): possible role of the environment. Neurotoxicology and teratology 36, 67–81.
18. Van Naarden Braun, K., Pettygrove, S., Daniels, J., Miller, L. *et al.* (2007) Evaluation of a methodology for a collaborative multiple source surveillance network for autism spectrum disorders. Autism and Developmental Disabilities Monitoring Network, 14 sites, United States, 2002. Morbidity and mortality weekly report, Surveillance summaries 56, 29–40.

19. Schendel, D.E., Bresnahan, M., Carter, K.W., Francis, R.W. *et al.* (2013) The International Collaboration for Autism Registry Epidemiology (iCARE): multinational registry-based investigations of autism risk factors and trends. Journal of autism and developmental disorders 43, 2650–2663.

20. Sasson, N.J., Lam, K.S., Childress, D., Parlier, M., Daniels, J.L., and Piven, J. (2013) The broad autism phenotype questionnaire: prevalence and diagnostic classification. Autism research 6, 134–143.

21. Sandin, S., Nygren, K.G., Iliadou, A., Hultman, C.M., and Reichenberg, A. (2013) Autism and mental retardation among offspring born after in vitro fertilization. Journal of the American Medical Association 310, 75–84.

22. Sun, X., Allison, C., Auyeung, B., Matthews, F.E., Baron-Cohen, S., and Brayne, C. (2013) The Mandarin Chinese version of the childhood autism spectrum test (CAST): Test-retest reliability. Research in developmental disabilities 34, 3267–3275.

23. Jonsson, L., Anckarsater, H., Zettergren, A., Westberg, L. *et al.* (2013) Association between ASMT and autistic-like traits in children from a Swedish nationwide cohort. Psychiatric genetics 24, 21–27.

24. Masoud, A., Roya, K., Mohammad-Esmaeil, M., Mahnaz, T. *et al.* (2013) Inequality in school readiness and autism among 6-year-old children across Iranian provinces: national health assessment survey results. Iranian journal of pediatrics 23, 71–78.

25. Sandin, S., Hultman, C.M., Kolevzon, A., Gross, R., MacCabe, J.H., and Reichenberg, A. (2012) Advancing maternal age is associated with increasing risk for autism: a review and meta-analysis. Journal of the American Academy of Child and Adolescent Psychiatry 51, 477–486, e471.

26. Parner, E.T., Baron-Cohen, S., Lauritsen, M.B., Jorgensen, M. *et al.* (2012) Parental age and autism spectrum disorders. Annals of epidemiology 22, 143–150.

27. Rahbar, M.H., Samms-Vaughan, M., Loveland, K.A., Pearson, D.A. *et al.* (2012) Maternal and paternal age are jointly associated with childhood autism in Jamaica. Journal of autism and developmental disorders 42, 1928–1938.

28. Puleo, C.M., Schmeidler, J., Reichenberg, A., Kolevzon, A. *et al.* (2012) Advancing paternal age and simplex autism. Autism 16, 367–380.

29. van Balkom, I.D., Bresnahan, M., Vuijk, P.J., Hubert, J., Susser, E., and Hoek, H.W. (2012) Paternal age and risk of autism in an ethnically diverse, non-industrialized setting: Aruba. PloS ONE 7, e45090.

30. Frye, R.E. and Rossignol, D.A. (2011) Mitochondrial dysfunction can connect the diverse medical symptoms associated with autism spectrum disorders. Pediatric research 69, 41R–47R.

31. Smith, M., Flodman, P.L., Gargus, J.J., Simon, M.T. *et al.* (2012) Mitochondrial and ion channel gene alterations in autism. Biochimica et biophysica acta 1817, 1796–1802.

32. Stein, T.P., Schluter, M.D., Steer, R.A., and Ming, X. (2013) Autism and phthalate metabolite glucuronidation. Journal of autism and developmental disorders 43, 2677–2685.

33. Edelson, S.B. and Cantor, D.S. (1998) Autism: xenobiotic influences. Toxicology and industrial health 14, 553–563.

34. James, S.J., Melnyk, S., Jernigan, S., Hubanks, A., Rose, S., and Gaylor, D.W. (2008) Abnormal transmethylation/transsulfuration metabolism and DNA hypomethylation among parents of children with autism. Journal of autism and developmental disorders 38, 1966–1975.

35. Deth, R., Muratore, C., Benzecry, J., Power-Charnitsky, V.A., and Waly, M. (2008) How environmental and genetic factors combine to cause autism: a redox/methylation hypothesis. Neurotoxicology 29, 190–201.

36. Kemper, T.L. and Bauman, M. (1998) Neuropathology of infantile autism. Journal of neuropathology and experimental neurology 57, 645–652.

37. Kemper, T.L. and Bauman, M.L. (1993) The contribution of neuropathologic studies to the understanding of autism. Neurologic clinics 11, 175–187.

38. Bailey, A., Luthert, P., Dean, A., Harding, B. *et al.* (1998) A clinicopathological study of autism. Brain 121 (Pt 5), 889–905.

39. Hazlett, H.C., Poe, M.D., Gerig, G., Styner, M. *et al.* (2011) Early brain overgrowth in autism associated with an increase in cortical surface area before age 2 years. Archives of general psychiatry 68, 467–476.

40. Jou, R.J., Minshew, N.J., Keshavan, M.S., Vitale, M.P., and Hardan, A.Y. (2010) Enlarged right superior temporal gyrus in children and adolescents with autism. Brain research 1360, 205–212.

41. Ke, X., Tang, T., Hong, S., Hang, Y. *et al.* (2009) White matter impairments in autism, evidence from voxel-based morphometry and diffusion tensor imaging. Brain research 1265, 171–177.

42. Keary, C.J., Minshew, N.J., Bansal, R., Goradia, D. *et al.* (2009) Corpus callosum volume and neurocognition in autism. Journal of autism and developmental disorders 39, 834–841.

43. McAlonan, G.M., Cheung, V., Cheung, C., Suckling, J. *et al.* (2005) Mapping the brain in autism. A voxel-based MRI study of volumetric differences and intercorrelations in autism. Brain 128, 268–276.

44. Mink, J.W. and McKinstry, R.C. (2002) Volumetric MRI in autism: Can high-tech craniometry provide neurobiological insights? Neurology 59, 158–159.

45. Bandari S., Wenzhuan H., Jilu, J., and Ming, X. (2013) The utility of standard brain magnetic resonance imaging in autistic children. Neurology 80 (Meeting Abstracts 1) P06.065.

46. Ghanizadeh, A., Sahraeizadeh, A., and Berk, M. (2013) A head-to-head comparison of aripiprazole and risperidone for safety and treating autistic disorders: a randomized double blind clinical trial. Child psychiatry and human development 45, 185–192.

47. Amminger, G.P., Berger, G.E., Schafer, M.R., Klier, C., Friedrich, M.H., and Feucht, M. (2007) Omega-3 fatty acids supplementation in children with autism: a double-blind randomized, placebo-controlled pilot study. Biological psychiatry 61, 551–553.

48. Gilbert, D.L. (2008) Regarding "omega-3 fatty acids supplementation in children with autism: a double-blind randomized, placebo-controlled pilot study." Biological psychiatry 63, e13, e15.

49. Bent, S., Bertoglio, K., Ashwood, P., Bostrom, A., and Hendren, R.L. (2011) A pilot randomized controlled trial of omega-3 fatty acids for autism spectrum disorder. Journal of autism and developmental disorders 41, 545–554.

50. Adams, J.B., Audhya, T., McDonough-Means, S., Rubin, R.A. *et al.* (2011) Effect of a vitamin/mineral supplement on children and adults with autism. BMC pediatrics 11, 111.

51. Bertoglio, K., Jill James, S., Deprey, L., Brule, N., and Hendren, R.L. (2010) Pilot study of the effect of methyl B12 treatment on behavioral and biomarker measures in children with autism. Journal of alternative and complementary medicine 16, 555–560.

52. Hardan, A.Y., Fung, L.K., Libove, R.A., Obukhanych, T.V. *et al.* (2012) A randomized controlled pilot trial of oral N-acetylcysteine in children with autism. Biological psychiatry 71, 956–961.

53. Critchfield, J.W., van Hemert, S., Ash, M., Mulder, L., and Ashwood, P. (2011) The potential role of probiotics in the management of childhood autism spectrum disorders. Gastroenterology research and practice 2011, E-Article ID 161358.

54. Tachibana, M., Kagitani-Shimono, K., Mohri, I., Yamamoto, T. *et al.* (2013) Long-term administration of intranasal oxytocin is a safe and promising therapy for early adolescent boys with autism spectrum disorders. Journal of child and adolescent psychopharmacology 23, 123–127.

55. Adams, J.B., Baral, M., Geis, E., Mitchell, J. *et al.* (2009) Safety and efficacy of oral DMSA therapy for children with autism spectrum disorders: part B, behavioral results. BMC clinical pharmacology 9, 17.

56. Rossignol, D.A., Rossignol, L.W., Smith, S., Schneider, C. *et al.* (2009) Hyperbaric treatment for children with autism: a multicenter, randomized, double-blind, controlled trial. BMC pediatrics 9, 21.

57. Ghanizadeh, A. (2012) Hyperbaric oxygen therapy for treatment of children with autism: a systematic review of randomized trials. Medical gas research 2, 13.

58. Srinivasan, S.M. and Bhat, A.N. (2013) A review of "music and movement" therapies for children with autism: embodied interventions for multisystem development. Frontiers in integrative neuroscience 7, 22.

59. Ming, X., Chen, X., Wang, X.T., Zhang, Z., Kang, V., and Zimmerman-Bier, B. (2012) Acupuncture for treatment of autism spectrum disorders. Evidence-based complementary and alternative medicine. E-Article ID 679845.

60. Lim, H.A. and Draper, E. (2011) The effects of music therapy incorporated with applied behavior analysis verbal behavior approach for children with autism spectrum disorders. Journal of music therapy 48, 532–550.

61. Cheuk, D.K., Wong, V., and Chen, W.X. (2011) Acupuncture for autism spectrum disorders (ASD). The Cochrane database of systematic reviews, CD007849.

62. Blaucok-Busch, E., Amin, O.R., Dessoki, H.H., and Rabah, T. (2012) Efficacy of DMSA therapy in a sample of Arab children with autistic spectrum disorder. Maedica 7, 214–221.

63. Allam, H., ElDine, N.G., and Helmy, G. (2008) Scalp acupuncture effect on language development in children with autism: a pilot study. Journal of alternative and complementary medicine 14, 109–114.

64. Virues-Ortega, J., Julio, F.M., and Pastor-Barriuso, R. (2013) The TEACCH program for children and adults with autism: a meta-analysis of intervention studies. Clinical psychology review 33, 940–953.

65. Wieder, S. and Greenspan, S.I. (2003) Climbing the symbolic ladder in the DIR model through floor time/interactive play. Autism 7, 425–435.

66. Callahan, K., Shukla-Mehta, S., Magee, S., and Wie, M. (2010) ABA versus TEACCH: the case for defining and validating comprehensive treatment models in autism. Journal of autism and developmental disorders 40, 74–88.

67. Foxx, R.M. (2008) Applied behavior analysis treatment of autism: the state of the art. Child and adolescent psychiatric clinics of North America 17, 821–834, ix.

68. Walsh, M.B. (2011) The top 10 reasons children with autism deserve ABA. Behavior analysis in practice 4, 72–79.

Chapter 2

1. Kemper, T.L. and Bauman, M. (1998) Neuropathology of infantile autism. Journal of neuropathology and experimental neurology 57, 645–652.

2. Ke, X., Tang, T., Hong, S., Hang, Y. et al. (2009) White matter impairments in autism, evidence from voxel-based morphometry and diffusion tensor imaging. Brain research 1265, 171–177.

3. Keary, C.J., Minshew, N.J., Bansal, R., Goradia, D. et al. (2009) Corpus callosum volume and neurocognition in autism. Journal of autism and developmental disorders 39, 834–841.

4. Kemper, T.L. and Bauman, M.L. (1993) The contribution of neuropathologic studies to the understanding of autism. Neurologic clinics 11, 175–187.

5. Bailey, A., Luthert, P., Dean, A., Harding, B. et al. (1998) A clinicopathological study of autism. Brain 121 (Pt 5), 889–905.

6. Yamasue, H. (2013) Function and structure in social brain regions can link oxytocin-receptor genes with autistic social behavior. Brain & development 35, 111–118.

7. Oblak, A., Gibbs, T.T., and Blatt, G.J. (2013) Reduced serotonin receptor subtypes in a limbic and a neocortical region in autism. Autism research 6, 571–583.

8. Tostes, M.H., Teixeira, H.C., Gattaz, W.F., Brandao, M.A., and Raposo, N.R. (2012) Altered neurotrophin, neuropeptide, cytokines and nitric oxide levels in autism. Pharmacopsychiatry 45, 241–243.

9. Choudhury, P.R., Lahiri, S., and Rajamma, U. (2012) Glutamate mediated signaling in the pathophysiology of autism spectrum disorders. Pharmacology, biochemistry, and behavior 100, 841–849.

10. Daly, E.M., Deeley, Q., Ecker, C., Craig, M. et al. (2012) Serotonin and the neural processing of facial emotions in adults with autism: an fMRI study using acute tryptophan depletion. Archives of general psychiatry 69, 1003–1013.

11. Enticott, P.G., Kennedy, H.A., Rinehart, N.J., Tonge, B.J., Bradshaw, J.L., and Fitzgerald, P.B. (2013) GABAergic activity in autism spectrum disorders: an investigation of cortical inhibition via transcranial magnetic stimulation. Neuropharmacology 68, 202–209.

12. Cuccaro, M.L., Tuchman, R.F., Hamilton, K.L., Wright, H.H. et al. (2012) Exploring the relationship between autism spectrum disorder and epilepsy using latent class cluster analysis. Journal of autism and developmental disorders 42, 1630–1641.

13. Woolfenden, S., Sarkozy, V., Ridley, G., Coory, M., and Williams, K. (2012) A systematic review of two outcomes in autism spectrum disorder: epilepsy and mortality. Developmental medicine and child neurology 54, 306–312.

14. Kanemura, H., Sano, F., Tando, T., Sugita, K., and Aihara, M. (2013) Can EEG characteristics predict development of epilepsy in autistic children? European journal of paediatric neurology 17, 232–237.

15. Berg, A.T. and Plioplys, S. (2012) Epilepsy and autism: Is there a special relationship? Epilepsy & behavior 23, 193–198.

16. Bolton, P.F., Carcani-Rathwell, I., Hutton, J., Goode, S., Howlin, P., and Rutter, M. (2011) Epilepsy in autism: features and correlates. British journal of psychiatry 198, 289–294.

17. Danielsson, S., Gillberg, I.C., Billstedt, E., Gillberg, C., and Olsson, I. (2005) Epilepsy in young adults with autism: a prospective population-based follow-up study of 120 individuals diagnosed in childhood. Epilepsia 46, 918–923.

18. Blardi, P., de Lalla, A., Sciuto, M.R., Di Rosa, C. et al. (2012) The co-occurrence of autism and epilepsy and the lack of a targeted therapeutical approach. Brain & development 34, 333.

19. Tuchman, R., Alessandri, M., and Cuccaro, M. (2010) Autism spectrum disorders and epilepsy: moving towards a comprehensive approach to treatment. Brain & development 32, 719–730.

20. Tuchman, R., Cuccaro, M., and Alessandri, M. (2010) Autism and epilepsy: historical perspective. Brain & development 32, 709–718.

21. Gesundheit, B., Rosenzweig, J.P., Naor, D., Lerer, B. et al. (2013) Immunological and autoimmune considerations of Autism Spectrum Disorders. Journal of autoimmunity 44, 1–7.

22. Sheldon, S.H., Ferber, R., and Kryger, M.H. (2005) Principles and Practice of Pediatric Sleep Medicine. Philadelphia, PA: W.B. Saunders.

23. Richdale, A.L. and Schreck, K.A. (2009) Sleep problems in autism spectrum disorders: prevalence, nature, and possible biopsychosocial aetiologies. Sleep medicine reviews 13, 403–411.

24. Krakowiak, P., Goodlin-Jones, B., Hertz-Picciotto, I., Croen, L.A., and Hansen, R.L. (2008) Sleep problems in children with autism spectrum disorders, developmental delays, and typical development: a population-based study. Journal of sleep research 17, 197–206.

25. Rapin, I. (1991) Autistic children: diagnosis and clinical features. Pediatrics 87, 751–760.

26. Gillberg, C. and Coleman, M. (1989) Early Symptoms in Autism. New York, NY: Plenum Press.

27. Ming, X. and Walters, A.S. (2009) Autism spectrum disorders, attention deficit/hyperactivity disorder, and sleep disorders. Current opinion in pulmonary medicine 15, 578–584.

28. Ming, X., Sun, Y.M., Nachajon, R.V., Brimacombe, M., and Walters, A.S. (2009) Prevalence of parasomnia in autistic children with sleep disorders. Clinical medicine: Pediatrics 3, 1–10.

29. Paavonen, E.J., Vehkalahti, K., Vanhala, R., von Wendt, L., Nieminen-von Wendt, T., and Aronen, E.T. (2008) Sleep in children with Asperger syndrome. Journal of autism and developmental disorders 38, 41–51.

30. Goodlin-Jones, B.L., Tang, K., Liu, J., and Anders, T.F. (2008) Sleep patterns in preschool-age children with autism, developmental delay, and typical development. Journal of the American Academy of Child and Adolescent Psychiatry 47, 930–938.

31. Jyonouchi, H., Sun, S., and Itokazu, N. (2002) Innate immunity associated with inflammatory responses and cytokine production against common dietary proteins in patients with autism spectrum disorder. Neuropsychobiology 46, 76–84.

32. Xue, M., Brimacombe, M., Chaaban, J., Zimmerman-Bier, B., and Wagner, G.C. (2008) Autism spectrum disorders: concurrent clinical disorders. Journal of child neurology 23, 6–13.

33. Malow, B.A., McGrew, S.G., Harvey, M., Henderson, L.M., and Stone, W.L. (2006) Impact of treating sleep apnea in a child with autism spectrum disorder. Pediatric neurology 34, 325–328.

34. Ming, X., Gordon, E., Kang, N., and Wagner, G.C. (2008) Use of clonidine in children with autism spectrum disorders. Brain & development 30, 454–460.

35. Lane, A.E., Young, R.L., Baker, A.E., and Angley, M.T. (2010) Sensory processing subtypes in autism: association with adaptive behavior. Journal of autism and developmental disorders 40, 112–122.

36. Tomchek, S.D. and Dunn, W. (2007) Sensory processing in children with and without autism: a comparative study using the short sensory profile. American journal of occupational therapy 61, 190–200.

37. Baranek, G.T., Boyd, B.A., Poe, M.D., David, F.J., and Watson, L.R. (2007) Hyperresponsive sensory patterns in young children with autism, developmental delay, and typical development. American journal of mental retardation 112, 233–245.

38. American Psychiatric Association (2013) *Diagnostic and Statistical Manual of Mental Disorders.* 5th Edition. Washington, DC: American Psychiatric Association.

39. McIntosh, D.N., Miller, L.J., Shyu, V., and Hagerman, R.J. (1999) Sensory-modulation disruption, electrodermal responses, and functional behaviors. Developmental medicine and child neurology 41, 608–615.

40. Schaaf, R.C., Miller, L.J., Seawell, D., and O'Keefe, S. (2003) Children with disturbances in sensory processing: a pilot study examining the role of the parasympathetic nervous system. American journal of occupational therapy 57, 442–449.

41. Reynolds, S., Lane, S.J., and Gennings, C. (2010) The moderating role of sensory overresponsivity in HPA activity: a pilot study with children diagnosed with ADHD. Journal of attention disorders 13, 468–478.

42. Chang, M.C., Parham, L.D., Blanche, E.I., Schell, A. *et al.* (2012) Autonomic and behavioral responses of children with autism to auditory stimuli. American journal of occupational therapy 66, 567–576.

43. Lane, S.J., Reynolds, S., and Dumenci, L. (2012) Sensory overresponsivity and anxiety in typically developing children and children with autism and attention deficit hyperactivity disorder: cause or coexistence? American journal of occupational therapy 66, 595–603.

44. Gillberg, C. and Coleman, M. (1989) *The Biology of the Autistic Syndromes.* London: Mac Keith Press.

45. Ming, X., Julu, P.O., Brimacombe, M., Connor, S., and Daniels, M.L. (2005) Reduced cardiac parasympathetic activity in children with autism. Brain & development 27, 509–516.

46. Ming, X., Bain, J.M., Smith, D., Brimacombe, M., Gold von-Simson, G., and Axelrod, F.B. (2011) Assessing autonomic dysfunction symptoms in children: a pilot study. Journal of child neurology 26, 420–427.

47. Cheshire, W.P. (2012) Highlights in clinical autonomic neuroscience: new insights into autonomic dysfunction in autism. Autonomic neuroscience: basic and clinical 171, 4–7.

48. Toichi, M. and Kamio, Y. (2003) Paradoxical autonomic response to mental tasks in autism. Journal of autism and developmental disorders 33, 417–426.

49. Chuang, C.Y., Han, W.R., Li, P.C., and Young, S.T. (2010) Effects of music therapy on subjective sensations and heart rate variability in treated cancer survivors: a pilot study. Complementary therapies in medicine 18, 224–226.

50. Orita, M., Hayashida, N., Shinkawa, T., Kudo, T. *et al.* (2012) Monitoring the autonomic nervous activity as the objective evaluation of music therapy for severely and multiply disabled children. Tohoku journal of experimental medicine 227, 185–189.

51. Telles, S., Singh, N., and Balkrishna, A. (2011) Heart rate variability changes during high frequency yoga breathing and breath awareness. BioPsychoSocial medicine 5, 4.

52. Telles, S., Raghavendra, B.R., Naveen, K.V., Manjunath, N.K., Kumar, S., and Subramanya, P. (2013) Changes in autonomic variables following two meditative states described in yoga texts. Journal of alternative and complementary medicine 19, 35–42.

53. Ming, X., Brimacombe, M., and Wagner, G.C. (2007) Prevalence of motor impairment in autism spectrum disorders. Brain & development 29, 565–570.

54. Cook, J.L., Blakemore, S.J., and Press, C. (2013) Atypical basic movement kinematics in autism spectrum conditions. Brain 136, 2816–2824.

55. Nickel, L.R., Thatcher, A.R., Keller, F., Wozniak, R.H., and Iverson, J.M. (2013) Posture development in infants at heightened vs. low risk for autism spectrum disorders. Infancy 18, 639–661.

56. Whyatt, C. and Craig, C. (2013) Sensory-motor problems in autism. Frontiers in integrative neuroscience 7, 51.

57. Yochum, C.L. and Wagner, G.C. (2009) Autism and Parkinson's disease: animal models and a common etiological mechanism. Chinese journal of physiology 52, 236–249.

58. Ming, X., Julu, P.O., Wark, J., Apartopoulos, F., and Hansen, S. (2004) Discordant mental and physical efforts in an autistic patient. Brain & development 26, 519–524.

Chapter 3

1. Simonoff, E., Pickles, A., Charman, T., Chandler, S., Loucas, T., and Baird, G. (2008) Psychiatric disorders in children with autism spectrum disorders: prevalence, comorbidity, and associated factors in a population-derived sample. Journal of the American Academy of Child and Adolescent Psychiatry 47, 921–929.

2. Fombonne, E. (1994) The Chartres Study: I. Prevalence of psychiatric disorders among French school-age children. British journal of psychiatry 164, 69–79.

3. Lewinsohn, P.M., Klein, D.N., and Seeley, J.R. (2000) Bipolar disorder during adolescence and young adulthood in a community sample. Bipolar disorders 2, 281–293.

4. Verhulst, F.C., van der Ende, J., Ferdinand, R.F., and Kasius, M.C. (1997) The prevalence of DSM-III-R diagnoses in a national sample of Dutch adolescents. Archives of general psychiatry 54, 329–336.

5. Rutter, M., Tizard, J., Yule, W., Graham, P., and Whitmore, K. (1976) Research report: Isle of Wight Studies, 1964–1974. Psychological medicine 6, 313–332.

6. van Steensel, F.J., Bogels, S.M., and Perrin, S. (2011) Anxiety disorders in children and adolescents with autistic spectrum disorders: a meta-analysis. Clinical child and family psychology review 14, 302–317.

7. White, S.W., Oswald, D., Ollendick, T., and Scahill, L. (2009) Anxiety in children and adolescents with autism spectrum disorders. Clinical psychology review 29, 216–229.

8. de Bruin, E.I., Ferdinand, R.F., Meester, S., de Nijs, P.F., and Verheij, F. (2007) High rates of psychiatric co-morbidity in PDD-NOS. Journal of autism and developmental disorders 37, 877–886.

9. Leyfer, O.T., Folstein, S.E., Bacalman, S., Davis, N.O. *et al.* (2006) Comorbid psychiatric disorders in children with autism: interview development and rates of disorders. Journal of autism and developmental disorders 36, 849–861.

10. Costello, E.J., Egger, H.L., and Angold, A. (2005) The developmental epidemiology of anxiety disorders: phenomenology, prevalence, and comorbidity. Child and adolescent psychiatric clinics of North America 14, 631–648, vii.

11. Gau, S.S., Ni, H.C., Shang, C.Y., Soong, W.T. *et al.* (2010) Psychiatric comorbidity among children and adolescents with and without persistent attention-deficit hyperactivity disorder. The Australian and New Zealand journal of psychiatry 44, 135–143.

12. Dekker, M.C. and Koot, H.M. (2003) DSM-IV disorders in children with borderline to moderate intellectual disability. I: Prevalence and impact. Journal of the American Academy of Child and Adolescent Psychiatry 42, 915–922.

13. Kuusikko, S., Pollock-Wurman, R., Jussila, K., Carter, A.S. *et al.* (2008) Social anxiety in high-functioning children and adolescents with Autism and Asperger syndrome. Journal of autism and developmental disorders 38, 1697–1709.

14. Lecavalier, L. (2006) Behavioral and emotional problems in young people with pervasive developmental disorders: relative prevalence, effects of subject characteristics, and empirical classification. Journal of autism and developmental disorders 36, 1101–1114.

15. Ford, T., Goodman, R., and Meltzer, H. (2003) The British Child and Adolescent Mental Health Survey 1999: the prevalence of DSM-IV disorders. Journal of the American Academy of Child and Adolescent Psychiatry 42, 1203–1211.

16. Frala, J.L., Leen-Feldner, E.W., Blumenthal, H., and Barreto, C.C. (2010) Relations among perceived control over anxiety-related events, worry, and generalized anxiety disorder in a sample of adolescents. Journal of abnormal child psychology 38, 237–247.

17. Sukhodolsky, D.G., Scahill, L., Gadow, K.D., Arnold, L.E. *et al.* (2008) Parent-rated anxiety symptoms in children with pervasive developmental disorders: frequency and association with core autism symptoms and cognitive functioning. Journal of abnormal child psychology 36, 117–128.

18. Witwer, A.N. and Lecavalier, L. (2010) Validity of comorbid psychiatric disorders in youngsters with autism spectrum disorders. Journal of developmental and physical disabilities 22, 367–380.

19. Weisbrot, D.M., Gadow, K.D., DeVincent, C.J., and Pomeroy, J. (2005) The presentation of anxiety in children with pervasive developmental disorders. Journal of child and adolescent psychopharmacology 15, 477–496.

20. Esbensen, A.J., Seltzer, M.M., Lam, K.S., and Bodfish, J.W. (2009) Age-related differences in restricted repetitive behaviors in autism spectrum disorders. Journal of autism and developmental disorders 39, 57–66.

21. Piven, J., Harper, J., Palmer, P., and Arndt, S. (1996) Course of behavioral change in autism: a retrospective study of high-IQ adolescents and adults. Journal of the American Academy of Child and Adolescent Psychiatry 35, 523–529.

22. McDougle, C.J., Kresch, L.E., Goodman, W.K., Naylor, S.T. et al. (1995) A case-controlled study of repetitive thoughts and behavior in adults with autistic disorder and obsessive-compulsive disorder. American journal of psychiatry 152, 772–777.

23. Russell, A.J., Mataix-Cols, D., Anson, M., and Murphy, D.G. (2005) Obsessions and compulsions in Asperger syndrome and high-functioning autism. British journal of psychiatry 186, 525–528.

24. Ghaziuddin, M., Weidmer-Mikhail, E., and Ghaziuddin, N. (1998) Comorbidity of Asperger syndrome: a preliminary report. Journal of intellectual disability research 42 (Pt 4), 279–283.

25. Ghaziuddin, M., Tsai, L., Naylor, M., and Ghaziuddin, N. (1992) Mood disorder in a group of self-cutting adolescents. Acta paedopsychiatrica 55, 103–105.

26. Lainhart, J.E. and Folstein, S.E. (1994) Affective disorders in people with autism: a review of published cases. Journal of autism and developmental disorders 24, 587–601.

27. Ghaziuddin, M., Ghaziuddin, N., and Greden, J. (2002) Depression in persons with autism: implications for research and clinical care. Journal of autism and developmental disorders 32, 299–306.

28. Frazier, J.A., Doyle, R., Chiu, S., and Coyle, J.T. (2002) Treating a child with Asperger's disorder and comorbid bipolar disorder. American journal of psychiatry 159, 13–21.

29. Gutkovich, Z.A., Carlson, G.A., Carlson, H.E., Coffey, B., and Wieland, N. (2007) Asperger's disorder and co-morbid bipolar disorder: diagnostic and treatment challenges. Journal of child and adolescent psychopharmacology 17, 247–255.

30. Komoto, J., Usui, S., and Hirata, J. (1984) Infantile autism and affective disorder. Journal of autism and developmental disorders 14, 81–84.

31. Wozniak, J., Biederman, J., Faraone, S.V., Frazier, J. et al. (1997) Mania in children with pervasive developmental disorder revisited. Journal of the American Academy of Child and Adolescent Psychiatry 36, 1552–1560.

32. Munesue, T., Ono, Y., Mutoh, K., Shimoda, K., Nakatani, H., and Kikuchi, M. (2008) High prevalence of bipolar disorder comorbidity in adolescents and young adults with high-functioning autism spectrum disorder: a preliminary study of 44 outpatients. Journal of affective disorders 111, 170–175.

33. Mazzone, L., Ruta, L., and Reale, L. (2012) Psychiatric comorbidities in Asperger syndrome and high functioning autism: diagnostic challenges. Annals of general psychiatry 11, 16.

34. Lovaas, O.I. (1987) Behavioral treatment and normal educational and intellectual functioning in young autistic children. Journal of consulting and clinical psychology 55, 3–9.

35. Lovaas, O.I. and Smith, T. (2003) Early and Intensive Behavioral Intervention in Autism. New York, NY: Guilford Press.

36. Green, G. (1996) Early behavioral intervention for autism: What does the research tell us? In C. Maurice, G. Green, and S. Luce (eds) Behavioural Interventions for Young Children with Autism (pp.29–44). Austin, TX: Pro-Ed.

37. McEachin, J.J., Smith, T., and Lovaas, O.I. (1993) Long-term outcome for children with autism who received early intensive behavioral treatment. American journal of mental retardation 97, 359–391.

38. Steward, K.K., Carr, J.E., and LeBlanc L.A. (2007) Evaluation of family-implemented behavioral skills training for teaching social skills to a child with Asperger's disorder. Clinical case studies 6, 252–262.

39. Williams White, S., Keonig, K., and Scahill, L. (2007) Social skills development in children with autism spectrum disorders: a review of the intervention research. Journal of autism and developmental disorders 37, 1858–1868.

40. Love, J.R., Carr, J.E., and LeBlanc, L.A. (2009) Functional assessment of problem behavior in children with autism spectrum disorders: a summary of 32 outpatient cases. Journal of autism and developmental disorders 39, 363–372.

41. Martins, Y., Young, R.L., and Robson, D.C. (2008) Feeding and eating behaviors in children with autism and typically developing children. Journal of autism and developmental disorders 38, 1878–1887.

42. Eldevik, S., Hastings, R.P., Hughes, J.C., Jahr, E., Eikeseth, S., and Cross, S. (2009) Meta-analysis of early intensive behavioral intervention for children with autism. Journal of clinical child and adolescent psychology 38, 439–450.

43. Rogers, S.J. and Vismara, L.A. (2008) Evidence-based comprehensive treatments for early autism. Journal of clinical child and adolescent psychology 37, 8–38.

44. LeBlanc, L.A. and Gillis, J.M. (2012) Behavioral interventions for children with autism spectrum disorders. Pediatric clinics of North America 59, 147–164, xi–xii.

45. Mandell, D.S. (2008) Psychiatric hospitalization among children with autism spectrum disorders. Journal of autism and developmental disorders 38, 1059–1065.

46. Hastings, R.P. and Brown, T. (2002) Coping strategies and the impact of challenging behaviors on special educators' burnout. Mental retardation 40, 148–156.

47. Tyrer, F., McGrother, C.W., Thorp, C.F., Donaldson, M. et al. (2006) Physical aggression towards others in adults with learning disabilities: prevalence and associated factors. Journal of intellectual disability research 50, 295–304.

48. Kaat, A.J. and Lecavalier, L. (2013) Disruptive behavior disorders in children and adolescents with autism spectrum disorders: a review of the prevalence, presentation, and treatment. Research in autism spectrum disorders 7, 1579–1594.

49. Brookman-Frazee, L.I., Taylor, R., and Garland, A.F. (2010) Characterizing community-based mental health services for children with autism spectrum disorders and disruptive behavior problems. Journal of autism and developmental disorders 40, 1188–1201.

50. Gabriels, R.L., Agnew, J.A., Beresford, C., Morrow, M.A., Mesibov, G., and Wamboldt, M. (2012) Improving psychiatric hospital care for pediatric patients with autism spectrum disorders and intellectual disabilities. Autism research and treatment, E-Article ID 685053.

51. Bass, M.M., Duchowny, C.A., and Llabre, M.M. (2009) The effect of therapeutic horseback riding on social functioning in children with autism. Journal of autism and developmental disorders 39, 1261–1267.

52. Winchester, P., Kendall, K., Peters, H., Sears, N., and Winkley, T. (2002) The effect of therapeutic horseback riding on gross motor function and gait speed in children who are developmentally delayed. Physical & occupational therapy in pediatrics 22, 37–50.

53. Sofronoff, K., Attwood, T., Hinton, S., and Levin, I. (2007) A randomized controlled trial of a cognitive behavioural intervention for anger management in children diagnosed with Asperger syndrome. Journal of autism and developmental disorders 37, 1203–1214.

54. Eyberg, S.M., Nelson, M.M., and Boggs, S.R. (2008) Evidence-based psychosocial treatments for children and adolescents with disruptive behavior. Journal of clinical child and adolescent psychology 53, 37, 215–237.

55. Eyberg, S.M., Boggs, S.R., and Algina, J. (1995) Parent-child interaction therapy: a psychosocial model for the treatment of young children with conduct problem behavior and their families. Psychopharmacology bulletin 31, 83–91.

56. Sanders, M. and Studman, L.J. (2003) Practitioner's manual for standard Stepping Stones Triple P. Brisbane: Triple P International Pty Ltd.

57. Bearss, K., Johnson, C., Handen, B., Smith, T., and Scahill, L. (2013) A pilot study of parent training in young children with autism spectrum disorders and disruptive behavior. Journal of autism and developmental disorders 43, 829–840.

58. Aman, M.G., McDougle, C.J., Scahill, L., Handen, B. et al. (2009) Medication and parent training in children with pervasive developmental disorders and serious behavior problems: results from a randomized clinical trial. Journal of the American Academy of Child and Adolescent Psychiatry 48, 1143–1154.

59. McIntyre, L.L. (2008) Parent training for young children with developmental disabilities: randomized controlled trial. American journal of mental retardation 113, 356–368.

60. Solomon, M., Ono, M., Timmer, S., and Goodlin-Jones, B. (2008) The effectiveness of parent-child interaction therapy for families of children on the autism spectrum. Journal of autism and developmental disorders 38, 1767–1776.

61. Roberts, C., Mazzucchelli, T., Studman, L., and Sanders, M.R. (2006) Behavioral family intervention for children with developmental disabilities and behavioral problems. Journal of clinical child and adolescent psychology 35, 180–193.

62. Whittingham, K., Sofronoff, K., Sheffield, J., and Sanders, M.R. (2009) Stepping Stones Triple P: an RCT of a parenting program with parents of a child diagnosed with an autism spectrum disorder. Journal of abnormal child psychology 37, 469–480.

63. Sofronoff, K., Attwood, T., and Hinton, S. (2005) A randomised controlled trial of a CBT intervention for anxiety in children with Asperger syndrome. Journal of child psychology and psychiatry, and allied disciplines 46, 1152–1160.

64. Chalfant, A.M., Rapee, R., and Carroll, L. (2007) Treating anxiety disorders in children with high functioning autism spectrum disorders: a controlled trial. Journal of autism and developmental disorders 37, 1842–1857.

65. Jesner, O.S., Aref-Adib, M., and Coren, E. (2007) Risperidone for autism spectrum disorder. The Cochrane database of systematic reviews, CD005040.

66. Ghanizadeh, A., Sahraeizadeh, A., and Berk, M. (2013) A head-to-head comparison of aripiprazole and risperidone for safety and treating autistic disorders: a randomized double blind clinical trial. Child psychiatry and human development 45, 185–192.

67. Williams, K., Brignell, A., Randall, M., Silove, N., and Hazell, P. (2013) Selective serotonin reuptake inhibitors (SSRIs) for autism spectrum disorders (ASD). The Cochrance database of systematic reviews 30, 8, CD004677.

Chapter 4

1. Coury, D.L., Ashwood, P., Fasano, A., Fuchs, G. *et al.* (2012) Gastrointestinal conditions in children with autism spectrum disorder: developing a research agenda. Pediatrics 130 (Suppl 2), S160–S168.

2. Gorrindo, P., Williams, K.C., Lee, E.B., Walker, L.S., McGrew, S.G., and Levitt, P. (2012) Gastrointestinal dysfunction in autism: parental report, clinical evaluation, and associated factors. Autism research 5, 101–108.

3. Buie, T., Campbell, D.B., Fuchs, G.J. 3rd, Furuta, G.T. *et al.* (2010) Evaluation, diagnosis, and treatment of gastrointestinal disorders in individuals with ASDs: a consensus report. Pediatrics 125 (Suppl 1), S1–S18.

4. Buie, T., Fuchs, G.J. 3rd, Furuta, G.T., Kooros, K. *et al.* (2010) Recommendations for evaluation and treatment of common gastrointestinal problems in children with ASDs. Pediatrics 125 (Suppl 1), S19–S29.

5. Maenner, M.J., Arneson, C.L., Levy, S.E., Kirby, R.S., Nicholas, J.S., and Durkin, M.S. (2012) Association between behavioral features and gastrointestinal problems among children with autism spectrum disorder. Journal of autism and developmental disorders 42, 1520–1525.

6. Nikolov, R.N., Bearss, K.E., Lettinga, J., Erickson, C. *et al.* (2009) Gastrointestinal symptoms in a sample of children with pervasive developmental disorders. Journal of autism and developmental disorders 39, 405–413.

7. Hill, I.D. (2005) What are the sensitivity and specificity of serologic tests for celiac disease? Do sensitivity and specificity vary in different populations? Gastroenterology 128, S25–S32.

8. Hill, I.D., Dirks, M.H., Liptak, G.S., Colletti, R.B. *et al.* (2005) Guideline for the diagnosis and treatment of celiac disease in children: recommendations of the North American Society for Pediatric Gastroenterology, Hepatology and Nutrition. Journal of pediatric gastroenterology and nutrition 40, 1–19.

9. Asperger, H. (1961) Psychopathology of children with coeliac disease. Ann Paediats 197, 346–351.

10. Genuis, S.J. and Bouchard, T.P. (2010) Celiac disease presenting as autism. Journal of child neurology 25, 114–119.

11. Ruggieri, M., Incorpora, G., Polizzi, A., Parano, E., Spina, M., and Pavone, P. (2008) Low prevalence of neurologic and psychiatric manifestations in children with gluten sensitivity. Journal of pediatrics 152, 244–249.

12. Lau, N.M., Green, P.H., Taylor, A.K., Hellberg, D. *et al.* (2013) Markers of celiac disease and gluten sensitivity in children with autism. PloS ONE 8, e66155.

13. Buie, T. (2013) The relationship of autism and gluten. Clinical therapeutics 35, 578–583.

14. Whiteley, P., Shattock, P., Knivsberg, A.M., Seim, A. *et al.* (2012) Gluten- and casein-free dietary intervention for autism spectrum conditions. Frontiers in human neuroscience 6, 344.

15. Millward, C., Ferriter, M., Calver, S., and Connell-Jones, G. (2008) Gluten- and casein-free diets for autistic spectrum disorder. The Cochrane database of systematic reviews, CD003498.

16. Boyce, B. (2011) Making menus friendly: marketing your food intolerance expertise. Journal of the American Dietetic Association 111, 1809–1812.

17. Boyce, J.A., Assa'ad, A., Burks, A.W., Jones, S.M. *et al.* (2011) Guidelines for the diagnosis and management of food allergy in the United States: summary of the NIAID-sponsored expert panel report. Nutrition 27, 253–267.

18. Burks, A.W., Casteel, H.B., Fiedorek, S.C., Williams, L.W., and Pumphrey, C.L. (1994) Prospective oral food challenge study of two soybean protein isolates in patients with possible milk or soy protein enterocolitis. Pediatric allergy and immunology 5, 40–45.

19. Williams, B.L., Hornig, M., Buie, T., Bauman, M.L. *et al.* (2011) Impaired carbohydrate digestion and transport and mucosal dysbiosis in the intestines of children with autism and gastrointestinal disturbances. PloS ONE 6, e24585.

20. Jyonouchi, H., Geng, L., Ruby, A., Reddy, C., and Zimmerman-Bier, B. (2005) Evaluation of an association between gastrointestinal symptoms and cytokine production against common dietary proteins in children with autism spectrum disorders. Journal of pediatrics 146, 605–610.

21. Dardennes, R.M., Al Anbar, N.N., Prado-Netto, A., Kaye, K., Contejean, Y., and Al Anbar, N.N. (2011) Treating the cause of illness rather than the symptoms: parental causal beliefs and treatment choices in autism spectrum disorder. Research in developmental disabilities 32, 1137–1146.

22. Gurney, J.G., McPheeters, M.L., and Davis, M.M. (2006) Parental report of health conditions and health care use among children with and without autism: national survey of children's health. Archives of pediatrics & adolescent medicine 160, 825–830.

23. Jyonouchi, H. (2010) Autism spectrum disorders and allergy: observation from a pediatric allergy/ immunology clinic. Expert review of clinical immunology 6, 397–411.

24. Emond, A., Emmett, P., Steer, C., and Golding, J. (2010) Feeding symptoms, dietary patterns, and growth in young children with autism spectrum disorders. Pediatrics 126, e337–e342.

25. Rhee, S.H., Pothoulakis, C., and Mayer, E.A. (2009) Principles and clinical implications of the brain–gut–enteric microbiota axis. Nature reviews gastroenterology & hepatology 6, 306–314.

26. Finegold, S.M., Molitoris, D., Song, Y., Liu, C. *et al.* (2002) Gastrointestinal microflora studies in late-onset autism. Clinical infectious diseases 35, S6–S16.

27. Song, Y., Liu, C., and Finegold, S.M. (2004) Real-time PCR quantitation of *Clostridia* in feces of autistic children. Applied and environmental microbiology 70, 6459–6465.

28. Parracho, H.M., Bingham, M.O., Gibson, G.R., and McCartney, A.L. (2005) Differences between the gut microflora of children with autistic spectrum disorders and that of healthy children. Journal of medical microbiology 54, 987–991.

29. Finegold, S.M., Dowd, S.E., Gontcharova, V., Liu, C. *et al.* (2010) Pyrosequencing study of fecal microflora of autistic and control children. Anaerobe 16, 444–453.

30. Adams, J.B., Johansen, L.J., Powell, L.D., Quig, D., and Rubin, R.A. (2011) Gastrointestinal flora and gastrointestinal status in children with autism: comparisons to typical children and correlation with autism severity. BMC gastroenterology 11, 22.

31. Gondalia, S.V., Palombo, E.A., Knowles, S.R., Cox, S.B., Meyer, D., and Austin, D.W. (2012) Molecular characterisation of gastrointestinal microbiota of children with autism (with and without gastrointestinal dysfunction) and their neurotypical siblings. Autism research 5, 419–427.

32. Mulle, J.G., Sharp, W.G., and Cubells, J.F. (2013) The gut microbiome: a new frontier in autism research. Current psychiatry reports 15, 337.

33. Critchfield, J.W., van Hemert, S., Ash, M., Mulder, L., and Ashwood, P. (2011) The potential role of probiotics in the management of childhood autism spectrum disorders. Gastroenterology research and practice, E-Article ID 161358.

34. Wakefield, A.J., Murch, S.H., Anthony, A., Linnell, J. *et al.* (1998) Ileal-lymphoid-nodular hyperplasia, non-specific colitis, and pervasive developmental disorder in children. Lancet 351, 637–641.

35. Taylor, B., Miller, E., Lingam, R., Andrews, N., Simmons, A., and Stowe, J. (2002) Measles, mumps, and rubella vaccination and bowel problems or developmental regression in children with autism: population study. British medical journal 324, 393–396.

36. D'Souza, Y., Fombonne, E., and Ward, B.J. (2006) No evidence of persisting measles virus in peripheral blood mononuclear cells from children with autism spectrum disorder. Pediatrics 118, 1664–1675.

37. Hornig, M., Briese, T., Buie, T., Bauman, M.L. *et al.* (2008) Lack of association between measles virus vaccine and autism with enteropathy: a case-control study. PloS ONE 3, e3140.

38. Ibrahim, S.H., Voigt, R.G., Katusic, S.K., Weaver, A.L., and Barbaresi, W.J. (2009) Incidence of gastrointestinal symptoms in children with autism: a population-based study. Pediatrics 124, 680–686.

39. Brown, A.C. and Mehl-Madrona, L. (2011) Autoimmune and gastrointestinal dysfunctions: Does a subset of children with autism reveal a broader connection? Expert review of gastroenterology & hepatology 5, 465–477.

Chapter 5

1. Carr, E.G. and Owen-Deschryver, J.S. (2007) Physical illness, pain, and problem behavior in minimally verbal people with developmental disabilities. Journal of autism developmental disorders 37, 413–424.

2. Boyce, J.A., Assa'ad, A., Burks, A.W., Jones, S.M. *et al.* (2010) Guidelines for the diagnosis and management of food allergy in the United States: report of the NIAID-sponsored expert panel. Journal of allergy and clinical immunology 126, S1–S58.

3. Burks, A.W., Jones, S.M., Boyce, J.A., Sicherer, S.H. *et al.* (2011) NIAID-sponsored 2010 guidelines for managing food allergy: applications in the pediatric population. Pediatrics 128, 955–965.

4. Jyonouchi, H. (2012) Non-IgE mediated food allergy: update of recent progress in mucosal immunity. Inflammation and allergy drug targets 11, 382–396.

5. Katelaris, C.H. (2010) Food allergy and oral allergy or pollen-food syndrome. Current opinion in allergy and clinical immunology 10, 246–251.

6. Peters, R.L., Gurrin, L.C., and Allen, K.J. (2011) The predictive value of skin prick testing for challenge-proven food allergy: a systematic review. Pediatric allergy and immunology 23, 347–352.

7. Garcia, B.E., Gamboa, P.M., Asturias, J.A., Lopez-Hoyos, M. *et al.* (2009) Guidelines on the clinical usefulness of determination of specific immunoglobulin E to foods. Journal of investigative allergology and clinical immunology 19, 423–432.

8. Liacouras, C.A., Furuta, G.T., Hirano, I., Atkins, D. *et al.* (2011) Eosinophilic esophagitis: updated consensus recommendations for children and adults. Journal of allergy and clinical immunology 128, 3–22, e26.

9. Caubet, J.C. and Nowak-Wegrzyn, A. (2011) Current understanding of the immune mechanisms of food protein-induced enterocolitis syndrome. Expert review of clinical immunology 7, 317–327.

10. Nomura, I., Morita, H., Hosokawa, S., Hoshina, H. *et al.* (2011) Four distinct subtypes of non-IgE-mediated gastrointestinal food allergies in neonates and infants, distinguished by their initial symptoms. Journal of allergy and clinical immunology 127, 685–688, e681–e688.

11. Jyonouchi, H. (2008) Non-IgE mediated food allergy. Inflammation and allergy drug targets 7, 173–180.

12. Hochwallner, H., Schulmeister, U., Swoboda, I., Twaroch, T.E. *et al.* (2011) Patients suffering from non-IgE-mediated cow's milk protein intolerance cannot be diagnosed based on IgG subclass or IgA responses to milk allergens. Allergy 66, 1201–1207.

13. Leonard, S.A. and Nowak-Wegrzyn, A. (2011) Food protein-induced enterocolitis syndrome: an update on natural history and review of management. Annals of allergy, asthma & immunology 107, 95–101, 162.

14. Caubet, J.C. and Nowak-Wegrzyn, A. (2011) Food protein-induced enterocolitis to hen's egg. Journal of allergy and clinical immunology 128, 1386–1388.

15. Coates, R.W., Weaver, K.R., Lloyd, R., Ceccacci, N., and Greenberg, M.R. (2011) Food protein-induced enterocolitis syndrome as a cause for infant hypotension. Western journal of emergency medicine 12, 512–514.

16. Mehr, S., Kakakios, A., Frith, K., and Kemp, A.S. (2009) Food protein-induced enterocolitis syndrome: 16-year experience. Pediatrics 123, e459–e464.

17. Jyonouchi, H., Geng, L., Ruby, A., and Reddy, C. (2007) Suboptimal Responses to Dietary Intervention in Children with Autism Spectrum Disorders and Non-IgE Mediated Food Allergy. In L.B. Zhao (ed.) Autism Research Advances (pp. 169–184). Hauppauge, NY: Nova Science Publishers.

18. Chang, T.W. and Pan, A.Y. (2008) Cumulative environmental changes, skewed antigen exposure, and the increase of allergy. Advances in immunology 98, 39–83.

19. Thornton, C.A., MacFarlane, T.V., and Holt, P.G. (2010) The hygiene hypothesis revisited: role of materno-fetal interactions. Current allergy and asthma reports 10, 444–452.

20. Tesse, R., Pandey, R.C., and Kabesch, M. (2011) Genetic variations in toll-like receptor pathway genes influence asthma and atopy. Allergy 66, 307–316.

21. Frei, R., Lauener, R.P., Crameri, R., and O'Mahony, L. (2012) Microbiota and dietary interactions: an update to the hygiene hypothesis? Allergy 67, 451–461.

22. Demoly, P., Calderon, M.A., Casale, T., Scadding, G. et al. (2013) Assessment of disease control in allergic rhinitis. Clinical translational allergy 3, 7.

23. Prokopakis, E., Vardouniotis, A., Kawauchi, H., Scadding, G. et al. (2013) The pathophysiology of the hygiene hypothesis. International journal of pediatric otorhinolaryngology 77, 1065–1071.

24. Salo, P.M., Calatroni, A., Gergen, P.J., Hoppin, J.A. et al. (2011) Allergy-related outcomes in relation to serum IgE: results from the National Health and Nutrition Examination Survey 2005–2006. Journal of allergy and clinical immunology 127, 1226–1235, e1227.

25. Gittler, J.K., Shemer, A., Suarez-Farinas, M., Fuentes-Duculan, J. et al. (2012) Progressive activation of T(H)2/T(H)22 cytokines and selective epidermal proteins characterizes acute and chronic atopic dermatitis. Journal of allergy and clinical immunology 130, 1344–1354.

26. Kabashima-Kubo, R., Nakamura, M., Sakabe, J., Sugita, K. et al. (2012) A group of atopic dermatitis without IgE elevation or barrier impairment shows a high Th1 frequency: possible immunological state of the intrinsic type. Journal of dermatological science 67, 37–43.

27. Lang, D.M. (2007) An overview of EPR3 asthma guidelines: What's different? Allergy and asthma proceedings 28, 620–627.

28. Di Bona, D., Plaia, A., Leto-Barone, M.S., La Piana, S., and Di Lorenzo, G. (2012) Efficacy of subcutaneous and sublingual immunotherapy with grass allergens for seasonal allergic rhinitis: a meta-analysis-based comparison. Journal of allergy and clinical immunology 130, 1097–1107, e1092.

29. Simons, F.E. (2010) Anaphylaxis. Journal of allergy and clinical immunology 125, S161–S181.

30. Simons, F.E. (2009) Anaphylaxis: recent advances in assessment and treatment. Journal of allergy and clinical immunology 124, 625–636.

31. Lieberman, P., Nicklas, R.A., Oppenheimer, J., Kemp, S.F. et al. (2010) The diagnosis and management of anaphylaxis practice parameter: 2010 update. Journal of allergy and clinical immunology 126, 477–480.

32. Kishimoto, T.K., Viswanathan, K., Ganguly, T., Elankumaran, S. et al. (2008) Contaminated heparin associated with adverse clinical events and activation of the contact system. New England journal of medicine 358, 2457–2467.

33. Perez-Rangel, I., Gonzalo-Garijo, M.A., Perez-Calderon, R., Zambonino, M.A., and Corrales-Vargas, S.I. (2013) Wheat-dependent exercise-induced anaphylaxis in elderly patients. Annals of allergy, asthma & immunology 110, 121–123.

34. Khan, D.A. and Solensky, R. (2010) Drug allergy. Journal of allergy and clinical immunology 125, S126–S137.

35. Vuurman, E.F., van Veggel, L.M., Uiterwijk, M.M., Leutner, D., and O'Hanlon, J.F. (1993) Seasonal allergic rhinitis and antihistamine effects on children's learning. Annals of allergy 71, 121–126.

36. Marshall, P.S., O'Hara, C., and Steinberg, P. (2000) Effects of seasonal allergic rhinitis on selected cognitive abilities. Annals of allergy, asthma & immunology 84, 403–410.

37. Walker, S., Khan-Wasti, S., Fletcher, M., Cullinan, P., Harris, J., and Sheikh, A. (2007) Seasonal allergic rhinitis is associated with a detrimental effect on examination performance in United Kingdom teenagers: case-control study. Journal of allergy and clinical immunology 120, 381–387.

38. Borres, M.P. (2009) Allergic rhinitis: more than just a stuffy nose. Acta paediatrica 98, 1088–1092.

39. Leger, D., Annesi-Maesano, I., Carat, F., Rugina, M. et al. (2006) Allergic rhinitis and its consequences on quality of sleep: an unexplored area. Archives of internal medicine 166, 1744–1748.

40. Brawley, A., Silverman, B., Kearney, S., Guanzon, D. et al. (2004) Allergic rhinitis in children with attention-deficit/hyperactivity disorder. Annals of allergy, asthma & immunology 92, 663–667.

41. Tsai, M.C., Lin, H.K., Lin, C.H., and Fu, L.S. (2011) Prevalence of attention deficit/hyperactivity disorder in pediatric allergic rhinitis: a nationwide population-based study. Allergy and asthma proceedings 32, 41–46.

42. Chen, M.H., Su, T.P., Chen, Y.S., Hsu, J.W. et al. (2012) Attention deficit hyperactivity disorder, tic disorder, and allergy: Is there a link? A nationwide population-based study. Journal of child psychology and psychiatry 54, 545–551.

43. Camfferman, D., Kennedy, J.D., Gold, M., Martin, A.J., Winwood, P., and Lushington, K. (2010) Eczema, sleep, and behavior in children. Journal of clinical sleep medicine 6, 581–588.

44. Schmitt, J., Apfelbacher, C., Heinrich, J., Weidinger, S., and Romanos, M. (2013) [Association of atopic eczema and attention-deficit/hyperactivity disorder: meta-analysis of epidemiologic studies]. Zeitschrift für Kinder- und Jugendpsychiatrie und Psychotherapie 41, 35–42.

45. Ponarovsky, B., Amital, D., Lazarov, A., Kotler, M., and Amital, H. (2011) Anxiety and depression in patients with allergic and non-allergic cutaneous disorders. International journal of dermatology 50, 1217–1222.

46. Garn, H. and Renz, H. (2007) Epidemiological and immunological evidence for the hygiene hypothesis. Immunobiology 212, 441–452.

47. Guerra, S. and Martinez, F.D. (2008) Asthma genetics: from linear to multifactorial approaches. Annual review of medicine 59, 327–341.

48. Stern, D.A., Morgan, W.J., Halonen, M., Wright, A.L., and Martinez, F.D. (2008) Wheezing and bronchial hyper-responsiveness in early childhood as predictors of newly diagnosed asthma in early adulthood: a longitudinal birth-cohort study. Lancet 372, 1058–1064.

49. Guerra, S., Sherrill, D.L., Kurzius-Spencer, M., Venker, C. et al. (2008) The course of persistent airflow limitation in subjects with and without asthma. Respiratory medicine 102, 1473–1482.

50. Spahn, J.D. and Covar, R. (2008) Clinical assessment of asthma progression in children and adults. Journal of allergy and clinical immunology 121, 548–557.

51. Borrego, L.M., Stocks, J., Leiria-Pinto, P., Peralta, I. et al. (2009) Lung function and clinical risk factors for asthma in infants and young children with recurrent wheeze. Thorax 64, 203–209.

52. Lougheed, M.D., Moosa, D., Finlayson, S., Hopman, W.M. et al. (2007) Impacts of a provincial asthma guidelines continuing medical education project: The Ontario Asthma Plan of Action's Provider Education in Asthma Care Project. Canadian respiratory journal 14, 111–117.

53. Fitzpatrick, A.M., Higgins, M., Holguin, F., Brown, L.A., and Teague, W.G. (2010) The molecular phenotype of severe asthma in children. Journal of allergy and clinical immunology 125, 851–857, e818.

54. Fitzpatrick, A.M., Teague, W.G., Meyers, D.A., Peters, S.P. et al. (2011) Heterogeneity of severe asthma in childhood: confirmation by cluster analysis of children in the National Institutes of Health/National Heart, Lung, and Blood Institute Severe Asthma Research Program. Journal of allergy and clinical immunology 127, 382–389, e1–e13.

55. Busse, W.W., Morgan, W.J., Gergen, P.J., Mitchell, H.E. et al. (2011) Randomized trial of omalizumab (anti-IgE) for asthma in inner-city children. New England journal of medicine 364, 1005–1015.

56. Wallace, D.V., Dykewicz, M.S., Bernstein, D.I., Blessing-Moore, J. *et al.* (2008) The diagnosis and management of rhinitis: an updated practice parameter. Journal of allergy and clinical immunology 122, S1–S84.

57. Sarin, S., Undem, B., Sanico, A., and Togias, A. (2006) The role of the nervous system in rhinitis. Journal of allergy and clinical immunology 118, 999–1016.

58. Ellis, A.K. and Keith, P.K. (2006) Nonallergic rhinitis with eosinophilia syndrome. Current allergy and asthma reports 6, 215–220.

59. Knipping, S., Holzhausen, H.J., Goetze, G., Riederer, A., and Bloching, M.B. (2007) Rhinitis medicamentosa: electron microscopic changes of human nasal mucosa. Otolaryngology—head and neck surgery 136, 57–61.

60. Hamilos, D.L. (2011) Chronic rhinosinusitis: epidemiology and medical management. Journal of allergy and clinical immunology 128, 693–707.

61. Meltzer, E.O. and Hamilos, D.L. (2011) Rhinosinusitis diagnosis and management for the clinician: a synopsis of recent consensus guidelines. Mayo Clinic proceedings 86, 427–443.

62. Hamilos, D.L. (2007) Chronic rhinosinusitis patterns of illness. Clincal reviews in allergy & immunology 20, 1–13.

63. Kalish, L.H., Arendts, G., Sacks, R., and Craig, J.C. (2009) Topical steroids in chronic rhinosinusitis without polyps: a systematic review and meta-analysis. Otolaryngology—head and neck surgery 141, 674–683.

64. Chan, Y. and Kuhn, F.A. (2009) An update on the classifications, diagnosis, and treatment of rhinosinusitis. Current opinion in otolaryngology & head and neck surgery 17, 204–208.

65. Pawankar, R. and Zernotti, M.E. (2009) Rhinosinusitis in children and asthma severity. Current opinion in allergy and clinical immunology 9, 151–153.

66. Jyonouchi, H. (2009) Food allergy and autism spectrum disorders: Is there a link? Current allergy and asthma reports 9, 194–201.

67. Yong, P.F., Thaventhiran, J.E., and Grimbacher, B. (2011) "A rose is a rose is a rose," but CVID is not CVID. Common variable immune deficiency (CVID): What do we know in 2011? Advances in immunology 111, 47–107.

68. van der Burg, M., van Zelm, M.C., Driessen, G.J., and van Dongen, J.J. (2012) New frontiers of primary antibody deficiencies. Cellular and molecular life sciences 69, 59–73.

69. Cunningham-Rundles, C. (2012) Human B cell defects in perspective. Immunology research 54, 227–232.

70. Jyonouchi, H., Geng, L., Streck, D.L., and Toruner, G.A. (2012) Immunological characterization and transcription profiling of peripheral blood (PB) monocytes in children with autism spectrum disorders (ASD) and specific polysaccharide antibody deficiency (SPAD): case study. Journal of neuroinflammation 9, 4.

71. Ozaras, N., Goksugur, N., Eroglu, S., Tabak, O., Canbakan, B., and Ozaras, R. (2012) Carbamazepine-induced hypogammaglobulinemia. Seizure 21, 229–231.

72. Gordins, P., Sloan, P., Spickett, G.P., and Staines, K.S. (2011) Oral hairy leukoplakia in a patient on long-term anticonvulsant treatment with lamotrigine. Oral surgery, oral medicine, oral pathology, oral radiology, and endodontology 111, e17–e23.

73. Hoshino, C. and Hoshi, T. (2011) Carbamazepine-induced agammagloblinaemia clinically mimicking diffuse panbronchiolitis. British medical journal case reports, ID1120103535.

74. Yamamoto, T., Uchiyama, T., Takahashi, H., Himuro, K., Kanai, K., and Kuwabara, S. (2010) B cell aplasia and hypogammaglobulinemia after carbamazepine treatment. Internal medicine 49, 707–708.

75. Okumura, A., Tsuge, I., Kamachi, Y., Negoro, T., and Watanabe, K. (2007) Transient hypogammaglobulinemia after antiepileptic drug hypersensitivity. Pediatric neurology 36, 342–344.

76. Azar, A.E. and Ballas, Z.K. (2008) Reversible panhypogammaglobulinemia associated with the antiepileptic agent levetiracetam. Annals of allergy, asthma & immunology 101, 108–109.

77. Swedo, S.E., Leckman, J.F., and Rose, N.R. (2012) From research subgroup to clinical syndrome: modifying the PANDAS criteria to describe PANS (pediatric acute-onset neuropsychiatric syndrome). Pediatrics & therapeutics 2, 113.

78. Swedo, S.E., Leonard, H.L., Garvey, M., Mittleman, B. *et al.* (1998) Pediatric autoimmune neuropsychiatric disorders associated with streptococcal infections: clinical description of the first 50 cases. American journal of psychiatry 155, 264–271.

79. Swedo, S.E. (1994) Sydenham's chorea. A model for childhood autoimmune neuropsychiatric disorders. Journal of the American Medical Association 272, 1788–1791.

80. Lin, H., Williams, K.A., Katsovich, L., Findley, D.B. *et al.* (2010) Streptococcal upper respiratory tract infections and psychosocial stress predict future tic and obsessive-compulsive symptom severity in children and adolescents with Tourette syndrome and obsessive-compulsive disorder. Biological psychiatry 67, 684–691.

81. Kurlan, R., Johnson, D., and Kaplan, E.L. (2008) Streptococcal infection and exacerbations of childhood tics and obsessive-compulsive symptoms: a prospective blinded cohort study. Pediatrics 121, 1188–1197.

82. Singer, H.S., Gause, C., Morris, C., and Lopez, P. (2008) Serial immune markers do not correlate with clinical exacerbations in pediatric autoimmune neuropsychiatric disorders associated with streptococcal infections. Pediatrics 121, 1198–1205.

83. Murphy, T.K., Kurlan, R., and Leckman, J. (2010) The immunobiology of Tourette's disorder, pediatric autoimmune neuropsychiatric disorders associated with *Streptococcus*, and related disorders: a way forward. Journal of child and adolescent psychopharmacology 20, 317–331.

84. Garvey, M.A., Perlmutter, S.J., Allen, A.J., Hamburger, S. *et al.* (1999) A pilot study of penicillin prophylaxis for neuropsychiatric exacerbations triggered by streptococcal infections. Biological psychiatry 45, 1564–1571.

85. Snider, L.A., Lougee, L., Slattery, M., Grant, P., and Swedo, S.E. (2005) Antibiotic prophylaxis with azithromycin or penicillin for childhood-onset neuropsychiatric disorders. Biological psychiatry 57, 788–792.

86. Sokol, M.S. (2000) Infection-triggered anorexia nervosa in children: clinical description of four cases. Journal of child and adolescent psychopharmacology 10, 133–145.

87. Murphy, T.K., Storch, E.A., Lewin, A.B., Edge, P.J., and Goodman, W.K. (2012) Clinical factors associated with pediatric autoimmune neuropsychiatric disorders associated with streptococcal infections. Journal of pediatrics 160, 314–319.

88. Deshmukh, V.M., Toelle, B.G., Usherwood, T., O'Grady, B., and Jenkins, C.R. (2007) Anxiety, panic and adult asthma: a cognitive-behavioral perspective. Respiratory medicine 101, 194–202.

89. Goodwin, R.D., Jacobi, F., and Thefeld, W. (2003) Mental disorders and asthma in the community. Archives of general psychiatry 60, 1125–1130.

90. Goodwin, R.D., Olfson, M., Shea, S., Lantigua, R.A. *et al.* (2003) Asthma and mental disorders in primary care. General hospital psychiatry 25, 479–483.

91. Goodwin, R.D., Fergusson, D.M., and Horwood, L.J. (2004) Asthma and depressive and anxiety disorders among young persons in the community. Psychological medicine 34, 1465–1474.

92. Hasler, G., Gergen, P.J., Kleinbaum, D.G., Ajdacic, V. *et al.* (2005) Asthma and panic in young adults: a 20-year prospective community study. American journal of respiratory and critical care medicine 171, 1224–1230.

93. Feldman, J.M., Ortega, A.N., McQuaid, E.L., and Canino, G. (2006) Comorbidity between asthma attacks and internalizing disorders among Puerto Rican children at one-year follow-up. Psychosomatics 47, 333–339.

94. Alati, R., O'Callaghan, M., Najman, J.M., Williams, G.M., Bor, W., and Lawlor, D.A. (2005) Asthma and internalizing behavior problems in adolescence: a longitudinal study. Psychosomatic medicine 67, 462–470.

95. Goodwin, R.D. and Eaton, W.W. (2003) Asthma and the risk of panic attacks among adults in the community. Psychological medicine 33, 879–885.

96. Craske, M.G., Poulton, R., Tsao, J.C., and Plotkin, D. (2001) Paths to panic disorder/agoraphobia: an exploratory analysis from age 3 to 21 in an unselected birth cohort. Journal of the American Academy of Child and Adolescent Psychiatry 40, 556–563.

97. Mogensen, N., Larsson, H., Lundholm, C., and Almqvist, C. (2011) Association between childhood asthma and ADHD symptoms in adolescence: a prospective population-based twin study. Allergy 66, 1224–1230.

98. Fasmer, O.B., Halmoy, A., Eagan, T.M., Oedegaard, K.J., and Haavik, J. (2011) Adult attention deficit hyperactivity disorder is associated with asthma. BMC psychiatry 11, 128.

99. Wasan, A., Fernandez, E., Jamison, R.N., and Bhattacharyya, N. (2007) Association of anxiety and depression with reported disease severity in patients undergoing evaluation for chronic rhinosinusitis. Annals of otology, rhinology & laryngology 116, 491–497.

100. Litvack, J.R., Mace, J., and Smith, T.L. (2011) Role of depression in outcomes of endoscopic sinus surgery. Otolaryngology—head and neck surgery 144, 446–451.

101. Sahlstrand-Johnson, P., Ohlsson, B., Von Buchwald, C., Jannert, M., and Ahlner-Elmqvist, M. (2011) A multi-centre study on quality of life and absenteeism in patients with CRS referred for endoscopic surgery. Rhinology 49, 420–428.

102. Jyonouchi, H., Geng, L., Streck, D.L., and Toruner, G.A. (2011) Children with autism spectrum disorders (ASD) who exhibit chronic gastrointestinal (GI) symptoms and marked fluctuation of behavioral symptoms exhibit distinct innate immune abnormalities and transcriptional profiles of peripheral blood (PB) monocytes. Journal of neuroimmunology 238, 73–80.

Chapter 6

1. Selwitz, R.H., Ismail, A.I., and Pitts, N.B. (2007) Dental caries. Lancet 369, 51–59.

2. Loo, C.Y., Graham, R.M., and Hughes, C.V. (2008) The caries experience and behavior of dental patients with autism spectrum disorder. Journal of the American Dental Association 139, 1518–1524.

3. van Houte, J. (1994) Role of micro-organisms in caries etiology. Journal of dental research 73, 672–681.

4. Jensen, M.E. (1999) Diet and dental caries. Dental clinics of North America 43, 615–633.

5. DeRouen, T.A., Martin, M.D., Leroux, B.G., Townes, B.D. et al. (2006) Neurobehavioral effects of dental amalgam in children: a randomized clinical trial. Journal of the American Medical Association 295, 1784–1792.

6. Browning, W.D. (2006) The benefits of glass ionomer self-adhesive materials in restorative dentistry. Compendium of continuing education in dentistry 27, 308–314.

7. Albandar, J.M. and Rams, T.E. (2002) Global epidemiology of periodontal diseases: an overview. Periodontology 2000, 29, 7–10.

8. Kaur, G., Verhamme, K.M., Dieleman, J.P., Vanrolleghem, A. et al. (2010) Association between calcium channel blockers and gingival hyperplasia. Journal of clinical periodontology 37, 625–630.

9. Eke, P.I., Dye, B.A., Wei, L., Thornton-Evans, G.O., Genco, R.J., and CDC Periodontal Disease Surveillance workgroup: Beck, J., Douglass, G., and Page, R. (2012) Prevalence of periodontitis in adults in the United States: 2009 and 2010. Journal of dental research 91, 914–920.

10. Prakasam, A., Elavarasu, S.S., and Natarajan, R.K. (2012) Antibiotics in the management of aggressive periodontitis. Journal of pharmacy & bioallied sciences 4, S252–S255.

11. Bogren, A., Teles, R.P., Torresyap, G., Haffajee, A.D., Socransky, S.S., and Wennstrom, J.L. (2008) Locally delivered doxycycline during supportive periodontal therapy: a 3-year study. Journal of periodontology 79, 827–835.

12. Ranjitkar, S., Smales, R.J., and Kaidonis, J.A. (2012) Oral manifestations of gastroesophageal reflux disease. Journal of gastroenterology and hepatology 27, 21–27.

13. Lang, R., White, P.J., Machalicek, W., Rispoli, M. et al. (2009) Treatment of bruxism in individuals with developmental disabilities: a systematic review. Research in developmental disabilities 30, 809–818.

14. Napeñas, J., Brennan, M., and Fox, P. (2009) Diagnosis and treatment of xerostomia (dry mouth). Odontology 97, 76–83.

15. Buie, T., Campbell, D.B., Fuchs, G.J. 3rd, Furuta, G.T. et al. (2010) Evaluation, diagnosis, and treatment of gastrointestinal disorders in individuals with ASDs: a consensus report. Pediatrics 125 (Suppl 1), S1–S18.

16. National Institue of Dental and Craniofacial Research (2013) *The Tooth Decay Process: How to Reverse It and Avoid a Cavity.* Available at www.nidcr.nih.gov/OralHealth/OralHealthInformation/ChildrensOralHealth/ToothDecayProcess.htm. Accessed on 12 November 2013.

17. American Dental Association (n.d.) *MouthHealthy.* Available at www.mouthhealthy.org. Accessed on 12 November 2013.

18. Sharma, N.C., Klukowska, M., Mielczarek, A., Grender, J.M., and Qaqish, J. (2012) A 4-week clinical comparison of a novel multi-directional power brush to a manual toothbrush in the reduction of gingivitis and plaque. American journal of dentistry 25 (Spec No A), 14A–20A.

19. Charles, J.M. (2010) Dental care in children with developmental disabilities: attention deficit disorder, intellectual disabilities, and autism. Journal of dentistry for children 77, 84–91.

20. DePaola, L.G. and Spolarich, A.E. (2007) Safety and efficacy of antimicrobial mouthrinses in clinical practice. American Dental Hygienists Association 81, 117.

21. Malamed, S.F. (2009) *Sedation: A Guide to Patient Management.* Philadelphia, PA: Elsevier Health Sciences.

22. Faulks, D., Hennequin, M., Albecker-Grappe, S., Maniere, M.C. *et al.* (2007) Sedation with 50% nitrous oxide/oxygen for outpatient dental treatment in individuals with intellectual disability. Developmental medicine and child neurology 49, 621–625.

23. Dougherty, N. (2009) The dental patient with special needs: a review of indications for treatment under general anesthesia. Special care in dentistry 29, 17–20.

Chapter 7

1. Abdul-Rahman, O.A. and Hudgins, L. (2006) The diagnostic utility of a genetics evaluation in children with pervasive developmental disorders. Genetics in medicine 8, 50–54.

2. Battaglia, A. and Carey, J.C. (2006) Etiologic yield of autistic spectrum disorders: a prospective study. American journal of medical genetics (Part C), Seminars in medical genetics 142C, 3–7.

3. Schaefer, G.B. and Lutz, R.E. (2006) Diagnostic yield in the clinical genetic evaluation of autism spectrum disorders. Genetics in medicine 8, 549–556.

4. Schaefer, G.B. and Mendelsohn, N.J. (2008) Clinical genetics evaluation in identifying the etiology of autism spectrum disorders. Genetics in medicine 10, 301–305.

5. Miles, J.H. (2011) Autism spectrum disorders: a genetics review. Genetics in medicine 13, 278–294.

6. Toriello, H.V. (2012) Approach to the genetic evaluation of the child with autism. Pediatric clinics of North America 59, 113–128, xi.

7. Narcisa, V., Discenza, M., Vaccari, E., Rosen-Sheidley, B., Hardan, A.Y., and Couchon, E. (2013) Parental interest in a genetic risk assessment test for autism spectrum disorders. Clinical pediatrics 52, 139–146.

8. McGrew, S.G., Peters, B.R., Crittendon, J.A., and Veenstra-Vanderweele, J. (2012) Diagnostic yield of chromosomal microarray analysis in an autism primary care practice: Which guidelines to implement? Journal of autism and developmental disorders 42, 1582–1591.

9. Bauer, S.C. and Msall, M.E. (2011) Genetic testing for autism spectrum disorders. Developmental disabilities research reviews 17, 3–8.

10. Shen, Y., Dies, K.A., Holm, I.A., Bridgemohan, C. *et al.* (2010) Clinical genetic testing for patients with autism spectrum disorders. Pediatrics 125, e727–e735.

Chapter 8

1. Wieder, S. and Greenspan, S.I. (2003) Climbing the symbolic ladder in the DIR model through floor time/interactive play. Autism 7, 425–435.

2. Bellini, S., Peters, J.K., Benner, L., and Hopf, A. (2007) A meta-analysis of school-based social skills interventions for children with autism spectrum disorders. Remedial and special education 28, 153–162.

3. Cuccaro, M.L., Tuchman, R.F., Hamilton, K.L., Wright, H.H. *et al.* (2012) Exploring the relationship between autism spectrum disorder and epilepsy using latent class cluster analysis. Journal of autism and developmental disorders 42, 1630–1641.

4. Woolfenden, S., Sarkozy, V., Ridley, G., Coory, M., and Williams, K. (2012) A systematic review of two outcomes in autism spectrum disorder: epilepsy and mortality. Developmental medicine and child neurology 54, 306–312.

5. Kanemura, H., Sano, F., Tando, T., Sugita, K., and Aihara, M. (2013) Can EEG characteristics predict development of epilepsy in autistic children? European journal of paediatric neurology 17, 232–237.

6. Rugino, T.A. and Samsock, T.C. (2002) Levetiracetam in autistic children: an open-label study. Journal of developmental and behavioral pediatrics 23, 225–230.

7. Wasserman, S., Iyengar, R., Chaplin, W.F., Watner, D. *et al.* (2006) Levetiracetam versus placebo in childhood and adolescent autism: a double-blind placebo-controlled study. International clinical psychopharmacology 21, 363–367.

8. Camacho, A., Espin, J.C., Nunez, N., and Simon, R. (2012) Levetiracetam-induced reversible autistic regression. Pediatric neurology 47, 65–67.

9. Uvebrant, P. and Bauziene, R. (1994) Intractable epilepsy in children. The efficacy of lamotrigine treatment, including non-seizure-related benefits. Neuropediatrics 25, 284–289.

10. Belsito, K.M., Law, P.A., Kirk, K.S., Landa, R.J., and Zimmerman, A.W. (2001) Lamotrigine therapy for autistic disorder: a randomized, double-blind, placebo-controlled trial. Journal of autism and developmental disorders 31, 175–181.

11. Hollander, E., Chaplin, W., Soorya, L., Wasserman, S. *et al.* (2010) Divalproex sodium vs placebo for the treatment of irritability in children and adolescents with autism spectrum disorders. Neuropsychopharmacology 35, 990–998.

12. Hollander, E., Soorya, L., Wasserman, S., Esposito, K., Chaplin, W., and Anagnostou, E. (2006) Divalproex sodium vs. placebo in the treatment of repetitive behaviours in autism spectrum disorder. International journal of neuropsychopharmacology 9, 209–213.

13. Canitano, R. (2005) Clinical experience with topiramate to counteract neuroleptic induced weight gain in 10 individuals with autistic spectrum disorders. Brain & development 27, 228–232.

14. Hardan, A.Y., Jou, R.J., and Handen, B.L. (2004) A retrospective assessment of topiramate in children and adolescents with pervasive developmental disorders. Journal of child and adolescent psychopharmacology 14, 426–432.

15. Rezaei, V., Mohammadi, M.R., Ghanizadeh, A., Sahraian, A. *et al.* (2010) Double-blind, placebo-controlled trial of risperidone plus topiramate in children with autistic disorder. Progress in neuro-psychopharmacology & biological psychiatry 34, 1269–1272.

16. Campbell, M., Anderson, L.T., Meier, M., Cohen, I.L. *et al.* (1978) A comparison of haloperidol and behavior therapy and their interaction in autistic children. Journal of the American Academy of Child Psychiatry 17, 640–655.

17. Cohen, I.L., Campbell, M., and Posner, D. (1980) A study of haloperidol in young autistic children: a within-subjects design using objective rating scales. Psychopharmacology bulletin 16, 63–65.

18. Campbell, M., Armenteros, J.L., Malone, R.P., Adams, P.B., Eisenberg, Z.W., and Overall, J.E. (1997) Neuroleptic-related dyskinesias in autistic children: a prospective, longitudinal study. Journal of the American Academy of Child and Adolescent Psychiatry 36, 835–843.

19. Shea, S., Turgay, A., Carroll, A., Schulz, M. *et al.* (2004) Risperidone in the treatment of disruptive behavioral symptoms in children with autistic and other pervasive developmental disorders. Pediatrics 114, e634–e641.

20. Marcus, R.N., Owen, R., Kamen, L., Manos, G. *et al.* (2009) A placebo-controlled, fixed-dose study of aripiprazole in children and adolescents with irritability associated with autistic disorder. Journal of the American Academy of Child and Adolescent Psychiatry 48, 1110–1119.

21. Richdale, A.L. and Schreck, K.A. (2009) Sleep problems in autism spectrum disorders: prevalence, nature, and possible biopsychosocial aetiologies. Sleep medicine reviews 13, 403–411.

22. Krakowiak, P., Goodlin-Jones, B., Hertz-Picciotto, I., Croen, L.A., and Hansen, R.L. (2008) Sleep problems in children with autism spectrum disorders, developmental delays, and typical development: a population-based study. Journal of sleep research 17, 197–206.

23. Sheldon, S.H., Ferber, R., and Kryger, M.H. (ed.) (2005) *Principles and Practice of Pediatric Sleep Medicine.* Philadelphia, PA: Elsevier Saunders.

24. Reed, H.E., McGrew, S.G., Artibee, K., Surdkya, K. *et al.* (2009) Parent-based sleep education workshops in autism. Journal of child neurology 24, 936–945.

25. Rossignol, D.A. and Frye, R.E. (2011) Melatonin in autism spectrum disorders: a systematic review and meta-analysis. Developmental medicine and child neurology 53, 783–792.

26. Garstang, J. and Wallis, M. (2006) Randomized controlled trial of melatonin for children with autistic spectrum disorders and sleep problems. Child: care, health and development 32, 585–589.

27. Giannotti, F., Cortesi, F., Cerquiglini, A., and Bernabei, P. (2006) An open-label study of controlled-release melatonin in treatment of sleep disorders in children with autism. Journal of autism and developmental disorders 36, 741–752.

28. Malow, B., Adkins, K.W., McGrew, S.G., Wang, L. *et al.* (2012) Melatonin for sleep in children with autism: a controlled trial examining dose, tolerability, and outcomes. Journal of autism and developmental disorders 42, 1729–1738.

29. Wright, B., Sims, D., Smart, S., Alwazeer, A. *et al.* (2011) Melatonin versus placebo in children with autism spectrum conditions and severe sleep problems not amenable to behaviour management strategies: a randomised controlled crossover trial. Journal of autism and developmental disorders 41, 175–184.

30. Malow, B.A., Byars, K., Johnson, K., Weiss, S. *et al.* (2012) A practice pathway for the identification, evaluation, and management of insomnia in children and adolescents with autism spectrum disorders. Pediatrics 130 (Suppl 2), S106–S124.

31. Ming, X., Gordon, E., Kang, N., and Wagner, G.C. (2008) Use of clonidine in children with autism spectrum disorders. Brain & development 30, 454–460.

32. McCracken, J.T., McGough, J., Shah, B., Cronin, P. *et al.* (2002) Risperidone in children with autism and serious behavioral problems. New England journal of medicine 347, 314–321.

33. Elbe, D. and Lalani, Z. (2012) Review of the pharmacotherapy of irritability of autism. Journal of the Canadian Academy of Child and Adolescent Psychiatry 21, 130–146.

34. Nagaraj, R., Singhi, P., and Malhi, P. (2006) Risperidone in children with autism: randomized, placebo-controlled, double-blind study. Journal of child neurology 21, 450–455.

35. Owen, R., Sikich, L., Marcus, R.N., Corey-Lisle, P. *et al.* (2009) Aripiprazole in the treatment of irritability in children and adolescents with autistic disorder. Pediatrics 124, 1533–1540.

36. Ghuman, J.K., Aman, M.G., Lecavalier, L., Riddle, M.A. *et al.* (2009) Randomized, placebo-controlled, crossover study of methylphenidate for attention-deficit/hyperactivity disorder symptoms in preschoolers with developmental disorders. Journal of child and adolescent psychopharmacology 19, 329–339.

37. Handen, B.L., Johnson, C.R., and Lubetsky, M. (2000) Efficacy of methylphenidate among children with autism and symptoms of attention-deficit hyperactivity disorder. Journal of autism and developmental disorders 30, 245–255.

38. Research Units on Pediatric Psychopharmacology Autism Network (2005) Randomized, controlled, crossover trial of methylphenidate in pervasive developmental disorders with hyperactivity. Archives of general psychiatry 62, 1266–1274.

39. Mahajan, R., Bernal, M.P., Panzer, R., Whitaker, A. *et al.* (2012) Clinical practice pathways for evaluation and medication choice for attention-deficit/hyperactivity disorder symptoms in autism spectrum disorders. Pediatrics 130 (Suppl 2), S125–S138.

40. Arnold, L.E., Aman, M.G., Cook, A.M., Witwer, A.N. *et al.* (2006) Atomoxetine for hyperactivity in autism spectrum disorders: placebo-controlled crossover pilot trial. Journal of the American Academy of Child and Adolescent Psychiatry 45, 1196–1205.

41. Jaselskis, C.A., Cook, E.H. Jr., Fletcher, K.E., and Leventhal, B.L. (1992) Clonidine treatment of hyperactive and impulsive children with autistic disorder. Journal of clinical psychopharmacology 12, 322–327.

42. King, B.H., Hollander, E., Sikich, L., McCracken, J.T. *et al.* (2009) Lack of efficacy of citalopram in children with autism spectrum disorders and high levels of repetitive behavior: citalopram ineffective in children with autism. Archives of general psychiatry 66, 583–590.

43. Hollander, E., Phillips, A., Chaplin, W., Zagursky, K. *et al.* (2005) A placebo controlled crossover trial of liquid fluoxetine on repetitive behaviors in childhood and adolescent autism. Neuropsychopharmacology 30, 582–589.

44. Hollander, E., Soorya, L., Chaplin, W., Anagnostou, E. *et al.* (2012) A double-blind placebo-controlled trial of fluoxetine for repetitive behaviors and global severity in adult autism spectrum disorders. American journal of psychiatry 169, 292–299.

45. McDougle, C.J., Naylor, S.T., Cohen, D.J., Volkmar, F.R., Heninger, G.R., and Price, L.H. (1996) A double-blind, placebo-controlled study of fluvoxamine in adults with autistic disorder. Archives of general psychiatry 53, 1001–1008.

46. McDougle, C.J., Kresch, L.E., and Posey, D.J. (2000) Repetitive thoughts and behavior in pervasive developmental disorders: treatment with serotonin reuptake inhibitors. Journal of autism and developmental disorders 30, 427–435.

47. Gordon, C.T., State, R.C., Nelson, J.E., Hamburger, S.D., and Rapoport, J.L. (1993) A double-blind comparison of clomipramine, desipramine, and placebo in the treatment of autistic disorder. Archives of general psychiatry 50, 441–447.

Chapter 9

1. Molloy, C.A. and Manning-Courtney, P. (2003) Prevalence of chronic gastrointestinal symptoms in children with autism and autistic spectrum disorders. Autism 7, 165–171.

2. Ibrahim, S.H., Voigt, R.G., Katusic, S.K., Weaver, A.L., and Barbaresi, W.J. (2009) Incidence of gastrointestinal symptoms in children with autism: a population-based study. Pediatrics 124, 680–686.

3. Smith, R.A., Farnworth, H., Wright, B., and Allgar, V. (2009) Are there more bowel symptoms in children with autism compared to normal children and children with other developmental and neurological disorders? A case control study. Autism 13, 343–355.

4. Rossignol, D.A. (2009) Novel and emerging treatments for autism spectrum disorders: a systematic review. Annals of clinical psychiatry 21, 213–236.

5. Pang, K.H. and Croaker, G.D. (2011) Constipation in children with autism and autistic spectrum disorder. Pediatric surgery international 27, 353–358.

6. Kushak, R.I., Lauwers, G.Y., Winter, H.S., and Buie, T.M. (2011) Intestinal disaccharidase activity in patients with autism: effect of age, gender, and intestinal inflammation. Autism 15, 285–294.

7. Gorrindo, P., Williams, K.C., Lee, E.B., Walker, L.S., McGrew, S.G., and Levitt, P. (2012) Gastrointestinal dysfunction in autism: parental report, clinical evaluation, and associated factors. Autism research 5, 101–108.

8. de Magistris, L., Familiari, V., Pascotto, A., Sapone, A. *et al.* (2010) Alterations of the intestinal barrier in patients with autism spectrum disorders and in their first-degree relatives. Journal of pediatric gastroenterology and nutrition 51, 418–424.

9. Finegold, S.M., Molitoris, D., Song, Y., Liu, C. *et al.* (2002) Gastrointestinal microflora studies in late-onset autism. Clinical infectious diseases 35, S6–S16.

10. Parracho, H.M., Bingham, M.O., Gibson, G.R., and McCartney, A.L. (2005) Differences between the gut microflora of children with autistic spectrum disorders and that of healthy children. Journal of medical microbiology 54, 987–991.

11. Finegold, S.M., Dowd, S.E., Gontcharova, V., Liu, C. *et al.* (2010) Pyrosequencing study of fecal microflora of autistic and control children. Anaerobe 16, 444–453.

12. Adams, J.B., Johansen, L.J., Powell, L.D., Quig, D., and Rubin, R.A. (2011) Gastrointestinal flora and gastrointestinal status in children with autism: comparisons to typical children and correlation with autism severity. BMC gastroenterology 11, 22.

13. Wang, L., Christophersen, C.T., Sorich, M.J., Gerber, J.P., Angley, M.T., and Conlon, M.A. (2011) Low relative abundances of the mucolytic bacterium *Akkermansia muciniphila* and *Bifidobacterium* spp. in feces of children with autism. Applied and environmental microbiology 77, 6718–6721.

14. Critchfield, J.W., van Hemert, S., Ash, M., Mulder, L., and Ashwood, P. (2011) The potential role of probiotics in the management of childhood autism spectrum disorders. Gastroenterology research and practic, E-Article ID 161358.

15. Van Cutsem, E., de Haas, S., Kang, Y.K., Ohtsu, A. *et al.* (2012) Bevacizumab in combination with chemotherapy as first-line therapy in advanced gastric cancer: a biomarker evaluation from the AVAGAST randomized phase III trial. Journal of clinical oncology 30, 2119–2127.

16. Kang, D.W., Park, J.G., Ilhan, Z.E., Wallstrom, G. *et al.* (2013) Reduced incidence of Prevotella and other fermenters in intestinal microflora of autistic children. PloS ONE 8, e68322.

17. Hanson, E., Kalish, L.A., Bunce, E., Curtis, C. *et al.* (2007) Use of complementary and alternative medicine among children diagnosed with autism spectrum disorder. Journal of autism and developmental disorders 37, 628.

18. Forman, J., Silverstein, J., Committee on Nutrition, Council on Environmental Health (2012) Organic foods: health and environmental advantages and disadvantages. Pediatrics 130, e1406–e1415.

19. Rudel, R.A., Gray, J.M., Engel, C.L., Rawsthorne, T.W. *et al.* (2011) Food packaging and bisphenol A and bis(2-ethyhexyl) phthalate exposure: findings from a dietary intervention. Environmental health perspectives 119, 914–920.

20. Geier, D.A., Kern, J.K., Garver, C.R., Adams, J.B., Audhya, T., and Geier, M.R. (2009) A prospective study of transsulfuration biomarkers in autistic disorders. Neurochemical research 34, 386–393.

21. Geier, D.A., Kern, J.K., Garver, C.R., Adams, J.B. *et al.* (2009) Biomarkers of environmental toxicity and susceptibility in autism. Journal of the neurological sciences 280, 101–108.

22. Stein, T.P., Schluter, M.D., Steer, R.A., and Ming, X. (2013) Autism and phthalate metabolite glucuronidation. Journal of autism and developmental disorders 43, 2677–2685.

23. Gu, F., Chauhan, V., and Chauhan, A. (2013) Impaired synthesis and antioxidant defense of glutathione in the cerebellum of autistic subjects: alterations in the activities and protein expression of glutathione-related enzymes. Free radical biology & medicine 65C, 488–496.

24. Roberts, E.M., English, P.B., Grether, J.K., Windham, G.C., Somberg, L., and Wolff, C. (2007) Maternal residence near agricultural pesticide applications and autism spectrum disorders among children in the California Central Valley. Environmental health perspectives 115, 1482–1489.

25. Reichelt, K.L., Ekrem, J., and Scott, H. (1990) Gluten, milk proteins and autism: dietary intervention effects on behavior and peptide secretion. Journal of applied nutrition 42, 12.

26. Vojdani, A., O'Bryan, T., Green, J.A., McCandless, J. *et al.* (2004) Immune response to dietary proteins, gliadin and cerebellar peptides in children with autism. Nutritional neuroscience 7, 151–161.

27. Kawashti, M.I., Amin, O.R., and Rowehy, N.G. (2006) Possible immunological disorders in autism: concomitant autoimmunity and immune tolerance. Egyptian journal of immunology 13, 99–104.

28. Lau, N.M., Green, P.H., Taylor, A.K., Hellberg, D. *et al.* (2013) Markers of celiac disease and gluten sensitivity in children with autism. PloS ONE 8, e66155.

29. Elder, J.H. (2008) The gluten-free, casein-free diet in autism: an overview with clinical implications. Nutrition in clinical practice 23, 583–588.

30. Harris, C. and Card, B. (2012) A pilot study to evaluate nutritional influences on gastrointestinal symptoms and behavior patterns in children with autism spectrum disorder. Complementary therapies in medicine 20, 437–440.

31. Pennesi, C.M. and Klein, L.C. (2012) Effectiveness of the gluten-free, casein-free diet for children diagnosed with autism spectrum disorder: based on parental report. Nutritional neuroscience 15, 85–91.

32. Knivsberg, A.M., Reichelt, K.L., Hoien, T., and Nodland, M. (2002) A randomised, controlled study of dietary intervention in autistic syndromes. Nutritional neuroscience 5, 251–261.

33. Whiteley, P., Haracopos, D., Knivsberg, A.M., Reichelt, K.L. *et al.* (2010) The ScanBrit randomised, controlled, single-blind study of a gluten- and casein-free dietary intervention for children with autism spectrum disorders. Nutritional neuroscience 13, 87–100.

34. Millward, C., Ferriter, M., Calver, S., and Connell-Jones, G. (2008) Gluten- and casein-free diets for autistic spectrum disorder. The Cochrane database of systematic reviews, CD003498.

35. Kossoff, E.H., Zupec-Kania, B.A., and Rho, J.M. (2009) Ketogenic diets: an update for child neurologists. Journal of child neurology 24, 979–988.

36. Evangeliou, A., Vlachonikolis, I., Mihailidou, H., Spilioti, M. *et al.* (2003) Application of a ketogenic diet in children with autistic behavior: pilot study. Journal of child neurology 18, 113–118.

37. Sharma, S., Sankhyan, N., Gulati, S., and Agarwala, A. (2012) Use of the modified Atkins diet in infantile spasms refractory to first-line treatment. Seizure 21, 45–48.

38. Sharma, S., Sankhyan, N., Gulati, S., and Agarwala, A. (2013) Use of the modified Atkins diet for treatment of refractory childhood epilepsy: a randomized controlled trial. Epilepsia 54, 481–486.

39. Haberlandt, E., Karall, D., Jud, V., Baumgartner, S.S. et al. (2013) Glucose transporter type 1 deficiency syndrome effectively treated with modified Atkins diet. Neuropediatrics 45, 117–119.

40. El-Rashidy, O.F., Nassar, M.F., Abdel-Hamid, I.A., Shatla, R.H. et al. (2013) Modified Atkins diet vs classic ketogenic formula in intractable epilepsy. Acta neurologica Scandinavica 128, 402–408.

41. Hyman, S.L., Stewart, P.A., Schmidt, B., Cain, U. et al. (2012) Nutrient intake from food in children with autism. Pediatrics 130 (Suppl 2), S145–S153.

42. Rimland, B. (1973) High Dosage Levels of Certain Vitamins in the Treatment of Children with Severe Mental Disorders. In D.R. Hawkins and L. Pauling (eds) Orthomolecular Psychiatry (pp. 513–538). San Francisco, CA: W.H. Freeman.

43. Rimland, B., Callaway, E., and Dreyfus, P. (1978) The effect of high doses of vitamin B6 on autistic children: a double-blind crossover study. American journal of psychiatry 135, 472–475.

44. Barthelemy, C., Garreau, B., Leddet, I., Sauvage, D. et al. (1980) [Biological and clinical effects of oral magnesium and associated magnesium–vitamin B6 administration on certain disorders observed in infantile autism (author's trans.)]. Therapie 35, 627–632.

45. Lelord, G., Callaway, E., and Muh, J.P. (1982) Clinical and biological effects of high doses of vitamin B6 and magnesium on autistic children. Acta vitaminologica et enzymologica 4, 27–44.

46. Martineau, J., Barthelemy, C., Cheliakine, C., and Lelord, G. (1988) An open middle-term study of combined vitamin B6–magnesium in a subgroup of autistic children selected on their sensitivity to this treatment. Journal of autism and developmental disorders 18, 435–447.

47. Kuriyama, S., Kamiyama, M., Watanabe, M., Tamahashi, S. et al. (2002) Pyridoxine treatment in a subgroup of children with pervasive developmental disorders. Developmental medicine and child neurology 44, 284–286.

48. Nye, C. and Brice, A. (2005) Combined vitamin B6–magnesium treatment in autism spectrum disorder. The Cochrane database of systematic reviews, CD003497.

49. Dalton, K. and Dalton, M.J. (1987) Characteristics of pyridoxine overdose neuropathy syndrome. Acta neurologica Scandinavica 76, 8–11.

50. James, S.J., Melnyk, S., Fuchs, G., Reid, T. et al. (2009) Efficacy of methylcobalamin and folinic acid treatment on glutathione redox status in children with autism. American journal of clinical nutrition 89, 425–430.

51. Bertoglio, K., Jill James, S., Deprey, L., Brule, N., and Hendren, R.L. (2010) Pilot study of the effect of methyl B12 treatment on behavioral and biomarker measures in children with autism. Journal of alternative and complementary medicine 16, 555–560.

52. Butler, C.C., Vidal-Alaball, J., Cannings-John, R., McCaddon, A. et al. (2006) Oral vitamin B12 versus intramuscular vitamin B12 for vitamin B12 deficiency: a systematic review of randomized controlled trials. Family practice 23, 279–285.

53. Kuzminski, A.M., Del Giacco, E.J., Allen, R.H., Stabler, S.P., and Lindenbaum, J. (1998) Effective treatment of cobalamin deficiency with oral cobalamin. Blood 92, 1191–1198.

54. Bolaman, Z., Kadikoylu, G., Yukselen, V., Yavasoglu, I., Barutca, S., and Senturk, T. (2003) Oral versus intramuscular cobalamin treatment in megaloblastic anemia: a single-center, prospective, randomized, open-label study. Clinical therapeutics 25, 3124–3134.

55. Yang, Y., Kalluri, H., and Banga, A.K. (2011) Effects of chemical and physical enhancement techniques on transdermal delivery of cyanocobalamin (vitamin B12) in vitro. Pharmaceutics 3, 11.

56. Ming, X., Stein, T.P., Brimacombe, M., Johnson, W.G., Lambert, G.H., and Wagner, G.C. (2005) Increased excretion of a lipid peroxidation biomarker in autism. Prostaglandins, leukotrienes, and essential fatty acids 73, 379–384.

57. James, S.J., Cutler, P., Melnyk, S., Jernigan, S. et al. (2004) Metabolic biomarkers of increased oxidative stress and impaired methylation capacity in children with autism. American journal of clinical nutrition 80, 1611–1617.

58. Dolske, M.C., Spollen, J., McKay, S., Lancashire, E., and Tolbert, L. (1993) A preliminary trial of ascorbic acid as supplemental therapy for autism. Progress in neuro-psychopharmacology & biological psychiatry 17, 765–774.

59. Suren, P., Roth, C., Bresnahan, M., Haugen, M. *et al.* (2013) Association between maternal use of folic acid supplements and risk of autism spectrum disorders in children. Journal of the American Medical Association 309, 570–577.

60. Mohammad, N.S., Jain, J.M., Chintakindi, K.P., Singh, R.P., Naik, U., and Akella, R.R. (2009) Aberrations in folate metabolic pathway and altered susceptibility to autism. Psychiatric genetics 19, 171–176.

61. Main, P.A., Angley, M.T., Thomas, P., O'Doherty, C.E., and Fenech, M. (2010) Folate and methionine metabolism in autism: a systematic review. American journal of clinical nutrition 91, 1598–1620.

62. Moretti, P., Sahoo, T., Hyland, K., Bottiglieri, T. *et al.* (2005) Cerebral folate deficiency with developmental delay, autism, and response to folinic acid. Neurology 64, 1088–1090.

63. Frye, R.E., Sequeira, J.M., Quadros, E.V., James, S.J., and Rossignol, D.A. (2013) Cerebral folate receptor autoantibodies in autism spectrum disorder. Molecular psychiatry 18, 369–381.

64. Frye, R.E., Huffman, L.C., and Elliott, G.R. (2010) Tetrahydrobiopterin as a novel therapeutic intervention for autism. Neurotherapeutics 7, 241–249.

65. Tani, Y., Fernell, E., Watanabe, Y., Kanai, T., and Langstrom, B. (1994) Decrease in 6R-5,6,7,8-tetrahydrobiopterin content in cerebrospinal fluid of autistic patients. Neuroscience letters 181, 169–172.

66. Fernell, E., Watanabe, Y., Adolfsson, I., Tani, Y. *et al.* (1997) Possible effects of tetrahydrobiopterin treatment in six children with autism: clinical and positron emission tomography data. A pilot study. Developmental medicine and child neurology 39, 313–318.

67. Danfors, T., von Knorring, A.L., Hartvig, P., Langstrom, B. *et al.* (2005) Tetrahydrobiopterin in the treatment of children with autistic disorder: a double-blind placebo-controlled crossover study. Journal of clinical psychopharmacology 25, 485–489.

68. Rossignol, D.A. and Frye, R.E. (2012) Mitochondrial dysfunction in autism spectrum disorders: a systematic review and meta-analysis. Molecular psychiatry 17, 25.

69. Frye, R.E., Melnyk, S., and Macfabe, D.F. (2013) Unique acyl-carnitine profiles are potential biomarkers for acquired mitochondrial disease in autism spectrum disorder. Translational psychiatry 3, e220.

70. Filipek, P.A., Juranek, J., Nguyen, M.T., Cummings, C., and Gargus, J.J. (2004) Relative carnitine deficiency in autism. Journal of autism and developmental disorders 34, 615–623.

71. Geier, D.A., Kern, J.K., Davis, G., King, P.G. *et al.* (2011) A prospective double-blind, randomized clinical trial of levocarnitine to treat autism spectrum disorders. Medical science monitor 17, PI15–PI23.

72. Fahmy, S.F., El-hamamsy, M.H., Zaki, O.K., and Badary, O.A. (2013) L-carnitine supplementation improves the behavioral symptoms in autistic children. Research in autism spectrum disorders 7, 8.

73. Chez, M.G., Buchanan, C.P., Aimonovitch, M.C., Becker, M. *et al.* (2002) Double-blind, placebo-controlled study of L-carnosine supplementation in children with autistic spectrum disorders. Journal of child neurology 17, 833–837.

74. Adams, J.B. and Holloway, C. (2004) Pilot study of a moderate dose multivitamin/mineral supplement for children with autistic spectrum disorder. Journal of alternative and complementary medicine 10, 1033–1039.

75. Adams, J.B., Audhya, T., McDonough-Means, S., Rubin, R.A. *et al.* (2011) Effect of a vitamin/mineral supplement on children and adults with autism. BMC pediatrics 11, 111.

76. Melke, J., Goubran Botros, H., Chaste, P., Betancur, C. *et al.* (2008) Abnormal melatonin synthesis in autism spectrum disorders. Molecular psychiatry 13, 90–98.

77. Giannotti, F., Cortesi, F., Cerquiglini, A., and Bernabei, P. (2006) An open-label study of controlled-release melatonin in treatment of sleep disorders in children with autism. Journal of autism and developmental disorders 36, 741–752.

78. Andersen, I.M., Kaczmarska, J., McGrew, S.G., and Malow, B.A. (2008) Melatonin for insomnia in children with autism spectrum disorders. Journal of child neurology 23, 482–485.

79. Wright, B., Sims, D., Smart, S., Alwazeer, A. *et al.* (2011) Melatonin versus placebo in children with autism spectrum conditions and severe sleep problems not amenable to behaviour management strategies: a randomised controlled crossover trial. Journal of autism and developmental disorders 41, 175–184.

80. Malow, B., Adkins, K.W., McGrew, S.G., Wang, L. *et al.* (2012) Melatonin for sleep in children with autism: a controlled trial examining dose, tolerability, and outcomes. Journal of autism and developmental disorders 42, 1729–1738.

81. Rossignol, D.A. and Frye, R.E. (2011) Melatonin in autism spectrum disorders: a systematic review and meta-analysis. Developmental medicine and child neurology 53, 783–792.

82. Simopoulos, A.P. (1991) Omega-3 fatty acids in health and disease and in growth and development. American journal of clinical nutrition 54, 438–463.

83. McNamara, R.K. and Carlson, S.E. (2006) Role of omega-3 fatty acids in brain development and function: potential implications for the pathogenesis and prevention of psychopathology. Prostaglandins, leukotrienes, and essential fatty acids 75, 329–349.

84. Mazza, M., Pomponi, M., Janiri, L., Bria, P., and Mazza, S. (2007) Omega-3 fatty acids and antioxidants in neurological and psychiatric diseases: an overview. Progress in neuropsychopharmacology & biological psychiatry 31, 12–26.

85. Innis, S.M. (2007) Dietary (n-3) fatty acids and brain development. Journal of nutrition 137, 855–859.

86. Wiest, M.M., German, J.B., Harvey, D.J., Watkins, S.M., and Hertz-Picciotto, I. (2009) Plasma fatty acid profiles in autism: a case-control study. Prostaglandins, leukotrienes, and essential fatty acids 80, 221–227.

87. Johnson, C.R., Handen, B.L., Zimmer, M., Sacco, K. (2010) Polyunsaturated fatty acid supplementation in young children with autism. Journal of developmental and physical disabilities 22, 11.

88. James, S., Montgomery, P., and Williams, K. (2011) Omega-3 fatty acids supplementation for autism spectrum disorders (ASD). The Cochrane database of systematic reviews, CD007992.

89. Amminger, G.P., Berger, G.E., Schafer, M.R., Klier, C., Friedrich, M.H., and Feucht, M. (2007) Omega-3 fatty acids supplementation in children with autism: a double-blind randomized, placebo-controlled pilot study. Biological psychiatry 61, 551–553.

90. Bent, S., Bertoglio, K., Ashwood, P., Bostrom, A., and Hendren, R.L. (2011) A pilot randomized controlled trial of omega-3 fatty acids for autism spectrum disorder. Journal of autism and developmental disorders 41, 545–554.

91. Iebba, V., Aloi, M., Civitelli, F., and Cucchiara, S. (2011) Gut microbiota and pediatric disease. Digestive diseases 29, 531–539.

92. Douglas-Escobar, M., Elliott, E., and Neu, J. (2013) Effect of intestinal microbial ecology on the developing brain. JAMA pediatrics 167, 374–379.

93. Finegold, S.M. (2011) State of the art; microbiology in health and disease. Intestinal bacterial flora in autism. Anaerobe 17, 367–368.

94. Thomas, D.W., Greer, F.R., American Academy of Pediatrics Committee on Nutrition, American Academy of Pediatrics Section on Gastroenterology, Hepatology, and Nutrition (2010) Probiotics and prebiotics in pediatrics. Pediatrics 126, 1217–1231.

95. Bin-Nun, A., Bromiker, R., Wilschanski, M., Kaplan, M. *et al.* (2005) Oral probiotics prevent necrotizing enterocolitis in very low birth weight neonates. Journal of pediatrics 147, 192–196.

96. Weizman, Z., Asli, G., and Alsheikh, A. (2005) Effect of a probiotic infant formula on infections in child care centers: comparison of two probiotic agents. Pediatrics 115, 5–9.

97. Bu, L.N., Chang, M.H., Ni, Y.H., Chen, H.L., and Cheng, C.C. (2007) *Lactobacillus casei rhamnosus* Lcr35 in children with chronic constipation. Pediatrics international 49, 485–490.

98. Bouvard, M.P., Leboyer, M., Launay, J.M., Recasens, C. *et al.* (1995) Low-dose naltrexone effects on plasma chemistries and clinical symptoms in autism: a double-blind, placebo-controlled study. Psychiatry research 58, 191–201.

99. Kolmen, B.K., Feldman, H.M., Handen, B.L., and Janosky, J.E. (1997) Naltrexone in young autistic children: replication study and learning measures. Journal of the American Academy of Child and Adolescent Psychiatry 36, 1570–1578.

100. Feldman, H.M., Kolmen, B.K., and Gonzaga, A.M. (1999) Naltrexone and communication skills in young children with autism. Journal of the American Academy of Child and Adolescent Psychiatry 38, 587–593.

101. Willemsen-Swinkels, S.H., Buitelaar, J.K., van Berckelaer-Onnes, I.A., and van Engeland, H. (1999) Six months continuation treatment in naltrexone-responsive children with autism: an open-label case-control design. Journal of autism and developmental disorders 29, 167–169.

102. Elchaar, G.M., Maisch, N.M., Augusto, L.M., and Wehring, H.J. (2006) Efficacy and safety of naltrexone use in pediatric patients with autistic disorder. Annals of pharmacotherapy 40, 1086–1095.

103. Willemsen-Swinkels, S.H., Buitelaar, J.K., Nijhof, G.J., and van England, H. (1995) Failure of naltrexone hydrochloride to reduce self-injurious and autistic behavior in mentally retarded adults. Double-blind placebo-controlled studies. Archives of general psychiatry 52, 766–773.

104. Dove, D., Warren, Z., McPheeters, M.L., Taylor, J.L., Sathe, N.A., and Veenstra-VanderWeele, J. (2012) Medications for adolescents and young adults with autism spectrum disorders: a systematic review. Pediatrics 130, 717–726.

105. Symons, F.J., Thompson, A., and Rodriguez, M.C. (2004) Self-injurious behavior and the efficacy of naltrexone treatment: a quantitative synthesis. Mental retardation and developmental disabilities research reviews 10, 193–200.

106. Singh, V.K. and Rivas, W.H. (2004) Prevalence of serum antibodies to caudate nucleus in autistic children. Neuroscience letters 355, 53–56.

107. Gupta, S., Aggarwal, S., and Heads, C. (1996) Dysregulated immune system in children with autism: beneficial effects of intravenous immune globulin on autistic characteristics. Journal of autism and developmental disorders 26, 439–452.

108. DelGiudice-Asch, G., Simon, L., Schmeidler, J., Cunningham-Rundles, C., and Hollander, E. (1999) A pilot open clinical trial of intravenous immunoglobulin in childhood autism. Journal of autism and developmental disorders 29, 157–160.

109. Gupta, S. (1999) Treatment of children with autism with intravenous immunoglobulin. Journal of child neurology 14, 203–205.

110. Birks, J. (2006) Cholinesterase inhibitors for Alzheimer's disease. The Cochrane database of systematic reviews, CD005593.

111. Handen, B.L., Johnson, C.R., McAuliffe-Bellin, S., Murray, P.J., and Hardan, A.Y. (2011) Safety and efficacy of donepezil in children and adolescents with autism: neuropsychological measures. Journal of child and adolescent psychopharmacology 21, 43–50.

112. Niederhofer, H., Staffen, W., and Mair, A. (2002) Galantamine may be effective in treating autistic disorder. British medical journal 325, 1422.

113. Nicolson, R., Craven-Thuss, B., and Smith, J. (2006) A prospective, open-label trial of galantamine in autistic disorder. Journal of child and adolescent psychopharmacology 16, 621–629.

114. Chez, M.G., Aimonovitch, M., Buchanan, T., Mrazek, S., and Tremb, R.J. (2004) Treating autistic spectrum disorders in children: utility of the cholinesterase inhibitor rivastigmine tartrate. Journal of child neurology 19, 165–169.

115. Krishnaswami, S., McPheeters, M.L., and Veenstra-Vanderweele, J. (2011) A systematic review of secretin for children with autism spectrum disorders. Pediatrics 127, e1322–e1325.

116. Horvath, K., Stefanatos, G., Sokolski, K.N., Wachtel, R., Nabors, L., and Tildon, J.T. (1998) Improved social and language skills after secretin administration in patients with autistic spectrum disorders. Journal of the Association for Academic Minority Physicians 9, 9–15.

117. Sandler, A.D., Sutton, K.A., DeWeese, J., Girardi, M.A., Sheppard, V., and Bodfish, J.W. (1999) Lack of benefit of a single dose of synthetic human secretin in the treatment of autism and pervasive developmental disorder. New England journal of medicine 341, 1801–1806.

118. Dunn-Geier, J., Ho, H.H., Auersperg, E., Doyle, D. et al. (2000) Effect of secretin on children with autism: a randomized controlled trial. Developmental medicine and child neurology 42, 796–802.

119. Chez, M.G., Buchanan, C.P., Bagan, B.T., Hammer, M.S. et al. (2000) Secretin and autism: a two-part clinical investigation. Journal of autism and developmental disorders 30, 87–94.

120. Owley, T., McMahon, W., Cook, E.H., Laulhere, T. et al. (2001) Multisite, double-blind, placebo-controlled trial of porcine secretin in autism. Journal of the American Academy of Child and Adolescent Psychiatry 40, 1293–1299.

121. Coniglio, S.J., Lewis, J.D., Lang, C., Burns, T.G. *et al.* (2001) A randomized, double-blind, placebo-controlled trial of single-dose intravenous secretin as treatment for children with autism. Journal of pediatrics 138, 649–655.

122. Roberts, W., Weaver, L., Brian, J., Bryson, S. *et al.* (2001) Repeated doses of porcine secretin in the treatment of autism: a randomized, placebo-controlled trial. Pediatrics 107, E71.

123. Molloy, C.A., Manning-Courtney, P., Swayne, S., Bean, J. *et al.* (2002) Lack of benefit of intravenous synthetic human secretin in the treatment of autism. Journal of autism and developmental disorders 32, 545–551.

124. Williams, K., Wray, J.A., and Wheeler, D.M. (2012) Intravenous secretin for autism spectrum disorders (ASD). The Cochrane database of systematic reviews 4, CD003495.

125. Sandler, R.H., Finegold, S.M., Bolte, E.R., Buchanan, C.P. *et al.* (2000) Short-term benefit from oral vancomycin treatment of regressive-onset autism. Journal of child neurology 15, 429–435.

126. Posey, D.J., Kem, D.L., Swiezy, N.B., Sweeten, T.L., Wiegand, R.E., and McDougle, C.J. (2004) A pilot study of D-cycloserine in subjects with autistic disorder. American journal of psychiatry 161, 2115–2117.

127. Reisberg, B., Doody, R., Stoffler, A., Schmitt, F. *et al.* (2003) Memantine in moderate-to-severe Alzheimer's disease. New England journal of medicine 348, 1333–1341.

128. Erickson, C.A. and Chambers, J.E. (2006) Memantine for disruptive behavior in autistic disorder. Journal of clinical psychiatry 67, 1000.

129. Owley, T., Salt, J., Guter, S., Grieve, A. *et al.* (2006) A prospective, open-label trial of memantine in the treatment of cognitive, behavioral, and memory dysfunction in pervasive developmental disorders. Journal of child and adolescent psychopharmacology 16, 517–524.

130. Chez, M.G., Burton, Q., Dowling, T., Chang, M., Khanna, P., and Kramer, C. (2007) Memantine as adjunctive therapy in children diagnosed with autistic spectrum disorders: an observation of initial clinical response and maintenance tolerability. Journal of child neurology 22, 574–579.

131. Erickson, C.A., Posey, D.J., Stigler, K.A., Mullett, J., Katschke, A.R., and McDougle, C.J. (2007) A retrospective study of memantine in children and adolescents with pervasive developmental disorders. Psychopharmacology 191, 141–147.

132. Smilkstein, M.J., Knapp, G.L., Kulig, K.W., and Rumack, B.H. (1988) Efficacy of oral N-acetylcysteine in the treatment of acetaminophen overdose. Analysis of the national multicenter study (1976 to 1985). New England journal of medicine 319, 1557–1562.

133. Aruoma, O.I., Halliwell, B., Hoey, B.M., and Butler, J. (1989) The antioxidant action of N-acetylcysteine: its reaction with hydrogen peroxide, hydroxyl radical, superoxide, and hypochlorous acid. Free radical biology & medicine 6, 593–597.

134. Hardan, A.Y., Fung, L.K., Libove, R.A., Obukhanych, T.V. *et al.* (2012) A randomized controlled pilot trial of oral N-acetylcysteine in children with autism. Biological psychiatry 71, 956–961.

135. Prichard, B.N. and Gillam, P.M. (1969) Treatment of hypertension with propranolol. British medical journal 1, 7–16.

136. Ratey, J.J., Bemporad, J., Sorgi, P., Bick, P. *et al.* (1987) Open trial effects of beta-blockers on speech and social behaviors in 8 autistic adults. Journal of autism and developmental disorders 17, 439–446.

137. Beversdorf, D.Q., Carpenter, A.L., Miller, R.F., Cios, J.S., and Hillier, A. (2008) Effect of propranolol on verbal problem solving in autism spectrum disorder. Neurocase 14, 378–383.

138. Narayanan, A., White, C.A., Saklayen, S., Scaduto, M.J. *et al.* (2010) Effect of propranolol on functional connectivity in autism spectrum disorder: a pilot study. Brain imaging and behavior 4, 189–197.

139. Beversdorf, D.Q., Saklayen, S., Higgins, K.F., Bodner, K.E., Kanne, S.M., and Christ, S.E. (2011) Effect of propranolol on word fluency in autism. Cognitive and behavioral neurology 24, 11–17.

140. Geier, D.A. and Geier, M.R. (2006) A prospective assessment of porphyrins in autistic disorders: a potential marker for heavy metal exposure. Neurotoxicity research 10, 57–64.

141. Geier, D.A. and Geier, M.R. (2007) A prospective study of mercury toxicity biomarkers in autistic spectrum disorders. Journal of toxicology and environmental health (Part A) 70, 1723–1730.

142. Blaucok-Busch, E., Amin, O.R., Dessoki, H.H., and Rabah, T. (2012) Efficacy of DMSA therapy in a sample of Arab children with autistic spectrum disorder. Maedica 7, 214–221.

143. De Palma, G., Catalani, S., Franco, A., Brighenti, M., and Apostoli, P. (2012) Lack of correlation between metallic elements analyzed in hair by ICP-MS and autism. Journal of autism and developmental disorders 42, 342–353.

144. Ip, P., Wong, V., Ho, M., Lee, J., and Wong, W. (2004) Mercury exposure in children with autistic spectrum disorder: case-control study. Journal of child neurology 19, 431–434.

145. Parker, S.K., Schwartz, B., Todd, J., and Pickering, L.K. (2004) Thimerosal-containing vaccines and autistic spectrum disorder: a critical review of published original data. Pediatrics 114, 793–804.

146. U.S. Food and Drug Administration (2013) *Thimerosal in Vaccines.* www.fda.gov/biologicsbloodvaccines/safetyavailability/vaccinesafety/ucm096228.

147. Nataf, R., Skorupka, C., Amet, L., Lam, A., Springbett, A., and Lathe, R. (2006) Porphyrinuria in childhood autistic disorder: implications for environmental toxicity. Toxicology and applied pharmacology 214, 99–108.

148. Bradstreet, J., Geier, D.A., Kartzinel, J.J., Adams, J.B., and Geier, M.R. (2003) A case-control study of mercury burden in children with autistic spectrum disorders. Journal of American physicians and surgeons 8, 4.

149. Cohen, D.J., Johnson, W.T., and Caparulo, B.K. (1976) Pica and elevated blood lead level in autistic and atypical children. American journal of diseases of children 130, 47–48.

150. Eppright, T.D., Sanfacon, J.A., and Horwitz, E.A. (1996) Attention deficit hyperactivity disorder, infantile autism, and elevated blood-lead: a possible relationship. Missouri medicine 93, 136–138.

151. Mitka, M. (2008) Chelation therapy trials halted. Journal of the American Medical Association 300, 2236.

152. Baxter, A.J. and Krenzelok, E.P. (2008) Pediatric fatality secondary to EDTA chelation. Clinical toxicology 46, 1083–1084.

153. Bouachour, G., Cronier, P., Gouello, J.P., Toulemonde, J.L., Talha, A., and Alquier, P. (1996) Hyperbaric oxygen therapy in the management of crush injuries: a randomized double-blind placebo-controlled clinical trial. Journal of trauma 41, 333–339.

154. Veltkamp, R., Warner, D.S., Domoki, F., Brinkhous, A.D., Toole, J.F., and Busija, D.W. (2000) Hyperbaric oxygen decreases infarct size and behavioral deficit after transient focal cerebral ischemia in rats. Brain research 853, 68–73.

155. Miljkovic-Lolic, M., Silbergleit, R., Fiskum, G., and Rosenthal, R.E. (2003) Neuroprotective effects of hyperbaric oxygen treatment in experimental focal cerebral ischemia are associated with reduced brain leukocyte myeloperoxidase activity. Brain research 971, 90–94.

156. Warren, J., Sacksteder, M.R., and Thuning, C.A. (1979) Therapeutic effect of prolonged hyperbaric oxygen in adjuvant arthritis of the rat. Arthritis and rheumatism 22, 334–339.

157. Luongo, C., Imperatore, F., Cuzzocrea, S., Filippelli, A. *et al.* (1998) Effects of hyperbaric oxygen exposure on a zymosan-induced shock model. Critical care medicine 26, 1972–1976.

158. Cuzzocrea, S., Imperatore, F., Costantino, G., Luongo, C. *et al.* (2000) Role of hyperbaric oxygen exposure in reduction of lipid peroxidation and in multiple organ failure induced by zymosan administration in the rat. Shock 13, 197–203.

159. Sumen, G., Cimsit, M., and Eroglu, L. (2001) Hyperbaric oxygen treatment reduces carrageenan-induced acute inflammation in rats. European journal of pharmacology 431, 265–268.

160. Tokar, B., Gundogan, A.H., Ilhan, H., Bildirici, K., Gultepe, M., and Elbuken, E. (2003) The effect of hyperbaric oxygen treatment on the inflammatory changes caused by intraperitoneal meconium. Pediatric surgery international 19, 673–676.

161. Vlodavsky, E., Palzur, E., and Soustiel, J.F. (2006) Hyperbaric oxygen therapy reduces neuroinflammation and expression of matrix metalloproteinase-9 in the rat model of traumatic brain injury. Neuropathology and applied neurobiology 32, 40–50.

162. Thom, S.R., Bhopale, V.M., Velazquez, O.C., Goldstein, L.J., Thom, L.H., and Buerk, D.G. (2006) Stem cell mobilization by hyperbaric oxygen. American journal of heart and circulatory physiology 290, H1378–H1386.

163. Rossignol, D.A. and Rossignol, L.W. (2006) Hyperbaric oxygen therapy may improve symptoms in autistic children. Medical hypotheses 67, 216–228.

164. Zilbovicius, M., Boddaert, N., Belin, P., Poline, J.B. *et al.* (2000) Temporal lobe dysfunction in childhood autism: a PET study. American journal of psychiatry 157, 1988–1993.

165. Wilcox, J., Tsuang, M.T., Ledger, E., Algeo, J., and Schnurr, T. (2002) Brain perfusion in autism varies with age. Neuropsychobiology 46, 13–16.

166. Rossignol, D.A. (2007) Hyperbaric oxygen therapy might improve certain pathophysiological findings in autism. Medical hypotheses 68, 1208–1227.

167. Rossignol, D.A. and Bradstreet, J.J. (2008) Evidence of mitochondrial dysfunction in autism and implications for treatment. American journal of biochemistry and biotechnology 4, 10.

168. Jyonouchi, H., Sun, S., and Le, H. (2001) Proinflammatory and regulatory cytokine production associated with innate and adaptive immune responses in children with autism spectrum disorders and developmental regression. Journal of neuroimmunology 120, 170–179.

169. Vargas, D.L., Nascimbene, C., Krishnan, C., Zimmerman, A.W., and Pardo, C.A. (2005) Neuroglial activation and neuroinflammation in the brain of patients with autism. Annals of neurology 57, 67–81.

170. Rossignol, D.A., Rossignol, L.W., James, S.J., Melnyk, S., and Mumper, E. (2007) The effects of hyperbaric oxygen therapy on oxidative stress, inflammation, and symptoms in children with autism: an open-label pilot study. BMC pediatrics 7, 36.

171. Chungpaibulpatana, J., Sumpatanarax, T., Thadakul, N., Chantharatreerat, C., Konkaew, M., and Aroonlimsawas, M. (2008) Hyperbaric oxygen therapy in Thai autistic children. Journal of the Medical Association of Thailand (*Chotmaihet thangphaet*) 91, 1232–1238.

172. Bent, S., Bertoglio, K., Ashwood, P., Nemeth, E., and Hendren, R.L. (2012) Hyperbaric oxygen therapy (HBOT) in children with autism spectrum disorder: a clinical trial. Journal of autism and developmental disorders 42, 1127–1132.

173. Rossignol, D.A., Rossignol, L.W., Smith, S., Schneider, C. *et al.* (2009) Hyperbaric treatment for children with autism: a multicenter, randomized, double-blind, controlled trial. BMC pediatrics 9, 21.

174. Granpeesheh, D., Tarbox, J., Dixon, D.R., Wilke, A.E., Allen, M.S., and Bradstreet, J.J. (2010) Randomized trial of hyperbaric oxygen therapy for children with autism. Research in autism spectrum disorders 4, 13.

175. Jepson, B., Granpeesheh, D., Tarbox, J., Olive, M.L. *et al.* (2011) Controlled evaluation of the effects of hyperbaric oxygen therapy on the behavior of 16 children with autism spectrum disorders. Journal of autism and developmental disorders 41, 575–588.

176. Ghanizadeh, A. (2012) Hyperbaric oxygen therapy for treatment of children with autism: a systematic review of randomized trials. Medical gas research 2, 13.

177. Fortis, P., Kornitzer, J., Goedert, K.M., and Barrett, A.M. (2009) Effect of prism adaptation on "aiming" spatial bias and functional abilities. Neurology 72, 1.

178. Barrett, B.T. (2009) A critical evaluation of the evidence supporting the practice of behavioural vision therapy. Ophthalmic & physiological optics 29, 4–25.

179. Carmody, D.P., Kaplan, M., and Gaydos, A.M. (2001) Spatial orientation adjustments in children with autism in Hong Kong. Child psychiatry and human development 31, 233–247.

180. Bettison, S. (1996) The long-term effects of auditory training on children with autism. Journal of autism and developmental disorders 26, 361–374.

181. Gillberg, C., Johansson, M., Steffenburg, S., and Berlin, O. (1997) Auditory integration training in children with autism: brief report of an open pilot study. Autism 1, 97.

182. Mudford, O.C., Cross, B.A., Breen, S., Cullen, C. *et al.* (2000) Auditory integration training for children with autism: no behavioral benefits detected. American journal of mental retardation 105, 118–129.

183. Sinha, Y., Silove, N., Hayen, A., and Williams, K. (2011) Auditory integration training and other sound therapies for autism spectrum disorders (ASD). The Cochrane database of systematic reviews, CD003681.

184. American Academy of Pediatrics Section on Complementary and Integrative Medicine, American Academy of Pediatric Council on Children with Disabilities, Zimmer, M., and Desch, L. (2012) Sensory integration therapies for children with developmental and behavioral disorders. Pediatrics 129, 1186–1189.

185. Wong, V.C. and Sun, J.G. (2010) Randomized controlled trial of acupuncture versus sham acupuncture in autism spectrum disorder. Journal of alternative and complementary medicine 16, 545–553.

186. Chen, W.X., Wu-Li, L., and Wong, V.C. (2008) Electroacupuncture for children with autism spectrum disorder: pilot study of 2 cases. Journal of alternative and complementary medicine 14, 1057–1065.

187. Wong, V.C. and Chen, W.X. (2010) Randomized controlled trial of electro-acupuncture for autism spectrum disorder. Alternative medicine review 15, 136–146.

188. Allam, H., ElDine, N.G., and Helmy, G. (2008) Scalp acupuncture effect on language development in children with autism: a pilot study. Journal of alternative and complementary medicine 14, 109–114.

189. Cheuk, D.K., Wong, V., and Chen, W.X. (2011) Acupuncture for autism spectrum disorders (ASD). The Cochrane database of systematic reviews, CD007849.

190. Yin, J.J., Lu, F., Ming, X.B., Qin, Z.H., and Ma, Y.J. (2012) Theoretical modeling and experiment of refractive index change in He+ ion-implanted KTP waveguide. Applied optics 51, 2400–2406.

191. Myers, S.M., Johnson, C.P., and American Academy of Pediatrics Council on Children With Disabilities (2007) Management of children with autism spectrum disorders. Pediatrics 120, 1162–1182.

Chapter 10

1. Hallmayer, J., Cleveland, S., Torres, A., Phillips, J. *et al.* (2011) Genetic heritability and shared environmental factors among twin pairs with autism. Archives of general psychiatry 68, 1095–1102.

2. Losh, M., Esserman, D., Anckarsater, H., Sullivan, P.F., and Lichtenstein, P. (2012) Lower birth weight indicates higher risk of autistic traits in discordant twin pairs. Psychological medicine 42, 1091–1102.

3. Rosenberg, R.E., Law, J.K., Yenokyan, G., McGready, J., Kaufmann, W.E., and Law, P.A. (2009) Characteristics and concordance of autism spectrum disorders among 277 twin pairs. Archives of pediatrics & adolescent medicine 163, 907–914.

4. Jyonouchi, H. (2010) Autism spectrum disorders and allergy: observation from a pediatric allergy/immunology clinic. Expert review of clinical immunology 6, 397–411.

5. Theoharides, T.C. (2009) Autism spectrum disorders and mastocytosis. International journal of immunopathology and pharmacology 22, 859–865.

6. Tareen, R.S. and Kamboj, M.K. (2012) Role of endocrine factors in autistic spectrum disorders. Pediatric clinics of North America 59, 75–88, x.

7. de Cock, M., Maas, Y.G., and van de Bor, M. (2012) Does perinatal exposure to endocrine disruptors induce autism spectrum and attention deficit hyperactivity disorders? Review. Acta paediatrica 101, 811–818.

8. Winneke, G. (2011) Developmental aspects of environmental neurotoxicology: lessons from lead and polychlorinated biphenyls. Journal of the neurological sciences 308, 9–15.

9. Kajta, M. and Wojtowicz, A. (2010) [Neurodevelopmental disorders in response to hormonally active environmental pollutants]. Przeglad lekarski 67, 1194–1199.

10. Hoshiko, S., Grether, J.K., Windham, G.C., Smith, D., and Fessel, K. (2011) Are thyroid hormone concentrations at birth associated with subsequent autism diagnosis? Autism research 4, 456–463.

11. Soldin, O.P., Lai, S., Lamm, S.H., and Mosee, S. (2003) Lack of a relation between human neonatal thyroxine and pediatric neurobehavioral disorders. Thyroid 13, 193–198.

12. Spratt, E.G., Nicholas, J.S., Brady, K.T., Carpenter, L.A. *et al.* (2012) Enhanced cortisol response to stress in children in autism. Journal of autism and developmental disorders 42, 75–81.

13. Corbett, B.A., Schupp, C.W., Levine, S., and Mendoza, S. (2009) Comparing cortisol, stress, and sensory sensitivity in children with autism. Autism research 2, 39–49.

14. Corbett, B.A., Mendoza, S., Wegelin, J.A., Carmean, V., and Levine, S. (2008) Variable cortisol circadian rhythms in children with autism and anticipatory stress. Journal of psychiatry & neuroscience 33, 227–234.

15. Rout, U.K. and Clausen, P. (2009) Common increase of GATA-3 level in PC-12 cells by three teratogens causing autism spectrum disorders. Neuroscience research 64, 162–169.

16. Miller, M.T., Stromland, K., Ventura, L., Johansson, M., Bandim, J.M., and Gillberg, C. (2005) Autism associated with conditions characterized by developmental errors in early embryogenesis: a mini review. International journal of developmental neuroscience 23, 201–219.

17. Rasalam, A.D., Hailey, H., Williams, J.H., Moore, S.J. et al. (2005) Characteristics of fetal anticonvulsant syndrome associated autistic disorder. Developmental medicine and child neurology 47, 551–555.

18. Ostrea, E.M., Morales, V., Ngoumgna, E., Prescilla, R. et al. (2002) Prevalence of fetal exposure to environmental toxins as determined by meconium analysis. Neurotoxicology 23, 329–339.

19. Bandim, J.M., Ventura, L.O., Miller, M.T., Almeida, H.C., and Costa, A.E. (2003) Autism and Mobius sequence: an exploratory study of children in northeastern Brazil. Arquivos de neuro-psiquiatria 61, 181–185.

20. Christianson, A.L., Chesler, N., and Kromberg, J.G. (1994) Fetal valproate syndrome: clinical and neuro-developmental features in two sibling pairs. Developmental medicine and child neurology 36, 361–369.

21. Ornoy, A. (2009) Valproic acid in pregnancy: How much are we endangering the embryo and fetus? Reproductive toxicology 28, 1–10.

22. Williams, G., King, J., Cunningham, M., Stephan, M., Kerr, B., and Hersh, J.H. (2001) Fetal valproate syndrome and autism: additional evidence of an association. Developmental medicine and child neurology 43, 202–206.

23. Williams, P.G. and Hersh, J.H. (1997) A male with fetal valproate syndrome and autism. Developmental medicine and child neurology 39, 632–634.

24. Moore, S.J., Turnpenny, P., Quinn, A., Glover, S. et al. (2000) A clinical study of 57 children with fetal anticonvulsant syndromes. Journal of medical genetics 37, 489–497.

25. Landrigan, P.J. (2010) What causes autism? Exploring the environmental contribution. Current opinion in pediatrics 22, 219–225.

26. Arndt, T.L., Stodgell, C.J., and Rodier, P.M. (2005) The teratology of autism. International Journal of developmental neuroscience 23, 189–199.

27. Engel, S.M., Miodovnik, A., Canfield, R.L., Zhu, C. et al. (2010) Prenatal phthalate exposure is associated with childhood behavior and executive functioning. Environmental health perspectives 118, 565–571.

28. Engel, S.M. and Daniels, J.L. (2011) On the complex relationship between genes and environment in the etiology of autism. Epidemiology 22, 486–488.

29. Hwang, H.M., Park, E.K., Young, T.M., and Hammock, B.D. (2008) Occurrence of endocrine-disrupting chemicals in indoor dust. Science of the total environment 404, 26–35.

30. Kimura-Kuroda, J., Nagata, I., and Kuroda, Y. (2007) Disrupting effects of hydroxy-polychlorinated biphenyl (PCB) congeners on neuronal development of cerebellar Purkinje cells: a possible causal factor for developmental brain disorders? Chemosphere 67, S412–S420.

31. Cheh, M.A., Millonig, J.H., Roselli, L.M., Ming, X. et al. (2006) En2 knockout mice display neurobehavioral and neurochemical alterations relevant to autism spectrum disorder. Brain research 1116, 166–176.

32. Yochum, C.L., Bhattacharya, P., Patti, L., Mirochnitchenko, O., and Wagner, G.C. (2010) Animal model of autism using GSTM1 knockout mice and early post-natal sodium valproate treatment. Behavioural brain research 210, 202–210.

33. Yochum, C.L., Dowling, P., Reuhl, K.R., Wagner, G.C., and Ming, X. (2008) VPA-induced apoptosis and behavioral deficits in neonatal mice. Brain research 1203, 126–132.

34. Palmer, R.F., Blanchard, S., Stein, Z., Mandell, D., and Miller, C. (2006) Environmental mercury release, special education rates, and autism disorder: an ecological study of Texas. Health & place 12, 203–209.

35. Palmer, R.F., Blanchard, S., and Wood, R. (2009) Proximity to point sources of environmental mercury release as a predictor of autism prevalence. Health & place 15, 18–24.

36. Ming, X., Brimacombe, M., Malek, J.H., Jani, N., and Wagner, G.C. (2008) Autism spectrum disorders and identified toxic land fills: co-occurrence across states. Environmental health insights 2, 55–59.

37. Windham, G.C., Zhang, L., Gunier, R., Croen, L.A., and Grether, J.K. (2006) Autism spectrum disorders in relation to distribution of hazardous air pollutants in the San Francisco bay area. Environmental health perspectives 114, 1438–1444.

38. Edelson, S.B. and Cantor, D.S. (1998) Autism: xenobiotic influences. Toxicology and industrial health 14, 553–563.

39. Edelson, S.B. and Cantor, D.S. (1998) Autism: xenobiotic influences. Toxicology and industrial health 14, 799–811.

40. Messer, A. (2010) Mini-review: polybrominated diphenyl ether (PBDE) flame retardants as potential autism risk factors. Physiology & behavior 100, 245–249.

41. Larsson, M., Weiss, B., Janson, S., Sundell, J., and Bornehag, C.G. (2009) Associations between indoor environmental factors and parental-reported autistic spectrum disorders in children 6–8 years of age. Neurotoxicology 30, 822–831.

42. Kalkbrenner, A.E., Daniels, J.L., Chen, J.C., Poole, C., Emch, M., and Morrissey, J. (2010) Perinatal exposure to hazardous air pollutants and autism spectrum disorders at age 8. Epidemiology 21, 631–641.

43. Waring, R.H. and Klovrza, L. (2000) Sulphur metabolism in autism. Journal of nutritional and environmental medicine 10, 25–32.

44. O'Reilly, B. and Waring, R.H. (2003) Enzyme and sulphur oxidation deficiencies in autistic children with known food and chemical intolerances. Journal of orthopaedic medicine 4, 198–200.

45. Edelson, S.B. and Cantor, D.S. (2000) The neurotoxic etiology of the autistic spectrum disorder: a replicative study. Toxicology & industrial health 16, 239–247.

46. Alberti, A., Pirrone, P., Elia, M., Waring, R.H., and Romano, C. (1999) Sulphation deficit in "low-functioning" autistic children: a pilot study. Biological psychiatry 46, 420–424.

47. James, S.J., Melnyk, S., Jernigan, S., Hubamks, A., Rose, S., and Gaylor, D.W. (2008) Abnormal methyllation-transulfuration metabolism and DNA hypomethylation among parents of children with autism. Journal of autism and developmental disorders 38, 1966–1975.

48. Armstrong, R.N. (1997) Structure, catalytic mechanism and evolution of the glutathione transferase. Chemical research in toxicology 10, 2–18.

49. Buyske, S., Williams, T.A., Mars, A.E., Stenroos, E.S. et al. (2006) Analysis of case-parent trios at a locus with a deletion allele: association of GSTM1 with autism. BMC genetics 7, 8.

50. Williams, T.A., Mars, A.E., Buyske, S.G., Stenroos, E.S. et al. (2007) Risk of autistic disorder in affected offspring of mothers with a glutathione S-transferase P1 haplotype. Archives of pediatrics & adolescent medicine 161, 356–361.

51. James, S.J., Cutler, P., Melnyk, S., Jernigan, S. et al. (2004) Metabolic biomarkers of increased oxidative stress and impaired methylation capacity in children with autism. American journal of clinical nutrition 80, 1611–1617.

52. Ming, X., Johnson, W.G., Stenroos, E.S., Mars, A., Lambert, G.H., and Buyske, S. (2010) Genetic variant of glutathione peroxidase 1 in autism. Brain & development 32, 105–109.

53. Ming, X., Stein, T.P., Brimacombe, M., Johnson, W.G., Lambert, G.H., and Wagner, G.C. (2005) Increased excretion of a lipid peroxidation biomarker in autism. Prostaglandins leukotrienes & essential fatty acids 73, 379–384.

54. Yao, Y., Walsh, W.J., McGinnis, W.R., and Pratico, D. (2006) Altered vascular phenotype in autism: correlation with oxidative stress. Archives of neurology 63, 1161–1164.

55. Schettler, T. (2006) Human exposure to phthalates via consumer products. International journal of andrology 29, 134–139.

56. Wittassek, M., Koch, H.M., Angerer, J., and Brüning, T. (2011) Assessing exposure to phthalates—the human biomonitoring approach. Molecular nutrition & food research 55, 7–31.

57. Testa, C., Nuti, F., Hayek, J., De Felice, C. et al. (2012) Di-(2-ethylhexyl) phthalate and autism spectrum disorders. ASN neuro 4, 223–229.

58. Stein, T.P., Schluter, M.D., Steer, R.A., and Ming, X. (2013) Autism and phthalate metabolite glucuronidation. Journal of autism and developmental disorders 43, 2677–2685.

59. Rudel, R.A. and Perovich, L.J. (2009) Endocrine disrupting chemicals in indoor and outdoor air. Atmospheric environment 43, 170–181.

60. Aurela, B., Kulmala, H., and Soderhjelm, L. (1999) Phthalates in paper and board packaging and their migration into Tenax and sugar. Food additives and contaminants 16, 571–577.

61. Rudel, R.A., Gray, J.M., Engel, C.L., Rawsthorne, T.W. *et al.* (2011) Food packaging and bisphenol A and bis(2-ethyhexyl) phthalate exposure: findings from a dietary intervention. Environmental health perspectives 119, 914–920.

62. Petersen, J.H. and Jensen, L.K. (2010) Phthalates and food-contact materials: enforcing the 2008 European Union plastics legislation. Food additives & contaminants (Part A), Chemistry, analysis, control, exposure & risk assessment 27, 1608–1616.

Chapter 11

1. Levisohn, P.M. (2007) The autism–epilepsy connection. Epilepsia 48 (Suppl 9), 33–35.

2. Spence, S.J. and Schneider, M.T. (2009) The role of epilepsy and epileptiform EEGs in autism spectrum disorders. Pediatric research 65, 599–606.

3. Coury, D. (2010) Medical treatment of autism spectrum disorders. Current opinion in neurology 23, 131–136.

4. Chez, M.G. (2008) *Autism and Its Medical Management: A Guide for Parents and Professionals.* London: Jessica Kingsley Publishers.

5. Olivie, H. (2012) The medical care of children with autism. European journal of pediatrics 171, 741–749.

6. Hazlett, H.C., Poe, M., Gerig, G., Smith, R.G. *et al.* (2005) Magnetic resonance imaging and head circumference study of brain size in autism: birth through age 2 years. Archives of general psychiatry 62, 1366–1376.

7. Stanfield, A.C., McIntosh, A.M., Spencer, M.D., Philip, R., Gaur, S., and Lawrie, S.M. (2008) Towards a neuroanatomy of autism: a systematic review and meta-analysis of structural magnetic resonance imaging studies. European psychiatry 23, 289–299.

8. Ancoli-Israel, S., Cole, R., Alessi, C., Chambers, M., Moorcroft, W., and Pollak, C.P. (2003) The role of actigraphy in the study of sleep and circadian rhythms. Sleep 26, 342–392.

9. Johnson, K.P. and Malow, B.A. (2008) Sleep in children with autism spectrum disorders. Current neurology and neuroscience reports 8, 155–161.

10. Ming, X. and Walters, A.S. (2009) Autism spectrum disorders, attention deficit/hyperactivity disorder, and sleep disorders. Current opinion in pulmonary medicine 15, 578–584.

11. Ibrahim, S.H., Voigt, R.G., Katusic, S.K., Weaver, A.L., and Barbaresi, W.J. (2009) Incidence of gastrointestinal symptoms in children with autism: a population-based study. Pediatrics 124, 680–686.

12. Rossignol, D.A. and Frye, R.E. (2012) Mitochondrial dysfunction in autism spectrum disorders: a systematic review and meta-analysis. Molecular psychiatry 17, 290–314.

Chapter 12

1. Medical Home Initiatives for Children With Special Needs Project Advisory Committee. American Academy of Psychiatry (2002) The medical home. Pediatrics 110, 184–186.

2. AAFP, A., ACP, and AOA (2010) Joint Principles for Medical Education of Physicians as Preparation for Practice in the Patient-Centered Medical Home. Available at www.acponline.org/running_practice/delivery_and_payment_models/pcmh/understanding/educ-joint-principles.pdf.

3. Sheldrick, R.C. and Perrin, E.C. (2010) Medical home services for children with behavioral health conditions. Journal of developmental and behavioral pediatrics 31, 92–99.

4. Ming, X., Hashim, A., Fleishman, S., West, T. *et al.* (2011) Access to specialty care in autism spectrum disorders: a pilot study of referral source. BMC health services research 11, 99.

5. Coury, D.L., Ashwood, P., Fasano, A., Fuchs, G. *et al.* (2012) Gastrointestinal conditions in children with autism spectrum disorder: developing a research agenda. Pediatrics 130 (Suppl 2), S160–S168.

Chapter 14

1. Neinstein, L., Gordon C., Katzman, D., Rosen, D., and Woods, E. (2008) *Adolescent Health Care: A Practical Guide.* Philadelphia, PA: Lippincott, Williams and Wilkins.
2. Feingold, D. (1992) Pediatric Endocrinology. In D. Feingold (ed.) *Atlas of Pediatric Physical Diagnosis,* 2nd Edition. Philadelphia, PA: W.B. Saunders.
3. Murphy, N.A. and Elias, E.R. (2006) Sexuality of children and adolescents with developmental disabilities. Pediatrics 118, 398–403.
4. Gardner, D. and Shoback, D. (eds) (2011) Physiology of Puberty. In *Greenspan's Basic and Clinical Endocrinology.* New York, NY: McGraw-Hill Medical.
5. Cortesi, F., Giannotti, F., Ivanenko, A., and Johnson, K. (2010) Sleep in children with autistic spectrum disorder. Sleep medicine 11, 659–664.
6. Coupey, S. (2000) *Primary Care of Adolescent Girls.* Philadelphia, PA: Hanley and Belfus.

Chapter 15

1. Wehman, P. (2006) *Life Beyond the Classroom: Transition Strategies for Young People with Disabilities.* Baltimore, MD: Brookes Publishing Company.
2. Cooley, W.C. and Sagerman, P.J. (2011) Supporting the health care transition from adolescence to adulthood in the medical home. Pediatrics 128, 182–200.
3. Ganz, M.L. (2007) The lifetime distribution of the incremental societal costs of autism. Archives of pediatrics & adolescent medicine 161, 343–349.
4. Myers, J.M. (2010) *How to Teach Lifeskills to Kids with Autism or Aspergers.* Arlington, TX: FutureHorizons.
5. Baker, J. (2005) *Preparing for Life: The Complete Guide for Transitioning to Adulthood for those with Autism and Asperger's Syndrome.* Arlington, TX: FutureHorizons.
6. Taylor, J.E. and Taylor, J.A. (2013) Person-centered planning: evidence-based practice, challenges, and potential for the 21st century. Journal of social work in disability & rehabilitation 12, 213–235.
7. Lerna, A., Esposito, D., Conson, M., Russo, L., and Massagli, A. (2012) Social-communicative effects of the Picture Exchange Communication System (PECS) in autism spectrum disorders. International journal of language & communication disorders 47, 609–617.

Chapter 16

1. American Psychiatric Association (2013) *Diagnostic and Statistical Manual of Mental Disorders.* 5th Edition. Washington, DC: American Psychiatric Association.
2. American Psychiatric Association (2000) *Diagnostic and Statistical Manual of Mental Disorders.* 4th Edition (text rev.). Washington, DC: American Psychiatric Association.
3. Unumb, L.S. and Unumb, D.R. (2011) *Autism and the Law: Cases, Statutes, and Materials.* Durham, NC: Carolina Academic Press.
4. www.parentcenterhub.org
5. Court Case (2009) Richardson Independent School Dist. v. Michael Z. In F3d. (United States Court of Appeals, Fifth Circuit), p.286.
6. Individuals with Disabilities Education Act (1990, reauthorized in 1997, 2004).

7. Price, C.S., Thompson, W.W., Goodson, B., Weintraub, E.S. *et al.* (2010) Prenatal and infant exposure to thimerosal from vaccines and immunoglobulins and risk of autism. Pediatrics 126, 656–664.

8. Stewart, A.M. (2009) When vaccine injury claims go to court. New England journal of medicine 360, 2498–2500.

9. Lerner, M.D., Haque, O.S., Northrup, E.C., Lawer, L., and Bursztajn, H.J. (2012) Emerging perspectives on adolescents and young adults with high-functioning autism spectrum disorders, violence, and criminal law. Journal of the American Academy of Psychiatry and the Law 40, 177–190.

10. Haskins, B.G. and Silva, J.A. (2006) Asperger's disorder and criminal behavior: forensic–psychiatric considerations. Journal of the American Academy of Psychiatry and the Law Online 34, 374–384.

11. Allen, D., Evans, C., Hider, A., Hawkins, S., Peckett, H., and Morgan, H. (2008) Offending behaviour in adults with Asperger syndrome. Journal of autism and developmental disorders 38, 748–758.

12. Dein, K. and Woodbury-Smith, M. (2010) Asperger syndrome and criminal behaviour. Advances in psychiatric treatment 16, 37–43.

13. Debbaudt, D. (2002) *Autism, Advocates and Law Enforcement Professionals: Recognizing and Reducing Risk Situations for People with Autism Spectrum Disorders.* London: Jessica Kingsley Publishers.

14. Hillbrand, M. and Sondik, T. (2012) Treatment and violence risk mitigation in high-functioning autism spectrum individuals. Journal of the American Academy of Psychiatry and the Law 40, 191–192.

Chapter 17

1. University of Virginia, Institutional Review Board. Available at www.virginia.edu/vpr/irb. Accessed on November 24, 2013.

2. James, S.J., Cutler, P., Melnyk, S., Jernigan, S. *et al.* (2004) Metabolic biomarkers of increased oxidative stress and impaired methylation capacity in children with autism. American journal of clinical nutrition 80, 1611–1617.

3. Ming, X., Stein, T.P., Brimacombe, M., Johnson, W.G., Lambert, G.H., and Wagner, G.C. (2005) Increased excretion of a lipid peroxidation biomarker in autism. Prostaglandins, leukotrienes, and essential fatty acids 73, 379–384.

4. Yao, Y., Walsh, W.J., McGinnis, W.R., and Pratico, D. (2006) Altered vascular phenotype in autism: correlation with oxidative stress. Archives of neurology 63, 1161–1164.

5. Ming, X., Julu, P.O., Brimacombe, M., Connor, S., and Daniels, M.L. (2005) Reduced cardiac parasympathetic activity in children with autism. Brain & development 27, 509–516.

6. Buie, T., Campbell, D.B., Fuchs, G.J. 3rd, Furuta, G.T. *et al.* (2010) Evaluation, diagnosis, and treatment of gastrointestinal disorders in individuals with ASDs: a consensus report. Pediatrics 125 (Suppl 1), S1–S18.

7. Jyonouchi, H., Geng, L., Streck, D.L., and Toruner, G.A. (2012) Immunological characterization and transcription profiling of peripheral blood (PB) monocytes in children with autism spectrum disorders (ASD) and specific polysaccharide antibody deficiency (SPAD): case study. Journal of neuroinflammation 9, 4.

8. Happe, F.G. (1994) Current psychological theories of autism: the "theory of mind" account and rival theories. Journal of child psychology and psychiatry, and allied disciplines 35, 215–229.

9. Schultz, R.T., Gauthier, I., Klin, A., Fulbright, R.K., Anderson, A.W., Volkmar, F. *et al.* (2000) Abnormal ventral temporal cortical activity during face discrimination among individuals with autism and Asperger syndrome. Archives of general psychiatry 57, 331–340.

10. Ming, X., Brimacombe, M., and Wagner, G.C. (2007) Prevalence of motor impairment in autism spectrum disorders. Brain & development 29, 565–570.

Index